STATE AND LOCAL
TAX POLICIES

STATE AND LOCAL TAX POLICIES

A Comparative Handbook

RONALD JOHN HY and
WILLIAM L. WAUGH, JR.

GREENWOOD PRESS
Westport, Connecticut • London

Library of Congress Cataloging-in-Publication Data

Hy, Ronald J. (Ronald John)
 State and local tax policies : a comparative handbook / Ronald
John Hy and William L. Waugh, Jr.
  p. cm.
 Includes bibliographical references and index.
 ISBN 0–313–28529–2 (alk. paper)
 1. Taxation—United States—States. 2. Local taxation—United
States. 3. Revenue—United States—States. I. Waugh, William L.
II. Title.
HJ2385.H9 1995
336.2'00973—dc20   94–30931

British Library Cataloguing in Publication Data is available.

Library of Congress Catalog Card Number: 94–30931
ISBN: 0–313–28529–2

First published in 1995

Greenwood Press, 88 Post Road West, Westport, CT 06881
An imprint of Greenwood Publishing Group, Inc.

Printed in the United States of America

The paper used in this book complies with the
Permanent Paper Standard issued by the National
Information Standards Organization (Z39.48–1984).

10 9 8 7 6 5 4 3 2 1

Copyright Acknowledgment

Appendix A has been excerpted from Ronald John Hy, "An Overview of Policy
Analysis Concepts," in William Coplin, ed., *Teaching Policy Analysis* (Lexington,
Mass.: Lexington Books, 1978). Reprinted by permission of the Policy Studies
Organization.

Contents

Exhibits   ix

Preface   xiii

1. Fiscal Outlook and Trends   1

    State Fiscal Profiles   9

    Spending Patterns   17

    Fiscal Outlook   19

    References   24

2. Overview of State and Local Taxes   25

    Tax Fairness   26

    Tax Base and Tax Rate   27

    Property Taxes   28

    General Sales Taxes   31

    Charges and Fees   32

    Utility Taxes   35

    Income, Wage, and Payroll Taxes   36

    Intergovernmental (State and Federal) Aid   40

    Long-Term Debt Financing   41

    Strategies for Balanced Tax Policies   48

Concluding Comments   48
References   50

3. **Income Taxes**   **51**

Tax Philosophy   53
Personal Income Taxes   53
Corporate Income Taxes   56
Trends in State and Local Income Taxation   58
Income Taxes and Tax Amnesty   76
Concluding Comments   78
References   79

4. **General Sales Taxes**   **81**

Tax Philosophy   82
Recent Trends in General Sales Taxation   84
Retail and Wholesale Sales Taxes   89
Agricultural Sales Taxes   96
Public Utility Taxes   100
Use Taxes   102
Site Determination   106
Sales and Use Tax Collection and Administration   106
Concluding Comments   107
References   108

5. **Excise and Consumption Taxes**   **111**

Tax Philosophy   112
Trends in Excise and Consumption Taxation   113
Selected Excise and Consumption Taxes   118
Consumption Taxes   126
References   146

6. **Property Taxes**   **149**

Tax Philosophy   151
Recent Trends in Property Taxation   152
Real Estate Property   154
Personal and Intangible Property Taxes   160
Assessment Process   162

Effects and Limitations of Property Taxes   164
Agricultural Property Taxes   166
Concluding Comments   175
References   178

7. **Severance Taxes**   **181**

Tax Philosophy   182
Trends in Severance Taxation   184
Types of Severance Taxes   184
Tax Exporting   194
Severance Tax Discrimination   195
Timber Taxes   198
Mineral Taxes   204
References   210

8. **Taxes and Economic Development**   **211**

Tax Incentive Philosophy   214
Recent Trends in Taxation and Economic Development 215
Interstate Tax Competition   222
Importance of State and Local Economies   223
Relationship Between Taxes and Economic Development 224
Concluding Comments   227
References   228

9. **Tax Administration**   **231**

Administrative Structures   232
Tax Collection   232
Tax Maintenance   236
Revenue Forecasting   242
Ingredients for Success   249
References   250

10. **Conclusion**   **251**

Own-Source Revenues   251
Tax Incidence   252
Types of Taxes   253
Exemptions, Deductions, and Credits   256

viii Contents

Interstate Differences   257
The Political Environment   259
References   263

Appendix A. Analyzing Taxes   **265**

Appendix B. Analytical Designs   **273**

**Appendix C. National and State Organizations and
  Information Sources**   **283**

Selected Bibliography   **293**

Index   **303**

Exhibits

1.1	Per Capita State Revenues, 1991	2
1.2	Per Capita Local Revenues, 1991	3
1.3	State and Local General Taxes per Capita, 1991	4
1.4	Percentage of State General Revenue Distribution by Source, 1986–1991	5
1.5	Percentage of Local Revenue Distribution by Source, 1986–1991	6
1.6	State and Local Revenue Sources	8
1.7	Regional Economy	10
1.8	Percent Growth of Population by Region, 1985–1992	11
1.9	Percent Growth of Nonfarm Employment by Region, 1985–1992	12
1.10	Percent Growth of Personal Income, 1985–1992	14
1.11	Percent Growth of Real Disposable Income by Region, 1985–1992	15
1.12	Percent Growth of Gross State Product, 1985–1992	16
1.13	Federal Aid as a Percentage of State and Local Revenues, 1978–1992	22
2.1	Example of Property Tax Computation	29
2.2	Example of Classification Rates	30

2.3	Selected Sales Tax Exemptions	32
2.4	Types of Local Government Fees, Charges, and Licenses	34
2.5	Example of Personal Income Tax Rates	37
2.6	Example of Corporate Income Tax Rates	39
2.7	Selected Financing Options	44
2.8	Strategies for Balanced Tax Policies	48
3.1	State Income Tax Revenues, FY 1991	59
3.2	Local Income and Payroll Taxes in FY 1991	63
3.3	Comparative Analysis of Four Types of Local Income Taxes	64
3.4	Local Income Tax Revenues, FY 1991	66
3.5	Income Tax Revenues per $1,000 Personal Income by Region	73
3.6	Individual Income Taxes as a Percentage of State Personal Income, 1988	74
3.7	Estimated Income Taxes for a Family of Four Earning $25,000 in 1990	75
4.1	Basic Local Sales Taxes: Combined Rates, Selected Cities, 1991	85
4.2	Sales Tax Revenues per $1,000 Personal Income by Region	88
4.3	General Sales and Gross Receipts Taxes as a Percentage of Personal Income, 1988	90
4.4	State Sales Taxes: Rates and Exemptions, 1991	92
4.5	Sales Tax Treatment of Feed and Seed, Fertilizer and Other Farm Chemicals, and Livestock	98
4.6	Sales Tax Treatment of Farm Machinery	99
4.7	Sales Tax on New Equipment and Implements	100
4.8	States with Mail Order Sales Tax Legislation	105
5.1	Examples of Indexing Motor Fuels Taxes	114
5.2	Major Excise Taxes as a Percentage of Total State and Local Collections, 1989–1990	115
5.3	Local Excise Revenues as a Percentage of Local Taxes	116
5.4	Excise Taxes as a Share of Income for a Family of Four, 1991	117
5.5	Motor Fuels Tax Revenues per $1,000 Personal Income by Region, 1986–1990	119
5.6	Comparison of State and Local Spending on Highway Finance, 1989	121

5.7	Basic Gasoline and Diesel Fuel Tax Rates by State, March 1994	122
5.8	Basic Cigarette Tax Rates, December 1993	125
5.9	Major Consumption Revenues, 1990	128
5.10	Lottery, Amusement, and Parimutuel Revenues, 1991	130
5.11	Parimutuel Revenues over Time	131
5.12	Racing Take-out Percent by State	132
5.13	State Lotteries, Net Proceeds, Fiscal Years 1980–1991	136
5.14	State Lottery Revenues, Annual Percentage Change, Fiscal Years 1980–1991	138
5.15	Earmarking of Net Lottery Proceeds, 1988	140
5.16	Charges as a Percentage of Local Revenues	144
6.1	Growth in Property Taxes for Counties	153
6.2	Property Taxes as a Percentage of Revenues, for Selected Years	154
6.3	Types of Property	155
6.4	Residential Property Tax Rates in Selected Large Cities, 1990	156
6.5	Basic Classifications of Real Property and Tangible Personal Property, 1991	158
6.6	Selected Features of Intangibles Taxation by State	161
6.7	Details of Intangibles Tax Base by State	162
6.8	Property Assessment Cycle	163
6.9	Estimated Property Tax Burden for a Family of Four, 1990	165
6.10	Property Taxes as a Percentage of Total Local Revenues	168
6.11	Property Taxes as a Percentage of Local Revenues by Region	169
6.12	Value of Acres in Farmland and Taxable Land and Buildings by Region, 1987	170
6.13	Percent Distribution of County Property Taxes by Population, 1989–1990	171
6.14	Steps Used to Calculate Net Income, Using a Five-Year Average	173
6.15	Land Value Assessment Process	174
6.16	Ten-Year Averaging Process	177
7.1	Severance Revenues as a Percentage of Total State Collections, 1950–1990	185
7.2	States Generating Most Severance Revenues	186

7.3	Steps in the Processing of Minerals and Mineral Fuels Between Severance and Use of Consumer Goods	187
7.4	Basic State Severance Tax Rates and Bases, 1992	188
7.5	Severance Revenues as a Percentage of Total Revenues	196
7.6	Earmarked Severance Taxes	198
7.7	Total Value of Timber Cut	200
7.8	Timber Production by Kind of Wood	201
7.9	Per Capita Consumption of Timber Products	203
7.10	Timber Data, 1990, in Thousands of Dollars, States with over 15 Million Acres	204
7.11	Timber Production by Region	205
7.12	States Generating Most Mineral Severance Revenues, 1990	208
7.13	Mining Production by Type of Minerals	209
8.1	Valuation of Site Selection Criteria by Firm Type	212
8.2	Employer Ratings of Importance of Factors for Locational Decisions	213
8.3	Employer Ratings of Importance of Maryland EZ Program Features	219
8.4	Program Participant Ratings of Maryland EZ Program Features	220
8.5	Employer Ratings of Importance of Nonfinancial Incentives	221
8.6	Statutory Provisions Governing Use of Tax Abatements	222
9.1	Tax Administration Structures	233
9.2	Typical Record Files for Property Taxes	235
9.3	Four Major Transactions Kept by Treasury Units	237
9.4	Characteristics of Investment Instruments	238
9.5	Long-Term, Seasonal, and Cyclical Patterns	243
9.6	Summary of Forecasting Practices	245
9.7	Econometric Forecasting Process	248
B.1	Pre/Post Design	275
B.2	Post Design	277
B.3	Trend Projection Design	280

Preface

A perusal of state and local finances indicates that states and localities have been experiencing slow revenue growth since 1983, causing them gradually to deplete their balances. And, without more rapid national economic growth, little improvement is expected. In addition to slow revenue growth, state and local governments are being compelled by lawsuits, court orders, unfunded and underfunded federal mandates, and constitutional requirements to spend more money each year. Additional fiscal tension is being placed on state and local revenues because of (1) the inability of revenue structures to capture economic growth (e.g., too many exemptions); (2) demographic growth that places considerable emphasis on additional spending for education, welfare, and the aged; (3) past fiscal decisions that have depleted reserves and pension funds; (4) implementation of one-time financing maneuvers; and (5) state and local competition for jobs that frequently leads to various tax abatements.

Consequently, state and local governments are facing serious financial problems that cannot be offset merely by decreasing expenditures to balance budgets. In fact, as entitlements become more commonplace, state and local budgets are being driven not so much by revenues as by mandated need—as evidenced by the Medicaid crisis experienced by state governments. Thus, decreasing expenditures is often not even a viable alternative.

For these and other reasons, state and local taxes are destined to become a hot topic in the years to come. Elected and appointed officials and concerned taxpayers already are showing a keen interest in taxes and their effects on existing revenue structures.

This felicitous interest nowadays focuses on incremental changes in existing tax rates and bases. Invariably, such tax inquisitiveness looks at the extent to which state and local tax policies deviate from national patterns. That is, what are other state and local governments doing?

This reference book, therefore, concentrates on state and local tax comparisons and discusses the impacts of various types of tax policies. This focus, we believe, addresses and clarifies the needs of those analyzing and dealing with various state and local tax policies. As this work will make clear, the choice of revenue sources by state and local governments is often guided less by economic considerations than by political and administrative reasons. Those political and administrative, as well as historical, influences on policy making are crucial to an understanding of both current and future policy options.

This comparative handbook provides an overview of state and local taxation, the current and future tax outlook across the nation, the role of taxes in economic development, and the administration of tax policies. It analyzes and compares major state and local taxes—income (personal and corporate), general sales (retail and wholesale taxes including those on food, medicine, and electricity), excise and consumption (motor fuel, tobacco, alcoholic beverages, lodging, amusements, parimutuels, and lotteries), property (residential, commercial, industrial, and agricultural), and severance taxes (timber and minerals). The handbook, moreover, examines the philosophy behind different taxes, recent trends, and current and future policy options. The volume is further enhanced by over ninety exhibits of statistical data. Appendices cover some tax policy analysis and evaluation techniques, and list key sources of information about state and local taxes. A selected bibliography for graduate and undergraduate students, public administrators, policy makers, economists, political scientists, as well as the general public, is included.

Since state and local taxes change at least annually, we encourage readers to keep up to date by reviewing some of the numerous tax policy publications, the most important of which are *State Tax Guide*, *Significant Features of Fiscal Federalism*, *State Government Finances*, *Government Finances*, and *State Government Tax Collections*.

Many persons have helped us prepare this book. Although it is impossible to cite each one individually, a few deserve special thinks. We are particularly indebted to Monte Venhaus, Kim Jackson, and Robin Wilson, all of the University of Arkansas at Little Rock. We are also grateful to our students at the University of Arkansas at Little Rock and Georgia State University who often pointed us in the right direction. Finally, this book is dedicated to our families as a way of thanking them for their patience, help, and love.

Needless to say, we are responsible for all errors and omissions.

Ronald John Hy
Little Rock, Arkansas

William L. Waugh, Jr.
Atlanta, Georgia

Fiscal Outlook
and Trends

Most discussions of tax policies focus on the federal government. But state and local tax policies deserve attention since they generate a considerable amount of money—about 13 percent of the gross national product since 1975. State and local revenues amounted to $849 billion in 1990, or 71 percent of the amount generated by the federal government. (Federal revenues in 1990 amounted to $1.2 trillion.) In addition, state and local governments spent a total of $834 billion in 1990, an increase of almost 10 percent from a year earlier. (Education alone accounted for over a third of this spending.)

Taxes are the principal own-source revenues of state and local governments. Exhibits 1.1 and 1.2 display per capita revenues generated by major revenue source for both states and localities. Although states, like localities, receive a tremendous amount of money via intergovernmental aid, states raise most of their dollars from personal income and sales and gross receipts taxes. Local governments, on the other hand, generate their own-source revenues mostly from property taxes, fines, and fees. As seen in Exhibit 1.3, of the fifty states, Alaska has the highest per capita state and local taxes, amounting to $4,441. Mississippi has the lowest per capita taxes, equaling $1,305.

Exhibits 1.4 and 1.5 display several tax trends. While intergovernmental aid for states is holding steady in terms of nominal dollars, real dollars are being reduced, although there was a slight increase in 1991. Thus, states are relying increasingly on personal income taxes, and charges, fines, and fees, while dependence on sales, gross receipts, and corporate taxes is declining. States are not depending on intergovernmental aid as an increasing source of revenue.

Reliance on intergovernmental aid is decreasing in part because states are

Exhibit 1.1
Per Capita State Revenues, 1991

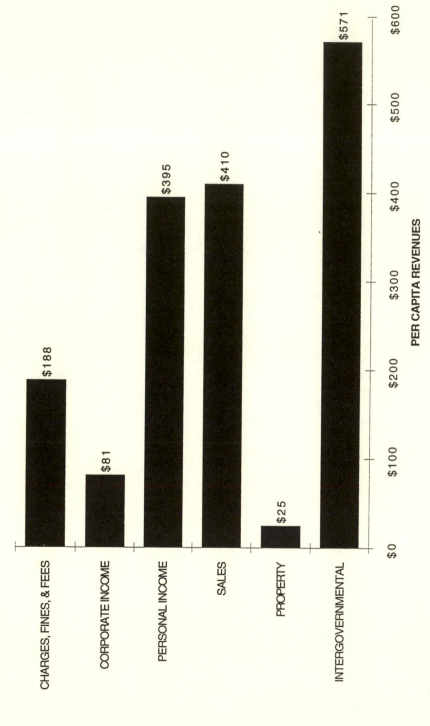

Source: ACIR, 1993: 102.

2

Exhibit 1.2
Per Capita Local Revenues, 1991

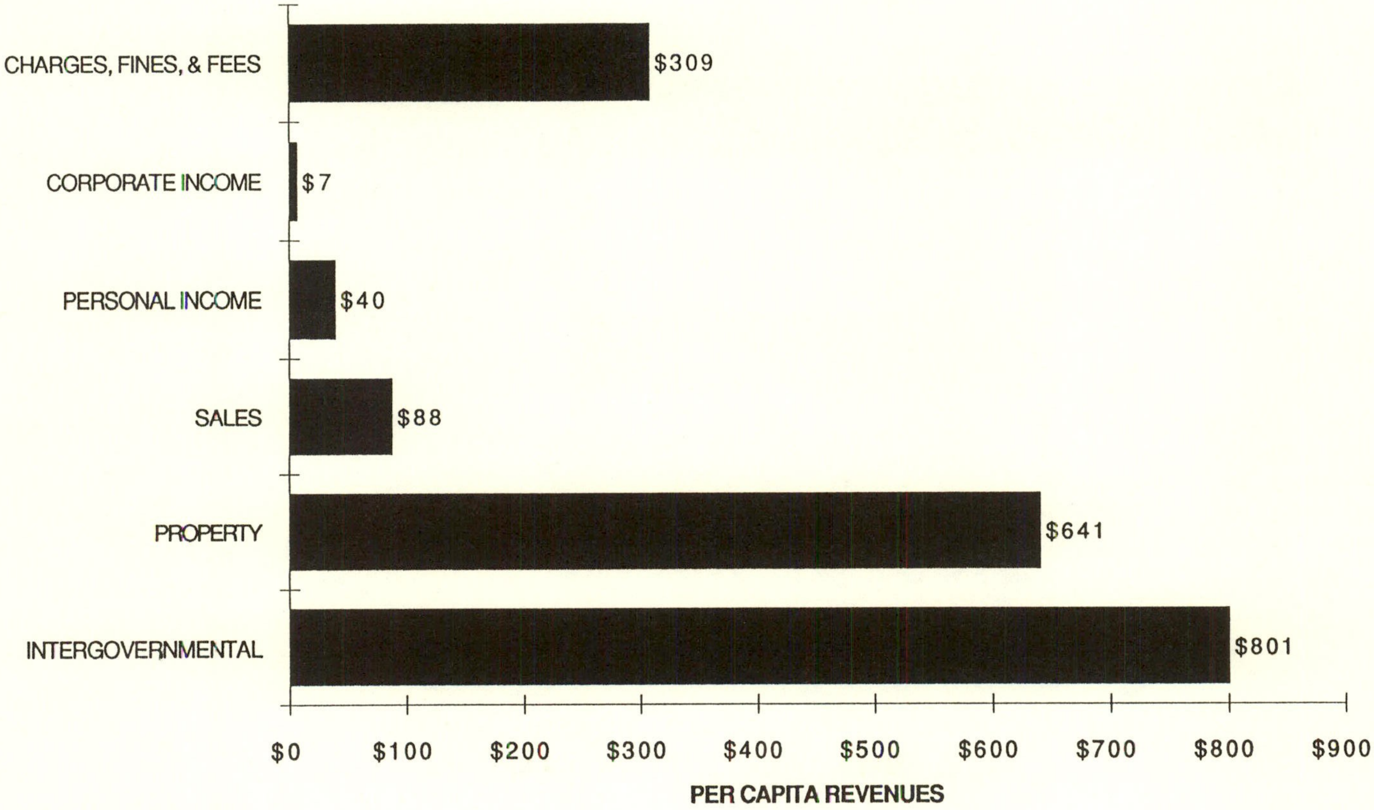

CHARGES, FINES, & FEES — $309
CORPORATE INCOME — $7
PERSONAL INCOME — $40
SALES — $88
PROPERTY — $641
INTERGOVERNMENTAL — $801

PER CAPITA REVENUES

$0 $100 $200 $300 $400 $500 $600 $700 $800 $900

Source: ACIR, 1993: 118.

Exhibit 1.3
State and Local General Taxes per Capita, 1991

Rank	State	Amount	Rank	State	Amount	Rank	State	Amount
1	Alaska	$4,411	17	Delaware	$2,081	34	North Dakota	$1,734
2	New York	$3,337	18	Maine	$2,033	35	Kentucky	$1,730
3	Hawaii	$2,867	19	Oregon	$2,017	36	New Mexico	$1,722
4	New Jersey	$2,778	20	Arizona	$2,004	37	North Carolina	$1,672
5	Connecticut	$2,667	21	Colorado	$1,960	38	Oklahoma	$1,671
6	Massachusetts	$2,469	22	Virginia	$1,960	39	Louisiana	$1,654
7	Minnesota	$2,348	23	Iowa	$1,947	40	West Virginia	$1,630
8	Maryland	$2,284	24	Nebraska	$1,944	41	Idaho	$1,604
9	California	$2,283	25	Nevada	$1,942	42	Utah	$1,601
10	Wyoming	$2,253	26	Kansas	$1,930	43	Missouri	$1,596
11	Washington	$2,236	27	New Hampshire	$1,915	44	South Carolina	$1,560
12	Wisconsin	$2,226	28	Pennsylvania	$1,887	45	South Dakota	$1,489
13	Illinois	$2,132	29	Ohio	$1,852	46	Montana	$1,468
14	Rhode Island	$2,132	30	Florida	$1,830	47	Tennessee	$1,410
15	Vermont	$2,121	31	Georgia	$1,797	48	Alabama	$1,364
16	Michigan	$2,106	32	Texas	$1,757	49	Arkansas	$1,335
	United States	**$2,088**	33	Indiana	$1,739	50	Mississippi	$1,305

Source: State Policy Reports, 1993b:11.

Exhibit 1.4
Percentage of State General Revenue Distribution by Source, 1986–1991

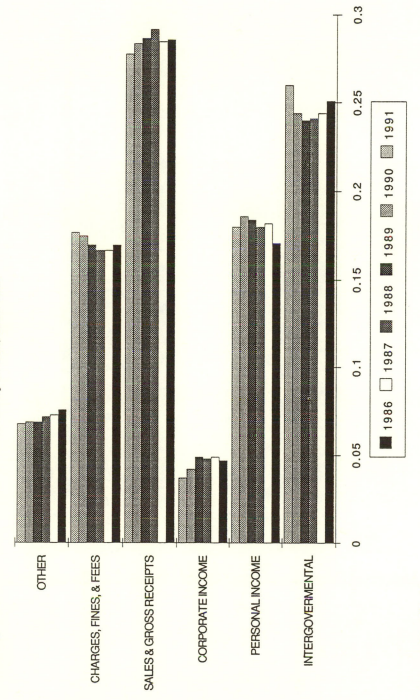

Source: ACIR, 1993: 71.

5

Exhibit 1.5
Percentage of Local Revenue Distribution by Source, 1986–1991

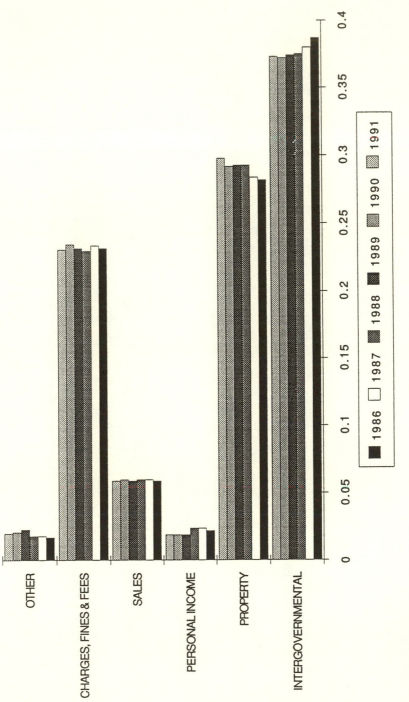

Source: ACIR, 1993: 73.

decreasing their efforts to help local governments finance their services (*State Policy Reports*, 1993b: 3). States are asking local governments to increase local property and sales taxes to balance local budgets.

The outlook for future state aid to local governments appears to be bleak because the changes during the past several years in state fiscal relations with local governments—excluding education—do not appear to be the result of state fiscal problems as much as they are long-term trends accelerated by state fiscal problems (*State Policy Reports*, 1993b: 4). State income and sales taxes simply are not generating sufficient revenues during times of sluggish economic growth. Local property tax revenues and federal aid, however, are largely immune from short-term economic conditions. Consequently, with some exceptions, states seem to be moving in the direction of discouraging state aid for general revenues for local governments, but encouraging the state takeover of functions that exact a heavy financial toll on local government revenues.

This situation is quite likely to continue for the foreseeable future because there are no signs that the economy is about to bottom out. Since 1990 states have rapidly depleted their balances. Fiscal experts tend to agree that state balances should be approximately 5 percent of the revenues collected. In 1993 state balances were about 1 percent of the collected revenues. This condition is fairly widespread, with only seven states in the 3 to 5 percent range and five states showing negative balances.

In 1992 state and local governments spent $42 billion more than they generated in revenues. Historically, this deficit is extremely high. The situation did not improve in 1993 since state and local government spending grew by 6.5 percent while revenues increased by only 5.6 percent (*State Policy Reports*, 1993b: 6). As shown in some of the preceding exhibits and in Exhibit 1.6, state and local governments rely to a considerable extent on federal funds to meet this accrued deficit. However, Congress is unlikely to continue to fund these governments at current levels. States and localities, therefore, will be forced to increase their own revenue sources in order to balance their budgets.

Many factors militate against any revenue increases. The primary one is that elected officials are especially aware of constituents' desires to avoid broad-based revenue increases. Most elected officials campaign on promises that revenue increases are a last resort, to be considered only after finding ways to reduce spending without negatively impacting essential services.

Despite this reluctance to raise taxes, however, conditions now exist that historically have signaled revenue increases at state and local levels. They are as follows:

• A recession that leads to major shortfalls in state and local revenues
• Reserves that have been depleted below traditional and sometimes statutory levels deemed appropriate
• Normal spending adjustments (e.g., pay raises) that have been skipped, creating pressures for expensive correctional actions

Exhibit 1.6
State and Local Revenue Sources

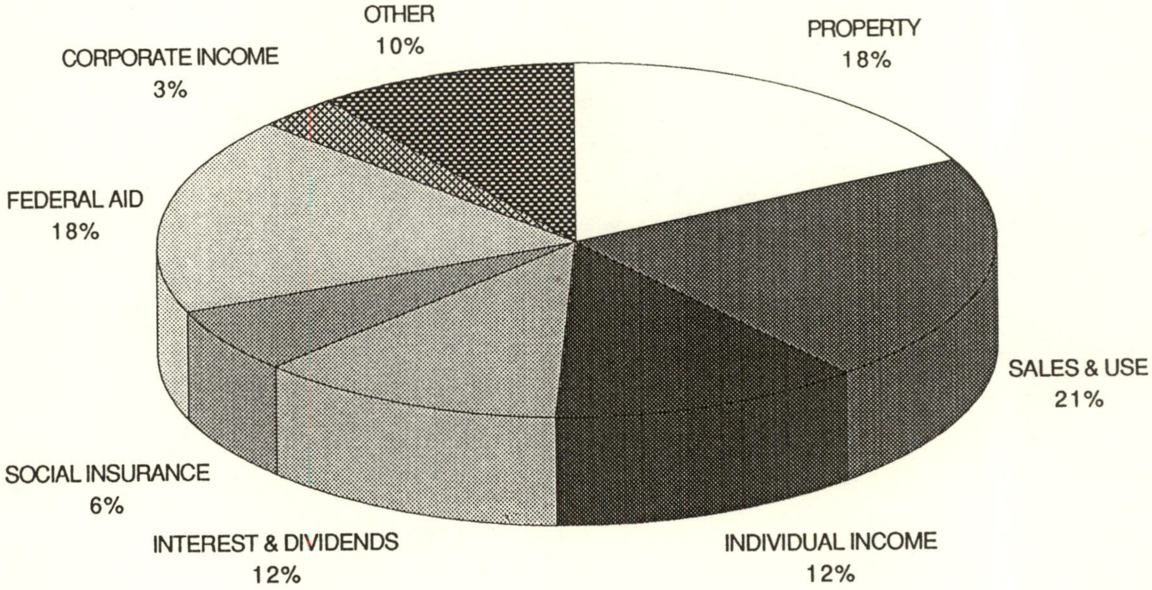

PROPERTY
18%

SALES & USE
21%

OTHER
10%

INDIVIDUAL INCOME
12%

CORPORATE INCOME
3%

INTEREST & DIVIDENDS
12%

FEDERAL AID
18%

SOCIAL INSURANCE
6%

Source: State Policy Reports, 1993a: 6.

- Actions that could increase revenues without increasing taxes (e.g., federal aid) seem unlikely

- Soaring costs, adverse judicial decisions, and federal aid cuts that have made state and local fiscal conditions extremely precarious. (*State Policy Reports*, 1993a: 2)

This case for increased revenues is best examined against the backdrop of established economic realities. Obviously, population growth, employment, income, and gross state product are fundamental to revenue increases. These factors change both the structure and function of revenue enhancement.

STATE FISCAL PROFILES

One of the major difficulties encountered in examining state and local tax policies is that there are fifty state governments and over 78,000 local governments (counties, cities, townships, school districts, and special districts), each with a different fiscal environment. In order to make sense of this fiscal diversity, the fifty state governments and over 78,000 local governments are grouped into nine regional economies based on Bureau of the Census configurations. Exhibit 1.7 illustrates these nine regional economies.

Although the economic performances of these regions undoubtedly vary, tax revenues depend on people, jobs, income, and fiscal capacity. An understanding of regional differences among these factors presents a clear backdrop for analyzing state and local tax policies.

Population Growth

The nationwide population growth rate between 1985 and 1992 was approximately 6 percent. Exhibit 1.8 depicts the population growth in each of the nine regions during this period. The highest growth rate was in the Pacific region (16%), followed by the Mountain (13%) and South Atlantic (12%) regions. The lowest growth rate (2%) was experienced by the Middle Atlantic states. Simply put, population growth is occurring predominantly in western and southern states.

Employment

Nationwide, nonfarm employment grew at a rate of 13 percent between 1985 and 1990. Exhibit 1.9 shows the nonfarm employment growth between 1985 and 1992. The employment growth, not unexpectedly, reflects population growth. The highest growth rates are in the Mountain (19%), East South Central (18%), and South Atlantic (17%) states. Conversely, nonfarm employment growth is lowest in the Middle Atlantic region (2%). The New England section

Exhibit 1.7
Regional Economy

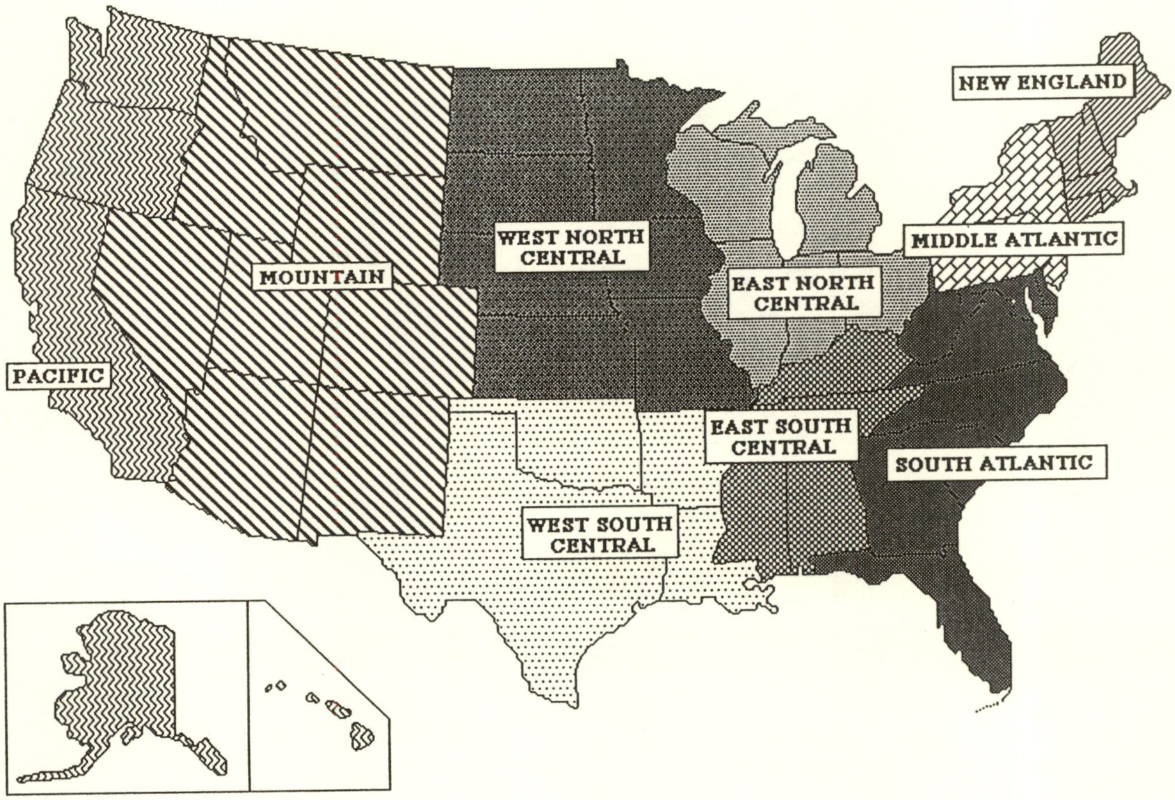

NEW ENGLAND

MIDDLE ATLANTIC

SOUTH ATLANTIC

EAST NORTH CENTRAL

EAST SOUTH CENTRAL

WEST NORTH CENTRAL

WEST SOUTH CENTRAL

MOUNTAIN

PACIFIC

10

Exhibit 1.8
Percent Growth of Population by Region, 1985–1992

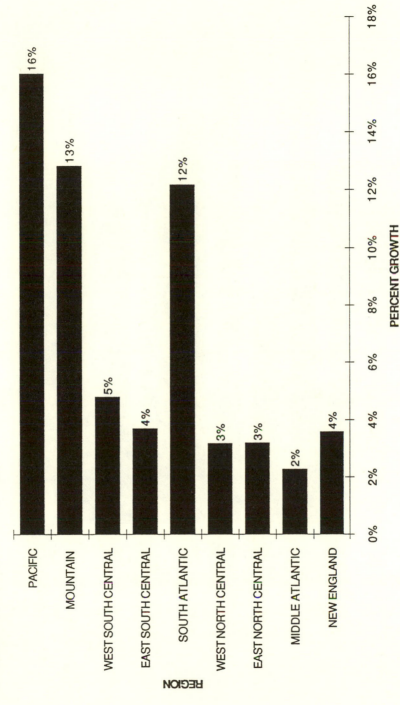

Source: U.S. Department of Commerce, 1993: 28.

11

Exhibit 1.9
Percent Growth of Nonfarm Employment by Region, 1985–1992

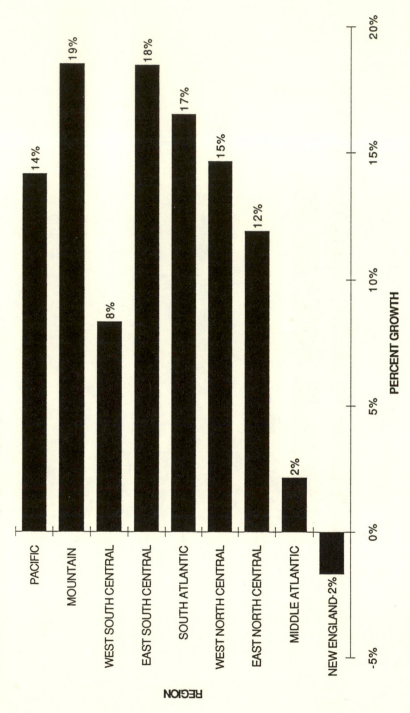

Source: U.S. Department of Commerce, 1993: 418.

of the country actually suffered a 2 percent decline in nonfarm employment over these years.

Income

People working translates into personal income, which in turn becomes state wealth, the primary base from which taxes are extracted. Between 1985 and 1992 growth in personal income nationwide was slightly over 13 percent. Exhibit 1.10 shows that the personal income growth rate was the highest in the South Atlantic (20%) and Pacific (16%) states, and the lowest among the West South Central states. Interestingly, the New England states, which experienced low population growth and a decrease in nonfarm employment, ranked among the highest in personal income growth.

Personal income, however, is only one aspect of state wealth. The rate of growth in real disposable income (income after taxes) also is consequential to the tax base. Exhibit 1.11 reveals that the greatest gains in real personal income were in the East South Central, Middle Atlantic, and New England states. The Pacific region, which had a sizable increase in nominal personal income, had a decrease in disposable income between 1985 and 1992. Nationwide, the growth rate of real disposable income was slightly more than 6 percent. Personal income growth in the Mountain and West South Central regions was largely limited to inflation during this period. These differences are due to tax increases in some states and differential inflation rates among state economies.

Gross State Product

Exhibit 1.12, which shows gross state product, incorporates population, employment, and income. It also includes factors such as manufacturing, construction, and investments that affect regional economies. Since gross state product (GSP) measures the level of a state's economic activity, it points to the importance of regional exports to these economies. GSP exhibits the extent to which export outside a region affect a region's economy. The more products that are produced within a region, the stronger the region's economy. The flow of income from exports also leads to growth of nonexport producing businesses and the outflow of goods and services from the region, the latter of which allows states to increase their tax bases and tax incidences by exporting taxes.

The South Atlantic, Middle Atlantic, and Pacific states boast the highest gross state product growth rates. The more vulnerable state economies are those in the West South Central, Mountain, and New England regions.

Concluding Comment

Major implications can be drawn from these exhibits of state fiscal profiles. With some exceptions, people, jobs, and wealth are moving south and west.

Exhibit 1.10
Percent Growth of Personal Income, 1985–1992 (in 1987 Dollars)

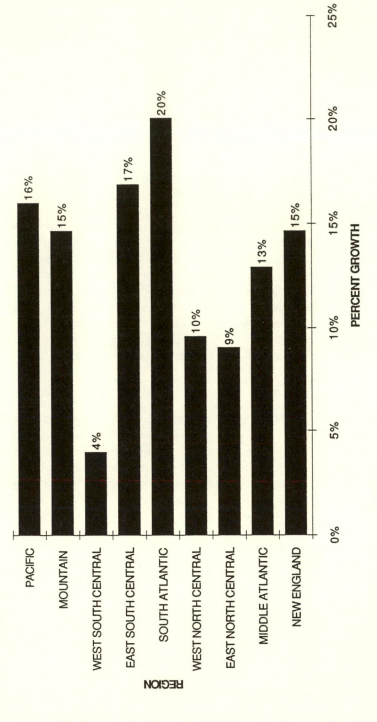

Source: U.S. Department of Commerce, 1993: 450.

14

Exhibit 1.11
Percent Growth of Real Disposable Income by Region, 1985–1992 (in 1987 Dollars)

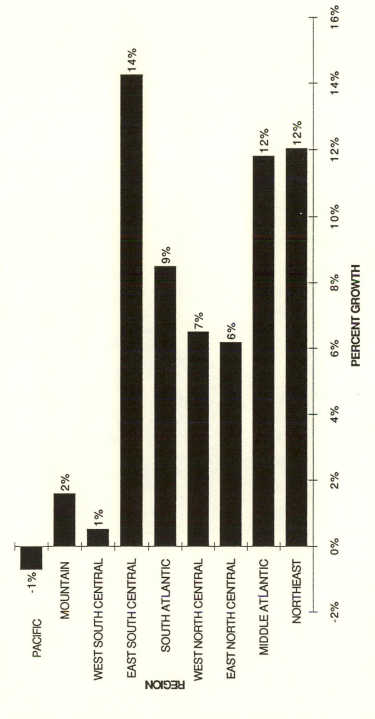

Source: U.S. Department of Commerce, 1993: 449.

Exhibit 1.12
Percent Growth of Gross State Product, 1985–1992 (in 1982 Dollars)

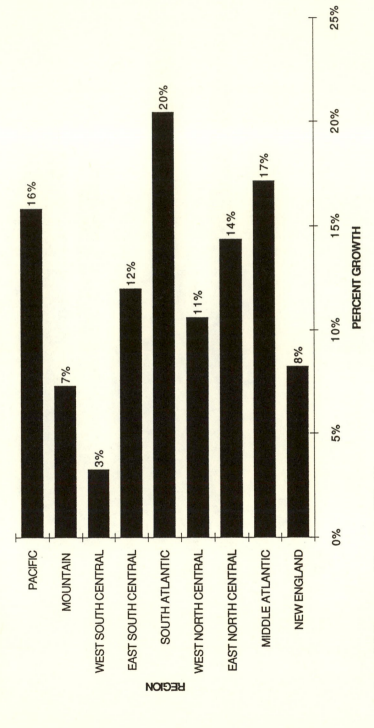

Source: U.S. Department of Commerce, 1993: 444.

States in these regions probably will have a growing tax base and may not have to raise taxes in order to meet moderate revenue needs. Conversely, other states may have to increase tax rates to meet moderate revenue needs.

SPENDING PATTERNS

Despite the increased need for revenues in the immediate future, state and local governments are confronted with serious taxpayer resistance. Simply put, taxpayers seem unwilling to pay higher taxes. This feeling became most prevalent when in 1978 California's voters accepted by a two to one margin (with 70 percent turnout) the infamous Proposition 13. That amendment to California's constitution cut state property taxes by approximately 57 percent. Although California was the epicenter of the "taxquake," it was not the only state where voters either rolled back taxes or rejected tax increases. In that year, taxpayers in Ohio, New Jersey, and Tennessee enacted various limitations on state and local spending. Similar moves have occurred since in most other states.

In spite of these antitax feelings, taxpayers still expect their governments to provide a vast array of goods and services, essentially determined by culture rather than by economics. Due to changing cultural values and expectations, state and local governments face soaring demands for increasingly costly public and private goods and services.

Public goods and services are those whose benefits cannot be withheld, even from persons not paying for them with tax dollars. These goods and services, which are normally financed by general taxes, can be enjoyed by more than one person without decreasing enjoyment by rival users. An example of a public service is police protection, which is financed by general revenues. Taxpayers and nontaxpayers alike benefit from this service—nontaxpayers are not excluded from police protection.

Private goods and services, on the other hand, are those whose benefits can be withheld from persons who do not pay for them. An illustration of a private good is municipal water. Nonpaying water users are eventually cut off from the city's water supply.

As demands for public and private goods and services rise, state and local governments must find ways to raise essential revenues. Obviously, increased demand for public and private goods and services costs money, lots of money. As a result, these governments must increase their tax bases and rates, reduce or eliminate services, and/or institute new taxes and bond indebtedness. Governments, therefore, must develop strategic spending patterns. Two factors affecting strategic spending patterns are (1) population growth and (2) changing attitudes about the degree of government involvement.

Population Growth

Spending, to be sure, is affected by the amount, type, and direction of population growth. The more residents a political jurisdiction has, the argument goes, the more goods and services it must provide. Still, population growth is not the only factor affecting spending, because spending has increased more drastically than either population or inflation (Savas, 1982: 12). More important to spending than population growth per se are the degree of urbanization and the composition of the population.

As people concentrate in a given area, they create more collective demands that must be met. For instance, as long as people live in areas with low population density, they have little need for zoning and water and sewerage systems; they can rely on wells and septic tanks. But as an area becomes densely populated, people need such regulations and systems. More police officers are required. Additional personnel are needed to monitor and control air and water pollution, to reduce noise, to investigate restaurants—and the list goes on. All these needs cost state and local governments money.

The composition of the population also affects government expenditures. When the population gets older and poorer, their needs increase. At the same time, an older and a poorer population erodes a government's tax base because these groups generally pay taxes at a lower rate than younger, more affluent groups. On the other hand, younger groups have their needs, too—primary, secondary, and higher education, for example.

Changing Attitudes about Government

Perhaps the most pervasive reason for growing governmental expenditures is the public's changing attitudes about government. People today expect state and local governments to do more without a concomitant increase in taxes, and to furnish goods and services that the private sector will not or cannot provide (often because they are unprofitable). Moreover, governments are expected to address and rectify a variety of social ills. The needs of the handicapped, poor, and aged are now met in part by state and local governments.

People tend to demand disproportionately more from state and local governments as their incomes (and taxes) rise. Wealthy sections of a community, for example, demand that more money be spent on educational programs, auxiliary facilities, and costly equipment for their schools. They expect better streets and recreational programs. At the same time, these people frequently vote *not* to increase taxes, a major funding source for these programs. As a result, there is an increasing incongruence between the public's changing attitudes about the role of government and their willingness to fund government with adequate financial resources.

Undeniably, governments are under strong pressure to increase their spending. The other side of the spending equation, as previously mentioned, is that the public is unlikely to favor increasing taxes to raise revenues needed to pay for goods and services. Despite the tension created by these two, government expenditures are increasing at a faster rate than revenues, even though the public's ability to pay more taxes is rising. The trick, then, is to find an equitable and productive way of drawing on that capacity.

FISCAL OUTLOOK

These tight fiscal conditions have produced retreats from past revenue policies. Higher than expected spending demands, often imposed on state and local governments by courts and entitlement programs, have frequently made it impossible for elected officials to avoid revenue increases. In order not to alienate voters, elected officials have spurned broad-based revenue increases in favor of specific taxes, especially in the form of fees, user charges, and excise taxes. Another tactic they have used is to assume a steadily growing economy—1.5 percent in real growth for 1994. Unfortunately, the economy is not growing at this rate, increasing the difference between revenues and expenditures. Significantly faster growth or rapid inflation would bail out most states and localities. However, neither is likely to happen. More likely, additional mandates for Medicaid, health care, social services, and pollution control—to name a few—will heighten the need for more revenues.

This fiscal outlook is leading to gross changes in the actions taken by state and local governments. According to Bland (1989: 5), state and local governments now as never before are addressing their need for:

- Greater financial self-sufficiency
- Increasing intergovernmental competition, both international and national, for new and expanding business investment
- Reducing distrust of government in economic and revenue matters
- Reducing economic uncertainty due to cyclical changes in the economy brought about by recession and inflation, sectoral shifts brought about by changes in technology and economic development, and population movement due to technology and job dislocations

At the same time, however, it must be remembered that state and local governments are limited in their ability to address revenue shortfalls. Almost all revenues are dependent on personal income, and increased revenues are dependent to a great extent on increased personal income. The fundamental change in this country's job market from manufacturing to high tech and services is not only beyond the control of state and local governments, but also leads to reduced personal income in real dollars. Consequently, jobs are not being lost temporarily because of a recession but rather lost permanently because of technology. About 70 percent of the manufacturing jobs lost in 1993 were managerial (*Wall Street Journal*, September 14, 1992). These good paying jobs, most of which are forever lost, might be replaced, but by lesser paying jobs, which in turn means that personal income and thus state and local revenues are reduced. No one knows which companies, much less which employees, will be around next year. State and local governments' ability to influence this process is relatively minor.

Need for Additional Revenues

States and localities today are facing long-term financial exigencies. Current services cannot possibly be maintained at existing funding levels. Government officials seeking to preserve current services have to develop ways to raise additional revenues, or those committed to holding the line on state and local revenues must figure out ways to curtail current services. If revenues are not raised, states and localities must avoid extensive new mandates in current programs. Unfortunately for states and localities, new mandates are seen as attractive by the federal government.

More important, however, state and local revenues are growing at a slower rate than current spending. In order for revenues to continue to flow into state and local governments at current levels, the economy must grow at an average rate in real gross domestic product of 2 percent or more, which, given current economic conditions, is more than can be expected.

The high growth rates experienced in the 1980s are not likely to occur in the 1990s because of the expected decline in the rate of the American workforce. Since 1988, the percent of persons in the workforce has declined from 67 percent to 66 percent. In addition, the influx of second income wage earners is slowing as the workforce becomes somewhat saturated. Since 1988, the female participation rate has leveled off at 57 percent.

Inasmuch as revenues normally are related strongly and positively to personal income, states with the highest per capita incomes tend to have the highest per capita taxes—even though the percentage of personal income taken by state and local taxes is declining (*State Policy Reports*, 1993b: 12). At the same time, it should be noted that states with lower personal incomes also have the highest tax burden—a greater percentage of their personal income goes toward paying taxes.

Complicating this situation is the fact that not all revenues are affected in the same manner by the economy. Oftentimes, state and local sales taxes lag behind personal income growth because an increasing percentage of personal income is being spent on exempted services. Excise taxes, especially those levied on tobacco, alcohol, and gasoline, also lag behind due to inflation. Personal income taxes, on the other hand, are growing faster than personal income because exemptions and deductions tend to flatten the dollars collected and many income taxes are generated via graduated rates (*State Policy Reports*, 1993a: 10).

Consequently, it may be virtually impossible for state and local governments not to increase revenues, given the expanding number of entitlement and court-ordered programs that must be funded. Unless drastic changes are made, education, corrections, and health care—primarily Medicaid—will require heavy state and local funding by the end of the 1990s. Money that states would ordinarily put into education and other social services is being siphoned off by increased costs of health care, Medicaid, and corrections.

The rising costs of public schools in the 1980s were heavily influenced by the reduction in average class sizes and the extension of years spent in public schools. The latter was due primarily to the widespread use of kindergartens, shifts to all-day kindergartens, and reduction in drop-out rates in secondary schools. In higher education students are staying in college longer, with concomitant increases in scholarships, loans, and tuition waivers. In addition, school enrollment will be increasing at more than 1 percent per year for the rest of this decade, a turnaround from the flattening enrollments that took the pressure off state budgets in the 1980s.

Corrections spending quadrupled during the 1980s. State costs increased from 19 cents per $100 of personal income to 40 cents per $100—a rate double that of overall economic growth (*Governing*, 1992: 25). These costs will continue to climb. Rising costs in the area of corrections are attributable in part to longer sentences as well as other policies affecting the rates of admissions to prisons and work-release programs.

Increased health care costs for state and local governments revolve around Medicaid. Health care costs are influenced by participation rates, number of services covered, and ease of getting on Medicaid rolls—all of which are increasing at unprecedented rates.

State revenues are not growing anywhere near as rapidly as the costs of health care. In Michigan, for example, revenue for 1993 is expected to increase between 5 percent and 6 percent. But state employee and retiree health care costs are going to grow at 22 percent, and Medicaid at 10 to 15 percent (*Governing*, 1992: 25).

As mentioned previously, state and local governments have spent more than they have raised for years. The federal government, through grants-in-aid and other assistance programs, has made up the difference. Now, however, the federal government is cutting back on assistance to states and localities. Exhibit 1.13 graphically depicts these federal cutbacks. In 1978 federal assistance to state and local governments constituted 22 percent of their revenues. By 1985 this share was down to 17.7 percent, and, by 1992 the federal share hovered around 16 percent. The growth in federal assistance that did occur was primarily in entitlement programs, which required increased contributions by states and localities from their own sources. Thus, the growth resulted in fewer discretionary dollars for state and local governments, just at the time that the federal government asked them to replace lost federal funds.

Not only is the federal government decreasing its fiscal support, but, as just illustrated, it is creating additional problems by passing unfunded mandates to state and local governments, forcing them to become more fiscally self-reliant. Then, too, shifts in the country's economic and demographic bases are exacerbating these problems.

The federal government is affecting state and local revenues in yet another

Exhibit 1.13
Federal Aid as a Percentage of State and Local Revenues, 1978–1992

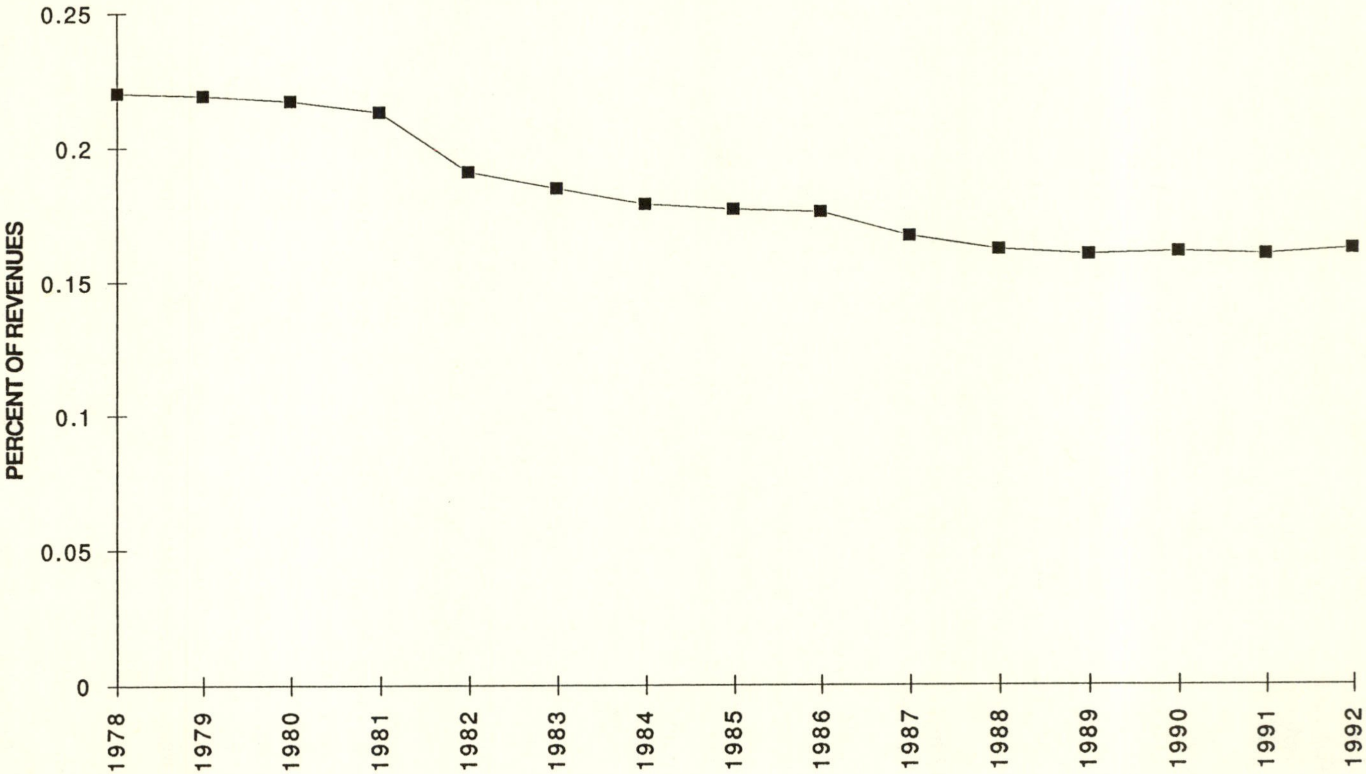

PERCENT OF REVENUES

Source: ACIR, 1993: 40.

way—by encroaching on their traditional tax bases. Since the early 1990s the federal government has been increasing excise taxes on a variety of products—particularly tobacco, alcohol, and gasoline—leaving very little room for states and localities to tap additional revenues from these sources. Moreover, the impact of these increases on state and local governments pales against the possibility of a federal sales tax or a national value-added tax. Either would strain the tax bases of states and localities.

As a result of these and other economic issues, long-term solutions for raising state and local revenues involve revamping revenue codes to bring in more revenue. In Arkansas alone, for example, the Office of Tax Research estimates that sales tax exemptions cost the state approximately $350 million per year, which amounts to 37 percent of the state's sales tax revenues. If exemptions were abolished, the state could raise additional revenues without increasing tax rates.

With regard to revenues, most state and local governments will need to fully address the major factors affecting their finances:

1. Economic stagnation
2. Sharply increasing demands on public services
3. Resumption of increases in school enrollment
4. Decreases in federal aid in terms of real dollars
5. Increases in federal mandates—especially in the areas of health care, solid waste disposal, sewage treatment, services for the disabled, and corrections

Thus, state and local finances are in relatively poor shape, with little prospect for immediate improvement without tax increases.

Revenue Enhancement

States are always looking for ways to acquire additional revenues without raising taxes. Fees and user charges are commonly used. Closing tax loopholes for sales and income taxes also is frequently employed. Whatever the form of revenue enhancement, it seems obvious that for now broad-based tax increases are not on the horizon.

According to *State Policy Reports* (1993b: 6), state tax commission studies indicate that the following six courses of action are the most popular ways of increasing state and local revenues in the 1990s.

1. *Apply sales taxes to more services and to health care providers.* Extending sales taxes to the consumption of services increases the sales tax base. Over the years a variety of services have been exempted, and the consumption patterns have been shifting from goods to services.

2. *Make business inputs subject to sales taxes.* Taxing purchases of machinery and equipment, raw materials, and consumable supplies, like applying sales taxes to services, would increase the sales tax base. However, this recommendation ordinarily conflicts with the trend to abate business taxes and with the desire to remove barriers to investment, all in the name of economic development.

3. *Allow local governments to increase certain types of taxes.* Permitting local option sales and/or income tax increases local revenues to pay for services no longer funded by state and federal governments.

4. *Encourage federal tax changes.* Having the federal government expand its income tax base would increase state (and some local) revenues without raising tax rates. Taxing a portion of employer and/or employee contributions to health insurance, eliminating deductions for mortgage payments exceeding a certain threshold, levying capital gains taxes at death, and limiting corporate deductions for excessive salaries and bonuses are some of the changes often suggested.

5. *Increase tobacco and alcoholic beverage taxes.* Raising these types of excise taxes is a standard recommendation of state and local health officials. Revenues from these sources are unlikely to increase over time, however, since their consumption continues to decline.

6. *Enhance environmental fees and taxes.* Taxing products that adversely affect environmental quality has traditionally been used to reduce or control pollution. Revenues can be augmented by raising gasoline or carbon taxes, solid and hazardous waste disposal fees, and fees on containers.

Broad-based tax increases generally are treated in this day and age as an unthinkable option in most states, particularly during election years. Increasing state taxes to relieve local property taxes is always popular. The concept is and will be especially hot in states under pressure from voters to reduce property taxes. Adopting sales taxes for local education also is viewed with mounting interest.

REFERENCES

Advisory Commission on Intergovernmental Relations (ACIR) (1993). *Significant Features of Fiscal Federalism.* Vol. 2. Washington, D.C.: ACIR.

Bland, Robert (1989). *A Revenue Guide for Local Government.* Washington, D.C.: International City Management Association.

Governing (1992). August.

State Policy Reports (1993a). Vol. 10.

State Policy Reports (1993b). Vol. 11.

U.S. Department of Commerce (1993). *Statistical Abstract of the United States, 1993.* Washington, D.C.: Bureau of the Census.

Wall Street Journal (1992). September 14.

Overview of State and Local Taxes

State and local governments are in a very real sense in competition for the tax dollar. In this competitive atmosphere, a rough—though not exclusive—division has developed among governments. The national government receives the bulk of its funds from corporate and individual income taxes. State governments rely heavily on income and sales taxes. Local governments derive most their funds from sales and property taxes, with increasing amounts coming from payroll taxes, charges, and fees.

Additionally, competition for tax resources is not confined to these three levels of governments; it occurs with even greater intensity among overlapping local governments. County governments, municipalities, school districts, and various special districts draw on the same taxpayers. Thus, the competition for the tax dollar is considerable, substantial, and in some cases quite vicious.

In order to effectively comprehend the impact these divisions have on state and local governments and special districts, one must understand why governments levy taxes as well as the tax structures themselves. Generally speaking, most people assume that governments collect taxes to generate money to pay for public and private goods and services. While this view undoubtedly is accurate, it is only one reason taxes are collected.

Taxes also are used to guide private spending and behavior in a way that will eventually increase tax revenues. For instance, by not taxing business and industry heavily, state and local governments hope to attract new businesses and expand existing ones, creating jobs and increasing the tax base in the process. By taxing items such as alcoholic beverages or tobacco, state and local governments not only generate revenues but also inhibit less desirable behavior. This latter objective is a particular function of some excise taxes, charges, fees, and fines.

TAX FAIRNESS

Tax equity is important to taxpayers. However, whether a tax is fair or not depends on whose ox is being gored, that is, who benefits and who loses. In a pluralistic political economy such as ours, there is no one objective standard of fairness because such a standard depends upon the values of the group doing the measuring. Every tax benefits and hurts some more than others.

Tax fairness consists of two dimensions, both of which can be stated as questions: What does "equal sacrifice" mean? Who determines what is funded? Tax fairness, then, is concerned not only with who pays and how much they pay, but also with who determines which items and programs are selected to be financed.

Basically, two approaches are used to demarcate tax fairness: ability to pay, and benefits received. While interactions between the two occur, they are usually perceived as mutually exclusive for the most part. Consequently, the degree of tax fairness depends on which of these two approaches individuals or groups most value. Governments try to use taxes that represent each of these values, thereby keeping everyone satisfied and dissatisfied simultaneously.

Ability to Pay

For many people the overriding value that determines tax fairness is *ability to pay*. The ability to pay concept reflects the idea that taxpayers should contribute to the support of public goods and services in proportion to their financial capacity. In other words, taxpayers with more income should pay proportionately more taxes (but how much more is the debatable point). The graduated income tax is based on the ability to pay concept. It should be noted, however, that local governments seldom rely heavily on the ability to pay concept because the national and state governments have preempted the use of this tax.

The ability to pay concept stresses "equal sacrifice." Equality in taxation normally is defined as equality of sacrifice (Mill, 1921: 804). The meaning of equal sacrifice, however, is problematical. John Stuart Mill and, later, other political economists transformed the term into a strictly subjective (though not necessarily inaccurate) concept focusing on the more general problem of income redistribution (Musgrave, 1959: 92). In other words, the extent to which equal sacrifice occurs is contingent on individual interpretation. Disagreement over the degree to which equal sacrifice is achieved is inevitable.

Taxes are assessed in some manner deemed equitable or just. Fairness is assumed to exist when taxes are distributed to minimize the total sacrifice involved. Such minimization is achieved by equating the sacrifices of all taxpayers. Put somewhat differently, tax fairness is based on the requirement that each taxpayer should suffer equally—a purely subjective decision.

So long as taxpayers and those allocating expenditures are congruent in their expenditure beliefs, taxpayers will support the ability to pay concept. However, when the expenditure beliefs become incongruent, taxpayers will not support the ability to pay concept. Taxpayers thus are left with two options: opposing further tax increases or supporting the benefits received concept of taxation.

Benefits Received

Another value applied to tax fairness is the *benefits received* concept, which suggests that those who benefit from publicly provided goods and services should bear the burden of their cost in proportion to the benefits received. Put another way, a tax is fair when individuals pay taxes on a percentage of the value they receive. The more benefits they receive, the more they should pay in taxes.

Flat rate taxes are among the most widely used taxes based on the benefits received concept. Flat rate taxes are seen as fair because every person, regardless of income, pays the same tax rate per unit. Flat rate taxes include the property tax, the sales tax, and flat rate wage and payroll taxes. An individual is taxed in proportion to his or her income, and income is regarded as an indirect measure of the amount of benefits individuals receive from society. Taxes, then, are seen as a price for services rendered by governments.

Individuals or groups pay the same tax rate, though the tax base may be different. For instance, the sales tax rate is the same for everyone, regardless of income. The rate also is the same regardless of item, although more expensive items obviously would generate more revenue than would less expensive items.

User charges, fees, and fines (such as fees for swimming pools and water rates) also are based on the benefits received concept. Revenues based on this concept are the most rapidly growing state and local revenues. The two predominant reasons for this thrust are that such revenues are easy and cheap to collect and that they are very popular with the public. Moreover, local governments are left with little choice but to use these revenue sources or raise sales and property taxes—an increasingly distasteful alternative.

TAX BASE AND TAX RATE

Regardless of the type of tax, the amount of tax paid is directly dependent upon both the tax base and the tax rate. The *tax base* is the price of the unit on which the tax is predicated. The *tax rate* is the amount of tax paid on each unit. A property tax, for instance, is based on the taxable (assessed) value of each piece of property, while the tax rate consists of the number of mills charged the property owner(s) per taxable valuation. For a sales tax, the base consists of the price of purchased goods, and the tax rate is the percentage of tax paid per dollar spent. When a shirt costs $15.00 (tax base) and the tax rate is 4 cents on the dollar, the amount of tax paid is 60 cents.

Own-source revenues can be enhanced by increasing either the tax base or the tax rate. For ambitious increases, the tax base and the tax rate can be increased simultaneously. A brief overview of the main types of taxes used by state and local governments follows.

PROPERTY TAXES

Historically, general property taxes have been the main source of revenue for all forms of local government. Though their relative importance has declined in the last ten years due primarily to a substantial boost in national and state aid and an increase in other revenue sources such as sales taxes, charges, and fees, state and local governments are beginning to rely more and more on property taxes to generate sufficient revenues. However, the extent to which local governments depend on property taxes varies widely. Generally speaking, property taxes finance a larger portion of services in small cities, suburbs, and counties than they do in central cities.

From a tax base standpoint, a well-balanced mix of residential, business, and industrial properties is desirable. (Parenthetically, residential real estate property normally raises only a portion of property tax revenues. Nationwide, business and industrial property taxes often contribute two to three times as much as residential property taxes.) A good mix is hard to attain. It is not uncommon to find large business and industrial complexes in one area, low and medium priced homes in another, and luxury housing in a third. Consequently, wealthy counties, for instance, often spend more on public services than less affluent counties, but not as much as their superior tax base would permit. Wealthy counties often have lower tax rates. Given a higher tax base, they can raise sufficient money with lower tax rates. The problem is that lower tax rates encourage business and industry to locate in their jurisdictions, thus creating unending fiscal crises. Because some local governments rely heavily on real property taxes, it is important to understand how the tax base and tax rate are ascertained.

Tax Base

The *tax base* is the unit upon which the tax is fixed. Real estate property (land and structures on the land) and motor vehicles comprise most of the property tax base. Another important element is the tangible property of business and industry, such as machinery, equipment, inventories, and other property owned by business firms. This is an exceedingly important source of revenue, even though approximately 53 percent of this type of property is tax-exempt for various reasons. In addition, real estate properties owned by governments and other tax-exempt organizations are not taxed (churches, schools, universities, and hospitals).

Exhibit 2.1
Example of Property Tax Computation

A.	Estimated market value of property (owner-occupied house)	$75,000
B.	Assessment ratio	.20
C.	Assessed value (A X B)	$15,000
D.	Homestead exemption	$5,000
E.	Taxable value (C X D)	$10,000
F.	Tax rate (50 mills = 5%)	.05
G.	Tax liability (E X F)	$500
H.	Effective tax rate (G/A)	.67%
I.	Percentage of assessed value	3.3%

The first and most important step in the development of the property tax base is to determine the market value of each piece of property. Essentially, the market value is based on sales data compiled from the surrounding area, as well as several physical (property, land, and locational) characteristics. *Property* characteristics include the number of bedrooms, bathrooms, and total rooms, square feet of living space, type of construction, age of structure, and attached garage. *Land* characteristics include the size and shape of the lot, as well as landscaping. *Locational* factors are type of neighborhood, distance from business district, type of school system, and view.

Property is seldom taxed at its market value. Rather, it normally is taxed at a percentage of its market value minus any allowable exemptions. In Exhibit 2.1, for instance, the market value of a house is estimated at $75,000. The house is taxed at 20 percent of its value, and there is a $5,000 homestead exemption granted by the state. Thus, the taxable value of the house is not $75,000, but $10,000.

Tax Rate

The amount of tax money collected from property tax depends on two factors: the tax base and the tax rate. (The *tax rate* is the amount of tax paid on each unit.) The property tax rate is expressed in terms of the number of mills per dollar or the number of dollars per thousand dollars. It is determined by dividing the levy by the total value of assessed taxable property. The tax rate shown in Exhibit 2.1 is 50 mills. To find out the amount of property tax due, one merely multiplies the tax rate (.05) by the taxable value ($10,000) to get a tax liability of $500.

Property Classifications and Tax Rates

All property is not taxed at the same assessment ratio. Different rates are used for different classes of property. For illustrative purposes, Exhibit 2.2 shows

Exhibit 2.2
Example of Classification Rates

Types of Property	Assessed Rates
Residential Rate	12%
Agriculture	30% of use value
Commercial and Industrial	
real property	30%
personal property	20%
machinery	20%
Oil and Gas Property	30%
Public Utilities	30%
Merchants' and Manufacturers' Inventory and Livestock	Exempt

property assessment rates. The assessment ratio for residential property is 12 percent of its market value as determined by appraisal. This includes homes, empty lots, and apartment buildings. Commercial and industrial real property are assessed at 30 percent, while commercial and industrial equipment and machinery are assessed at 20 percent of their depreciated value.

In this example, property used to produce income—generally nonresidential buildings, oil, gas, and coal properties, and public utility properties—is assessed for taxes at 30 percent of its market value. Farmland is assessed at 30 percent of its use value (its ability to return income to owners). Farm machinery, livestock, and merchants' and manufacturers' inventories are exempt from property taxes. The rationale for taxing at a percentage of market value rather than at market value is that as long as the same percentage of assessment is applied to all similar property, the tax borne by each property owner is not distorted enough to make a significant difference in market values and tax collection discrepancies.

Assessment of Tax Base

The major problem in determining property tax liability is that most property, regardless of classification, is not appraised on-site annually. In fact, the period of time between on-site appraisals may be as long as ten to fifteen years. This means that the assessment ratios probably are not based on true market values of the property and the improvements on it. Most assessors do not have sufficient staff, time, or money to keep market values current. Assessors, however, can, and often do, update property without site visits. They base new assessments on current sales figures of comparable property in the area. In addition, with the increasingly widespread use of Computer Aided Mass Assessment (CAMA) software, many states and larger localities are able to keep assessments up to date.

Notwithstanding, assessment abuses and inequities do exist and are fairly widespread. Setting the market value of property low is the most common abuse. Property owners pay less tax, thereby reducing government revenues and limiting its capacity to borrow money, since the amount governments can borrow is often fixed by state legislatures at a percentage of assessed valuation.

Though much criticized, real property taxes appeal to local governments and are likely to remain the mainstay of their revenues, especially since they are one of the few taxes that have not been preempted by national and state governments. Besides, they are somewhat easy to collect—land and buildings cannot be hidden or moved, as can personal property. They are also less complicated and less expensive to administer than sales or wage taxes.

GENERAL SALES TAXES

A post–World War II innovation is the general sales tax, now used by most state and local governments and many special districts. The sales tax is a proportional (flat rate) tax, which means that everyone, regardless of income, pays the same amount on all goods and services subject to the tax. As a result, low income people normally pay a higher percentage of their income in sales tax than do those with moderate and high incomes.

To alleviate some of this disparity, many states and localities exempt some necessities from the sales tax, such as food, prescription drugs, and utilities. Exhibit 2.3 lists some exemptions other than those just mentioned. In addition, some states permit persons to use the amount they paid in sales tax as credit toward the state income tax, a move designed to help low income families.

In most cases general sales taxes are *ad valorem*; that is, they are a percentage of the value of the purchased goods and services. For example, when a person buys a stereo system for $100 and the county has a 1 percent sales tax, the county will receive $1 in sales tax revenues. Sales taxes, which are based on the benefits received concept of tax fairness, do not take into account incomes of the purchasers. (Because of this feature, sales taxes are frequently criticized for being regressive.)

Another characteristic of the sales tax is that the local sales tax usually is piggybacked with the state sales tax, thus reducing collection costs. Put another way, the local sales tax is levied on retail purchasers and in most cases simply added to the state sales tax, collected by the state, and returned to the local government by the state. For instance, if a county levies a 1 percent sales tax and the state levies a 4 percent sales tax *and if the tax base and exemptions are identical* (as they usually are), the county can enter into an agreement with the state to permit merchants to collect a 5 percent sales tax, which is sent (usually monthly) to the state. The state then remits 1 percent to the county, after subtracting a predetermined service fee, say 2.6 percent of the amount collected, from the 1 percent sales tax.

Exhibit 2.3
Selected Sales Tax Exemptions

1. Sale of newspapers, advertising space in newspapers and publications, and billboard advertising services.
2. Machinery and equipment used directly in the manufacturing process which are purchased for a new manufacturing facility or to replace existing equipment. Quality control equipment and ancillary production equipment may be classified as "used directly" for purposes of the exemption, and machinery and equipment required by Arkansas law to be purchased for air or water pollution control are also exempt.
3. Natural gas, L.P. gas and electricity purchased by a processor or mining company in or in connection with the open pit underground mining or processing of bauxite.
4. Electricity used in the production of aluminum metal by electrolytic reduction process.
5. Barges, towboats and vessels of at least 50-ton load displacement.
6. Feedstuffs, vaccines, medications and medicinal preparations used in the commercial production of livestock and poultry.
7. Agricultural fertilizer, limestone and chemicals used in the commercial production of agricultural products.
8. Sewer, sanitation and garbage service charges.
9. Drugs and oxygen sold pursuant to a prescription.
10. New or used farm equipment or machinery, used exclusively and directly for the agricultural production of food or fiber as a business.
11. Sales of aircraft manufactured or substantially completed in Arkansas and sold to a purchaser for use outside the state.
12. Repair services performed on watches and clocks shipped from outside the state and, after service, returned to the state of origin.
13. Repair or maintenance services performed on railroad cars, parts or equipment brought into the state only to be repaired, refurbished, modified or converted.
14. Value of trade-in allowance of old automobile parts (core charges) when deducted from the original selling price.
15. Legally purchased with food stamps.

Source: University of Arkansas at Little Rock, Regional Economics Analysis, 1990.

The basic advantage of the general sales tax is that it is quite easy and inexpensive to collect. The principal problem is that the amount of money that the sales tax will yield from one year to the next is difficult to estimate inasmuch as it depends primarily on business cycles and inflation rates.

In summary, the sales tax is an important source of revenue because it provides a substantial amount of money to state and local governments. Consequently, it is here to stay even though it is noticeably regressive.

CHARGES AND FEES

State and local governments are deriving an expanding proportion of their income from charges and fees, which are based on the benefits received concept of tax fairness. *Charges*, often called *user charges*, are similar to prices charged for privately produced goods and services in that they represent payment for goods and services persons would not receive if they did not pay for them. *Fees* represent compensation paid to governments for expenses incurred in providing services. The costs of paving a street or installing curbs are examples of fees. (Not all private goods and services are subjected to user charges and fees. Some, such as education, meet societal rather than private needs and are thus considered common services and funded from general tax dollars.)

In two respects, however, user charges and fees differ from charges for privately produced goods and services. First, user charges and fees, unlike private charges, do not always cover the full cost of the goods and services. Second, user charges and fees frequently are levied for some good or service that users may really not want. For instance, property owners may be required to pay for a building permit to allow them to make physical improvements on their domiciles whether they want to or not. Exhibit 2.4 is a list of typical user charges and fees. Normally, charges, fees, and licenses are assessed similar to market prices, but they may involve a subsidy to specific users. Payments are voluntary, and, depending on the types of service, the amount charged will depend on individual demand, administrative costs, volume, location, and population density.

Nationwide, according to the United States Bureau of the Census, charges and fees now amount to approximately 21 percent of the total revenues of municipal budgets. Such financing is especially widespread in cities with less than 250,000 people, where user charges and fees provide more than 40 percent of the operating revenues.

Increased reliance on user charges and fees is quite salable to taxpayers because they take the burden off the general taxpayer and put it on users of the service. In addition, charges and fees, like sales taxes, permit governments to export taxes (extend their tax base beyond their political jurisdiction). For instance, a water bill is based on the number of gallons of water used, regardless of where the user lives. In fact, often users who live outside the providing jurisdiction pay a slightly higher rate than residents for the same amount of goods. The same principle is applied to sewage disposal, garbage collection, and other such services.

Since user charges and fees are applied to private services (those from which a person can be excluded for nonpayment), persons are free to decide which services, and how much of each, they want, depending of course on their ability to pay for them. In brief, then, people normally can choose any combination of services within the constraints of their income.

User charges and fees tend to be applied to private services when at least one of the following conditions is met: (1) the service would be wasted if there were no charges; (2) the service directly and measurably benefits particular individuals (or families); or (3) the charges and fees are relatively inexpensive to collect (Bollens and Schmandt, 1970: 263).

Invariably, money generated from user charges and fees is placed in restricted

Exhibit 2.4
Types of Local Government Fees, Charges, and Licenses

Police protection
Special patrol service fees
Fees for fingerprints, copies
Payments for extra police services for stadiums, theaters, circuses
Transportation
Subway and bus fares
Bridge tolls
Landing and departure fees
Hangar rentals
Parking meter receipts
Health and hospitals
Inoculation charges
X-ray charges
Hospital charges
Ambulance charges
Concessions rentals
Education
Charges for books
Charges for gymnasium uniforms
Recreation
Greens fees
Parking charges
Admission fees or charges
Permit charges for tennis courts
Specific recreation services
Picnic stove fees
Stadium gate tickets
Stadium club fees
Park development charges
Sanitation
Domestic and commercial trash collection fees
Industrial waste charges
Sewerage
Sewerage system fees
Other public utility operations
Water meter permits
Water services charges
Electricity rates
Telephone booth rentals
Street tree fees
Tract map filing fees
Street lighting installations
Convention center revenues
Commodity sales

Salvage materials
Sales of maps
Sales of codes
Licenses and fees
Advertising vehicles
Amusements (ferris wheels, etc.)
Billiard and pool halls
Bowling alleys
Circuses and carnivals
Coal dealers
Commercial combustion
Dances
Dog tags
Duplicate dog tags
Electricians—first class
Electricians—second class
Film storage
Food peddlers
Hucksters and intinerant peddlers
Heating equipment contractors
Loading zone permits
Lumber dealers
Pawnbrokers
Plumbers—first class
Plumbers—second class
Pest eradicators
Poultry dealers
Produce dealers—itinerant
Pushcarts
Secondhand dealers
Sign inspection
Solicitations
Shooting galleries
Taxis
Taxi transfer licenses
Taxi drivers
Theaters
Trees—Christmas
Vending—coin
Vault cleaners
Sound trucks
Refuse haulers
Landfills
Sightseeing buses
Wrecking licenses

funds. That is, the money collected must be spent for a particular purpose and cannot be put into the general fund. For instance, water receipts must be spent within the Water Department, recreation receipts on recreational facilities, and so forth. Property and sales tax revenues, on the other hand, are customarily placed in the general fund and can be spent for any legitimate purpose.

With intergovernmental aid unlikely to increase substantially anytime in the near future, with citizen demands for increased services, and with property and sales taxes stabilizing, user charges and fees will continue to be an essential element in state and local government finance.

Enterprise Funds

Enterprise funds are fees collected for special purposes. Some governments provide particular goods and services to the public for a fee. The funds accumulated from these services are commonly called enterprise funds. The principal government enterprises relate to water, sewerage and water pollution, and parking. Normally, the net incomes from these enterprises are deposited in restricted accounts; they cannot be spent for any purpose other than that enterprise. (Special taxes such as assessments, intergovernmental aid, and court fines also tend to be restricted money.) Many services formerly provided without charge to residents are being turned into enterprise funds because state and local governments can no longer pay the service costs from general taxes.

UTILITY TAXES

Utilities pay property taxes on land they occupy. In addition, however, they pay *utility taxes*, which are reimbursements from privately owned public utilities for rental of government property. Taxes (and charges) are imposed on utility companies for infrastructure impact and government services needed to accommodate the delivery of utility products.

For example, a municipality and an electric company often enter into an agreement concerning the delivery of electricity to the municipality's residents. Under such an agreement the municipality grants the electric company the right to run its power lines on municipal land and to be the sole provider of electricity. In return, the electric company pays the municipality fees based on usage, most of which are passed on to consumers.

Other sources of utility taxes are telephone services, cable television, garbage disposal services, and transportation. For a government of approximately 150,000 residents, utility taxes typically produce about $5 million—for example, $2.5 million for electricity, $2 million for gas, and $200,000 for cable television. Based on usage, the amount of money produced from utility taxes—like sales taxes—is quite variable from year to year. Mild summers and winters result in lower sales of gas and electricity, for example.

INCOME, WAGE, AND PAYROLL TAXES

Income taxes are a much less important revenue source for state and local government than for the federal government. Overall, personal income taxes produce approximately 19 percent of state and local revenues, and corporate income taxes provide about 5 percent. Of course, the amount varies from state to state and locality to locality.

The primary reason that state and local governments do not depend heavily on income taxes is that such taxes are more appropriately levied by governments whose political boundaries are coincident with the extent of the market. Since the marketplace exists beyond the political boundaries of state and local governments, persons and corporations can "escape" their income tax levies, whereas persons and corporations cannot escape federal income taxes unless they move to another country, and even then their incomes might be taxed. Accordingly, a division of tax incidence occurs at state and local levels. States tend to rely on personal and corporate income taxes, while local governments, if they tax personal income, rely on wage and payroll taxes.

Personal Income Taxes

A *personal income tax* is a tax on the earnings of resident and nonresident individuals and estates and trusts. Total income is rarely taxed. Rather, taxes are levied on an amount called *taxable income*, which is the amount left after exemptions, allowable adjustments, and credits have been subtracted from the total earnings. *Earnings* consist of wages, salaries, tips, interest income, dividends, refunds from other taxes, alimony, rents, royalties, capital gains, taxable pensions, farm income, and unemployment income. *Exemptions* are credits given for financially supporting dependents, the aged, and the handicapped. *Allowable adjustments* include things such as moving and business expenses, alimony paid, and nontaxable retirement funds. Tax *credits* are usually given for expenses related to child, disabled, elderly, and dependent care, medical and dental care, and residential energy costs. Credits also may be given for interest and taxes paid (state and local income, real estate, motor vehicle, and sometimes sales taxes).

States seldom assess taxable incomes at a flat rate. Normally the rates are progressive; tax rates increase as incomes increase. Exhibit 2.5 gives an example of personal income tax rates.

To make the personal income tax even more progressive, states often exempt persons earning less than a specified amount per year from paying income taxes. For instance, those making less than $5,000 a year may not be required to pay any state income tax. Some benefits deemed essential may be excluded from being classified as earnings. The principal exclusion is fringe benefits, primarily health and insurance premiums and Social Security payments.

Exhibit 2.5
Example of Personal Income Tax Rates

Resident individuals, estates and trusts, and nonresident individuals, estates and trusts, deriving income from within the state are subject to a tax on their net income at the following rates:

Net Taxable Income	Rate	Net Taxable Income	Rate
First $2,999	1%	Next $6,000	4.5%
Next $3,000	2.5%	Next $10,000	6%
Next $3,000	3.5%	$25,000 or over	7%

To arrive at next taxable income the taxpayer may elect to either itemize deductions or to sue the standard deduction of $1,000 or 10 percent of gross income, whichever is the lesser. Federal income tax is not deductible from income subject to Arkansas individual income tax.

A credit is allowed resident individuals for the amount of income tax paid to any other state not to exceed what the tax would be on out-of-state income calculated at Arkansas income tax rates. The following personal tax credits are allowed:

1. Single individuals, $20,000, blind and/or deaf taxpayers, additional $20,000; taxpayers 65 years or older, additional $20.00 credit.

2. Head of family, $40,000.

3. Dependents with gross income of less than $3,000.

4. Fiduciaries, $20.00.

5. Age 65 special: $20.00 for Arkansas residents 65 or older not claiming a deduction for employer sponsored pension.

Certain resident low income persons are exempt from Arkansas personal income tax. They range from single individuals with gross incomes of $3,000 or less, to married couples or family heads having two or more dependent children and gross incomes of $5,000 or less; there are alternative lower tax liabilities on the first $100 of income in excess of the basic exemptions.

An appealing feature of the personal income tax is that the rate applies to the taxable income of persons residing within a state regardless of where they work. (A credit of some sort usually is given when residents of the taxing state pay income taxes to another state.) Those who work within the state but live outside it also pay income taxes in the state in which they work. Consequently, the personal income tax, like sales taxes and user charges and fees, is a means of exporting taxes; that is, of recouping some costs of services the state furnishes to nonresident workers.

Corporate Income Taxes

A *corporate income tax* is applied to the *net earnings* of corporations. Deductions are allowed for operating costs, charitable contributions, and a variety of economic development incentives, such as creating jobs and locating in particular geographical areas. Normally, the tax applies to its total corporate profits, including earnings retained by the firm as well as those paid in dividends to stockholders. Exhibit 2.6 is an example of basic corporate income tax rates.

Calculating the amount of corporate income tax is complicated because corporations usually conduct business in more than one state (and often in more than a single country), and all but five states have a corporate income tax. (The exceptions are Nevada, South Dakota, Texas, Washington, and Wyoming.) Consequently, for multistate corporations, it is difficult to know exactly how much income clearly originated in each state, as well as how much of a firm's profits should be taxed in each state.

To answer these questions, most states adopt a formula for allocating profits. The formula computes the average percentage of the total property, total payroll, and total sales in a state and then assigns that percentage total to the total profits taxable in each state. While such computations are relatively simple, they are normally less than precise because most states lack sufficient audit staff to verify the percentages; they accept the calculations supplied by corporations. The corporate income tax is a way for states to be compensated for benefits furnished to corporations. However, a sizable portion of the corporate income tax is shifted to consumers in the form of higher prices.

Wage and Payroll Taxes

Approximately 4,000 local governmental units levy some form of wage or payroll tax. However, since there are over 78,000 local governmental units in the United States, one can readily see that wage or payroll taxes are not widely used. Only thirty-two cities with populations over 50,000 have some kind of wage or payroll tax. Most are located in only six states: Kentucky, Michigan, Missouri, Ohio, Pennsylvania, and New York. (The wage or payroll tax probably is not used by more municipalities for fear that it may influence individuals and businesses to move elsewhere.)

A *wage tax* generally is a percentage of the gross wages or salaries of individuals and is collected and appropriated at the place of residence. Normally, the tax rate, whether fixed or variable, is relatively low—no more than 2 percent on gross earnings. The wage tax is not an income tax, although many refer to it as such. The tax is based only on gross earnings and generally excludes rental income, capital gains, interest, deductions, and exemptions—sources of income commonly subject to state and national income taxes.

A *payroll tax*, on the other hand, is a wage tax collected and appropriated at the workplace. A wage tax benefits the area where people live, while the payroll

Exhibit 2.6
Example of Corporate Income Tax Rates

Domestic corporations and all foreign corporations doing business within the state are subject to tax on net income at the following rates:

> First $ 3,000 - 1%
> Next $ 3,000 - 2%
> Next $ 5,000 - 3%
> Next $14,000 - 5%
> Over $25,000 - 6%

When business income is derived from activity which is taxable both within and without Arkansas, it is apportioned for taxation according to percent of property and payrolls utilized in the state and sales attributable to Arkansas pursuant to the multistate tax compact.

The following example shows the method of apportioning business income to Arkansas, and the computations of tax due to state for a hypothetical firm:

1. Business income amounts to $1,250,000.
2. Apportionment method based on the three-factor formula:

	Everywhere	Arkansas	Percent in Arkansas
Plant, property and equipment (beginning of year)	$3,100,000	$ 750,000	
Plant, property and equipment (end of year)	3,300,000	850,000	
Total	6,400,000	1,600,000	
Average (÷2)	3,200,000	800,000	25%
Payrolls	900,000	3,750,000	24%
Sales and other apportionable income	25,000,000	3,750,000	15%
Sum of Percentages			60%
Average (÷3)			20%

3. Income subject to tax in Arkansas is the total income multiplied by the average of the sum of percentages in Arkansas ($1,250,000 X 20% = $250,000).

4. Arkansas state income tax computations based on $250,000 and Arkansas tax rates:

	Income Amount	Amount of Tax
Amount taxable at 1% (first $3,000)	$ 3,000	$ 30
Amount taxable at 2% (next $3,000)	3,000	60
Amount taxable at 3% (next $5,000)	5,000	150
Amount taxable at 5% (next $14,000)	14,000	700
Amount taxable at 6% (next $25,000)	225,000	13,500
Total	$250,000	$14,440

A corporation other than a Subchapter S Corporation doing business in Arkansas and sustaining a net operating loss for a tax year beginning on or after January 1, 1987, may carry forward the loss to the next succeeding taxable year and annually, thereafter, for a total period of five years next succeeding the year of such loss and deduct it from gross taxable income.

tax benefits the area where people work. Problems occur when people work in one area but reside in another. Differing benefits obviously accrue to local governments from each of the two types of taxes depending on where individuals live and work.

One way out of this quagmire is to split tax receipts. For instance, those who live and work in the city pay the full wage or payroll tax, say 1 percent. However, those who work in the city and live outside it or live in the city and work outside it pay only half the tax—half of 1 percent—to each jurisdiction.

Excluding other forms of income and not permitting deductions and exemptions means that wage and payroll taxes are based on benefits received rather than on ability to pay. It is this benefits received approach that is used to justify taxing nonresidents of a jurisdiction. As long as wage and payroll taxes are based on the benefits received concept, the major question is not whether nonresidents should pay, but how much they should pay compared to residents— one-fourth, one-half, or three-fourths. As with sales taxes and user charges and fees, wage and payroll taxes are means of extending the tax bases of governments, enabling them to recoup some costs of services furnished to nonresident workers.

Wage and payroll taxes are more popular than an income tax with local governments because the cost of collecting and enforcing an income tax is prohibitive, whereas the cost of collecting taxes on salaries and wages is relatively low. Remember, to collect such taxes, governments must establish tax rolls, prepare tax return forms, hire clerical and audit personnel, and monitor compliance. To collect taxes on income separate from salaries and wages also would require additional expenses that probably would not be worth the effort.

INTERGOVERNMENTAL (STATE AND FEDERAL) AID

By the early 1990s, all state and local governments had to cope with increasingly inadequate revenues. Some transferred certain services to other governmental units and/or special districts. Cincinnati, for instance, divested itself of its courts, its university, and its hospital. Baltimore shifted its social services to the state (Schultze, 1985: 185).

Shifting services, however, is only one way to transfer funds. The more widely used method is for the federal government to give money to state and local governments and for state governments to give money to local governments to deliver goods and services. By 1991 federal aid to state and local governments alone amounted to about $143 billion. States also increased their aid to local governments to the tune of approximately $80 billion. Federal aid is granted to communities for a variety of projects dealing primarily with highways and streets, welfare, elementary and secondary education, hospitals, mental health, libraries, airports, public housing, and urban redevelopment. Basically, federal aid is given to state and local governments to implement particular national goals.

State aid, on the other hand, generally is earmarked to support services deemed essential but which localities alone cannot afford. State aid includes various project grants, manipulation of tax rate ceilings, and technical assistance programs such as police training and computer sharing. States also help local governments financially by imposing and collecting taxes which then are returned proportionally to them (sales, liquor, cigarette, and gasoline taxes).

Intergovernmental aid benefits both services and individuals. Medicaid, for instance, is a service funded by federal and state monies, while Aid to Families with Dependent Children (AFDC) payments subsidize individuals. With the exception of Medicaid, intergovernmental aid for services has been declining in terms of real dollars for the past fifteen years. Intergovernmental aid for individuals, on the other hand, has been growing rapidly during the same time period.

LONG-TERM DEBT FINANCING

Besides taxes, charges, and fees, state and local governments enhance their revenues via astute short- and long-term borrowing. By reducing costs of borrowing, governments can maximize the amount of money available for other uses. The amount of debt governments can incur is limited typically by state law and/or the state constitution since the authority to borrow comes from the state.

In certain limited situations, a local government may receive the power to borrow money independent of the state. When Congress passes legislation, it may use a local government as an agent to implement that legislation. In such a situation, a government, therefore, obtains the power to act, including the power to borrow money if necessary. Since federal laws supersede state provisions, a state cannot prevent a local government from borrowing money, even when state laws directly prohibit such action. For instance, in 1953 Tacoma, Washington, was licensed by the Federal Power Commission to construct a dam in contravention of state of Washington law. The state of Washington tried to stop Tacoma from borrowing money to construct the dam and was overruled by the federal courts. But an exception like this is rare; state laws normally control most local bond issues.

To keep the cost of borrowing money to a minimum, most state and local government bonds are exempt from various forms of state and federal taxes, such as personal and corporate income taxes. Because those who purchase such bonds do not pay taxes on the interest earned, they are willing to buy bonds carrying a lower interest rate. As a result, governments can borrow money at a cheaper rate than private businesses can.

Although recent court cases suggest a gradual erosion of the immunity from taxation doctrine, courts have ruled that the federal government cannot constrain any state's financial decisions affecting the delivery of services. These rulings might well include the taxation of interest on state and local bond issues, since such taxation clearly would increase the cost of financing services, which in turn might affect the local decision-making process.

It also should be understood that most projects financed with general obligation bonds entail the issuance of temporary loans pending the completion of the project. Temporary loans are needed because most states restrict the amount of the general obligation bond to the total cost of the project, which generally is unknown until the project is completed. Temporary loans are used to finance the project in the meantime, then paid off with the money from the general obligation bond.

Types of Bonds

There are three basic types of bonds state and local governments can issue: general obligation bonds, revenue bonds, and industrial development bonds.

General Obligation Bonds. The principal and interest on these bonds are backed by the full faith, credit, and resources of the state and/or local government. The money to pay off these bonds comes either from a general tax levy or from special assessments levied on the properties benefited by the improvements.

For example, when a county decides to build a civic center, the money to build it frequently comes from a mileage increase assessed on all the property in the county. An example of a special assessment is the development of a benefit district. Here, only the property located within such a district is assessed. Of course, the money collected from that assessment is spent only within the district. If the special assessment cannot pay for the cost of the improvements, however, the state and/or local government is required to pay the unpaid balance.

Since general obligation bonds are backed by the government's resources, most states feel a need to regulate how much money a community can borrow. These restrictions generally limit the total amount of general obligation debt a government can incur. (Special public service projects—hospital construction, for instance—often are exempt from such restrictions.)

Revenue Bonds. These bonds are paid solely from revenues produced by the project being financed. Revenue bonds normally are not subject to debt limitation laws. Consequently, governments increasingly are relying on revenue bonds to finance projects. (As previously mentioned, many states have laws restricting the amount local governments can borrow. One way to circumvent many of these state laws is to use revenue rather than general obligation bonds.)

Most revenue bonds are used to finance private services. In specific terms, this means that most revenue bonds are issued to finance utility improvements. The term *utility*, however, is defined quite broadly. For instance, utility can mean any publicly owned utility, instrumentality or facility of a revenue producing character including but not limited to plants, facilities and instrumentalities for the purpose of supplying natural or manufactured gas, water or electric light and offstreet parking facilities and sewage disposal plants, facilities and interceptor sewers.

Industrial Development Bonds. These bonds, often called industrial revenue bonds, are issued by governments to stimulate economic development. Industrial development bonds, which have been around since the 1930s, provide low cost financing for businesses and induce new businesses to locate in states and localities that offer them. Since government bonds are usually tax exempt, governments can borrow money at a cheaper rate than can the private sector. They then use the money from the sale of these bonds to build or improve industrial or commercial facilities. These facilities are then leased to business enterprises at a rent sufficient to pay for the principal and interest on the bond, or the money is loaned directly to the businesses. In either case, businesses obtain the benefit of a tax-exempt loan.

In the past the Internal Revenue Service allowed development bonds to be used to finance not only small industrial and commercial businesses, but also rental housing, mass transit, convention and sport facilities, utilities, airports, and marine terminals, and in general any business that has a public purpose, as defined by each state's laws.

For a number of years the Internal Revenue Service looked extremely favorably on development bonds. But in the early 1970s, legislation was introduced to curb their use. The United States Department of the Treasury opposes development bonds on the grounds that the federal government is subsidizing private business and losing tax revenues in the process. In addition, Treasury argues, the increasing use of these bonds is driving up the cost of other types of government bonds. Hence, state and local governments pay more money to build schools, streets, and sewers because they pay high interest rates on general obligation and revenue bonds.

Methods of Sale. Bonds, regardless of type, are sold by state and local governments to investors through underwriters who assume the burden of selling bonds by putting together a syndicate of buyers. For this, underwriters charge a fee.

Bonds can be sold either by competitive bids or negotiation, though most bonds are sold via competitive bids because state and local governments usually are required to do so by state law. After bid specifications and detailed market information are drawn up, a bid is let. With competitive bids, the lowest bidder usually gets to purchase the bond.

However, sometimes a bond is let through a *negotiated sale*. Simply put, state and local governments and underwriters negotiate the specifications, timing, and types of bonds to be issued in hopes of obtaining the most favorable deal. Since a variety of factors affect bond purchases, negotiated sales attempt to sell bonds in the most favorable environment to get the best possible interest rates. Negotiated sales are particularly effective for governments that do not have a high credit rating. Exhibit 2.7 illustrates some debt financing options.

Exhibit 2.7
Selected Financing Options

	GENERAL OBLIGATION BONDS	REVENUE BONDS	SHORT-TERM BORROWING
DESCRIPTION	Traditional "plain vanilla" bonds backed by the full faith and credit of the issuing unit of government. The bonds are secured by an unconditional pledge of the issuing government to levy unlimited taxes to retire the bonds.	Principal and interest on the bonds are payable exclusively from the earning of a public enterprise such as water or sewerage systems. No taxes are levied or pledged as a backup.	Short-term borrowing instruments with maturities generally less than one year such as bond, tax, or revenue anticipation notes. Tax revenues or future bond proceeds pledged as security.
PURPOSE	Used by governments to finance capital projects which exhibit community-wide benefits that should be paid for by present and future residents.	To provide front-end financing for facilities that can pay for themselves over the investment's useful life from project revenues.	To take advantage of lower short-term interest rates at start of project. Also used to manage cash-flow requirements.
MARKET ACCEPTANCE	Traditional, well-known form of tax-exempt borrowing.	Highly dependent on service or project to be financed. Greater risk than for general obligation bonds.	Notes purchased by investors unwilling to commit long-term funds.
ADVANTAGES	● Due to strong security features, the interest rates of G.O. supported bonds are generally the lowest available. ● More marketable debt due to higher security. ● Opportunity to invest proceeds of bond issue.	● Credit analysis is straightforward. ● Users pay for facility. ● Default on issue does not burden local taxpayers. ● Usually not need for bond referendum. ● Often not subject to debt ceiling. ● Promotes sound financial management.	● Can be sign of astute financial management. ● Ability to lower total project costs through lower interest costs. ● Short-term borrowing generally does not require voters' approval, though subsequent long-term bond sale may.
DISADVANTAGES	● Credit analysis is complex. ● May require voter approval. ● May create need to raise taxes. ● Time lags increase construction cost. ● Subject to debt ceiling. ● If paid by property taxes, cost of facilities may not be paid for by project beneficiaries.	● Generally higher interest costs. ● Bonds usually contain restrictive covenants which may restrict operations.	● Threat of becoming overburdened with short-term debt. ● Increases issuer's risk, for the use of bond anticipation notes assumes that long-term rates will fall.

	COMPOUND COUPON BONDS	ZERO COUPON BONDS	VARIABLE RATE BONDS
DESCRIPTION	Long-term securities sold at par. Semi-annual interest accrues to investor at a compounded rate but is not paid until maturity.	Bonds that pay no interest prior to maturity. They are sold at a substantial discount from their face value, similar to a U.S. Government Series E savings bond.	Floating rate security wherein the interest rate is tied to one or more market interest rates, such as a percentage of the prime rate or U.S. Treasury Bill rate. The bonds or notes usually have a specified floor and ceiling on the rates. The cost of borrowing becomes variable rather than a fixed cost to the issuer.
PURPOSE	Similar to zero coupon bonds; allows issuer to defer interest payments until maturity. Lowers interest costs.	To lower interest costs to issuers and enable them to defer interest payments on the obligation until maturity.	To obtain lower interest rates by assuming a share of the investor's market risk.
MARKET ACCEPTANCE	Issuer assumes investor's reinvestment risk.	Investors value the ability to "lock in" a fixed rate of return as reinvestment risk is borne by issuer.	Popular with investors in a volatile market, for the floating rate preserves the market value of the bond.
ADVANTAGES	● Lowers interest costs to issuer. ● All debt service deferred until maturity. ● Reduced administrative costs. ● Investors guaranteed a fixed yield to maturity.	● Lowers interest costs to issuers. ● Payment of interest is deferred. ● Investors guaranteed a fixed yield to maturity. ● Low initial investment popular with individual investors.	● Lowers interest costs to issuers. ● Allows issuers to sell bonds to a broader market. ● Investor's capital value of bonds is protected.
DISADVANTAGES	● Balloon payment at end must be planned for by establishing a sinking fund. ● High cost of calling bonds for redemption prior to maturity.	● Some states may prohibit deep discounting of bonds. ● Issuers receive much less cash up front. ● May be difficult concept to sell to the public. ● The balloon payment may increase credit risk. ● Legal question of debt limit calculation may inhibit sale.	● Issuers face great uncertainty in debt service planning. ● Requires greater expertise in administration.

Exhibit 2.7 (Continued)

	TAX-EXEMPT COMMERCIAL PAPER	LEASE-PURCHASE	OPERATING LEASE
DESCRIPTION	Extremely short-term promissory notes with average maturity of 45 days. Notes are intended to be rolled over continuously for periods that may exceed one year.	An installment or conditional sales contract under which the governmental use of the equipment or property subject to the contract agrees to make payments of a purchase price plus interest over a period of years. Government retains the right to purchase the asset at the end of the lease for a nominal amount.	An arrangement through which the lessee (the governmental unit) acquires use of an asset for only a portion of its useful life. The lessor may or may not be responsible for maintenance, insurance, and taxes. Type of lease used in a sale-leaseback transaction.
PURPOSE	Lower borrowing costs to issuers with continuous need for short-term funds.	To enable governmental units to acquire assets without incurring debt as legally defined.	To enable governments to use facilities or equipment for a public purpose without having to purchase the asset.
MARKET ACCEPTANCE	Preferred by investors concerned with rapid liquidity. Tax-exempt money market funds are large purchasers.	If properly structured, interest income can be considered tax-exempt. Third-party lenders are often involved.	Ownership for tax purposes is transferred from public to private body. Investors can depreciate the asset and possibly receive investment tax credit. Form of tax shelter.
ADVANTAGES	• Interest rates are lowest available. • Relatively easy to increase amounts outstanding. • Maturities may be tailored to specific needs of issuer or investor.	• Preservation of debt capacity for other purposes. • No need for bond referendum. • Ownership reverts to government with little or no additional cost. • Usually not subject to debt limitations. • Because interest portions of lease payments are tax-exempt, acquisition costs may be lower.	• Frees up funds for other purposes. • Sale price in a sale-leaseback adds to city revenue. • Lease obligation not considered as debt. • May be less expensive way to obtain mass transit vehicles or to renovate public buildings than G.O. financing.
DISADVANTAGES	• High initial costs. • Requires daily staff commitment. • Letter or line of credit necessary. • Generally accepted $25 million minimum.	• Higher interest rates than debt financing. • Lease payments subject to annual appropriations. • Narrower market than traditional debt instruments. • No opportunity to invest proceeds of bond issue. • Purposes may be limited.	• Government is not acquiring an equity interest in asset. • The private owner expects fair compensation for use of leased asset. • In sale-leaseback, repurchase price at end of lease is uncertain. • Sale of public property may not show up as an asset.

46

	PUT OPTION BONDS	BONDS WITH WARRANTS
DESCRIPTION	A long-term bond which provides the investor the option of redeeming the issue well in advance of the stated maturity. The "put" creates a potentially shorter term obligation.	A warrant is a feature that provides the investor with an option to purchase additional bonds at a specified interest rate during a specific period.
PURPOSE	Lowers the cost of borrowing as long-term issue has characteristics of a short-term obligation.	To provide issuers with a method for lowering initial interest costs.
MARKET ACCEPTANCE	Investors value liquidity and protection from a major drop in market value.	Investors are willing to accept a lower rate of interest on the premise that interest rates will decline in the period for which the warrent is valid.
ADVANTAGES	● Lowers interest costs to issuers. ● Allows issuers to sell bonds to a broader market.	● Lowers interest cost to issuers. ● Warrants may be detached from bonds and sold separately, creating new market. ● Broadens market for debt to include speculative purchasers.
DISADVANTAGES	● May require back-up credit from a major financial institution. ● Increases level of uncertainty in debt service planning. ● Significant risk exposure in having sufficient funds available to redeem debt if put is exercised.	● Issuers must be prepared to issue additional bonds. ● If warrants are exercised, issuer must pay higher than prevailing interest rate.

Source: Hough and Petersen, 1983: 17.

STRATEGIES FOR BALANCED TAX POLICIES

Over the years, state and local governments have sought to (1) diversify their revenue sources and (2) export as many taxes as possible. This pursuit has led to increased dependency on property, income, sales, and excise taxes. This, in turn, has further intensified the need to look at tax incidence (who pays) and tax equity (fairness). Thus, an incentive for a balanced state and local tax system is quickly developing.

According to Kleine and Shannon (1985: 20), the case for a balanced state and local tax system rests on two basic assumptions. First, most state and local governments are affected by increasing interstate tax competition coupled with an uncertain economic environment. Second, because of competition and economic uncertainties, most of these governments must—if they have not already—develop tax strategies. Such strategies can best be implemented with moderate use of income, sales, and property taxes, coupled with a proportional distribution of the tax burden and safeguards for low income taxpayers. Exhibit 2.8 lists specific tax strategies state and local governments should seriously consider.

CONCLUDING COMMENTS

State and local governments exist to furnish public and private goods and services to their residents. To pay for these services they collect money in the form of taxes and charges. By reducing the cost of long-term financing, governments indirectly increase the amount of money available to them.

Finance involves a highly developed, complex array of interrelated factors. With the increasing federal deficit and the problems accruing from it, state and local governments will have to search for creative ways to cut expenditures, deliver goods and services, increase revenues, and raise capital.

Exhibit 2.8
Strategies for Balanced Tax Policies

Personal Income Tax

1. Should provide 20 to 30 percent of all state-local tax revenue.
2. Should offer personal exemptions or credits at least as generous as the federal income tax exemptions.
3. Should minimize the number of deductions allowed for state income taxes.
4. Should be indexed for inflation.
5. Should share the proceeds of the personal income tax with local governments or permit local income taxation.
6. Should *not* have rates markedly higher than rates in surrounding area.

Exhibit 2.8 (Continued)

Sales Tax

1. Should provide 20 to 30 percent of all state-local tax revenue.
2. Should exempt foods, drugs, and utilities or provide tax credits for purchase of these items.
3. Should tax most services as well as goods.
4. Should share proceeds of sales tax with local governments or allow them to levy sales taxes.
5. Should maintain a strong audit and enforcement program to protect integrity of tax base.
6. Should *not* be out of line with surrounding states.

Property Tax

1. Should provide 20 to 30 percent of all state-local tax revenues.
2. Should force state and local governments to work together to insure that property tax burden does not become excessive.
3. Should finance a "circuit breaker" property tax relief program to shield low income taxpayers from excessive tax burdens.
4. Should be assessed on average at no less than 80 percent of full market value.
5. Should include a mechanism to prevent automatic increases in revenues from inflation-induced assessment increases.

Business Taxes

1. Should be broad based with some consideration of ability to pay.
2. Should be applicable to all forms of business organizations.
3. Should provide immediate write-off for capital investment and dispense with special tax inducements.
4. Should keep the number of separate taxes within the business tax system as low as possible.
5. Should use a stable tax base.
6. Should furnish funding to local governments to allow local repeal of personal property tax on inventories.
7. Should have moderate rates for unemployment insurance and workers' compensation as well as for general business taxes.

Excise Taxes

1. Should be levied on value (ad valorem tax).
2. Should use restraint in setting rates.
3. Should share proceeds with excise audit programs.

Source: Kleine, and Shannon, 1985: 5–18.

REFERENCES

Bollens, John, and Henry Schmandt (1970). *The Metropolis: Its People, Politics, and Economic Life*. New York: Harper and Row.

Bradford, David, and Wallace Oates (1974). "Suburban Exploitation of Central Cities." In Harold Hochman and George Peterson, eds., *Redistribution Through Public Choice*. New York: Columbia University Press.

Hough, Wesley, and John Petersen (1983). *State Constraints on Local Capital Financing*. Washington, D.C.: Municipal Finance Officers Association.

Kleine, Robert, and John Shannon (1985). *Characteristics of a Balanced and Moderate State-Local Revenue System*. Denver: National Conference of State Legislatures.

Mill, John Stuart (1921). *Principles of Political Economy*. London: Ashley, Longmans, and Green.

Musgrave, Richard (1959). *The Theory of Public Finance: A Study in Political Economy*. New York: McGraw-Hill.

Savas, E. S. (1982). *Privatizing the Public Sector*. Chatham, N.J.: Chatham House.

Schreiber, Arthur, and Richard Clemmer (1982). *Economics of Urban Problems: An Introduction*. Boston: Houghton Mifflin.

Schultze, William (1985). *Urban Politics: A Political Economy Approach*. Englewood Cliffs, N.J.: Prentice-Hall.

3

Income Taxes

The income tax was established on the ability to pay concept. As a result, most income taxes are designed to be progressive, meaning that they are based on vertical equity, which holds that persons with greater ability to pay should pay more than those with less ability. A tax is progressive, then, when high income taxpayers pay a greater percentage of their income in taxes than do low income taxpayers. Conversely, as tax is regressive when low income taxpayers pay a higher percentage of their incomes in taxes than do persons with larger incomes. In keeping with this progressivity concept, most states also exempt very low income persons from income taxation.

Graduated personal and corporate income taxes are increasingly being viewed as an appropriate and effective means of assuring progressivity and elasticity in state and local revenues. That is, progressive income taxes assure cost equity to taxpayers and are more responsive to economic changes than are most other broad-based taxes. This latter characteristic reduces the need for state officials to go to the voters year after year to increase tax rates or to introduce new taxes, charges, or fees. While the movement toward tax indexing has tended to reduce the elasticity of nonprogressive taxes, graduated income taxes are still more progressive than most of the other revenue sources available to state and local governments (Hansen, 1983: 415). Income taxes, as well, are less likely to be earmarked for special purposes—unlike gasoline taxes, which are typically designated for road building, or lottery revenues, which may be committed for education. Thus, income taxes provide state and local governments with more spending flexibility.

Notwithstanding these advantages, income taxes are generally less popular than sales taxes among state and local governments because of the costs and difficulty of administering collections; and they are less popular among citizens because of the nature of the tax (i.e., large annual payments, expense of compliance, and costs in time and money for recordkeeping and filing tax forms). In other words, ease of payment and collection may outweigh other concerns, including the actual tax rate, for many citizens (Hansen, 1983: 415).

That graduated, progressive income tax rates place a greater burden on higher income groups than do sales and property taxes also tends to reduce political support for income taxes among the more politically influential segments of the population. Studies of voting behavior indicate generally greater participation by citizens in higher income categories. Voting studies also show proportionally greater participation among citizens on fixed incomes—those whose incomes either do not increase at all or that simply keep up with the inflation rate— whose purchasing power decreases with inflation, and whose tax obligations may erode an increasing percentage of their income due to inflation (Wolfinger and Rosenstone, 1980: 20–26; Rosenstone and Hansen, 1993: 134–135). Perhaps the greatest criticism of income taxes among more affluent taxpayers is that they are levied on their investment income even though businesses have paid corporate income taxes on the same income. In short, it is argued, income from business investments is taxed twice.

There is also some fear that corporate income taxes will inhibit economic development and lead to the migration of businesses to states with lower tax rates. Very little evidence, however, supports the notion that taxes weigh that heavily in business site selection decisions, although lowered taxes may be a popular item for local business interests (Hansen, 1983: 145; Pischak, 1989: 305; Waugh and Waugh, 1988a: 218–220; Waugh and Waugh, 1988b: 113; also see Chapter 8 herein, ''Taxes and Economic Development''). Indeed, it is highly unlikely that minor differences in income tax rates have any significant impact on the economic viability or locational decisions of local businesses. Tax costs are usually passed on to consumers or workers. The costs and availability of appropriately skilled labor, raw materials, and transportation are far larger concerns for relocating and expanding businesses (Waugh and Waugh, 1988b). Corporate income taxes do, however, pose slightly different problems for businesses because they normally are levied on net profits that are calculated after the fiscal year rather than at the point of sale or during earlier stages of production. Thus, it is more difficult to pass income tax costs on to customers, since some of those costs are unknown at the time prices are set. If shifted, these costs have to be passed on to consumers in succeeding years.

For counties and municipalities experiencing increased political and administrative responsibility without corresponding increases in taxing and borrowing authority, an income tax offers potentially new resources via tax exporting. This tax shifting is particularly crucial for central cities and larger urban areas where the costs of maintaining services have not generally been borne by those employed locally. Because local revenue systems have relied on property and sales taxes, both of which are associated more closely with places of residence than with places of employment, wage and payroll taxes designed to capture needed revenue from those working in the community are growing in popularity. These taxes also offer the advantage of being more popular with the local electorate because the commuting workers live and vote elsewhere.

TAX PHILOSOPHY

The basic philosophy of personal and corporate income taxation is simple— tax those most able to pay. Since income represents a flow of capital (i.e., wealth of individuals and corporations), income taxes are generally designed to capture some portion of that flow to be used for government purposes. In some measure, income taxes may be viewed as payments extracted from those individuals and corporations that have benefited most from the American economic system. Progressive income taxes have also been described as antirevolution taxes to the extent that they are designed to redistribute wealth. Much of revenue generated is used to provide social and economic safety nets for the less affluent members of society. In other words, a considerable portion of income tax revenues may be used to lessen the disparities between the richest and poorest segments of society and to lessen the likelihood of political conflict, especially violent conflict, between rich and poor.

The design of income taxes, however, may lessen the redistributive benefits when definitions of taxable income give advantages to some groups over others or when tax rates are not applied uniformly. The nominal tax rate defines the prescribed level of taxation within an income group. Deductions, exemptions, and other adjustments to income that affect the definition of taxable income may (and often do) raise or lower the effective tax rates for individuals, families, or corporations. Advantages are gained by those who can exclude at least a portion of their income or redefine at least some of it as nontaxable income. How and where income is taxed may also advantage or disadvantage particular taxpayers or even permit some to avoid income taxes altogether.

PERSONAL INCOME TAXES

For the most part, state and local income tax structures are similar to those of the federal government. That is, adjusted gross income (AGI) is used as a base to determine taxable income (TI) and ultimately to calculate the taxes due. AGI typically includes personal income with miscellaneous earnings, such as interest income, and excludes some income, such as Social Security payments. TI is calculated from AGI with reductions based on the state or local revenue system's specified deductions and exemptions from income.

Debate concerning taxable income is constant, with some tax experts arguing that the base from which the tax is determined should be as broad as possible and represent the individual's or business' comprehensive income (Hyman,

1983: 500). Stated another way, the argument is that all sources of income should be considered in setting the income base upon which the tax is levied. This economic definition of income is predicated on the notion that numerous sources of income having monetary value or affecting a taxpayer's net worth are not being taxed. Gifts and transfer payments like unemployment benefits, for example, are not generally included in calculations of income. The proponents of the comprehensive income position would strictly interpret income to include almost everything that has monetary value.

Often the comprehensive income debate is tied to the discussion of flat tax rates, that is, a greatly simplified income tax system using a larger tax base and a single tax rate for all taxpayers (Pechman, 1989: 61). It also has been a recurring theme in tax reform proposals since World War II (Pechman, 1989: 76–77). At the federal level, President Reagan's very short-lived recommendations to end the federal tax deduction for mortgage interest payments and to tax employer contributions for health insurance are examples of reforms designed to broaden the definition of income, as are the more recent proposals to limit or end the issue of tax-free state and municipal bonds. Needless to say, income deductions and exclusions from income are jealously defended by strong and influential political interests.

The very political nature of the tax system is evident in the tax preferences given certain segments of society. The clearest examples of preferences in the federal and state income tax systems are the deductions for those over sixty-five years of age, the blind, and those with dependent children. The number of preferences granted in an income tax system encourages legislatures to begin estimating *tax expenditures*, which are revenues lost due to preferences granted or permitted and which are in effect indirect contributions to or expenditures for the affected taxpayers. Reducing a person's tax obligation is essentially the same as giving that person money, in other words.

Tax preferences are certainly not unusual. Income tax systems in the United States are characterized by "loopholes" that permit tax avoidance, exclusions of certain forms of income from the calculation of AGI, exemptions from all or some tax liability, and credits offered to certain groups or for desired behaviors. Exclusions of income from TI are typically granted for such things as income-in-kind and imputed income (where dollar values may be difficult to calculate), transfers such as food stamps and social welfare payments, income from the sale of property (capital gains), interest on municipal bonds, and pension contributions. Exemptions are typically offered for some portion of personal income through standard deductions for individuals and families, itemized deductions for business expenses, and so forth. Tax credits are offered for a variety of categories, such as child care and energy-related investments (Hyman, 1983: 512).

In other words, the use of the income tax system to encourage expenditures for charitable and cultural activities, to improve equity among citizens by subsidizing child care and health care, and to support other kinds of desired behaviors complicates the determination of TI and affects the abilities of citizens to understand and to comply with the procedural requirements in determining their taxes. Notwithstanding the confusion that results from tax expenditures, the redistributive impacts may be desirable and difficult to achieve by other means, and their impacts are unknown.

At the state level, most revenue loss is due to home mortgage interest deductions and other deductions. However, those who do not itemize—generally low income persons—cannot take advantage of deductions, even though they often pay taxes, contribute to charities, and have interest expenses. The ability to itemize gives upper income taxpayers a distinct advantage. The following list, while not all-inclusive, includes the most commonly used state deductions and exemptions:

• Personal tax credits for each dependent, including the taxpayer and spouse
• Gasoline, auto license tag, and drivers' license fees
• Medical and dental expenses
• Charitable and political contributions
• Energy-saving expenditures
• Insurance premiums
• At risk limitations for losses for which taxpayers were at risk
• Net operating loss carry-forwards
• Portion of retirement incomes
• Child care credit
• Investment interest expenses
• Business and travel expenses
• Checkoffs for earmarked contributions

Income tax systems also raise a number of structural issues, such as how to treat families. In the United States, income splitting permits consideration of the incomes of husband and wife individually, although community property states are more likely to consider family incomes as a unit. The personal deduction or standard deduction supplements the amount of each individual's income that is exempted from taxation and subsidizes such things as contributions to charity, payments for insurance, expenditures for health care, and payments of taxes to other jurisdictions. Other exemption issues include the treatment of theft and fire losses, the timing of capital gains and losses, reconciling corporate and personal taxes on the same income, the effects of inflation, and fluctuating incomes that are not neatly fitted into the usual twelve-month period for calculating income (Pechman, 1989: 53).

The aforementioned concerns are also applicable to local income taxes. However, municipalities, counties, and special districts most often rely on payroll taxes, withholding a set percentage (usually 1 percent) of earned income without adjustments to income. Payroll taxes do not include nonwage income, such as interest or pension payments or rents. (That is the case in nine of the fourteen states that permit local governments to levy income taxes.) The alternative for municipalities and counties is to use the adjusted gross income figures from state or federal tax returns to calculate local tax liability (ACIR, 1988: 19).

Another issue is whether local income taxes will be collected by state revenue authorities or by local authorities. The former reduces administrative costs to the local government and compliance costs to the taxpayer (by reducing the number of forms and payments), but it is still easier for localities to collect payroll taxes via withholding than to rely on state authorities to collect payroll taxes. A few municipalities share collection agencies, and in Ohio a few large jurisdictions provide collection facilities for smaller governments nearby.

CORPORATE INCOME TAXES

The corporate income tax has been in existence since 1909, but the rationale for taxing corporate income has always been subject to considerable debate. Corporate taxes are products of compromises between those who think that corporate income should be taxed like any other income and those who believe that corporate income should not be taxed more than once. The fact that corporate income is taxed once when earned by a corporation and again when stockholders are paid dividends is seen as *double taxation*. The tax also is seen as inhibiting capital investment by siphoning off income that might be reinvested, thus reducing state economic growth.

Incorporation of businesses under state law permits them to be treated as taxpayers in much the same way as individuals. Without benefit of incorporation, owners of firms pay personal taxes on their firm's income. Indeed, it is argued by some experts that corporate income taxes should be eliminated altogether in favor of personal income, rather than taxing business income twice. The problem is that corporate income can be put back into the firm as undistributed corporate profits and, while it increases personal and corporate assets, the income—as nonpersonal income—would not be subject to taxation (Hyman, 1983: 529).

Other issues raised by corporate income taxes include opportunity costs of capital which cannot be deducted from income in calculating tax liability, the tax treatment of depreciation of assets, the provision for inflation affecting the cost of capital, and tax preferences. Getting true estimates of capital costs is very difficult, and the easiest course may simply be to deduct capital invested at a particular time or for a particular purpose without dealing with opportunity costs. Depreciation of capital assets can be computed in a number of ways, some of which encourage investment and/or reinvestment in such assets, or others which do not permit speedy recovery of costs. The impact of inflation on the costs of capital can be assessed with some accuracy, but the resulting adjustment of estimates of capital investment would complicate the estimation of tax liabilities.

As with personal income taxes, states and localities do often offer tax preferences to certain kinds of businesses. Depletion allowances compensate firms for using nonrenewable raw materials or natural resources. States and localities may show decided preferences in their corporate tax structures for firms with high equipment costs, such as permitting an accelerated depreciation of assets. Agricultural states, for example, may be generous in letting businesses depreciate very expensive farm equipment.

More states are now looking at consumption instead of income as a basis for corporate taxation. At issue for state officials is the potential to export some corporate tax burden to citizens of other states. With a consumption tax, the after-tax rates of the return on all marginal investments equal the pretax rates of return. In addition, states wish to capture revenues within the state, and to assure that the revenues will be paid within that state rather than elsewhere. (These concerns are even more pronounced in the debate over value-added taxes—VATs—which are essentially sales taxes on the value that a product increases during each step of the production process.)

In sum, as corporate income taxes have evolved, they have become more and more complex. Current corporate income taxes also are seriously flawed because they do not raise revenues simply, fairly, or efficiently. The tax is not simple, since it is sheltered in complex sets of rules and regulations which impose sizable compliance costs on taxpayers. Corporations, for instance, cannot deduct imputed interest from expansion financed by retained earnings. They also cannot deduct dividend payment as a cost. These types of regulations, coupled with many others, increase the monitoring costs for governments.

In addition, these taxes complicate investment decisions by forcing corporations to rely on tax codes rather than on business acumen. The continuous addition and deletion of deductions and exemptions have made it difficult for businesses to determine their financial and investment plans. The tax is unfair because it imposes varying tax burdens on businesses depending on the industry and the mix of its capital assets. Advantage is held by the businesses or industries that have been most influential in the state legislature.

Capital Gains

Capital gains result from the sales of assets such as stocks, bonds, and real estate that have increased in value over time. States generally tax income derived from these assets at a lower rate than they do other forms of income. Of the forty-one states that tax capital gains, thirty-four have some form of favorable treatment, taxing only 40 or 50 percent of capital gains income.

The preferential treatment of capital gains income is one of the most heatedly debated income tax policies. Tax breaks are intended to encourage investment by returning more money to investors. The equity problem created by capital gains stems from the fact that low and middle income persons who earn most of their money from wages and salaries are taxed on 100 percent of their income, while upper income persons who derive a good portion of their income from capital gains are taxed at 40 percent or 50 percent of it. This tax break, therefore, conflicts with the vertical equity concept on which most personal income taxes are based—those with greater ability to pay actually pay less. Nationwide, approximately 45 percent of capital gains breaks go to persons earning more than $100,000.

This tax break means that states lose revenues. And a state can never be certain that the lost revenues will be spent or invested within the state to encourage local development and/or to produce jobs.

TRENDS IN STATE AND LOCAL INCOME TAXATION

The Bureau of the Census has estimated that 18 percent of state revenues and 1.9 percent of local revenues were derived from income taxes on individuals in 1991—down from 15.9 percent and 3.1 percent, respectively, in 1980 (ACIR, 1993: 71, 73). At the same time, income taxes on corporations accounted for 3.7 percent of state general revenue in 1991—down from 5.7 percent in 1980 (ACIR, 1993: 71, 73). Exhibit 3.1 shows fiscal year 1991 percentages in terms of total collections from personal and corporate income taxes, percentages of total revenues, per capita collections, and percent of personal income, by region and state. The data clearly show much less reliance on income taxes in the Southwest and Southeast than in other sections of the country. In terms of personal income paid in income taxes, Oregon collects the greatest percentage (4.1%), followed by Hawaii (3.8%). The highest percentage of corporate income collected is by Alaska (2.2%), followed by Delaware and Michigan (both .9%).

Clearly, state and local governments have in the past relied less on income taxes than has the federal government. Economists, in fact, argue that the effective implementation of income taxes requires geographic taxing boundaries that correspond closely with the boundaries of the market from which the taxes are extracted (Buchanan and Flowers, 1987: 324–325). In the simplest terms, it is often extremely difficult to assign a location to earnings and other business transactions. For example, a salesperson may earn his or her salary in one community, be paid in another community, and live in still a third. The question is whether income taxes should be paid where the salaries are earned, where they are paid, or where the individuals are living.

When the issue is income from real estate rentals or stocks and bonds, the locus of earnings may be even more ambiguous. Many of the same kinds of problems exist in assigning a location to business transactions and profits. Indeed, the federal government itself has had difficulties dealing with multinational corporations and individuals involved in transnational business operations. The marketplace is frequently defined in international terms, and the location of

Exhibit 3.1
State Income Tax Revenues, FY 1991

Region and State	Total Revenue	Income Tax Revenue		% of Total Revenue		Per Capita		% Of Personal Income	
		Individual Income	Corporation Income	Individual Income	Corporation Income	Individual Income	Corporation Income	Individual Income	Corporation Income
United States	$551,721.7	$99,278.9	$20,356.9	18.0	3.7	$395	$81	2.1	0.4
New England	$34,948.6	$7,122.5	$1,507.1	20.4	4.3	$540	$114	2.4	0.5
Connecticut	$8,745.4	$474.6	$515.9	5.4	5.9	$144	$157	0.6	0.6
Maine	$2,901.5	$580.7	$76.1	20.0	2.6	$471	$62	0.6	0.4
Massachusetts	$17,459.6	$5,343.4	$719.6	30.6	4.1	$891	$120	2.8	0.4
New Hampshire	$1,701.5	$36.9	$122.2	2.2	7.2	$33	$111	0.2	0.5
Rhode Island	$2,592.3	$429.2	$46.0	16.6	1.8	$427	$46	2.3	0.2
Vermont	$1,548.2	$257.5	$27.4	16.6	1.8	$454	$48	2.6	0.3
Mideast	$109,976.8	$24,540.5	$4,450.9	22.3	4.0	$567	$103	2.6	0.5
Delaware	$2,226.7	$461.7	$122.5	20.7	5.5	$679	$180	3.3	0.9
Maryland	$10,604.7	$2,731.0	$255.5	27.6	2.4	$603	$53	2.8	0.2
New Jersey	$20,055.8	$3,391.0	$1,030.6	16.9	5.1	$437	$133	1.8	0.5
New York	$54,934.6	$14,482.1	$2,030.3	26.4	3.7	$802	$112	3.6	0.5
Pennsylvania	$22,154.9	$3,274.7	$1,012.0	14.8	4.6	$274	$85	1.5	0.5
Great Lakes	$87,117.9	$17,730.3	$3,915.4	20.4	4.5	$418	$92	2.3	0.5
Illinois	$21,800.8	$4,538.5	$940.8	20.8	4.3	$393	$82	2.0	0.4
Indiana	$11,222.4	$2,184.0	$310.4	19.5	2.8	$389	$55	2.3	0.3
Michigan	$20,891.0	$3,787.2	$1,593.1	18.1	7.6	$404	$170	2.2	0.9
Ohio	$21,378.5	$4,217.2	$630.2	19.7	2.9	$385	$58	2.2	0.3
Wisconsin	$11,825.1	$3,003.4	$440.9	25.4	3.7	$606	$89	3.5	0.5
Plains	$37,613.5	$7,745.5	$1,269.3	20.6	3.4	$435	$71	2.5	0.4
Iowa	$6,200.5	$1,343.6	$201.9	21.7	3.3	$481	$72	2.9	0.4
Kansas	$4,724.2	$880.7	$213.0	18.6	4.5	$353	$85	2.0	0.5
Minnesota	$11,642.5	$2,974.6	$458.3	25.5	3.9	$671	$103	3.6	0.6
Missouri	$8,660.7	$1,829.2	$224.8	21.1	2.6	$355	$44	2.1	0.3
Nebraska	$3,219.1	$603.1	$81.9	18.7	2.5	$379	$51	2.2	0.3
North Dakota	$1,755.0	$114.3	$50.9	6.5	2.9	$180	$80	1.2	0.5
South Dakota	$1,411.6	n.l.	$38.6	n.l.	2.7	n.l.	$55	n.l.	0.4

Exhibit 3.1 (Continued)

Region and State	Total Revenue	Income Tax Revenue		% of Total Revenue		Per Capita		% Of Personal Income	
		Individual Income	Corporation Income	Individual Income	Corporation Income	Individual Income	Corporation Income	Individual Income	Corporation Income
Southeast	$114,790.3	$16,722.8	$3,548.3	14.6	3.1	$278	$59	1.7	0.4
Alabama	$8,173.3	$1,174.2	$168.3	14.4	2.1	$287	$41	1.9	0.3
Arkansas	$4,306.7	$793.9	$122.2	18.4	2.8	$335	$52	2.4	0.4
Florida	$22,079.6	n.t.	$582.1	n.t.	2.6	n.t.	$44	n.t.	0.2
Georgia	$11,863.6	$2,947.7	$416.6	24.8	3.5	$445	$63	2.7	0.4
Kentucky	$8,705.6	$1,693.3	$219.4	19.5	3.7	$456	$86	3.1	0.6
Louisiana	$9,409.9	$803.6	$326.7	8.5	3.5	$189	$77	1.3	0.5
Mississippi	$4,948.9	$479.6	$139.8	9.7	2.8	$185	$54	1.5	0.4
North Carolina	$12,927.2	$3,534.5	$500.0	27.3	3.9	$525	$74	3.2	0.5
South Carolina	$7,407.6	$1,386.6	$151.4	18.7	2.0	$390	$43	2.6	0.3
Tennessee	$8,384.8	$97.0	$345.5	1.2	4.1	$20	$70	0.1	0.4
Virginia	$12,431.3	$3,236.0	$285.1	26.0	2.3	$515	$45	2.6	0.2
West Virginia	$4,151.7	$576.3	$191.2	13.9	4.6	$320	$106	2.3	0.8
Southwest	$47,349.2	$2,833.4	$378.9	6.0	0.8	$110	$15	0.7	0.1
Arizona	$7,543.6	$1,245.6	$192.3	16.5	2.5	$332	$51	2.1	0.3
New Mexico	$4,332.2	$369.5	$49.0	8.5	1.1	$239	$32	1.7	0.2
Oklahoma	$6,654.8	$1,218.3	$137.6	18.3	2.1	$384	$43	2.6	0.3
Texas	$28,818.6	n.t.	n.t.	n.t.	n.t.	n.t.	n.t.	n.t.	n.t.
Rocky Mountain	$15,662.2	$2,?10.3	$327.5	18.6	2.1	$390	$44	2.4	0.3
Colorado	$6,225.7	$1,466.3	$114.5	23.6	1.8	$434	$34	2.4	0.2
Idaho	$2,147.6	$446.1	$59.7	20.8	2.8	$429	$57	2.9	0.4
Montana	$1,885.8	$283.0	$70.8	15.0	3.8	$350	$87	2.4	0.6
Utah	$3,662.1	$714.9	$82.5	19.5	2.3	$404	$47	2.9	0.3
Wyoming	$1,741.0	n.t.	n.t.	n.t.	n.t.	n.t.	n.t.	n.t.	n.t.
Far West	$94,241.8	$18,800.9	$4,589.6	19.9	4.9	$475	$116	2.4	0.6
California	$72,675.5	$16,817.2	$4,440.5	23.1	6.1	$554	$146	2.7	0.7
Nevada	$2,463.3	n.t.	n.t.	n.t.	n.t.	n.t.	n.t.	n.t.	n.t.
Oregon	$6,353.3	$1,983.7	$149.1	31.2	2.3	$679	$51	4.1	0.3
Washington	$12,749.7	n.t.	n.t.	n.t.	n.t.	n.t.	n.t.	n.t.	n.t.

Region and State	Total Revenue	Income Tax Revenue		% of Total Revenue		Per Capita		% Of Personal Income	
		Individual Income	Corporation Income	Individual Income	Corporation Income	Individual Income	Corporation Income	Individual Income	Corporation Income
Alaska	$5,673.5	n.t.	$253.6	n.t.	4.5	n.t.	$445	n.t.	2.2
Hawaii	$4,348.0	$872.7	$116.4	20.1	2.7	$768	$102	3.8	0.5

n.t.—no tax

- represents zero

< - rounds to zero

Includes selective sales and gross receipts taxes, license taxes, death and gift taxes, severance taxes, and other taxes.

Includes interest earnings, special assessments, sale of property, lottery revenues, and other general revenues.

District of Columbia excluded. The Bureau of the Census classifies the District of Columbia as a municipality.

Alaska and Hawaii are excluded from Far West regional totals, but are included in U.S. totals.

Source: ACIR, 1993: 101.

61

earnings is often very unclear to revenue collectors (and even irrelevant to the firms themselves). Some analysts recommend that state and local governments choose alternative bases for taxation, such as property and/or sales, and leave income taxes to the federal government (Buchanan and Flowers, 1987: 326).

Notwithstanding these problems, most states and a growing number of local governments have chosen to tax income because they need to develop more progressive tax structures. But the manner in which the taxes have been structured usually reflects the problems inherent in attributing a geographic location to income earned. As will be illustrated later in this chapter, decisions have to be made concerning the locus of income so that taxpayers are not taxed more than once on the same income, or able to escape taxation entirely because of jurisdictional confusion.

State Income Taxes

State income taxes predate the federal tax. Wisconsin implemented the first income tax in the United States in 1911. However, only a few states, including New York, Oregon, Wisconsin, Massachusetts, and Delaware, have used income taxes as their principal revenue source (Palmer, 1977: 121–122), although that is changing as states and communities are reducing their reliance on property taxes.

Forty-four states currently have a tax on personal income, and forty-six have a tax on corporate net income (Buchanan and Flowers, 1987: 325; see Exhibit 3.1 for fiscal year 1991 income tax data). The maximum marginal rates of taxation on personal incomes are generally low compared to either the federal personal income rates or to state corporate income rates. These marginal rates range from 2 to 16 percent. The difficulties of determining where income was earned and the need to assure ease of administration have given states a strong incentive to tie their tax rates and procedures to those of the federal government. Nebraska, Rhode Island, and Vermont have simply chosen to make their personal income taxes a percentage of an individual's federal tax payment (Hansen, 1983: 423; Buchanan and Flowers, 1987: 325).

Most states, however, have very different rate brackets, exemptions, deductions, and credits, although many still use the federal income and tax liability estimates as benchmarks for estimating state and local income and tax liability. Corporate income tax rates, on the other hand, tend to be proportional rather than progressive. In recognizing the ideal of keeping tax structures simple, states generally assess corporations at a percentage of their net earnings regardless of the magnitude of those earnings. Simply put, the rates are flat rather than progressive. Then, too, state and local governments also consider the importance of simple and clear tax compliance procedures, primarily because they usually lack the resources to enforce strict compliance. Administrative concerns may be the reason that corporations have been subject to local income taxes only in the District of Columbia and New York City (ACIR, 1993: 114–115).

Exhibit 3.2
Local Income and Payroll Taxes in FY 1991 (millions)

State	Individual Income Tax	% of Own Source Tax	Corporate Income Tax	% of Own Source Tax
Alabama (1)	54.5	1.0	0	0
Delaware (1)	24.1	2.5	0	0
District of Columbia (1)	615.7	12.9	133.6	2.8
Illinois (1)	2.3	>.1	0	0
Indiana (2)	310.2	3.2	0	0
Kentucky (1,2)	355.2	7.3	0	0
Maryland (1,2)	1392.8	15.5	0	0
Michigan (1)	387.8	2.0	0	0
Missouri (1)	216.9	2.9	0	0
New York (1)	2842.1	4.2	1752.0	2.6
Ohio (1,3)	1895.4	9.2	0	0
Pennsylvania (1,3)	1961.6	8.9	0	0
Texas (1)	0.2	>.1	0	0

Local taxing jurisdictions:

(1) one or more cities

(2) one or more counties

(3) one or more school districts

Source: ACIR, 1993: 114–117.

Local Income Taxes

The preference for simple income tax structures certainly holds true for local governments. Most local income taxes are assessed at a flat (proportional) rate based on gross income (Buchanan and Flowers, 1987: 325). A 1988 estimate by the Advisory Commission on Intergovernmental Relations (ACIR, 1988: 9–10) held that, in 1987, 3,550 local governments and special districts in fourteen states had some form of income, wage, or payroll tax. Exhibits 3.2 and 3.3 show the major features of local income and payroll taxes and a comparison of four types of local income taxes.

Pennsylvania was the first state to permit local income taxes. In 1932 the state legislature permitted the city of Philadelphia to tax the incomes of residents without regard to where the income was earned, and nonresidents working in the city. (Philadelphia's flat rate of approximately 4.3 percent currently is the highest local rate in the United States). In 1947 the Pennsylvania state legislature extended the authority to levy income taxes to other local governments, but the rate of tax permitted to those governments is limited to 1 percent. Where a

Exhibit 3.3
Comparative Analysis of Four Types of Local Income Taxes

	Local Wage or Payroll Tax	Local Income Tax Tied to Federal or State Tax		Locally Designed Progressive Tax
		Percentage of State Income Tax Liability	Flat Rate On Federal Adjusted Gross Income	
	1A	1B	1C	1D
Examples of Usage	Most common: found in nine of 14 states using local income taxes.	Maryland Counties	Indiana Counties	New York City
	2A	2B	2C	2D
General Characteristics	Flat rate on wages and salaries, no exemptions, no deductions.	Includes the exemption and deduction pattern of the state income tax; also has the broader definition of taxable income set forth in 2B.	No exemptions or deductions but has a much broader definition of taxable income than set forth in 2A.	Locally set exemptions and deductions patterned on broad definition of income.
	3A	3B	3C	3D
Tax Base	It does not tax all forms of income. It also fails to shield subsistence income from taxation.	Taxes all forms of income. It also shields subsistence income from taxation.	It taxes all forms of income. However, it fails to shield subsistence income from taxation.	Taxes all forms of income. It also shields subsistence income from taxation.
	4A	4B	4C	4D
Taxpayer Compliance Requirements	Minimal: Only self employed have to file returns.	Fairly Light: Just one added calculation on the state income tax return.	Fairly Light: However, all taxpayers must file a simplified return.	Heavier: More calculations required.
	5A	5B	5C	5D
Revenue Yield During Periods of Economic Growth	Will grow automatically at same rate as the community's wage and salary base.	Will grow automatically at a somewhat faster rate than the growth in the community's income.	Will grow automatically at same rate as the community's income.	Will grow automatically at a somewhat faster rate than the growth in the community's income.
	6A	6B	6C	6D
Revenue Yield During Periods of Economic Recession	Will decline automatically at same rate as the community's wage and salary base.	Will decline automatically at a somewhat faster rate than the drop in the community's income.	Will decline automatically at same rate as the drop in the community's income.	Will decline automatically at a somewhat faster rate than the drop in community's income.

Source: ACIR, 1988: 6.

municipality and a school district both levy income taxes, the rate still cannot exceed 1 percent and must be divided evenly between the two jurisdictions. While all municipalities can tax nonresidents, school districts cannot. And taxpayers working in one municipality and residing in another have to pay taxes only where they live. Because municipalities typically tax at the maximum 1 percent limit and have to give credit for taxes paid to other municipalities based on residence, taxpayers do not have to pay any more than 1 percent in local income taxes. The only exception to that rule is the city of Philadelphia, which does not have to credit taxes paid elsewhere (Stull and Stull, 1991: 183). Thus, suburbanites who work in Philadelphia may have to pay taxes to the city and to their suburban municipalities and/or school districts.

The adoption of local income taxes was given impetus during the late 1960s and the 1970s and was largely a response by large cities to their shrinking dependence on property taxes and to the need to capture taxes from commuters working in the city and living in the suburbs. Most of the income taxes have been of the payroll variety, with Detroit being the first (1962) to design a piggyback tax. (The Detroit and New York City income taxes are each unique.) In 1967 Maryland mandated county and Baltimore city income taxes with rates of 20 to 50 percent of the state tax liability. Most of the counties have chosen the highest allowable rate (ACIR, 1988: 9–10).

In 1991, local income taxes were levied in 12 states. Excluding Pennsylvania, 636 cities, 178 counties, and 59 school districts levied income taxes. An additional 2,824 cities, boroughs, towns, townships, and school districts levied such a tax in Pennsylvania (ACIR, 1993: 77). The major features of specific local income and payroll taxes, including the range of rates in 1988 and responsibility for administering the taxes, are outlined in Exhibit 3.2.

Local taxes on personal income represented only 2 percent of local tax revenues in 1970, 1.9 percent in 1980, and 1.9 percent in 1991. However, personal income taxes in 1991 provided over $10 billion in revenue to local governments, up from $1.6 billion in 1970 (ACIR, 1993: 72–73). In 1991, too, personal income taxes provided 15.5 percent of local own-source revenues (excluding intergovernmental transfers) in Maryland and 12.9 percent in the District of Columbia. The percentages were slightly lower in Ohio (9.2 percent) and Pennsylvania (8.9 percent). Exhibit 3.4 provides data on local income tax revenues, percentages of total revenue, per capita revenue, and percentage of personal income by state and region. It is again noteworthy that only local governments in Maryland and the District of Columbia levy local corporate income taxes, and those taxes bring in only 2.8 percent of the District's own-source revenue and 2.6 percent of Maryland's local government revenue.

Local income and wage taxes consist of three basic varieties:

- *Wage, payroll, or earned income taxes,* which usually are based on a flat rate and collected through payroll withholding
- *Piggyback taxes,* which are usually based on the state income tax liability or the adjusted gross income reported for federal income taxes
- *Locale specific, broad-based income taxes* having their own rate structure and definitions of taxable income

The *payroll tax* generally lacks deductions or exemptions from income, thus it is easy to calculate and, being collected by the employer via withholding, easy to administer. But with flat rates and no adjustments to income, local payroll taxes do tend to be more regressive than federal or state graduated in-

Exhibit 3.4
Local Income Tax Revenues, FY 1991

Region and State	Total Revenue	Income Tax Revenue		% of Total Revenue		Per Capita		% of Personal Income	
		Individual Income	Corporation Income	Individual Income	Corporation Income	Individual Income	Corporation Income	Individual Income	Corporation Income
United States	$541,790.9	$10,061.9	$1,885.6	1.9	0.3	$40.0	$7.0	0.2	<
New England	$24,808.0	n.t.	n.t.	n.t.	n.t.	n.t.	n.t.	n.t.	n.t.
Connecticut	$612.5	n.t.	n.t.	n.t.	n.t.	n.t.	n.t.	n.t.	n.t.
Maine	$1,958.2	n.t.	n.t.	n.t.	n.t.	n.t.	n.t.	n.t.	n.t.
Massachusetts	$11,782.2	n.t.	n.t.	n.t.	n.t.	n.t.	n.t.	n.t.	n.t.
New Hampshire	$2,014.6	n.t.	n.t.	n.t.	n.t.	n.t.	n.t.	n.t.	n.t.
Rhode Island	$1,531.8	n.t.	n.t.	n.t.	n.t.	n.t.	n.t.	n.t.	n.t.
Vermont	$908.7	n.t.	n.t.	n.t.	n.t.	n.t.	n.t.	n.t.	n.t.
Mideast	$122,795.6	$2,842.1	$1,885.6	5.6	1.5	$156.0	$43.0	0.7	0.2
Delaware	$982.3	$24.1	n.t.	2.5	n.t.	$35.0	n.t.	0.2	n.t.
District of Columbia	$4,758.1	$615.7	$133.6	12.9	2.8	$1,035.0	$225.0	4.3	0.9
Maryland	$8,982.0	$1,392.8	n.t.	15.5	n.t.	$287.0	n.t.	1.3	n.t.
New Jersey	$18,523.6	n.t.	n.t.	n.t.	n.t.	n.t.	n.t.	n.t.	n.t.
New York	$67,408.1	$2,842.1	$1,752.0	4.2	2.6	$157.0	$97.0	0.7	0.4
Pennsylvania	$22,141.5	$1,961.6	n.t.	8.9	n.t.	$164.0	n.t.	0.9	n.t.
Great Lakes	$83,917.2	$2,595.6	n.t.	3.1	n.t.	$61.0	n.t.	0.3	n.t.
Illinois	$23,097.9	$2.3	n.t.	<	n.t.	+	n.t.	0	n.t.
Indiana	$9,828.6	$310.2	n.t.	3.2	n.t.	$55.0	n.t.	0.3	n.t.
Michigan	$19,515.0	$387.8	n.t.	2	n.t.	$41.0	n.t.	0.2	n.t.
Ohio	$20,620.4	$1,895.4	n.t.	9.2	n.t.	$173.0	n.t.	1	n.t.
Wisconsin	$10,855.1	n.t.	n.t.	n.t.	n.t.	n.t.	n.t.	n.t.	n.t.

Region and State	Total Revenue	Income Tax Revenue		% of Total Revenue		Per Capita		% of Personal Income	
		Individual Income	Corporation Income	Individual Income	Corporation Income	Individual Income	Corporation Income	Individual Income	Corporation Income
Plains	$34,308.0	$220.1	n.t.	0.6	n.t.	$12.0	n.t.	0.1	n.t.
Iowa	$5,223.8	$3.1	n.t.	0.1	n.t.	$1.0	n.t.	<	n.t.
Kansas	$4,700.2	n.t.	n.t.	n.t.	n.t.	n.t.	n.t.	n.t.	n.t.
Minnesota	$11,885.0	n.t.	n.t.	n.t.	n.t.	n.t.	n.t.	n.t.	n.t.
Missouri	$7,491.6	$216.9	n.t.	2.9	n.t.	$42.0	n.t.	0.2	n.t.
Nebraska	$3,003.3	n.t.	n.t.	n.t.	n.t.	n.t.	n.t.	n.t.	n.t.
North Dakota	$1,020.3	n.t.	n.t.	n.t.	n.t.	n.t.	n.t.	n.t.	n.t.
South Dakota	$984.0	<	n.t.	<	n.t.	+	n.t.	<	n.t.
Southeast	$106,381.7	$409.7	n.t.	0.4	n.t.	$7.0	n.t.	<	n.t.
Alabama	$5,660.1	$54.5	n.t.	1	n.t.	$13.0	n.t.	0.1	n.t.
Arkansas	$2,796.6	n.t.	n.t.	n.t.	n.t.	n.t.	n.t.	n.t.	n.t.
Florida	$29,857.3	n.t.	n.t.	n.t.	n.t.	n.t.	n.t.	n.t.	n.t.
Georgia	$13,209.5	n.t.	n.t.	n.t.	n.t.	n.t.	n.t.	n.t.	n.t.
Kentucky	$4,871.7	$355.2	n.t.	7.3	n.t.	$96.0	n.t.	0.6	n.t.
Louisiana	$7,389.2	<	n.t.	<	n.t.	+	n.t.	<	n.t.

Exhibit 3.4 (Continued)

Region and State	Total Revenue	Income Tax Revenue		% of Total Revenue		Per Capita		% of Personal Income	
		Individual Income	Corporation Income	Individual Income	Corporation Income	Individual Income	Corporation Income	Individual Income	Corporation Income
Mississippi	$3,985.5	n.t.	n.t.	n.t.	n.t.	n.t.	n.t.	n.t.	n.t.
North Carolina	$12,096.6	n.t.	n.t.	n.t.	n.t.	n.t.	n.t.	n.t.	n.t.
South Carolina	$5,212.9	n.t.	n.t.	n.t.	n.t.	n.t.	n.t.	n.t.	n.t.
Tennessee	$7,386.5	✓	n.t.	✓	n.t.	+	n.t.	✓	n.t.
Virginia	$11,575.5	✓	n.t.	✓	n.t.	+	n.t.	✓	n.t.
West Virginia	$2,340.5	n.t.	n.t.	n.t.	n.t.	n.t.	n.t.	n.t.	n.t.
Southwest	$47,285.3	$0.2	n.t.	✓	n.t.	+	n.t.	✓	n.t.
Arizona	$7,979.9	n.t.	n.t.	n.t.	n.t.	n.t.	n.t.	✓	n.t.
New Mexico	$2,732.3	n.t.	n.t.	n.t.	n.t.	n.t.	n.t.	n.t.	n.t.
Oklahoma	$4,686.6	n.t.	n.t.	n.t.	n.t.	n.t.	n.t.	n.t.	n.t.
Texas	$31,886.5	$0.2	n.t.	✓	n.t.	+	n.t.	n.t.	n.t.

Region and State	Total Revenue	Income Tax Revenue		% of Total Revenue		Per Capita		% of Personal Income	
		Individual Income	Corporation Income	Individual Income	Corporation Income	Individual Income	Corporation Income	Individual Income	Corporation Income
Rocky Mountain	$14,633.0	n.t.	n.t.	n.t.	n.t.	n.t.	n.t.	n.t.	n.t.
Colorado	$7,575.9	n.t.	n.t.	n.t.	n.t.	n.t.	n.t.	n.t.	n.t.
Idaho	$1,599.0	n.t.	n.t.	n.t.	n.t.	n.t.	n.t.	n.t.	n.t.
Montana	$1,345.3	n.t.	n.t.	n.t.	n.t.	n.t.	n.t.	n.t.	n.t.
Utah	$2,789.8	n.t.	n.t.	n.t.	n.t.	n.t.	n.t.	n.t.	n.t.
Wyoming	$1,323.0	n.t.	n.t.	n.t.	n.t.	n.t.	n.t.	n.t.	n.t.
Far West	$104,283.2	n.t.	n.t.	n.t.	n.t.	n.t.	n.t.	n.t.	n.t.
California	$84,489.3	n.t.	n.t.	n.t.	n.t.	n.t.	n.t.	n.t.	n.t.
Nevada	$2,993.1	n.t.	n.t.	n.t.	n.t.	n.t.	n.t.	n.t.	n.t.
Oregon	$6,118.6	n.t.	n.t.	n.t.	n.t.	n.t.	n.t.	n.t.	n.t.
Washington	$10,682.2	n.t.	n.t.	n.t.	n.t.	n.t.	n.t.	n.t.	n.t.

Exhibit 3.4 (Continued)

Region and State	Total Revenue	Income Tax Revenue		% of Total Revenue		Per Capita		% of Personal Income	
		Individual Income	Corporation Income	Individual Income	Corporation Income	Individual Income	Corporation Income	Individual Income	Corporation Income
Alaska	$2,281.4	n.t.	n.t.	n.t.	n.t.	n.t.	n.t.	n.t.	n.t.
Hawaii	$1,097.5	n.t.	n.t.	n.t.	n.t.	n.t.	n.t.	n.t.	n.t.

n.t.—no tax

- represents zero

< - rounds to zero

Includes selective sales and gross receipts taxes, license taxes, death and gift taxes, severance taxes, and other taxes.

Includes interest earnings, special assessments, sale of property, lottery revenues, and other general revenues.

District of Columbia excluded. The Bureau of the Census classifies the District of Columbia as a municipality.

Alaska and Hawaii are excluded from Far West regional totals, but are included in U.S. totals.

Source: ACIR, 1993: 101.

come taxes. Alabama, Arkansas, California, Delaware, Kentucky, Missouri, New Jersey, Ohio, Oregon, and Pennsylvania permit local payroll taxes (even if called something else in California, New Jersey, and Oregon).

In 1992 the city of Philadelphia joined five states (California, New York, Illinois, Minnesota, and Missouri) in imposing a payroll tax on out-of-state professional athletes and coaches. Using rosters, newspapers, and media guides, officials identified over 4,500 professional athletes and coaches who worked in the city during the year. The government prorated each salary by the number of days in the season, multiplied the daily salary by the number of days that the team played in Philadelphia to figure out taxable income, and applied a tax rate of 6 percent to arrive at the tax due. Atlanta Braves pitcher Tom Glavine, for example, with a salary of $2.925 million for the 1992 season ($17,005 a day over the 172-day season), was billed $6,122 in payroll taxes for the six days that the Braves played the Phillies in Philadelphia (Rosenberg, 1992: E1).

Piggyback taxes are based on the adjusted gross income reported on federal income tax returns. These kinds of piggyback taxes are less repressive than income taxes based on gross income without adjustments. They also are much easier to administer than taxes requiring entirely separate calculations of taxable income and tax liability. The state of Michigan and the city of Yonkers, New York, piggyback on federal tax rates and bases. Iowa and Maryland, on the other hand, piggyback local taxes on state graduated rates and bases.

A *broad-based locally designed income tax* is used in New York City. The same deductions and exemptions are used as those permitted in the New York State tax system, but a separate, graduated rate schedule is used for calculating local tax liability. Since 1976 residents of New York City have been able to calculate and pay their city income taxes with the state forms, without having to file separate city income tax forms (ACIR, 1988: 5, 8).

The general features of each of these types of local income taxes are compared in Exhibit 3.3. The most important considerations for local governments and for taxpayers may be the simplicity of tax structures, the somewhat low costs of compliance (particularly for local wage and payroll taxes and the local income taxes tied to state or federal returns), and the stable revenue afforded local governments during periods of economic growth or decline.

Local income tax rates are generally low and flat in nature, ranging from .25 percent in some Ohio school districts to over 4 percent in the city of Philadelphia. Municipal rates are typically in the 1 to 3 percent range. New York City's rates range from 1.5 percent to 3.5 percent for residents, with a .45 percent rate for nonresidents. Some localities, such as Ohio, exempt nonresidents from local income taxation for school districts, while other localities, such as some cities in Pennsylvania, set lower school district rates for nonresidents (ACIR, 1988: 14, 16).

The importance of local income taxes is growing. In fiscal year 1991, local income tax revenues were approximately $12 billion, including $10 billion in personal taxes and $1.9 billion in corporate taxes (ACIR, 1993: 114). That is a substantial increase from the approximately $8.5 billion in income tax revenues raised by local governments in 1986. As Exhibit 3.2 indicates, the importance of the local income tax varies considerably among jurisdictions; while not widespread, it is generating more and more revenues where it is used. Income taxes are major sources of revenue for many U.S. cities and have been the principal own-source revenues for the cities of Canton, Cleveland, Columbus, Dayton, and Toledo, Ohio (ACIR, 1988: 15).

Differences in how states and localities rely on income taxes are evident in Exhibit 3.5. Income taxes are comparatively low in the South, where states have tended to hold taxes low generally, with more reliance on sales taxes. Exhibit 3.6 categorizes states according to how they levy income taxes as a percentage of personal income. The highest percentages are generally found in the Northeast and upper Midwest. Much the same pattern holds true in Exhibit 3.7, which categorizes the states according to the estimated income taxes for a family of four earning $25,000 in 1990. Clearly there is wide variance in the propensities of states and localities to adopt income taxes, as well as in the rates applied.

Most state legislatures have been reluctant to grant authority for local income taxation, and legislatures that have authorized such taxes clearly are the same ones that have been most willing to expand other forms of local autonomy and authority. Because large central cities and large urban and suburban counties have to be more creative in their search for revenues and have to look for ways to capture additional tax revenues from their suburban rings, interest in income taxes is likely to grow. At the same time, more ambitious tax proposals are not as popular as minute increases in property tax millage and sales tax rates. Moreover, the prospect of persuading suburban electorates to support urban-targeted taxes appears remote.

Indexing Income Taxes

Generally speaking, inflation causes taxable income, whether personal or corporate, to expand more rapidly than real income. During periods of high inflation, therefore, taxable incomes rise more rapidly than the inflation rate, creating tax increases without legislative or constitutional actions by governments or electoral approval by taxpayers.

To rectify such hidden tax increases, many legislatures have been or are indexing tax brackets. Indexing means that real tax liabilities increase only when income increases more rapidly than the inflation rate. When income increases less than the inflation rate, tax liabilities actually decrease.

A simple example illustrates the indexing problem. Consider a family of four whose total personal income increased from $25,000 to $27,500 during a year in which the inflation rate was 10 percent. Although real income in terms of purchasing power remained the same, the family jumped from a 6 percent to an 8 percent tax bracket and increased its tax liability without increasing its purchasing power.

Exhibit 3.5
Income Tax Revenues per $1,000 Personal Income by Region

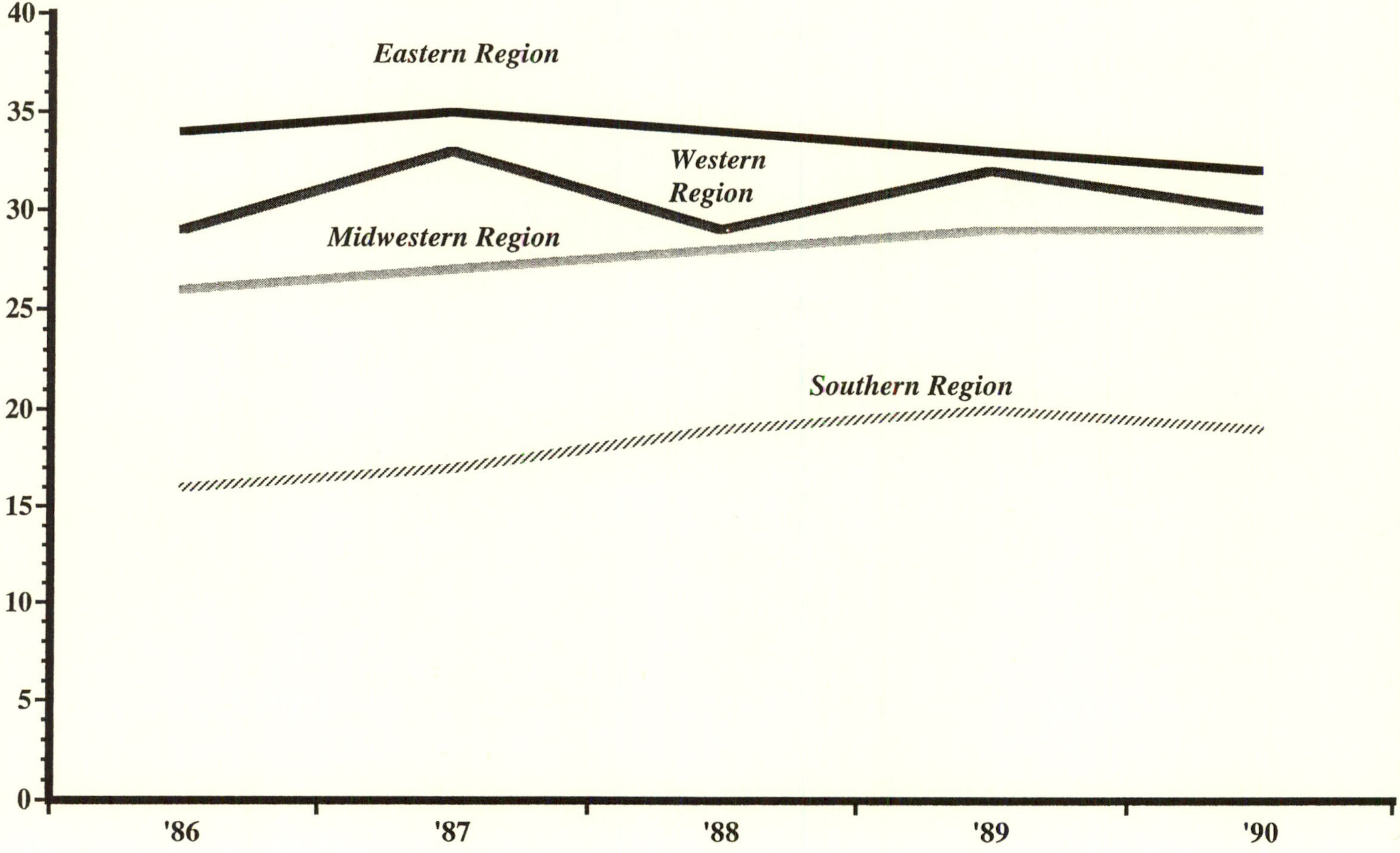

Exhibit 3.6
Individual Income Taxes as a Percentage of State Personal Income, 1988

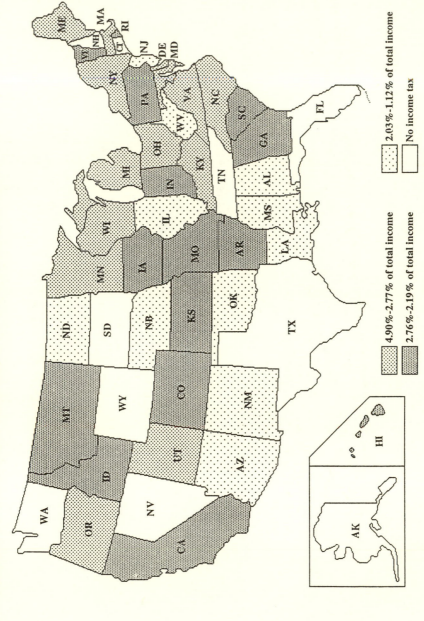

Source: Commerce Clearing House, 1991: 4015. Reproduced with permission from the CCH *Multi-State Tax Guide,* copyright 1991, published and copyrighted by Commerce Clearing House, Inc., 2700 Lake Cook Road, Riverwoods, Illinois 60015.

Exhibit 3.7
Estimated Income Taxes for a Family of Four Earning $25,000 in 1990

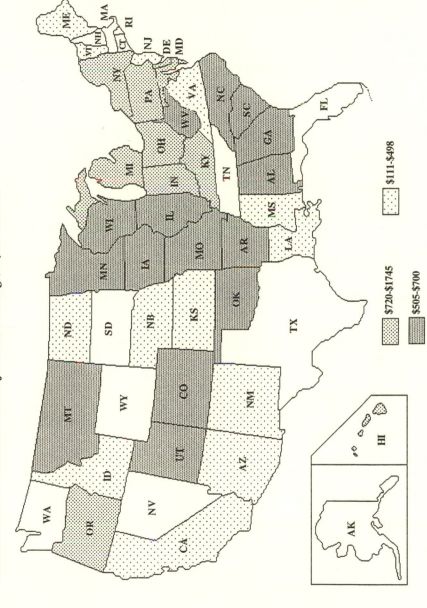

$720-$1745

$505-$700

$111-$498

Source: District of Columbia, 1991: 35.

The family's tax bill increased more than the inflation rate (10 percent) because it moved into a higher income tax bracket. At 6 percent, the family's tax liability is $1,650. A 10 percent increase in this liability would mean that the tax liability would be $1,815. However, by moving into the 8 percent tax bracket, the family's liability is $2,200—or $385 more than it would be if the tax bill were increased by only the inflation rate.

Another major problem with indexing involves which index to use. Most frequently, the Consumer Price Index (CPI) developed by the Bureau of Labor Statistics is used to measure the cost of living—even though the bureau continually stresses that that is not the purpose of the index. The CPI measures only the cost of buying a market basket of goods and services for the average urban consumer. It also includes costs for housing and durable goods credit purchases, both of which inflate most persons' cost of living. Thus, the CPI overstates cost of living increases for most people. In addition, as prices increase, consumers can, and do, change their buying habits. Unfortunately, the CPI does not account for changes in the pattern of purchases. Consequently, before seriously considering indexing, legislative bodies are advised to develop their own cost of living index, though this is extremely difficult and expensive.

Indexing doubtless removes an increasing, but often hidden, tax burden on low and middle income taxpayers. While taxpayers undoubtedly benefit from indexing, regardless of the index used, indexing also has its costs. Loss of government revenue is the most serious cost. Indexing significantly reduces revenues during periods of rapid inflation, which, it should be noted, is also when state and local governments need more money to purchase the goods and services whose costs have increased because of the same inflationary pressures. Governments' primary fear of indexing, hence, is that it will add to deficits, especially during times of high inflation. The only way to increase revenues under indexing is to increase tax rates. An interesting side-effect, then, is that indexing increases voters' control over tax rates.

INCOME TAXES AND TAX AMNESTY

Delinquent revenues are a major problem for state and local governments. Tax amnesty has been adopted by a number of state and local governments as a means of collecting delinquent taxes. It has been a particularly attractive option for governments seeking immediate revenue gains from personal and corporate income taxes since the economic turmoil of the 1970s and 1980s. Lacking or having little capacity for tax enforcement and monitoring and, in some cases, having only vague estimates of the amounts delinquent, government officials have used offers of general amnesty from prosecution to encourage known delinquents to pay their taxes and unknown evaders to identify themselves and pay up as well. Unlike property taxes, which are based on a recorded estimate of property value, assessment of taxes by government agents, and provision for the seizure of property when taxes are not paid, income tax estimations are dependent upon taxpayer-reported information, which is exceedingly difficult for state and local governments to monitor.

In fact, the public's expectation generally has been that the most committed tax evaders, those who choose to evade some or all their tax liabilities very deliberately and for whom tax evasion is a long term pattern of behavior, will not respond to tax amnesty programs. The committed tax evaders will likely fear audits of earlier returns which could result in very large tax liabilities. But it is also expected that the marginal tax evaders (i.e., those who cheat on their taxes and may feel some guilt or fear of being caught, and those who underreport income by accident and wish to avoid being prosecuted) may take the opportunity to be forgiven for their indiscretions. As a consequence, there are few expectations of large payoffs in most tax amnesty programs (Fisher, Goddeeris, and Young, 1989).

Nonetheless, the utility of tax amnesty programs has been at least partially affirmed by experience. A three-month tax amnesty program in Massachusetts from October 17, 1983, to January 17, 1984, netted an estimated $58 million from 40,000 to 50,000 delinquent taxpayers. A two-month program in Arizona netted an estimated $6 million from 10,000 taxpayers. State programs in Missouri and North Dakota netted $853,000 and $150,000, respectively. Municipal programs in New York City and Philadelphia netted $43 million and $30 million, respectively. The 1992 amnesty program in Georgia recovered $30 million of an estimated $300 million in lost tax revenue.

The fear that amnesties might encourage delinquency (i.e, taxpayers may simply underreport income or not file at all in anticipation of amnesties) does not seem justified (Steiss, 1989: 99). Nor does it seem that amnesties encourage as widespread a response as some governments have anticipated.

A study by Fisher, Goddeeris, and Young (1989) of the income tax amnesty program in Michigan focused on whether such programs encourage payment of taxes that authorities would not otherwise receive and whether the revenue gains will be long term. The researchers generally expected that structural aspects of the program would influence willingness to participate. More specifically, they felt that the threat of much more stringent enforcement procedures and stricter penalties (i.e., increasing the likelihood of apprehension by authorities) as well as the provision of confidentiality for those self-identifying as tax delinquents or evaders (i.e., avoidance of social stigma as lawbreakers) would increase compliance. The experience from other states also suggested that most of the payments of delinquent accounts would be less than $100, and the most common delinquencies would be for only one year and more often for nonfiling rather than erroneous filing. In most respects, those availing themselves of the opportunity offered by the state of Michigan were very much like other taxpayers in terms of filing status, resident status, and other demographic factors. There were some indications that the participants on average may have had higher adjusted gross incomes than the general taxpaying population, but the difference was not great and might be explained by other factors. Indeed, 72 percent paid for only one year of delinquency and 42 percent paid less than $100 per year. The delinquent amounts were so small that detection by enforcement agencies would have been extremely difficult, if not impossible. There was no single profile of evaders; their characteristics and reasons for evading taxes varied tremendously.

In short, tax amnesties have brought immediate revenue dividends to some states and municipalities, but are of limited utility in identifying tax evaders and in encouraging continuing tax compliance (and continuing revenue gains). Consequently, the value of income tax amnesties is quite limited.

CONCLUDING COMMENTS

The rationale for income taxes is clear; most are based on the ability to pay. How income taxes are structured affects the progressivity and the effectiveness of the tax system. State and local governments, moreover, have had to be creative in their hunt for needed revenues to support services. The unwillingness, and at times the inability, of residents to pay additional property taxes has fueled the search for alternative revenue sources. For local governments, the pursuit of commuters, those who take advantage of local services but tend to pay their taxes elsewhere, has focused attention on the paychecks earned in the cities and cashed in the suburbs.

While a few states still do not levy income taxes, relying instead on revenues generated by gambling, tourism, oil production, or the more traditional property and sales taxes, most states are having to diversify their revenue sources as hedges against business slumps, fluctuating energy costs, rapid growth, industrial decline, or other economic disturbances. Similarly, local governments are seeking more diverse revenue sources to fund local programs, to support state and federally mandated programs, and to reduce reliance on property and sales taxes. For local governments, broad, but low, wage or payroll taxes may well prove easier to implement than more complex income taxes.

The progressive and elastic nature of income taxes has great appeal. The trend is toward greater reliance on income taxes by both state and local governments, as well as toward greater tax simplification to facilitate taxpayer compliance and government monitoring. To some extent, simplification efforts may increase interest in reducing the number of adjustments to income. Political pressures, however, will not make it easy to eliminate current deductions. Moreover, the temptation offered political leaders to use income taxes to accomplish policy goals, such as business investment and home-buying, will likely remain.

Officials at all level of government are becoming increasingly concerned about making taxes more progressive, reducing the erosion of tax bases, and reducing the income elasticity of taxes. Correspondingly:

- Personal income and general sales taxes are the pillars of state tax systems.
- Corporate income tax revenues as a percentage of personal income are declining.
- Severance taxes are rising at a rate three times that of personal income.

- Revenues from excise taxes are growing relatively slowly.
- State revenues as a percentage of personal income are declining.

It is to these other revenue sources that we now turn.

REFERENCES

Advisory Commission on Intergovernmental Relations (ACIR) (1988). *Local Revenue Diversification: Local Income Taxes.* Washington, D.C.: ACIR.
——— (1993). *Significant Features of Fiscal Federalism.* Vol. 2. Washington, D.C.: ACIR.
Buchanan, James M., and Marilyn R. Flowers (1987). *The Public Finances.* 6th ed. Homewood, Ill.: Richard D. Irwin.
District of Columbia (1991). *Tax Rates and Tax Burdens in the District of Columbia: A Nationwide Comparison.* Washington, D.C.: Department of Finance and Revenue.
Fisher, Ronald C., John H. Goddeeris, and James C. Young (1989). "Participation in Tax Amnesties: The Individual Income Tax." *National Tax Journal,* 42.
Hansen, Susan B. (1983). "Extraction: The Politics of State Taxation." In Virginia Gray, Herbert Jacob, and Kenneth N. Vines, eds., *The American States: A Comparative Analysis.* Boston: Little, Brown.
Hyman, David N. (1983). *Public Finance: A Contemporary Application of Theory to Policy.* Chicago: Dryden Press.
Palmer, Kenneth T. (1977). *State Politics in the United States.* 2nd ed. New York: St. Martin's Press.
Pechman, Joseph (1989). *Tax Reform: The Rich and the Poor.* 2nd ed. Washington, D.C.: Brookings Institution.
Pischak, Kathryn A. (1989). "State Economic Development Incentives: What's Available? What Works?" *Municipal Finance Journal,* 10.
Rosen, Harvey S. (1985). *Public Finance.* Homewood, Ill.: Richard D. Irwin.
Rosenberg, I. J. (1992). "Philadelphia a Taxing Place to Play." *Atlanta Journal/Atlanta Constitution,* September 16, p. E1.
Rosenstone, Steven, and John Mark Hansen (1993). *Participation and Democracy in America.* New York: Macmillan.
Steiss, Alan Walter (1989). *Financial Management in Public Organizations.* Pacific Grove, Calif.: Brooks/Cole.
Stull, William J., and Judith C. Stull (1991). "Capitalization of Local Income Taxes." *Journal of Urban Economics,* 29.
Waugh, William L., and Deborah M. Waugh (1988a). "Baiting the Hook: Targeting Economic Development Monies More Effectively." *Public Administration Quarterly,* 12, Summer.
——— (1988b). "Economic Development Programs of State and Local Governments and the Site Selection Decisions of Smaller Firms." In Richard J. Judd, William T. Greenwood, and Fred W. Becker, eds., *Small Business in a Regulated Economy.* New York: Quorum Books.
Wolfinger, Raymond, and Steven Rosenstone (1980). *Who Votes?* New Haven, Conn.: Yale University Press.

4

General Sales Taxes

One of the first things that foreign visitors notice when shopping in the United States is that they pay more for an item, sometimes much more, than the amount shown on the price tag. That is, they notice the difference that the sales tax makes in a purchase price. That difference is seldom noted by Americans, except when the amount of the purchase and the resulting tax are relatively large or when they barely have enough money to make a purchase. Indeed, Americans have come to expect the added cost of sales taxes when they shop. In most respects, those observations simply state the obvious, but they are also important in understanding the appeal of general sales taxes to state and local officials as a major source of revenue. While large amounts of revenue are collected, sales tax rates do not engender the same levels of political opposition and often hostility as income and property tax. Sales taxes seldom are noticed by shoppers, are widely accepted, and generally have little effect on their spending habits.

The first state sales taxes were levied in the 1930s, and the first local sales tax was levied in New York City in 1934 (Hyman, 1983: 566). Initially, state and local sales taxes were selectively levied and resembled today's excise taxes. However, by the 1940s selective sales taxes on items such as tobacco, alcohol, and gasoline peaked as more general taxes on retail and wholesale sales became more commonly used by state governments (Bingham, et al., 1978: 6). At local levels, the key development in the application of local sales taxes, according to John F. Due and John L. Mikesell (1983: 267), was the introduction of state-administered local sales taxes by Mississippi in 1950. State assumption of the burden of administering the local tax made effective use of the taxes possible. Today, general sales taxes are the most important source of revenue for state governments (Buchanan and Flowers, 1987: 342) and the second most important source of revenue after property taxes, for local governments (Bland, 1989: 55).

The major advantage of general sales taxes is that they efficiently generate high levels of revenue at relatively low rates of taxation (Buchanan and Flowers, 1987: 348). That is, even low sales tax rates produce considerable revenue because of the breadth of the tax base. Moreover, relatively low sales tax rates are easier to sell to the electorate than are higher property and income tax rates. In addition, well-designed sales taxes compel nonresident shoppers to pay a portion of the local taxes (Bland, 1989: 55), so at least some portion of the tax burden is shifted to nonresidents.

Another advantage of sales taxes is that they can be collected readily and effectively. Because sales taxes generally are collected by retail businesses rather than by government agencies, they are among the easiest and most efficient taxes to collect. In exchange for collecting and remitting sales tax revenues, most states (except Alaska, Arizona, and Minnesota) compensate retailers by providing a discount of 1 to 5 percent of the taxes collected (Due and Mikesell, 1983: 289).

The two major disadvantages of sales taxes are their general regressivity— although economists differ on just how regressive sales taxes are (if at all)— and their responsiveness to fluctuations in business cycles. In general, sales taxes are assumed to place a greater burden on those who spend the largest percentages of their income on taxable items (Browning and Browning, 1994: 346; Hyman, 1993: 350). Just how regressive sales taxes are depends on the extent to which the burden is passed from sellers to consumers, which differs according to the goods or services being sold.

Because sales taxes are based on purchases, revenues rise when business activity increases and drop when activity decreases during normal seasonal business cycles. These fluctuations can cause problems when a government is overly dependent on sales taxes for its operating budget. Cash flow problems may result from the cyclic revenue shortfalls. Moreover, exempting food from sales taxes removes the most stable category of sales from the tax base, making sales taxes even more responsive to business cycles (Bland, 1989: 58). Since sales taxes are commonly used to retire debt and to pay off bonds, this unstable cash flow can create major headaches for local government officials (Due and Mikesell, 1983: 281).

TAX PHILOSOPHY

A sales tax is fundamentally a tax on consumption. More specifically, it is a tax on a commodity, whether it be a product or a service, purchased for consumption. A general sales tax uses the same tax rate for all, or most, commodities, as opposed to a selective sales tax (or excise tax), which is levied on specific commodities only, or to a differential commodity tax, which applies different rates to different commodities. A sales tax typically is either a unit tax—one levied per unit purchased (such as a gallon of gasoline or a fifth of whiskey)—or an ad valorem tax—one based on a percentage of the basic purchase price of a commodity (Rosen, 1985: 543–544).

Most often, general sales taxes are levied as single-stage, ad valorem taxes on retail sales and collected by retailers themselves. Multistage sales taxes or turnover taxes levied on manufactured products or on wholesale and retail sales are uncommon in the United States, although such value-added taxes are increasingly being considered by all governments (Buchanan and Flowers, 1987: 342–343). For instance, a firm purchases raw materials worth $1 million. The market value of these material increases to $2 million by the time the firm completes its processing. The firm's contribution to the value of a product is $1 million, which represents the firm's contribution in the production of a product, or its value added. Value added includes the value of labor services, the rent paid for the use of capital and land, the interest paid on borrowed capital, royalties and leases paid, and direct taxes paid to governments.

If the value added tax is 4.5 percent, the tax calculation is as follows:

Market value	$2 million
Initial cost of materials	$1 million
Value added	$1 million
Tax levied	.045
Tax liability	$45,000

In addition, general sales taxes typically are not fully comprehensive in the scope of economic transactions covered and are not based on final consumption (Hyman, 1983: 565). Indeed, most state and local governments exempt services and some consumer sales from the tax base.

The distinctions between single-stage and multistage taxes and between more or less comprehensive sales taxes are important in terms of which income groups bear the greatest tax burdens. Research suggests that multistage or turnover taxes may be less regressive because lower income consumers are more likely to buy commodities that have been processed less, such as food and clothing, and fewer commodities that have been processed many times, such as electronic equipment. To the extent that lower income consumers tend to spend larger percentages of their income on food and clothing that are taxed at lower rates, the turnover taxes may be less regressive than single-stage general sales taxes (Hyman, 1983: 569). Economists also suggest that turnover taxes may encourage the vertical integration of production-distribution systems, minimizing the transfers or turnovers from one firm to another (Buchanan and Flowers, 1987: 342). Less comprehensive sales taxes (i.e., those exempting such items as food, clothing, and prescription drugs) may lessen regressivity by not taxing items that represent major expenses for lower income consumers (Buchanan and Flowers, 1987: 349).

RECENT TRENDS IN GENERAL SALES TAXATION

Except for increases in tax rates and bases, not much has changed in recent decades with respect to general sales taxes at the state level. In 1970 sales and gross receipt taxes brought in $3.7 billion, approximately 35 percent of total revenues, for state governments. In 1991 they brought in over $153 billion for state governments, although that much larger figure represented only about 28 percent of total revenues (ACIR, 1993: 70). While reliance on sales taxes may be decreasing somewhat in comparison to other revenue sources, their importance is still substantial.

The best predictor of reliance on sales taxes tends to be past history; those who adopted sales taxes earliest are generally those with the highest levels of reliances on them (Bingham, et al., 1978: 155). Recent trends at the local level, however, indicate expanded reliance on general sales tax revenues. In 1970 sales taxes accounted for just over $3 billion in local revenue; in 1991 that figure was over $32 billion. Sales taxes represented 3.8 percent of local government revenue in 1970 and 5.9 percent in 1991 (ACIR, 1993: 72–73).

Almost 5,500 cities and 1,250 counties levy general sales taxes, and more are choosing to do so as state laws expand local taxing authority. In 1987 thirteen states collected sales taxes and transferred a portion of the tax revenues to their city and/or county governments. Twenty-nine states permitted local governments to levy sales taxes directly, twenty-three allowed municipalities to tax, and twenty-five permitted counties to do so.

Local authority to levy sales taxes is granted in a number of ways. It is permitted by local home rule provisions in Colorado, Illinois, and North Dakota and through business licensing powers in Alabama and Arizona (Bland, 1989: 55–57). Increasingly, special districts—such as school districts in Louisiana—and rapid transit districts are adopting sales taxes to diversify their revenue sources; but most still rely heavily on property taxes (Bingham, et al., 1978: 100).

Exhibit 4.1 lists the basic general sales tax rates in 1991 for the fifty states, the District of Columbia, and selected cities. State rates are almost uniformly higher than county, city, and other government rates. The wide variation in rates is also noteworthy. Alaska, Delaware, Montana, New Hampshire, and Oregon have no state general sales taxes at all. Connecticut, Delaware, Hawaii, Idaho, Indiana, Maine, Maryland, Massachusetts, Michigan, Mississippi, Montana, New Hampshire, New Jersey, Oregon, Pennsylvania, Rhode Island, South Carolina, Vermont, and West Virginia have no local general sales taxes. Most states, however, have some mix of state and local sales taxes.

The form and use of general sales taxes vary radically from state to state and from locality to locality. For example, in addition to providing revenue for general purposes, sales taxes frequently are earmarked to support specific activities:

Exhibit 4.1
Basic Local Sales Taxes: Combined Rates, Selected Cities, 1991

State	City (County)	State Tax	County Tax	City Tax	Other Tax	Combined State-Local Tax Rate
Alabama	Birmingham (Jefferson)	4.0	1.0	2.0	1.0	8.0
	Mobile (Mobile)	4.0	1.0	3.0	1.5	9.5
Alaska	Juneau (Juneau)	--		4.0		4.0
Arizona	Phoenix (Maricopa)	5.0	0.5	1.2	0.5	7.2
	Tucson (Pima)	5.0		2.0		7.0
Arkansas	Little Rock (Pulaski)	4.5	1.0			5.5
	Pine Bluff (Jefferson)	4.0		1.0		5.0
California	Los Angeles (Los Angeles)	6.0	1.25		1.0	8.25
	Sacramento (Sacramento)	6.0	1.25		0.5	7.75
	San Diego (San Diego)	6.0	1.25		1.0	8.25
	San Francisco (San Francisco)	6.0	1.25		1.0	8.25
Colorado	Colorado Springs (El Paso)	3.0	1.0	2.5	0.6	7.10
	Denver (Denver)	3.0		3.5	0.6	7.10
Connecticut	No local general sales taxes					
Delaware	No state or local general sales taxes					
District of Columbia				6.0		6.0
Florida	Jackson County	6.0	1.0			7.0
	Jefferson County	6.0	1.0			7.0
Georgia	Atlanta (Fulton)	4.0	1.0		1.0	6.0
	Columbus (Muscogee)	4.0	1.0			5.0
	Savannah (Chatham)	4.0	1.0			5.0
Hawaii	No local general sales taxes	4.0				4.0
Idaho	No local general sales taxes	5.0				5.0
Illinois	Chicago (Cook)	6.25		1.0	0.75	8.0
	Peoria (Peoria)	6.25		1.0		7.25
Indiana	No local general sales taxes	5.0				5.0
Iowa	Des Moines	4.0	1.0			5.0
Kansas	Kansas City (Wyandotte)	4.25	1.0	1.0		6.25
	Topeka (Shawnee)	4.25		1.0		5.25
	Wichita (Sedgwick)	4.25	1.0			5.25
Kentucky	No local general sales taxes	6.0				6.0
Louisiana	Baton Rouge (E. Baton Rouge)	4.0	4.0			8.0
	New Orleans (Orleans)	4.0	5.0			9.0
	Shreveport (Caddo)	4.0	2.5	2.5		9.0
Maine	No local general sales taxes	6.0				6.0
Maryland	No local general sales taxes	5.0				5.0
Massachusetts	No local general sales taxes	5.0				5.0
Michigan	No local general sales taxes	4.0				4.0
Minnesota	Duluth (St. Louis)	6.5		1.0		7.5
	Minneapolis (Hennepin)	6.5		0.5		7.0

Exhibit 4.1 (Continued)

State	City (County)	State Tax	County Tax	City Tax	Other Tax	Combined State-Local Tax Rate
Mississippi	No local general sales taxes	6.0				6.0
Missouri	Kansas City (Jackson)	4.225	0.75	1.0	0.5	6.475
	St. Louis City	4.225		1.0		5.225
Montana	No local general sales taxes	---				---
Nebraska	Lincoln (Lancaster)	5.0		1.5		6.5
	Omaha (Douglas)	5.0		1.5		6.5
Nevada	Las Vegas (Clark)	6.5	0.5			7.0
	Reno (Washoe)	6.5	0.25			6.75
New Hampshire	No state or local general sales taxes	--				--
New Jersey	No state or local general sales taxes	7.0				7.0
New Mexico	Albuquerque (Bernalillo)	5.0		0.75		5.75
	Santa Fe (Santa Fe)	5.0		0.875		5.875
New York	Buffalo (Erie)	4.0	4.0			8.0
	New York City	4.0		4.25		8.25
	Rochester (Monroe)	4.0	3.0			7.0
	Yonkers (Westchester)	4.0	1.5	2.5	0.25	8.25
North Carolina	Charlotte (Mecklenburg)	4.0				4.0
	Greensboro (Guilford)	4.0				4.0
	Raleigh (Wake)	4.0				4.0
North Dakota	Bismarck (Burleigh)	5.0		1.0		6.0
Ohio	Cincinnati (Hamilton)	5.0	0.5			5.5
	Cleveland (Cuyahoga)	5.0	1.0		1.0	7.0
	Columbus (Franklin)	5.0	0.5		0.25	5.75
	Dayton (Montgomery)	5.0	1.0		0.5	6.5
	Toledo (Lucas)	5.0	1.0			6.0
Oklahoma	Oklahoma City (Canadian)	4.5		2.875		7.375
	Tulsa (Tulsa)	4.5		3.0		7.5
Oregon	No state or local general sales taxes	--				--
Pennsylvania	No state or local general sales taxes	6.0				6.0
Rhode Island	No state or local general sales taxes	7.0				7.0
South Carolina	No state or local general sales taxes	5.0				5.0
South Dakota	Sioux Falls (Minnehaha)	4.0		2.0		6.0
	Pierre (Hughes)	4.0		1.0		5.0
Tennessee	Memphis (Shelby)	5.5	2.25			7.75
	Nashville (Davidson)	5.5	2.25			7.75
Texas	Austin (Travis)	6.25		1.0	.75	8.0
	Dallas (Dallas)	6.25		1.0	1.0	8.25
	Fort Worth (Tarrant)	6.25		1.0	0.5	7.75
	Houston (Harris)	6.25		1.0	1.0	8.25

Exhibit 4.1 (Continued)

State	City (County)	State Tax	County Tax	City Tax	Other Tax	Combined State-Local Tax Rate
Utah	Salt Lake City (Salt Lake)	5.0	1.0		0.25	6.25
Vermont	No local general sales taxes	5.0				5.0
Virginia	Alexandria	3.5		1.0		4.5
	Richmond	3.5		1.0		4.5
	Arlington County	3.5	1.0			4.5
	Fairfax County	3.5	1.0			4.5
	Prince William County	3.5	1.0			4.5
	Virginia Beach	3.5		1.0		4.5
Washington	Seattle (King)	6.5		1.7		8.2
	Spokane (Spokane)	6.5		1.4		7.9
West Virginia	No local general sales taxes	6.0				6.0
Wisconsin	Madison (Dane)	5.0	0.5			5.5
	Milwaukee (Milwaukee)	5.0	0.5			5.5
Wyoming	Cheyenne (Laramie)	3.0	1.0		1.0	5.0

Source: ACIR, 1992: 98.

- Capital improvements (including infrastructure) in Arkansas, Colorado, Florida, and Wyoming
- Public mass transit districts in Colorado, Hawaii, Nevada, New York, Ohio, Utah, and Washington
- Highways in Colorado and Nevada
- Public education in Georgia
- The Kansas and Missouri culture district in Kansas
- Tourism development in Nevada
- Indigent hospital care and county fire protection for unincorporated areas in New Mexico (ACIR, 1992: 99–101)

There also are a number of other ways states permit localities and special districts to use general sales taxes. Some states and localities grant authority for sales taxation to special districts, such as the Metropolitan Commuter Transit District, which is supported by taxes in New York City and neighboring counties. Arkansas permits localities to impose special taxes for set periods of time to finance capital improvements. Florida authorizes a local surtax on the state tax for up to fifteen years to finance infrastructure improvements. A number of states allow local governments to levy sales taxes for the purpose of reducing local property taxes. In Texas that intention is explicitly written into law (ACIR, 1992: 99–101). While this listing certainly is not all-inclusive, it illustrates the variety of uses of sales tax revenues.

The relationship between sales tax revenues and personal income is shown in Exhibit 4.2. Clearly, sales taxes tend to be higher as a percentage of income in the South and West than in the Midwest and East, and the differentials have

Exhibit 4.2
Sales Tax Revenues per $1,000 Personal Income by Region

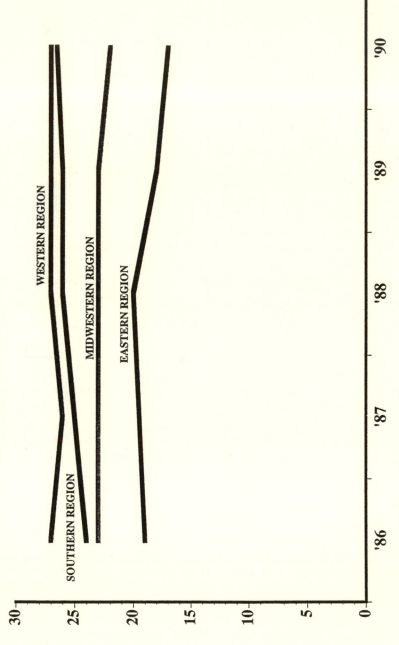

Source: Fiscal and Tax Research Division, 1991: 14.

been increasing slightly over the past few years. States are grouped according to general sales taxes (including gross receipts taxes) as a percentage of personal income are illustrated in Exhibit 4.3. While the regional patterns generally are discernible, the specific rankings provide a better perspective, particularly on those states that differ significantly from their neighbors, such as New York, Connecticut, and South Dakota, with their comparatively higher sales taxes. The advantage of states that do not levy sales taxes over neighbors with relatively high sales taxes would appear intrinsically clear, but the impact of sales taxes on the location and kinds of purchases is still unclear.

The collection and administration of general sales taxes has taken several forms, particularly in terms of assuring interlocal coordination of tax collections. North Carolina, for example, permits only counties to levy sales taxes, but revenues are to be shared with cities. South Dakota permits only municipalities to levy sales taxes, while Wisconsin permits only counties to do so. In California, both cities and counties can levy sales taxes; but city rates take precedence, so county rates cannot be so high that when added to the city rates they exceed state limits. In Tennessee, precedence is given to county rates. In Louisiana and Texas, city and county rates are simply added together (Bland, 1989: 63). Thus, the general sales tax rate in Shreveport is 9 percent (4 percent state and 2.5 percent each for city and county), and in Texas many municipalities have rates in excess of 8 percent (ACIR, 1992: 89–90).

RETAIL AND WHOLESALE SALES TAXES

Conventional wisdom concerning retail sales taxes is that the greater the differential tax rates between states or localities, the greater the likelihood consumers will make purchases to minimize their tax liability. An early study of New York City's sales tax showed that a tax 1 percent higher than that of a neighboring community could reduce the sales tax revenues by 6 percent (Mikesell, 1970: 211; Due and Mikesell, 1983: 315). A more recent study of smaller cities indicated that a 1 percent differential could lower sales tax revenues by 3.1 percent (Mikesell and Zorn, 1986: 335). While slight differences in sales tax rates have little effect on consumer shopping patterns for small ticket items, extensive tax bases and high rates seem to affect spending patterns for large ticket items. Thus, the border city problem, as it is called, encourages governments to avoid tax differentials in excess of about 1 percent (Bland, 1989: 60–61).

In 1992, for example, Tennessee officials proposed raising that state's sales tax rate .5 percent to 6 percent which, when added to a local rate that can be as high as one-half of the state rate, could have created a combined rate of 9 percent in some communities. Critics warned that the differential between a 9 percent Tennessee rate and the rates of 6.5 percent in Arkansas–Little Rock, 6 percent in Georgia-Atlanta, 6 percent in Mississippi, 6 percent in Kentucky, and 6 percent in North Carolina–Charlotte would encourage consumers to leave the state to shop for expensive items. Given that retail activity also means jobs, the

Exhibit 4.3
General Sales and Gross Receipts Taxes as a Percentage of Personal Income, 1988

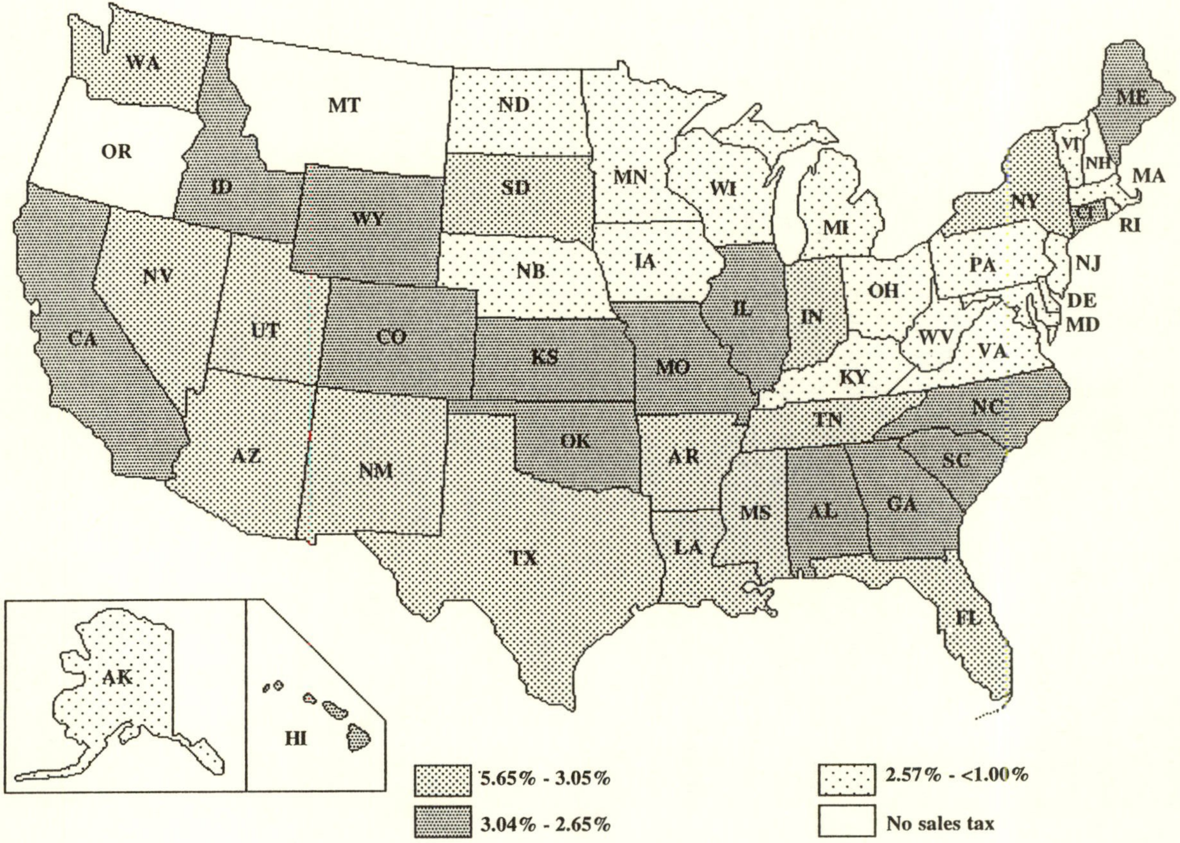

5.65% - 3.05%	2.57% - <1.00%
3.04% - 2.65%	No sales tax

negative impact on Tennessee would be all the greater (*Atlanta Constitution*, 1992). But there obviously are limits on how far shoppers will travel to save a few cents or dollars on purchases. These limits vary proportionately with the costs of items and with differential tax rates. That is, the more expensive the item, the more consumers will pay in taxes, and the further they will travel to purchase it in a location with a lower differential tax rate.

More dramatically, exemptions of certain items from taxation in some states and communities can increase the impact of tax differential even more, luring shoppers to the communities offering the exemptions. Hence, New York shoppers may drive to New Jersey to buy their clothing because New Jersey exempts clothing from taxation, while New York does not (Rosen, 1985: 457).

Exemptions

The exemption issue is important to an understanding of the forms and impact of general sales taxes. Basic tax rates and major tax-exempt items are listed in Exhibit 4.4. It shows considerable and significant differences in which purchases are subject to sales taxes. For example, while Colorado and Minnesota exempt food purchases from state sales taxes, Denver and Minneapolis levy local taxes on restaurant food—defined as immediate or on-premise consumption (ACIR, 1992: 100–101). The wide variance in sales tax application further complicates the measurement of their impact. For instance, in New York City, tickets to Broadway productions are exempt from taxation, but tickets to supporting events are not. In New York State, purchases of all flags, except state flags, are taxed (Rosen, 1985: 457).

As Exhibit 4.4 indicates, a majority of states offer sales tax exemptions for food (26 states), prescription medicines (44 states), consumer electric and gas utilities (26 states), custom computer programs (29 states), installation services (29 states), and sale of materials to manufacturers, producers, and processors (45 states). Other items listed as more likely to be taxed by most states are clothing, telecommunication services, and materials sold to contractors and repairers (ACIR, 1992: 90). The listing of exempted and taxed items in Exhibit 4.4 provides a profile of state effort to reduce the regressivity of general sales taxes by exempting those items that represent the largest categories of expense for lower income households (food, clothing, and utilities). The listing also provides information about state decisions concerning purchases made for resale in terms of the provision (or lack thereof) of exemption for materials purchased by contractors, repairers, and producers of goods. And the listing represents artifacts of state political processes in terms of specific items that are exempted (or not exempted) from state sales taxation. For example, sales by contractors, while taxed in forty-three states, are exempted from taxes when contractors are selling to the U.S. government (ACIR, 1992: 89–91). This provision, which appears uniform among states, acts to put in-state contractor bids for federal contracts on an equal footing (ACIR, 1992: 91).

Exhibit 4.4
State Sales Taxes: Rates and Exemptions, 1991

State	Tax Rate	Food	Pre-scription Drugs	Consumer Electric and Gas Utilities	Clothing	Tele-communication Services	Custom Computer Programs	Repair Charges	Install-ation Service	Sale of Materials to— Contrac-tors	Sale of Materials to— Manufacturers, Producers, Processors	Repairers	States Granting Related Tax Credit
Alabama	4		X				X	X	X		X		
Alaska						No state sales tax							
Arizona	5	X	X				X	X	X	X	X		
Arkansas	4.5		X	X					X		X		
California	6	X	X	X		X	X	X	X		X		
Colorado	3	X	X				X	X	X		X		
Connecticut	6	X	X	X	X				X		X		
Delaware						No state sales tax							
District of Columbia	6	X	X	X		X	X		X		X	X	
Florida	6	X	X	X			X	X	X		X	X	
Georgia	4		X								X		
Hawaii	4		X	X									X
Idaho	5		X	X		X	X	X	X		X	X	X
Illinois	6.25	X	X				X	X	X	X	X	X	
Indiana	5	X	X				X	X	X		X		
Iowa	4	X	X				X		X		X	X	
Kansas	4.25		X	X			X				X		X
Kentucky	6	X	X				X	X	X		X		
Louisiana	4		X				X		X		X		
Maine	6	X	X	X				X	X		X		
Maryland	5	X	X				X	X	X		X		
Massachusetts	5	X	X	X	X		X	X	X		X		
Michigan	4	X	X				X	X	X		X		
Minnesota	6.5	X	X		X		X	X	X		X		
Mississippi	6		X										
Missouri	4.225		X	X			X	X	X		X		

State	Tax Rate	Food	Pre-scription Drugs	Consumer Electric and Gas Utilities	Clothing	Tele-commu-nication Services	Custom Computer Programs	Repair Charges	Install-ation Service	Sale of Materials to— Contrac-tors	Sale of Materials to— Manufacturers, Producers, Processors	Sale of Materials to— Repairers	States Granting Related Tax Credit
Montana	No state sales tax												
Nebraska	5	X	X						X		X		
Nevada	6.5	X	X	X		X		X	X		X		
New Hampshire	No state sales tax												
New Jersey	7	X	X	X	X	X	X				X		
New Mexico	5										X	X	X
New York	4	X	X	X			X	X	X		X	X	
North Carolina	4		X				X	X	X		X	X	
North Dakota	5	X	X	X			X	X	X		X		
Ohio	5	X	X	X		X			X		X	X	
Oklahoma	4.5	X	X	X			X	X	X		X		X
Oregon	No state sales tax												
Pennsylvania	6	X	X		X		X	X	X		X	X	
Rhode Island	7	X	X	X	X		X	X	X		X		
South Carolina	5		X	X							X		
South Dakota	4		X								X		X
Tennessee	5.5	X	X	X							X	X	
Texas	6.25	X	X	X							X	X	
Utah	5		X				X	X	X		X	X	
Vermont	5	X	X	X		X	X	X	X		X		X
Virginia	3.5		X	X		X	X	X	X		X	X	
Washington	6.5	X	X				X	X		X	X		
West Virginia	6		X	X							X	X	
Wisconsin	5	X	X	X			X				X		
Wyoming	3		X								X		X
Total Exempting		27	44	24	6	8	29	25	29	3	45	13	n.a.
Total Taxing		20	2	20	40	36	17	21	17	43	1	33	n.a.

Source: ACIR, 1992: 89.

93

Food. Food consumed at home is exempt from general sales taxes in twenty-six states and taxed in twenty others. Most states do not exempt restaurant purchases of food and beverages for on-premise consumption unless all food is exempt from sales taxes. (Localities may still tax sales of food not sold principally for home consumption.) In resort communities and states with large tourist industries, sales taxes on restaurant food can serve to shift a significant portion of the tax burden to nonresidents. The exemption of food purchased for home consumption, too, reduces the regressivity of sales taxes. Rather than exemptions, some states use other means to lessen regressivity. For example, Louisiana taxes food at 3 percent and other items at 4 percent, and Illinois taxes food at 1 percent and other items at 6.25 percent. Other states, such as Hawaii, provide income tax credits to lower income taxpayers to offset their sales tax payments (ACIR, 1992: 91).

Prescription Medicine. Prescription medicines are exempt from general sales taxes in forty-four states and taxed in only two states. Here, too, the purpose of the exemption is to reduce the general regressivity of sales taxes for low income households and/or elderly residents on fixed incomes. Alabama, for example, exempts prescription medicines from taxation for persons over sixty-five years of age, and New Mexico provides an income tax credit for taxpayers with an adjusted gross income of less than $10,000 (ACIR, 1992: 91).

Gas and Electric Utilities. Gas and electricity are exempted from sales taxes in twenty-six states and taxed in twenty others. Where utilities are taxed, there are numerous mechanisms designed to reduce the burden to lower income households. For example:

- Arkansas exempts the first 500 kilowatt hours of electricity each month for residential consumers with incomes not exceeding $12,000 per year.
- Maine exempts the first 750 kilowatt hours of electricity each month, without regard to income.
- Minnesota and Wisconsin exempt all residential use of gas or electricity for heating from November through April.
- Utah limits utility sales tax rates to 2 percent for residential customers.
- Washington exempts sales of natural and manufactured gas. (ACIR, 1992: 91)

By contrast, Texas and Oklahoma, large gas producing states where fuel costs are comparatively low, permit their local governments to tax gas and electricity (ACIR, 1992: 91).

Consumer Services. While sales taxes are widely and frequently levied on the sale of goods, they seldom are levied on services. Indeed, the almost universal exemption of consumer services from taxation by state and local governments is one of the largest impediments, if not the largest, to the development of more comprehensive sales tax structures and represents a tremendous loss of revenues. Currently, Hawaii, New Mexico, and South Dakota levy a tax on services.

Everything from accounting and legal services to haircuts and dry cleaning is taxed. Tennessee, Texas, and Mississippi tax fewer services (*Atlanta Journal/ Constitution*, 1991: G6), but lists of taxable business and personal services are expanding, and the reasons are easy to understand. In a small state like Arkansas the loss of revenues from service exemptions is estimated at slightly more than $354 million. Losses, to be sure, are more extensive in larger states. The enormous growth of the service sector, indeed, suggests that the continued exemption of services will be a more and more hotly contested political issue as governments seek other revenue sources.

The short-lived service sales tax in Florida in 1987 is the most often cited example of a failure of such an expansion of a sales tax base. The reasons for the repeal of the Florida tax do not provide persuasive arguments against sales taxes on services, however (Francis, 1988: 129–130). The tax was enacted by the Florida state legislature with relatively little opposition. The legislature had spent years trying to expand revenue sources to meet the service and infrastructure needs of Florida's burgeoning population. In the process, the legislature had questioned a number of sales tax exemptions before settling on a service tax. The notion of taxing all service transactions, without exemptions for sales among businesses (i.e., wholesale sales), was all the more appealing because of the potential size of the tax base. The passage of the tax bill, requiring approval of both houses of the legislature and the governor, prevented several interest groups from protecting their own exemptions (Francis, 1988: 130–131). That is, the bill first provided for the taxation of all services, and then was amended to exclude certain services, instead of listing specific services to be taxed and requiring the legislature to exempt each item specifically. The very breadth of the tax base limited the influence of business and other interests.

Revenues from sales taxes on all services were expected to be $4.2 billion in fiscal year 1989. When the legislature reduced the number of taxable services to 45 percent of the total that might have been taxed, revenue estimates were greatly reduced. The legislature's granting of exemptions further confused the issue of what kinds of services should and should not be taxed. Levying taxes on haircuts, but not on accounting services, for example, was difficult to justify (Francis, 1988: 133).

The lack of distinction between final sales and wholesale sales also was problematical. The meaning of final sale is much less clear with services, although the distinction between items purchased for internal use by a firm (i.e., their use in producing goods and/or services that then will in turn be sold) and those purchased for resale to customers is made when taxing sales of some goods. For many states and local governments, however, the distinction is not so clearly drawn, and business purchases may be subject to sales taxes regardless of their use. The collection of sales taxes by nongovernmental agents unfamiliar with those more subtle distinctions increases the likelihood of confusion. The Florida statute provided five criteria for determining the exception of a service from taxation based on its ultimate resale, but problems still remained (Francis, 1988: 135–136).

Additional problems arose over the use tax on services purchased outside of Florida but used within the state. The discussion of use taxes below deals more specifically with the problem of taxing goods and services purchased outside of the taxing unit. Suffice it to say here that the issue greatly complicated the application of Florida's tax on services. In the absence of tangible property, most services are taxed at the location at which most of the cost of delivering the service is realized. The cost of compliance was the greatest concern of taxpayers, particularly multistate corporations (Francis, 1988: 139–140).

When the Florida tax on services was repealed in December 1987, a higher general sales tax rate was approved to replace some of the lost revenues. The failure of the tax was likely due to the antitax climate among the electorate, media opposition to the tax on advertising, and ineffective defense of the tax by the state's political leadership (Francis, 1988: 142–145).

Pressure for additional state and local revenue sources militates against continued exemption of services. Given that affluent taxpayers tend to use more personal services than do the less affluent, the tax can be used to lessen the regressivity of state and local taxes, and perhaps to replace taxes on such items as food. The Florida experience, however, does suggest that a broadly based service tax will provide greater revenue and, if rates are commensurately low and exemptions are few, will reduce political opposition.

AGRICULTURAL SALES TAXES

Just as preferential treatment exists in the taxation of farm or agricultural property, sales tax preferences are also given to compensate farmers for the risks and uncertainties involved in agricultural production. In some measure, the preferences are intended to encourage mechanization, technological development, and resource mobilization, that is, to increase production. But they are also a reflection of the political influence of agricultural interests in most states. While agricultural interests have lost much of their clout in many state capitals today, they once exercised powerful influence on state and local tax policies, and those historical taxing patterns have not been erased.

Generally, sales tax exemptions for farming are viewed as inputs into the agricultural process, and thus are treated like manufacturing exemptions. Taken together, states exempt a vast array of agriculture-related products and machinery from sales taxes. For example, the sales of livestock, seed, feed, pesticides, fertilizers, and farm fuels and electricity are exempt either in part or entirely from sales taxes, though their treatment varies from state to state. Recent trends involve exempting farm machinery and equipment from sales taxes, much as manufacturing machinery is exempt.

The following list—though not all-inclusive—contains the products most commonly exempted:

- Lubricating oils, diesel fuels, and gasoline

- Fertilizers, herbicides, and pesticides

- Seeds, meals, and feeds

- Livestock and poultry

- Vegetables, plants, shoots, and slips

- Production materials

- Sawdust, wood chips, and shavings

- Gross receipts from the sale of agricultural products

- Trucks, tractor-trailers, or semitrailers purchased or leased for farm operations

- Leases and rentals of farm machinery and equipment

Exhibits 4.5 and 4.6 show how states treat the most important inputs of agricultural production—feed, seed, fertilizer and other farm chemicals, livestock, and farm machinery. All states with general sales taxes exempt feed, seed, most fertilizers, and livestock. Thirty states exempt farm machinery and equipment from sales taxes, while fourteen tax them at a reduced rate. (Five states do not levy general sales taxes.)

Sales tax exemptions of farm machinery and equipment and on cattle and calves seem to affect all states. Exemptions on poultry, however, appear to affect state and local governments in the Midwest and South more than in other states. And sales tax exemptions on hogs and pigs tend to have an impact on even fewer state and local governments, primarily those in the upper Midwest.

Exhibit 4.7 illustrates the typical sales tax savings of a farm whose owners purchased some power machinery and irrigation equipment. If the owners were required to pay a 5 percent sales tax on the purchased items, they would pay $37,397 in sales taxes. In other words, the state subsidized the farmer to the tune of $37,397. By the late 1980s, the adoption of sales tax exemptions by state and local governments had become almost universal and provided effective tax relief for agricultural producers.

Preferential treatment for agricultural products was adopted primarily because states regarded such taxes as indirect business taxes. These taxes, economic theory suggests, should be borne by consumers of the products. However, they are not. Instead, this preferential treatment entailed losses of tax dollars to both states and local governments and placed additional relative tax burdens on non-farmers. The extent to which these treatments impact state and local governments depends on the relative importance of the agricultural sector to the state and local economies. The challenge is for state and local governments to weigh the benefits of subsidizing the agricultural sector and to find equitable ways to replace lost revenues.

Exhibit 4.5
Sales Tax Treatment of Feed and Seed, Fertilizer and Other Farm Chemicals, and Livestock

| | | Sales Tax Treatment | |
| | | Fertilizer and | |
State	Feed/Seed	Other Chemicals	Livestock
Alabama	Exempt	Exempt	Exempt
Arizona	Exempt	Tax	Exempt
Arkansas	Exempt	Exempt	Exempt
California	Exempt	Exempt	Exempt
Colorado	Exempt	Exempt fertilizer only	Exempt
Connecticut	Exempt	Exempt	Exempt
Florida	Exempt	Exempt	Exempt
Georgia	Exempt	Exempt	Exempt
Hawaii	Tax	Tax	Tax
Idaho	Exempt	Exempt	Exempt
Illinois	Exempt	Exempt	Exempt
Indiana	Exempt	Exempt	Exempt
Iowa	Exempt	Exempt	Exempt
Kansas	Exempt	Exempt	Exempt
Kentucky	Exempt	Exempt	Exempt
Louisiana	Exempt	Exempt	Exempt
Maine	Exempt	Exempt	Exempt
Maryland	Exempt	Exempt	Exempt
Massachusetts	Exempt	Exempt	Exempt
Michigan	Exempt	Exempt	Exempt
Minnesota	Exempt	Exempt	Exempt
Mississippi	Exempt	Exempt	Exempt
Missouri	Exempt	Exempt	Exempt
Nebraska	Exempt	Exempt	Exempt
Nevada	Exempt	Exempt	Exempt
New Jersey	Exempt	Exempt	Exempt
New Mexico	Exempt	Exempt	Exempt
New York	Exempt	Exempt	Exempt
North Carolina	Exempt	Exempt	Exempt
North Dakota	Exempt	Exempt	Exempt
Ohio	Exempt	Exempt	Exempt
Oklahoma	Exempt	Exempt	Exempt
Pennsylvania	Exempt	Exempt	Exempt
Rhode Island	Exempt	Exempt	Exempt
South Carolina	Exempt	Exempt	Exempt
South Dakota	Exempt	Exempt	Exempt
Tennessee	Exempt	Exempt	Exempt
Texas	Exempt	Exempt	Exempt
Utah	Exempt	Exempt	Exempt
Vermont	Exempt	Exempt	Exempt
Virginia	Exempt	Exempt	Exempt
Washington	Exempt	Exempt	Exempt
West Virginia	Exempt	Exempt	Exempt
Wisconsin	Exempt	Exempt	Exempt
Wyoming	Exempt	Exempt	Exempt

States without a general sales tax: Alaska; Delaware; Montana; New Hampshire; Oregon

Source: Compiled by Arkansas' Bureau of Legislative Research, Office of Tax Research, 1992.

Exhibit 4.6
Sales Tax Treatment of Farm Machinery

State	Sales Tax Treatment
Alabama	Taxable at 1.5%
Arizona	Exempt (new) - used machinery taxed at 5%
Arkansas	Exempt
California	Taxable at 4.75%
Colorado	Taxable at 3%
Connecticut	Exempt
Florida	Taxable at 3% - rental taxed at 4%
Georgia	Exempt
Hawaii	Taxable at 4%
Idaho	Exempt
Illinois	Exempt
Indiana	Exempt
Iowa	Exempt
Kansas	Exempt
Kentucky	Exempt
Louisiana	Partial exemption
Maine	Exempt
Maryland	Exempt
Massachusetts	Exempt
Michigan	Exempt
Minnesota	Taxed at 2%
Mississippi	Farm equipment (tractors) at 1%; self-propelled equipment at 3% implements and other equipment at 6%
Missouri	Exempt
Nebraska	Taxed at 3.5%
Nevada	Taxed at 5.75%
New Jersey	Exempt
New Mexico	4.75% on 50% of sale price
New York	Exempt
North Carolina	$80 maximum tax per article
North Dakota	Taxed at 3.5%
Ohio	Exempt
Oklahoma	Exempt
Pennsylvania	Exempt
Rhode Island	Exempt
South Carolina	Exempt
South Dakota	Taxed at 3% on trade-in difference
Tennessee	Exempt
Texas	Exempt
Utah	Exempt
Vermont	Exempt
Virginia	Exempt
Washington	Taxed at 6.5%
West Virginia	Exempt
Wisconsin	Exempt
Wyoming	Taxed at 3%

States without a general sales tax: Alaska; Delaware; Montana; New Hampshire; Oregon

Source: Compiled by Arkansas' Bureau of Legislative Research, Office of Tax Research, 1992.

Exhibit 4.7
Sales Tax on New Equipment and Implements

Power Equipment and Implements	Estimated Purchase Price	5% Gross Receipts Tax
2 Tractor - 85 hp	$27,500 each	$2,750
Tractor AC, DW 140 hp	50,180	2,509
Combine, 4WD Rice 253 hp	122,970	6,148
Triple K 26.67'	13,750	687
Blade - 8' Rear Mount	1,700	85
Disk, MC 9.0"	15,250	762
Ditcher, Rear Mount	1,800	90
Field Cultivator	10,950	547
Levee Disk with Box Seeder	3,750	187
Planter, 8-Row @ 30"	12,570	628
Roller (Byfold)	6,500	325
2 Row Cultivator, 8-Row	5,930 each	593
Sprayer, Saddle Mtd. BC	3,130	156
Sprayer, Dir., 8-Row	2,500	125
Stalkcutter	3,080	154
Total Power Equipment and Implements =		$15,746

IRRIGATION EQUIPMENT

Wells and Pumps	$255,760	$12,788
Power Units	58,500	2,925
Underground Pipe	118,754	5,938
Total Irrigation		$21,651
Grand Total		$37,397

PUBLIC UTILITY TAXES

Most public utilities are privately owned and government regulated. Private businesses operating as legal monopolies own and operate public utilities and sell their products either directly to the public or indirectly through government owned utilities. Electricity, for example, may be bought from a privately owned utility by a municipal electric company and then sold to the city's residents. The major exceptions are water and public transit, where a great majority of municipalities with populations of over 5,000 own and operate their own water supply and distribution systems as well as their transportation systems.

A public utility, then, is a privately or publicly owned and operated business that has been granted a monopoly position in its own markets by a government. It is protected from competition by law so that it is the sole provider of a product within a geographic region. Businesses supplying the public with electricity, natural gas, water, cable television and sometimes solid waste disposal often are classified as public utilities by governments.

Governments grant certain businesses such exclusive rights because public utilities are natural monopolies—ones that occur because the nature of the business is such that greater efficiency is achieved through sole production, provision, and distribution of a product. Required capital investment is so large that only one business can operate profitably. If competition were allowed, it is possible that no business could afford to provide the product, which government has deemed essential.

Such an arrangement also means that consumers who are dissatisfied with the product cannot go to a competitive provider. This monopolistic position enjoyed by a business allows it—if unchecked—to charge different customers different prices. Furthermore, the public utility can charge a higher rate for a product than would otherwise be the case if there was a competitive marketplace. To constrain such potential abuses, governments closely regulate (or should closely regulate) public utilities to ensure that each customer pays a rate equal to the cost incurred by the business plus a "reasonable" profit. A reasonable profit is one that allows a business to attract sufficient capital to be able to replace and expand its plant and equipment.

Over 88 percent of the revenues raised from public utility taxes are generated by local governments. It should also be noted that, for statistical reporting purposes, state owned and operated liquor stores are a public utility. In seventeen states, some, if not all, alcoholic beverages are sold in state liquor stores. The state establishes a markup over inventory to recover its operating costs, as well as a predetermined profit ratio. Consequently, liquor profit is included with public utility revenues in the seventeen states that operate liquor stores, and alcoholic beverage revenues will be slightly underreported.

Since the mid-1980s, state public utility revenues have not increased significantly. Most state governments keep their utility revenues in the general fund. Only twelve states earmark their public utility revenues. Alaska, New Jersey, North Carolina, and Ohio designate a portion of their revenues for local government use. Alabama, Florida, Oklahoma, and Texas earmark a portion of theirs for education. Thirty-seven states do not specifically set aside their public utility revenues for prescribed purposes.

Rates

Generally, public utility tax rates are levied as a fixed percentage of gross earnings or receipts. In a few states, the rates are graduated. In addition, some states subject capital, stocks, or net income to taxation. It also should be noted that rates normally are higher when the utility tax is collected in lieu of property taxes. By taxing gross earnings or receipts, governments can make their tax base broader, because the tax is levied on all earnings before any expenditures or exemptions are deducted. If the tax is a fee for the use of public rights-of-way, tax exempt businesses still have to pay the tax, thus broadening the tax base.

Public utilities operating only in one state are taxed on their entire earnings or receipts; those functioning in more than one state are taxed in proportion to their gross earnings or receipts from sources in the state compared to their total earnings or receipts from all sources (Commerce Clearing House, 1991: 8006). Normally, states may not levy taxes on costs of transporting products between states, but may tax intrastate transportation costs. Moreover, license fees frequently are levied at fixed rates, some are graduated according to the population of the locality in which the utility is located.

Local government dependence on public utility revenues varies considerably. Local governments use the power to regulate the use of land within their jurisdictions as the basis for levying utility taxes. They levy a gross earnings or receipts tax on utilities for the privilege of using their land (right-of-way). Like state utility revenues, rates are a fixed percentage of gross earnings or receipts, though additional fees may be charged.

Stability

Besides being quite regressive (i.e., lower income families pay a higher proportion of their incomes on utility products), public utility revenues may not be very stable as sources of government income. The tax base is vulnerable to economic downturns and weather patterns. Economically, the stability of utility revenues depends on the tax base. For instance, utilities that supply primarily residential consumers are much more stable than those that service industrial consumers. Weather, of course, is uncontrollable. Inordinately warm winters or excessively cold summers mean less electricity usage and, in turn, fewer tax revenues. Governments, therefore, need to be cautious about relying too much on such uncertain revenue sources, although not all utilities are unstable.

USE TAXES

Very simply, use taxes are levied on goods and/or services that are purchased out of state or out of town, but used or consumed within the state or locality. Use taxes permit states and localities to regain tax monies lost when firms or individuals choose to make purchases elsewhere to avoid local taxes or simply to avail themselves of lower prices. Most states have situs rules to determine the location of use or consumption of goods or services. That is, they most frequently base their determination on the location at which goods or services are transferred from the seller to the purchaser (i.e., where delivery was taken). Transportation costs, tax laws relating to the length of time goods remain in particular locations, and offsetting state taxes generally discourage firms from trying to avoid taxation in a particular state (Francis, 1988: 137). Most often, it is simply less expensive to accept the tax liability in the state in which the goods or services will be located than to attempt an elaborate scheme to void the taxes.

Mail Order and Direct Marketing

In 1967 the U.S. Supreme Court allowed mail order and direct marketing companies to avoid state sales and use taxes appreciably when it ruled that out-of-state firms with no physical presence in a state are not required to collect and remit a state's sales and use taxes. This ruling meant that states lost an estimated $3.3 billion in 1992 in sales and use tax revenues. In addition:

• Based on a complex formula ACIR determined that for the average sales tax state, the 1990 potential use tax revenue loss was $63.2 million.

• If states that impose a local sales tax were allowed to collect that tax, the revenue potential from mail order sales was estimated to be $3.45 billion in 1992.

• If all local governments with sales taxes were allowed to collect taxes on mail orders, the revenue potential was estimated to be $3.91 billion in 1992. (ACIR, 1991: 1)

The following example represents the way mail order and direct marketing revenues are lost. If consumers in Mississippi purchase commodities at a local retail store, the retail establishment collects sales taxes and remits them to the state. If those same consumers, on the other hand, buy from Sears catalogue headquarters in Chicago, Sears will collect a use tax from them and remit the revenues back to the state. In either case state sales and use taxes will be collected. However, if consumers in Mississippi buy from a catalogue center that has no business locations in the state, the catalogue center will not collect sales or use taxes, and the state will not collect those taxes.

In the late 1980s, states began to challenge the mail order industry's interpretations of the scope of the Supreme Court's 1967 decision. On May 26, 1992, the U.S. Supreme Court ruled in *Quill Corporation v. North Dakota* that a state cannot tax a business that does not have a physical presence in that state. The decision was based on the commerce clause of the Constitution, rather than on the due process clause on which a similar 1967 decision was based. The *Quill* decision opened the door for Congress to pass specific legislation regarding state taxation of mail order sales (Hellerstein, 1992: 120; Cloud, 1992: 1522). A decision in favor of North Dakota might cost mail order houses as much as $20 billion in back taxes (Colford, 1992: 4; Savage, 1992: 14).

As of 1990, more than half of the states that collect sales and use taxes have legislation aimed at taxing mail order marketers. The reasons states have taken such an active role are threefold. In the first place, a substantial amount of revenues now lost can be collected. Second, states hope their actions will compel the Supreme Court to overturn, or at least narrow, their previous ruling. Finally, states hope to goad Congress into action on this matter of lost revenues (ACIR, 1990: 1).

The nature of state efforts to collect mail order and direct marketing sales and use taxes varies broadly. To date, most states rely on voluntary compliance.

Many businesses comply because they do not want to incur a substantial tax liability in the event that their interpretations of their tax exemptions are overruled by the courts. With significant changes occurring in direct marketing, the applicability of the 1967 Supreme Court decision remains unclear.

Also, to be on the safe side, many such firms are complying voluntarily because physical presence is being redefined, albeit slowly. Regular and systematic solicitation, cable television advertising, toll-free telephone numbers, and credit card acceptances may now be viewed as a business presence (Morse and Zimmerman, 1990: 7).

Legislative puissance varies, but may be classified into four levels of activity (Morse and Zimmerman, 1990: 15):

- *Aggressive*—Seeking compliance through tax audits, threat of audit, and/or litigation
- *Active*—Notifying firms of tax liability, collecting revenues via voluntary compliance, sometimes involving interstate compacts
- *Inactive*—Collecting only after authorization by federal or court action
- *Contingent*—Collecting required only after federal legislation allows for it

Exhibit 4.8 lists states which correspond to these classifications.

In addition to individual state actions, some states are entering into multi- or bistate compacts to force voluntary compliance. At present, these efforts are viewed as complementary to and not a substitute for individual state actions. Yet they too may ultimately facilitate changes in current mail order and direct marketing taxation. Five such compacts presently exist (Morse and Zimmerman, 1990: 15):

- Tri-State Compact on Sales and Use Tax: Connecticut, Massachusetts, and Rhode Island
- Great Lakes States Tax Compact: Illinois, Indiana, Michigan, Minnesota, and Ohio
- Midwest Sales Tax compact: Illinois, Iowa, Kansas, Michigan, Minnesota, Nebraska, and South Dakota
- Southeastern Association of Tax Administrators Agreement to Exchange Sales and Use Tax Information: Alabama, Arkansas, Florida, Georgia, Kentucky, Louisiana, Mississippi, North Carolina, South Carolina, Tennessee, Virginia, and West Virginia
- An agreement among Ohio, Pennsylvania, and West Virginia

The most significant and far-reaching bistate agreements are between New York and New Jersey and New York and Connecticut. Firms in these states are pressured to comply lest the states in which they are located fine them.

Most mail order and direct marketing businesses are conducted by large firms, where compliance costs are not onerous. Such costs, however, appear to be a significant problem for small firms, which do not account for the bulk of mail

Exhibit 4.8
States with Mail Order Sales Tax Legislation

STATE	YEAR ENACTED	ENFORCEMENT STATUS
Arkansas	1987	Active
Arizona	1989	Active
California	1985,87	Aggressive
Colorado	1990	Contingent
Connecticut	1988,89	Aggressive
Florida	1987	Inactive
Georgia	1990	Contingent
Idaho	1989	Active
Illinois	1989	Inactive
Iowa	1988	Active
Kansas	1990	Contingent
Kentucky	1988	Active
Louisiana	1987	Contingent
Maine	1990	Contingent
Massachusetts	1988	Inactive
Minnesota	1988	Aggressive
Mississippi	1988	Contingent
Missouri	1990	Contingent
Nebraska	1987	Active
Nevada	1989	Active
New Mexico	1990	Contingent
New York	1989	Active
North Carolina	1988	Active
North Dakota	1987	Aggressive
Ohio	1987,90	Active
Oklahoma	1986	Inactive
South Carolina	1987, 89	Active
South Dakota	1987	Inactive
Tennessee	1988	Aggressive
Texas	1987,89	Inactive
Utah	1990	Contingent
Vermont	1990	Contingent
Washington	1986,89	Active
West Virginia	1989	Active

Source: Morse and Zimmerman, 1990: 4. Reprinted with permission of The National Conference of State Legislatures.

order business. An often suggested solution entails enacting a national, single uniform rate on all mail order and direct marketing businesses and remitting the revenues proportionately to the states. Another alternative is to exempt small firms.

So far, however, businesses have been able to effectively resist state taxing jurisdictions. Nevertheless, this new source of money looks especially attractive to states that are relying increasingly on sales and use revenues. They are unlikely to give up easily.

SITE DETERMINATION

Sales and use taxes on services pose problems because location is difficult to pinpoint. While products are sold at definite, known locations, services often are not. A service may be delivered in another state, particularly if that state does not tax services. The criteria for legal determination of the location of service delivery often are related to a firm's real property, tangible personal property, or market. When a direct link to a business operation is lacking, the location is generally determined by using an average of the ratios of in-state sales to total sales, in-state property to total property, and in-state payroll to total payroll. The tax would be determined by multiplying the purchase price by the percentage (average ratio) and applying the state tax rate (Francis, 1988: 138).

The problems inherent in defining locations of sale, delivery, and/or use of goods and services make it very difficult for a local government to administer a use tax effectively. State officials can more easily administer such taxes and distribute revenue based on known business locations and prorate them based upon the jurisdictions involved in the sale, or a set formula for allocating such revenues (Due and Mikesell, 1983: 313–314).

SALES AND USE TAX COLLECTION AND ADMINISTRATION

States generally collect, via vendors, their own sales and use taxes as well as local sales and use taxes, when the local tax base is identical to that of the state. (States, of course, charge local governments for this service before they remit collections to the localities.) Despite the obvious advantages of state collected and administered sales and use taxes, some larger local governments still choose to collect and administer their own sales and use taxes. Common problems with locally collected and administered taxes include the following:

- Duplication of administration for state and local taxes, including collection, audit, and enforcement of tax laws, can occur.
- The likelihood of overlapping tax rates by different local governments increases when there is no state coordination.
- Jurisdictional confusion, particularly with transactions that cross boundaries, may leave some transactions untaxed and others taxed more than once.
- Nonuniform tax bases cause difficulties when there are differences in the kinds of transactions taxed.

In short, local administration of general sales and use taxes may speed up the cash flow to local coffers but may well cost more and require more supplemental administrative wherewithal than local governments can afford or provide.

By contrast, collection and administration of general sales and use taxes by the state has numerous advantages:

- Vendors or retailers can be used as transaction sites, making it more efficient to collect taxes.
- Technological advances in data processing make it possible to remit revenues to localities at least quarterly, if not monthly, and to minimize collection costs (i.e., holding vendor compensation to no more than 1 percent).
- Local duplication of state use tax captures sales tax revenue from interstate purchases.
- Vendor compensation expenses for local taxes are avoided.
- Redistribution of revenues to different local governments and special districts is facilitated. (Due and Mikesell, 1983: 313–314)

Then, too, state collection and administration encourages commonality in the state and local tax bases, exemptions, and rates; it encourages tax simplicity.

CONCLUDING COMMENTS

General sales and use taxes are the most important source of revenue for state government and the second most important source for local government, and their importance is growing for special districts and other governmental units. Typically, these taxes are levied on retail sales and collected by retailers.

The primary advantage of general sales and use taxes is that relatively large amounts of revenues are generated with relatively low tax rates and small bases. Key to revenue potential and low rates is the comprehensiveness of the tax base, although few state and local governments attempt to tax services (even though that is likely to change in the near future).

The disadvantages include the uncertainty of revenue collections when sales and use taxes are so closely tied to business cycles and economic growth, and the general regressivity of sales taxes. The sales and use tax burden is heaviest on lower income households, although some of the burden is reduced if food, clothing, utilities, and other items that represent larger expenses to lower income households are exempted from taxation. Indeed, most states do exempt food purchased for home consumption, prescription drugs, and gas and electricity from sales and use taxes.

Local sales and use taxes are usually collected and administered by state governments to minimize confusion over tax bases and tax rates and to minimize administrative costs. State and local governments frequently dedicate these revenues to specific purposes, such as financing capital improvements and mass transit systems, and sometimes implement sales taxes for specific, short-term objectives, such as to retire debt or to construct a particular project.

General sales and use taxes are more attractive to state and local governments than are most other forms of taxation because consumers find the taxes relatively painless. Persons do not receive large tax bills quarterly or annually as they do with income and property taxes. Indeed, increases in sales and use tax rates and bases are often approved explicitly or implicitly to provide property tax relief. The negative impact of these taxes on lower income households, however, does suggest that limits should be placed on the rates imposed and on the commodities taxed. Excessively high tax rates, too, can encourage the flight of shoppers to retail firms outside of the city, county, or state with the high rates, thus reducing revenues and employment. In short, there are limits to the revenue potential of general sales and use taxes, particularly as more and more general purpose and special purpose governments adopt them.

The competition among county and municipal governments now to levy utility taxes on cable television service, particularly since the Federal Communications Commission has opened the door for much more local regulation of cable service, is a good illustration of the future for sales and use taxes. As cable television ceases to be considered an amenity, the pressure for greater taxation of services will give way to pressures for greater regulation to assure broad public access, just as happened with electrical power. That is one of the dilemmas of taxing consumption—it influences who can afford to consume.

REFERENCES

Advisory Commission on Intergovernmental Relations (ACIR) (1986). *State and Local Taxation of Out-of-State Mail Order Sales.* Washington, D.C.: ACIR.

———— (1990). *Significant Features of Fiscal Federalism.* Vol. 2. Washington, D.C.: ACIR.

———— (1991). *State Taxation of Interstate Mail Order Sales: Estimates of Revenue Potential, 1990–1992.* Washington, D.C.: ACIR.

———— (1992). *Significant Features of Fiscal Federalism.* Vol. 1. Washington, D.C.: ACIR.

———— (1993). *Significant Features of Fiscal Federalism.* Vol. 2. Washington, D.C.: ACIR.

Atlanta Constitution (1992). "Shoppers Skirt Tennessee Sales Tax." February 24, p. A3.

Atlanta Journal/Constitution (1991). "Tax Dog Shampoos, Hairdos." November 17, p. G6.

Bingham, Richard D., et al. (1978). "The Impact of the Socioeconomic Environment upon Revenue Policy." In Richard D. Bingham, Brett W. Hawkins, and F. Ted Hebert, eds. *The Politics of Raising State and Local Revenue.* New York: Praeger.

Bingham, Richard D., Brett W. Hawkins, and Kraig Rodenbeck (1978). "Selected Current Issues in the Use of State and Local Revenue Sources." In Richard D. Bingham, Brett W. Hawkins, and F. Ted Hebert, *The Politics of Raising State and Local Revenue.* New York: Praeger.

Bland, Robert (1989). *A Revenue Guide for Local Government.* Washington, D.C.: International City Management Association.

Browning, Edgar K., and Jacquelene M. Browning (1994). *Public Finance and the Price System,* 4th ed. New York: Macmillan.

Buchanan, James M., and Marilyn R. Flowers (1987). *The Public Finances*. 6th ed. Homewood, Ill.: Richard D. Irwin.

Chicoine, David (1986). "Farm Taxes." In Steven D. Gold, ed., *Reforming State Tax Systems*. Denver: National Conference of State Legislatures.

Cloud, David S. (1992). "High Court Points to Congress for Mail Order Tax Ruling," *Congressional Quarterly Weekly Report*, 50, May.

Colford, Steven W. (1992). "Landmark Case May Bring Mailers Tax Bill of $20B," *Advertising Age*, 63, January 6.

Commerce Clearing House (1991). *State Tax Guide: All States*. Chicago: Commerce Clearing House.

Due, John F., and John L. Mikesell (1983). *Sales Taxation: State and Local Structure and Administration*. Baltimore: Johns Hopkins University Press.

Fiscal and Tax Research (1991), *Comparative Revenues, 1985 Through 1989, and Revenue Forecasts*, Little Rock: Bureau of Legislative Research, State of Arkansas.

Francis, James (1988). "The Florida Sales Tax on Services: What Really Went Wrong?" In Steven D. Gold, ed., *The Unfinished Agenda for State Tax Reform*. Washington, D.C.: National Conference of State Legislatures.

Hellerstein, Walter (1992). "Supreme Court Says No State Use Tax," *The National Journal of Taxation*, 77, August.

Hyman, David N. (1983). *Public Finance: A Contemporary Application of Theory to Policy*. New York: Dryden Press.

Mikesell, John (1991). *Fiscal Administration: Analysis and Applications for the Public Sector*, 3rd ed. Chicago: Dorsey Press.

Mikesell, John, and C. Kurt Zorn (1986). "Impact of the Sales Tax Rate on Its Base: Evidence from a Small Town," *Public Finance Quarterly*, July.

Morse, Ann, and Christopher Zimmerman (1990). *Efforts to Collect Sales Tax on Interstate Mail-Order Sales: Recent State Legislation*. Denver: National Conference of State Legislatures.

Rosen, Harvey S. (1985). *Public Finance*. Homewood, Ill.: Richard D. Irwin.

Savage, David G. (1992). "Legal Confusion over Mail-Order Taxes," *State Legislatures*, 18, August.

U.S. Department of Commerce, Bureau of the Census (1990). *Agricultural Atlas of the United States*. Vol. 2. Washington, D.C.: Bureau of the Census.

———— (1992). *County Government Finances: 1989–90*. Washington, D.C.: Bureau of the Census.

Excise and Consumption Taxes

Excise and consumption taxes, unlike personal and corporate income taxes, are *expenditure taxes*. Theoretically, an expenditure tax is based on the belief that consumption is an index of a person's ability to pay. The greater one's ability to pay, the more one purchases.

The dominant expenditure taxes used by state and local governments are general sales and use taxes, which were described in the preceding chapter. Other important types of expenditure taxes are excise and consumption taxes, both of which are actually selective sales taxes. (These two types of taxes account for over 10 percent of total state revenues.) The principal advantage of ad valorem-based excise and consumption taxes (as well as sales and use taxes) for the taxing authority is that the impact of inflation is mitigated. These tax bases do need not to be adjusted to the inflation rate because it is done automatically by current pricing.

Excise and consumption taxes are actually selective sales taxes. General sales and use taxes are ad valorem levies of a fixed percent on the retail value of the purchases. True sales and use taxes are levied only on purchases made at their final stage and are collected from sellers. These taxes usually are added to the retail prices of the purchases, with sellers acting as collection agents of the government.

Excise and consumption taxes are levied on designated types of purchases such as motor fuels, tobacco, and alcoholic beverages. These taxes are designed to raise revenues, though some also are intended to discourage certain types of consumption. Moreover, excise and consumption tax revenues frequently are earmarked for particular purposes while sales and use tax revenues generally are deposited in the government's general funds (Hyman, 1987: 506).

TAX PHILOSOPHY

Generally speaking, excise and consumption taxes are based on the benefits received philosophy discussed earlier, which holds that only those persons who benefit from the use of a product should pay the taxes levied on that product.

Ordinarily, excise taxes are paid by manufacturers, wholesalers, or retailers and passed on to consumers via higher product prices. In a highly competitive marketplace where higher prices might decrease usage, the tax may not be passed on to consumers but rather to the owners in the form of lower prices, resulting in lower profits, or to workers in the form of lower wages.

Excise—and to some extent, consumption—taxes are designed to compensate state and local governments for additional services furnished to consumers of the product. Consequently, most of these revenues are dedicated for specific purposes, usually, but not always, related to product use. For instance, motor fuels taxes normally are designed for construction and maintenance of highways, roads, and bridges.

Sumptuary Taxes

A specific type of excise tax is a sumptuary or sin tax, levied, theoretically at least, to discourage consumption of certain nonessential products such as alcohol or tobacco. Reducing consumption of such products supposedly will help consumers become more healthy and thus less of a drain on the health care system.

Sumptuary taxes are intended to increase the cost of the product enough to help dissuade persons from purchasing it. Whether these taxes are effective depends on the responsiveness of use to price. In reality, current tax rates normally are insufficient to discourage use of products, although some studies suggest that taxes on cigarettes may be positively related to a decrease in usage. Generally speaking, however, sumptuary taxes are increased in small incremental units which seldom discourage usage. Adding an additional penny to the existing 24 cent per pack tax on cigarettes hardly discourages usage. If, on the other hand, a state were to increase its tax an additional $4.50 per pack, that might be sufficient to discourage usage. Put differently, when consumers insist on purchasing a sumptuary product despite price, the tax will have little, if any, effect on reducing the number of purchases. Consequently, taxes on sumptuary products will yield somewhat stable revenues as long as taxes are increased in small increments. Sumptuary taxes, are currently used to regulate consumption and to earmark revenues for socially desirable purposes. For example, tobacco taxes frequently are earmarked for aiding the aged; motor fuels taxes are designated for highway, road, and bridge construction and maintenance.

Tax Rates

Although considerable variation exists among the tax rates of state and local governments, excise and consumption taxes are assessed on either a per unit or an ad valorem basis. Most excise and consumption taxes are assessed on a per unit basis. Examples of per unit levies are 21 cents per gallon of gasoline and 24 cents per pack of twenty cigarettes. Luxury taxes, on the other hand, are levied as a percentage of the value of the product (ad valorem).

A major problem with per unit charges is that revenues can decline during periods of inflation because unit consumption may not keep up with inflation. When this occurs, states normally need to increase revenues from these sources because the revenues are earmarked and the recipients of these funds need them. The most obvious way to increase per unit taxes is to increase rates. However, since per unit taxes are set by state law, legislatures are required to pass new laws every time an increase in per unit rates is desired.

An option adopted by a few states—and discussed by many—is to index per unit tax rates. Indexed rates are adjusted administratively in response to one or more indexing factors, such as the Consumer Price Index. The rates increase or decrease in response to the value of the product. Indexing prevents inflation from eroding the purchasing power of revenues and, just as important, does not require legislative approval every time a rate index needs to be increased (or decreased). Exhibit 5.1 illustrates some ways in which states index motor fuels.

Another widely discussed alternative is to tax on an ad valorem rather than on a per unit basis. Ad valorem taxes are inflation sensitive. They often are not significantly affected by inflation since ad valorem taxes are based on the purchase price, which normally keeps up with inflation. In fact, as inflation increases, the unit purchase price increases and ad valorem revenues—which are a percentage of the unit price—also increase. Simply put, during inflationary times either of these two options allows state and local governments to increase revenues without increasing rates.

TRENDS IN EXCISE AND CONSUMPTION TAXATION

Excise and consumption taxes do not generate nearly as much money as income or sales taxes. Exhibit 5.2 shows the major excise taxes as a percentage of total state collections. While motor fuels and tobacco taxes generate the most money, neither yields much. Motor fuel taxes generate less than 10 percent of the total collections, while tobacco taxes produce less than 2 percent.

Most excise and consumption revenues are collected by state rather than local governments. Local governments do not rely much on such revenues because they are quite expensive to collect, making them relatively inefficient taxes. Besides, local governments often are discouraged by their state from levying excise and consumption taxes. From a state's point of view, the argument is that local governments already receive benefits from these revenues because a

Exhibit 5.1
Examples of Indexing Motor Fuels Taxes

INDEXING FACTORS	SOURCE FOR INDEXING FACTORS
Average Retail or Wholesale Price, Less State and Federal Taxes	Prices in February and August from State Sales and Use Returns
Weighted Average Wholesale Tank Wagon Prices, Less Federal Taxes	Price for First Month of Previous Quarter
Percentage Change in State Sales of Taxable Fuel and National Highway Maintenance and Construction Costs Index	Vendor Reports for Previoius Fiscal Year, From Federal Highway Administration
Average Cost of Fuel Purchased by the State, Less state and Federal Taxes	Price for First Month of Previous Quarter
Percentage Change in Consumer Price Index	Labor Statistics Report of Consumer Price Index

Source: Adapted from Bowman and Mikesell, 1983: 169.

portion of the collected revenues is rebated to local governments. For example, local governments receive a proportion of motor fuels revenues for street and road maintenance.

Although excise and consumption taxes are not widely used by local governments, forty-five states permit local governments to levy such taxes. As Exhibit 5.3 indicates, where levied, these taxes represent minor sources of revenue. Excise and consumption taxes are used predominantly by cities. Approximately 84 percent of local revenues from excise and consumption taxes are collected by cities. The largest such revenue producer is public utilities, which generate almost 93 percent of the revenues collected by local governments (U.S. Department of Commerce, 1991b: 78).

Other taxes popular among local governments are alcohol and tobacco taxes as well as taxes on food and lodging. But these taxes, which almost always are shifted to consumers, generate a negligible amount of total tax dollars for localities.

It also should be pointed out that regardless of the tax rate or the basis of assessment, excise and consumption taxes are quite regressive. Exhibit 5.4 displays this regressivity. As income for a family of four rises, the percentage of income paid as excise and consumption taxes decreases. Families with a household income of less than $13,000, for instance, pay almost 2 percent of their income in excise and consumption taxes. By contrast, families making $54,000

Exhibit 5.2
Major Excise Taxes as a Percentage of Total State and Local Collections, 1989–1990

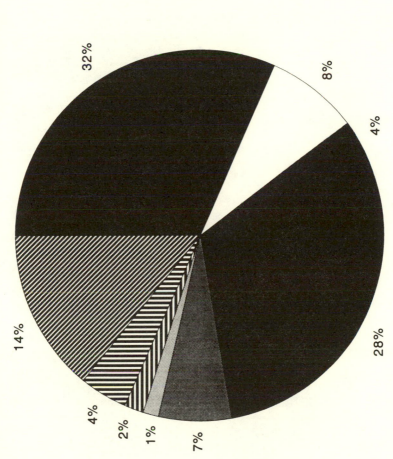

Source: Fiscal and Tax Research, 1991: 3.

Exhibit 5.3
Local Excise Revenues as a Percentage of Local Taxes

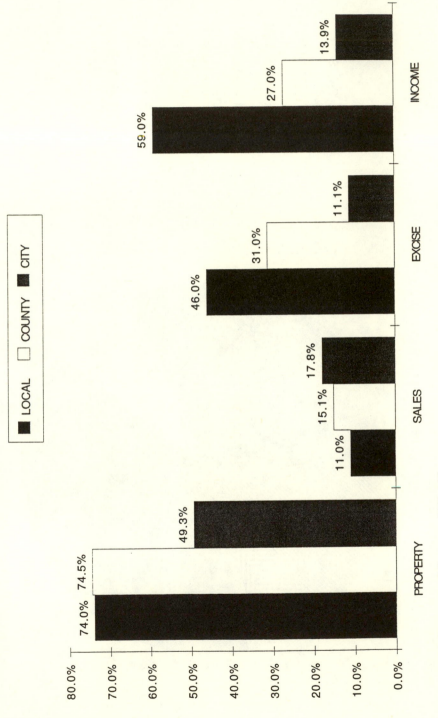

Source: U.S. Department of Commerce, 1991a: 46.

116

Exhibit 5.4
Excise Taxes as a Share of Income for a Family of Four, 1991

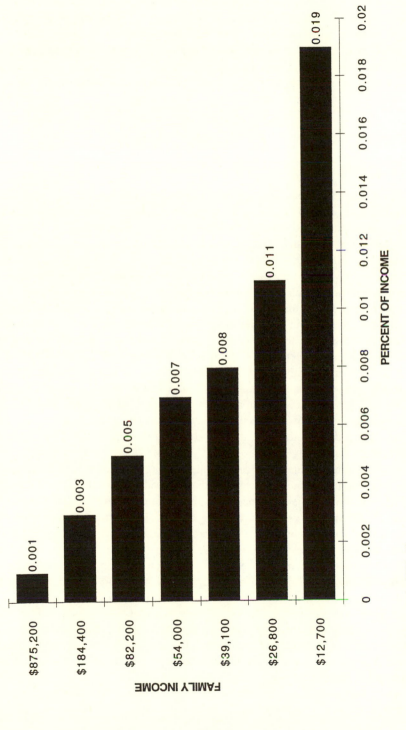

Source: McIntyre et al., 1991: 18.

117

per year pay less than half that amount in such taxes. Of all the excise and consumption taxes, tobacco and alcoholic beverage taxes are the most regressive, while taxes on food and lodgings are the least regressive.

While time and space do not permit the examination all excise and consumption taxes used by state and local governments, the remainder of this chapter focuses on the six taxes that generate the most revenue—motor fuels, tobacco, alcohol, food and lodging, amusements and gambling, and user charges and fees.

SELECTED EXCISE AND CONSUMPTION TAXES

Motor Fuel

Motor fuels taxes are imposed by governments on the storage, distribution, sale, and use of gasoline and other motor vehicle fuels. Lubricating oils, kerosene, marine fuels, and aviation fuels also are taxed. Fees for inspecting various petroleum products usually are included in motor fuels revenues. The state generates about 70 percent of these revenues from motor fuels taxes and about 15 percent from vehicle registration, operators' license fees, charges on common carriers, and other such charges (Snell, 1991: 5).

Exhibit 5.5 shows that motor fuels revenues per $1,000 of personal income are highest in states in the southern tier of the country. While reliance is increasing somewhat in the midwestern region, dependence on such taxes as revenue generators in other parts of the country is decreasing slightly. Wholesalers and retailers are usually responsible for paying these taxes, although they are normally shifted to consumers. In addition, dealers may be subject to other motor fuel related excise taxes and fees which also may be passed on to consumers. Regardless of who actually pays the taxes, virtually all motor fuels revenues are dedicated to the design, construction, and maintenance of highways, roads, and bridges.

Forty percent of state and local capital spending, for example, is for construction and maintenance of highways, roads, and bridges. About one-quarter of the money for these projects comes from motor fuels revenues levied inside the state. Of the money generated by state and local governments, state revenues account for approximately three-quarters of the revenues, while local governments account for the remaining quarter.

Earmarking motor fuels revenues for the construction and maintenance of highways, roads, and bridges has always had widespread appeal as a practical application of the benefits received concept; that is, persons who benefit from a product should pay for that product. Forty-four states designate at least some motor fuel revenues for state highways and mass transit. Thirty-one states distribute funds generated from motor vehicle registration and operators' licenses for such purposes. Local governments also benefit from earmarked motor fuels receipts. Eighteen states earmark motor fuels receipts for local governments, whereas thirteen states designate a portion of revenues from motor vehicle registration for local governments (Fabricius and Snell, 1990: 52).

Exhibit 5.5
Motor Fuels Tax Revenues per $1,000 Personal Income by Region, 1986–1990

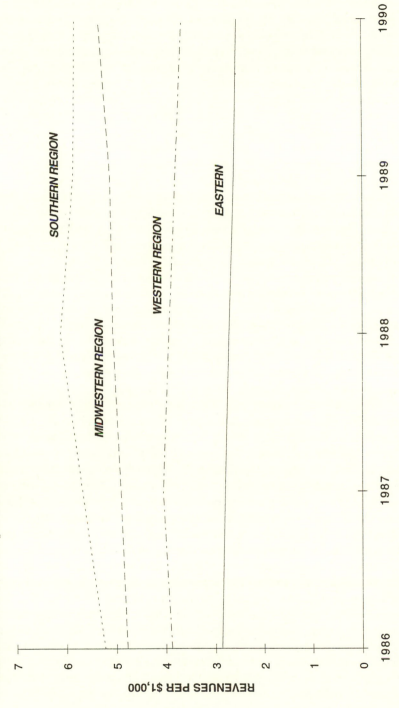

Source: Fiscal and Tax Research, 1990: 24.

Inasmuch as motor fuels taxes are based in part on the benefits received concept of public financing, the revenues benefit motor vehicle users either directly or indirectly. There are some important exceptions, however. In the first place, benefits are divided disproportionately among motor vehicle users. Taxes are based on volume usage (e.g., gallons) rather than on frequency of usage and/or weight of vehicle. Heavier vehicles, for instance, are more likely, than lighter vehicles to damage highways, roads, and bridges, thus increasing construction and maintenance costs. Even though heavier vehicle users may pay incrementally higher taxes, they still do not pay for all respective damage costs. As a result, lighter vehicle users pay for damage created by heavier vehicle users. Put differently, heavier vehicle users benefit more from motor fuels taxes than do lighter vehicle users because the former pay proportionately less tax.

Second, money collected from such taxes may not be distributed according to usage. Normally, over half the motor vehicle traffic within a state occurs in or around metropolitan areas. Yet less than half the tax dollars are redistributed to those areas. Despite these two exceptions, motor fuels taxes still are assumed to be based on the benefits received concept of taxation.

Economic realities make traditional motor fuels excise taxes—a flat rate levy per gallon—an increasingly inadequate way to fund highway, road, and bridge construction and maintenance. More and more, states are appropriating less from their general funds and more from motor fuels revenues, making repeated rate increases necessary to maintain existing levels of expenditure. In 1989, eighteen legislatures raised motor fuels taxes; six did so in 1990, and fifteen in 1991. All but five states raised the diesel rates by the same amount as gasoline. As a result, the median diesel rate now is 17 cents per gallon.

The primary reason that motor fuels taxes are continually increased is that they do not increase in proportion to the value of the product on which they are levied. Unlike sales taxes, motor fuels revenues do not increase when prices increase. As a matter of fact, the opposite often happens. As prices of motor fuels increase, the amount of purchases decreases and revenues fall, slowing or reversing the growth of tax collections. Consequently, alternative taxing structures such as those mentioned earlier in the chapter—indexing of per unit rates or taxing on an ad valorem basis—have been adopted in a few states.

States with dense population distributions are affected less by the inelasticity of motor fuels taxes than states with smaller populations. California, for instance, generates $125 million per penny of motor fuels tax, whereas Alaska collects only $2 million per penny. Therefore, states with less dense populations have the most expensive highway and road systems in terms of per capita expenditures. Exhibit 5.6 shows that on both per capita and personal income bases, Alaska, Wyoming, North Dakota, and South Dakota have the most expensive highway systems in the country. California, the District of Columbia, Massachusetts, and Hawaii, by contrast, have the least expensive systems.

It also should be noted that motor fuels taxes are quite regressive. The Tax Foundation published a study in 1989 showing that, except for tobacco taxes,

Exhibit 5.6
Comparison of State and Local Spending on Highway Finance, 1989

		Per Capita Expenditure	Rank	Expenditure per $100 of Personal Income	Rank
New England	Connecticut	$373	6	$1.61	30
	Maine	275	22	1.83	19
	Massachusetts	188	47	0.90	49
	N. Hampshire	291	19	1.50	33
	Rhode Island	240	29	1.42	34
	Vermont	358	8	2.34	10
Middle Atlantic	Delaware	327	12	1.89	17
	D.C.	181	49	0.82	50
	Maryland	317	14	1.61	29
	New Jersey	271	24	1.22	45
	New York	249	27	1.26	44
	Pennsylvania	227	33	1.41	35
Great Lakes	Illinois	241	28	1.37	38
	Indiana	191	45	1.29	43
	Michigan	193	43	1.18	47
	Ohio	187	48	1.21	46
	Wisconsin	273	23	1.78	21
Plains	Iowa	344	11	2.40	9
	Kansas	293	18	1.87	18
	Minnesota	353	10	2.14	13
	Missouri	208	40	1.36	39
	Nebraska	304	17	2.09	14
	No. Dakota	374	5	3.03	3
	So. Dakota	382	4	3.03	4
Southeast	Alabama	212	37	1.66	27
	Arkansas	192	44	1.58	32
	Florida	228	32	1.38	37
	Georgia	203	41	1.33	40
	Kentucky	280	21	2.19	12
	Louisiana	209	39	1.71	25
	Mississippi	212	38	1.92	16
	No. Carolina	199	42	1.40	36
	So. Carolina	167	50	1.30	42
	Tennessee	224	35	1.61	28
	Virginia	320	13	1.81	20
	West Virginia	226	34	1.95	15
Southwest	Arizona	391	3	2.61	7
	New Mexico	364	7	2.93	5
	Oklahoma	235	30	1.77	22
	Texas	251	26	1.70	26
Rocky Mountain	Colorado	283	20	1.72	24
	Idaho	308	16	2.44	8
	Montana	354	9	2.75	6
	Utah	271	25	2.21	11
	Wyoming	568	2	4.13	2
Far West	California	145	51	0.77	51
	Nevada	314	15	1.76	23
	Oregon	235	31	1.59	31
	Washington	217	36	1.33	41
	Alaska	1113	1	5.78	1
	Hawaii	188	46	1.12	48
U.S. Average		**$236**		**$1.43**	

Source: "State and Local Highway Finance: Where Does the Money Come from and Why Isn't There Enough?" National Conference of State Legislatures LFP #78, 1991.

Exhibit 5.7
Basic Gasoline and Diesel Fuel Tax Rates by State, March 1994

	Gasoline	Diesel Fuel		Gasoline	Diesel Fuel
Alabama	16¢	17¢	Mississippi.	18¢	18¢
Alaska	8¢	8¢	Missouri	13¢	13¢
Arizona	18¢	18¢	Montana	24¢	24¢
Arkansas	18.5¢	18.5¢	Nebraska..	26¢	26¢
California	18¢	18¢	Nevada	22.5¢	27¢
Colorado	22¢	18¢	New Hampshire	18¢	18¢
Connecticut	30¢	18¢	New Jersey	10.5¢	13.5¢
Delaware	22¢	19¢	New Mexico	22¢	18¢
District of Columbia	20¢	20¢	New York.	8¢	10¢
Florida.	4¢	4¢	North Carolina	22¢	22¢
Georgia	7.5¢	7.5¢	North Dakota	18¢	18¢
Hawaii			Ohio	22¢	22¢
Hawaii County	24.8¢	24.8¢	Oklahoma	16¢	13¢
Honolulu County	32.5¢	32.5¢	Oregon	24¢	24¢
Kauai County	26¢	26¢	Pennsylvania	12¢	12¢
Maui County	27¢	27¢	Rhode Island	28¢	28¢
Idaho.	21¢	21¢	South Carolina	16¢	16¢
Illinois.	19¢	21.5¢	South Dakota	18¢	18¢
Indiana	15¢	16¢	Tennessee	20¢	17¢
Iowa	20¢	22.5¢	Texas	20¢	20¢
Kansas	18¢	20¢	Utah	19¢	19¢
Kentucky	15¢	12¢	Vermont	15¢	16¢
Louisiana	20¢	20¢	Virginia	17.5¢	16¢
Maine	19¢	20¢	Washington	23¢	23¢
Maryland	23.5¢	24.3¢	West Virginia	20.5¢	20.5¢
Massachusetts	21¢	21¢	Wisconsin	23.2¢	22.2¢
Michigan	15¢	15¢	Wyoming	9¢	9¢
Minnesota	20¢	20¢			

Source: Commerce Clearing House, 1994: 4015. Reproduced with permission from the *State Tax Guide*, published and copyrighted by CCH Incorporated, 2700 Lake Cook Road, Riverwoods, Illinois 60015.

motor fuels taxes are more regressive than any other excise tax. Motor fuels taxes consume 1.9 percent of the total income of households earning less than $10,000 per year. At $50,000 per year that figure shrinks to 0.5 percent (Snell, 1991:7).

Rates. Exhibit 5.7 lists the basic gasoline and diesel fuel rates for each state. Basic rates range from 8 cents per gallon in Alaska to 30 cents a gallon in Connecticut.

Although states set their rates, some states have entered into reciprocal agreements to standardize the administration and collection of motor fuels taxes. For instance, an International Fuel Tax Agreement has been entered into by the states of Arizona, Colorado, Idaho, Indiana, Minnesota, Missouri, Nebraska, North Dakota, Oklahoma, South Dakota, Utah, Washington, Wisconsin, and Wyoming. The purpose of the agreement is (1) to make uniform the administration of motor fuels use taxation laws with respect to motor vehicles operated interstate, (2) to enable participating jurisdictions to act cooperatively and to provide mutual assistance in the administration and collection of motor fuels use taxes, and (3) to establish and maintain the concept of one license and administering base jurisdiction for each license and to provide that a license's base jurisdiction will be the administrator of this agreement and execute all its provisions. (Commerce Clearing House, 1992: 4012)

In addition, regional fuel tax agreements have been implemented in Maine, New Hampshire, and Vermont to make the administration of motor fuels taxes uniform and to allow the states to assist in the collection of taxes (Commerce Clearing House, 1991: 4013).

Local Usage. Motor fuels taxes are levied primarily by federal and state governments. Local governments in twelve states do tax motor fuels, generating a relatively insignificant proportion of their revenues—just over 3 percent. Besides, since the 1980s both counties and cities have reduced their dependence on motor fuels revenues.

Of all local governments, counties use motor fuels taxes most. Counties generated, on the average, 8.1 cents in revenue from fuels taxes for every dollar produced from property taxes. By comparison, cities generated 7.6 cents in revenue from fuels taxes for every dollar produced from property taxes (Bland, 1989: 80).

The central deterrent to the more widespread use of motor fuels taxes by local governments is their heavy use by federal and state governments. There is considerable fear by local officials that additional taxes will increase the purchase price of fuels to the point that consumers will patronize filling stations outside their jurisdictions. In addition, local governments also realize that such taxes generate little revenue, making them inefficient to collect and costly to administer. In any case, local governments receive a substantial proportion of the motor fuels revenues collected by their state for road and bridge construction and maintenance.

Tobacco

Tobacco taxes have long been part of state and local revenue structures and are regarded as one of the most productive and socially justified of the excise taxes. They are collected by wholesalers and retailers and passed on predominantly to consuming adults. These taxes are a relatively stable source of revenue even during economic downturns. This inelasticity allows governments to tax tobacco, an otherwise cheap product, quite heavily.

Although tobacco consumption has been falling dramatically and substantially over the last ten years, the demand for product is still relatively inelastic. The major reason for the reduction of tobacco consumption apparently is not increases in taxes but rather the adoption of healthier lifestyles. That is, people are not smoking as much because they understand the health risks involved.

Tobacco taxes actually are stamp taxes; that is, wholesalers and retailers purchase stamps, which are sold by states in an effort to insure that each product is taxed only once. The cost of these tax stamps then is passed on to consumers in the form of higher prices. Besides these taxes, wholesalers, retailers, vending machine owners, and manufacturers frequently are subject to a variety of license and permit fees. In a few states, the fees correspond to the amount of sales. Because payment of taxes and fees is made to the state prior to sale of the product, tobacco revenues are unusually efficient to collect and administer.

Most states designate tobacco taxes for local government, education, and health and welfare programs. Approximately ten states earmark tobacco revenues for local governments, eight allocate revenues to educational programs, and nine specify health and human service programs. Other activities receiving some money from these taxes are state pension funds, debt and building funds, and conservation programs.

Rates. All states tax cigarettes; some also tax a variety of smoking and chewing tobacco products. Different products, however, often are taxed at different rates and even on different bases. For instance, cigarettes are taxed on the weight and the dimension of cigarette packs in which they are packaged. Cigars, on the other hand, are taxed according to retail price.

Tax rates vary considerably among states, from 2.5 cents per pack in Virginia to 65 cents per pack in Washington, D.C. Exhibit 5.8 lists the basic per pack cigarette rates by state. These rates change often, as states raise their tax rates on cigarettes frequently. Generally speaking, not a year goes by that some state does not increase taxes on cigarettes and/or other tobacco products. The median state rate is about 21 cents per pack of cigarettes (Alt, 1990: 312).

In 1991, twelve states increased their tobacco taxes and none reduced them. The largest increases occurred in Pennsylvania and Washington, D.C., where taxes were raised by 13 cents per pack. North Carolina, at the time the state with the lowest tobacco taxes, increased taxes from 2 cents to 5 cents a pack (Eckl et al., 1991: 26).

Alcoholic Beverages

Excise taxes on alcoholic beverages are lucrative sources of revenues, yielding states well over a billion dollars annually. Besides generating revenues, these taxes, like taxes on tobacco products, have a sumptuary purpose, since alcohol usage entails enormous social costs borne frequently by society. Consequently, governments normally do not hesitate to enact heavy levies on alcoholic beverages. Tax rates often are higher for products with higher alcoholic content; for example, taxes on distilled liquor may be higher per unit than taxes on beer.

Exhibit 5.8
Basic Cigarette Tax Rates, December 1993 (per pack of 20)

State	Cigarette Tax (per pack of 20)
Alabama	16.5 cents
Alaska	29
Arizona	18
Arkansas	31.5
California	37
Colorado	20
Connecticut	47
Delaware	24
District of Columbia	65
Florida	33.9
Georgia	12
Hawaii	60
Idaho	18
Illinois	44
Indiana	15.5
Iowa	36
Kansas	24
Kentucky	3
Louisiana	20
Maine	36
Maryland	16
Massachusetts	51
Michigan	25
Minnesota	48
Mississippi	18
Missouri	17
Montana	18
Nebraska	34
Nevada	35
New Hampshire	25
New Jersey	40
New Mexico	21
New York	56
North Carolina	5
North Dakota	44
Ohio	24
Oklahoma	23
Oregon	38
Pennsylvania	31
Rhode Island	44
South Carolina	7
South Dakota	23
Tennessee	13
Texas	41
Utah	26.5
Vermont	20
Virginia	2.5
Washington	54
West Virginia	17
Wisconsin	38
Wyoming	12

Source: Commerce Clearing House, 1993: 5515. Reproduced with permission from the *State Tax Guide*, published and copyrighted by CCH Incorporated, 2700 Lake Cook Road, Riverwoods, Illinois 60015.

This practice is designed to discourage consumption of products with high alcoholic content.

Like tobacco taxes, alcoholic beverage taxes are administratively efficient to collect. Taxes, by and large, are paid by purchasing from the state stamps that are then affixed to packages and containers. This means that the tax is paid by dealers who then shift it to consumers. If purchasers buy products without affixed stamps, they are directly subject to the tax on alcoholic beverages.

By the late 1980s, twenty-eight states earmarked a portion of their revenues. Twenty-two states designated some of these revenues for local governments, and fifteen earmarked them for health and human service programs. Six states designated revenues for educational programs (Fabricius and Snell, 1990: 49).

Rates. Almost all alcoholic beverages are subject to excise taxes. Rates, however, vary remarkably both within and among states. Moreover, taxes on distilled liquors normally are higher than taxes on beer, with intervening rates for mixed beverages. Beverages commonly are classified as beer, wine, and distilled liquors, depending on alcoholic content. Different rates are levied on products within each classification.

Besides excise taxes, license fees are imposed on wholesalers, retailers, importers, and other dispensers of alcoholic beverages. These fees are usually fixed, although they sometimes are assessed on a per unit basis. Distillers and brewers pay the highest fees. Fees are proportionately lower for wholesalers, retailers, and other dispensers. Generally speaking, the higher the alcoholic content, the higher the fees. License fees, whether fixed or per volume, are paid annually.

State Monopolies. Some states have established state operated monopolies to handle the purchase and sale of alcoholic beverages, particularly distilled liquors. In seventeen states some—if not all—sales of alcoholic beverages are made in state owned and operated stores. States operate the stores in much the same way local governments operate water departments. They establish a markup over inventory costs to cover operating expenses as well as to make a profit. These monopolies are regulated by control boards or commissions. States with such monopolies usually derive revenues from sales rather than from taxes and license fees, although a few states do collect taxes from purchasers.

Revenues from such state monopolies, it should be noted, are not listed as alcoholic excise taxes, but as utility taxes, since such businesses are seen as public monopolies. Consequently, states with such arrangements report only a portion of their alcohol revenues as such; the remainder are reported as utility revenues. (And it often is difficult to separate revenues from liquor stores from other utility revenues.)

CONSUMPTION TAXES

Food and Lodging

Although revenues produced from taxes on food and lodging are much lower than those generated by other excise and consumption taxes, state and local governments are beginning to see the value of food and lodging taxes. Almost all states as well as local governments in thirty-eight states use such taxes, as do over 80 percent of the largest cities in the country (Bland, 1989: 77).

These taxes are levied on prepared meals, selected food items, and hotel and motel prices, ostensibly to compensate governments for expanded services furnished to tourists, such as roads, public transit use, and police and fire protection. Consumers of these products also pay sales taxes in addition to the food and lodging taxes. Lodging taxes, unlike food taxes, primarily are exported beyond the taxing jurisdiction because residents seldom stay in hotels and motels near home. Residents, however, do pay taxes on prepared food. State laws almost always limit the maximum rate local governments can levy. These rates typically range from 4 to 6 percent of the value of the taxable product (Bland, 1989: 77).

Amusements

Taxes on admissions to events and facilities have been used widely since the 1970s, almost exclusively by local governments. Amusement taxes are based on the assumption that some spending is less essential than other spending; and less essential spending can be taxed at a relatively low rate without interfering with consumption patterns and/or volume. It is further assumed that governments, not consumers, should decide what spending is essential and what is less essential. The problem, of course, is that the same product may be essential to one person and nonessential to another.

For the most part, these taxes are ad valorem excises ranging from 1 to 10 percent of the admission price. Revenues from these taxes normally are quite small except in localities with major entertainment events and facilities. Amusement taxes do not generate a high proportion of the total budgets for either state or local governments, for two basic reasons. First, there are not many commercial amusement establishments compared to the number of retail stores and the total amount of their transactions. Second, and in some ways more important, many only collect a portion of the tax by making only part of the ticket price subject to taxation. They divide the price of the ticket into two parts: the price of the admission to an event, which is taxable, and a charge for the length of use, which is not subject to taxation. This process simply reduces the amount of revenues governments can collect.

Approximately 33 percent of state sales and gross receipts revenues come from excise and other selective sales taxes. Exhibit 5.9 illustrates that of that amount less than 1 percent comes from amusement taxes. Exhibit 5.10 further shows that amusement tax revenues have remained somewhat stable since the late 1980s.

Parimutuels

Some states derive revenues directly from parimutuel activities in addition to collecting sales and income taxes from bettors (consumers). More precisely, a

Exhibit 5.9
Major Consumption Revenues, 1990

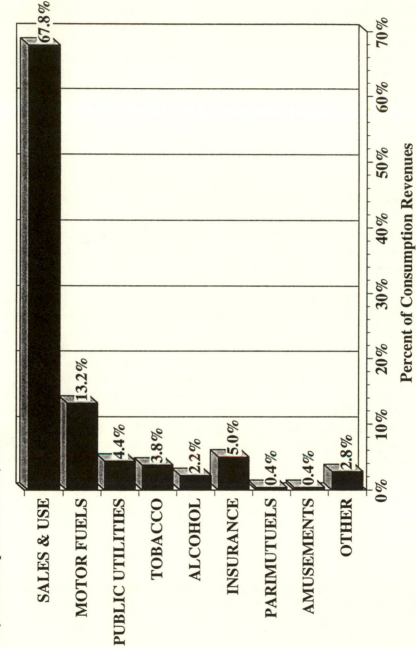

Percent of Consumption Revenues

Source: Book of the States, 1992–93, 1992: 414. Copyright 1992. The Council of State Governments. Reprinted with permission from The Book of the States.

number of states have legalized gambling on horse and dog racing and tax both successful and unsuccessful patrons as well as track owners, who generally pass the tax on to consumers in the form of smaller purses (which affect the quality of the racing product) or smaller betting pools. (Illegal gambling, of course, escapes state taxation.)

Successful consumers are subject to income taxes on winnings, while all consumers must pay at least admission taxes, which are levied as a percentage of the entrance price. Money also is produced from nonparimutuel receipts such as parking, concessions, and racing publications, and these services often are taxed via sales taxes. The primary source of revenue, however, is a tax on the handle (wagers) paid by track owners, who are part of a billion dollar racing industry.

Exhibit 5.10 shows that parimutuel revenues, like amusement revenues, produce proportionally little gaming money, though the former generate slightly more tax dollars for states. Moreover, the amount of tax dollars produced by parimutuels has been falling since the mid-1980s.

Exhibit 5.11 shows that of the two major sources of parimutuel revenues, horse racing generates far more money than greyhound racing. In addition, lesser amounts come from unclaimed tickets and various fees and fines to which all gambling establishments are subject (Certain games, most notably bingo, frequently are exempt by state law.)

Rates. Exhibit 5.12 lists the various parimutuel rates associated with horse and greyhound racing. Some states levy a flat rate, say 6 percent, on the total handle. A few states levy a graduated rate, such as 5 percent on handles up to $20 million and 6 percent on handles above that amount. Parimutuel revenues, therefore, depend primarily on the size of the handle. Despite this relationship, evidence indicates that the tax rate does not affect the amount wagered because the ratio of possible profit to loss has very little to do with the placing of bets, although the racing industry suggests otherwise.

Lotteries

Since the early 1970s lotteries—games of chance operated as monopolies by states to generate revenues—have become a small, but certainly not an insignificant, source of revenue for many state governments, netting over $8 billion in 1992 or just under 36 percent of gross sales. Although widely used, lotteries contribute a small amount to total state finances, usually less than 2 percent. Except in a few states, they fail to raise enough revenue to make tax increases unnecessary, despite claims by lottery proponents. Lotteries do—as illustrated in Exhibit 5.10—generate more than either amusement or parimutuel taxes, but not nearly so much as other excise taxes. In the early 1990s, for example, lotteries generated twelve times more money than either amusement or parimutuel taxes.

Lotteries were common revenue mechanisms in the colonial period and during the first century of American government, but were outlawed in the late 1800s

Exhibit 5.10
Lottery, Amusement, and Parimutuel Revenues, 1991

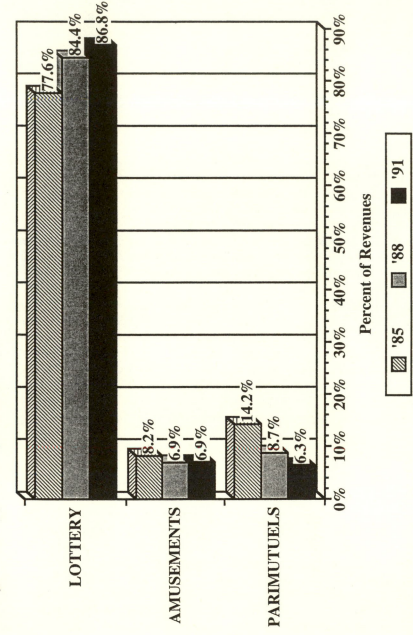

Percent of Revenues

'85 '88 '91

Source: U.S. Department of Commerce, 1992: 13, 16.

130

Exhibit 5.11
Parimutuel Revenues over Time

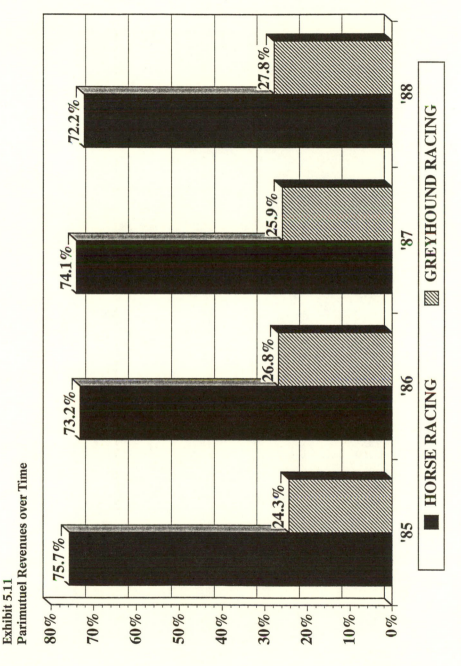

Source: Compiled by Arkansas Bureau of Legislative Research, Office of Tax Research, 1992.

Exhibit 5.12
Racing Take-out Percent by State

STATE	WPS (1 Animal)	Multiple (2 Animals)	Exotic (3 or More)
ARIZONA	19%	21%	25%
ARKANSAS	17%	21%	21%
ALABAMA (BIRMINGHAM)	17%	21%	23%
CALIFORNIA	15%	19.75%	19.75%
COLORADO	18.5%	21.5%	21.5%
DELAWARE	17%	19%	25%
FLORIDA	18.1%	22%	22%
IDAHO	20%	20%	20%
ILLINOIS	17%	20.5%	25%
IOWA	16%	20%	20%
KANSAS	18%	22%	22%
KENTUCKY (OVER 900,000 DAILY AVG.)	16%	19%	19%
KENTUCKY (UNDER 900,000 DAILY AVG.)	17.5%	19%	19%
LOUISIANA	17%	20.5%	25%
MAINE	16%	25%	25%
MARYLAND	17%	19%	25%
MASSACHUSETTS	19%	19%	19%
MICHIGAN	17%	20.5%	25%
MINNESOTA	17%	23%	23%
MISSOURI	18%	20%	25%
MONTANA	20%	22%	22%
NEBRASKA (RACING MORE THAN 4 DAYS/WEEK)	15%	20%	20%
NEBRASKA (RACING 4 OR LESS DAYS/WEEK)	18%	20%	20%
NEVADA	18%	18%	18%
NEW HAMPSHIRE	19%	26%	26%
NEW JERSEY	17%	19%	25%
NEW MEXICO	18.75%	18.75%	18.75%
NEW YORK (MYRA TRACKS)	17%	17%	25%
NEW YORK (Finger Lakes)	18%	20%	25%
NORTH DAKOTA	18.25%	18.25%	18.25%
OHIO	18%	21.5%	21.5%
OKLAHOMA	18%	20%	25%
OREGON	18%	22%	22%
PENNSYLVANIA	17%	20%	35%
PENNSYLVANIA (DAILY LESS THAN 300,000)	19%	20%	35%
SOUTH DAKOTA	18%	18%	18%
TENNESSEE	17%	20.5%	25%
TEXAS	18%	20%	20%
VERMONT	18%	25%	25%
(ON SUNDAY)	19%	25%	25%
WASHINGTON	15%	20.5%	24.5%
WEST VIRGINIA	17.25%	19%	25%
WISCONSIN	17%	23%	23%
WYOMING	19.9%	19.9%	19.9%

Exhibit 5.12 (Continued)

Greyhound Racing

STATE	WPS (1 Animal)	MULTIPLE (2 Animals)	EXOTIC (3 or more)
ALABAMA			
(Green County)	19%	19%	21%
(Macon County)	18%	18%	18%
(Mobile County)	19%	19%	21%
ARIZONA	19%	21%	25%
ARKANSAS	18%	18%	18%
COLORADO	15%	15%	15%
CONNECTICUT	19%	19%	19%
FLORIDA	17.6%	21%	23%
IDAHO	20%	20%	20%
IOWA	16%	20%	20%
KANSAS	18%	22%	22%
MASSACHUSETTS	19%	19%	19%
NEW HAMPSHIRE	19%	26%	26%
OREGON	16.5%	16.5%	18.5%
RHODE ISLAND	18%	18%	18%
SOUTH DAKOTA	18.25%	22%	22%
TEXAS	18%	20%	20%
VERMONT	20%	25%	25%
WEST VIRGINIA	16.3%	19%	21%
WISCONSIN	17%	23%	23%

Source: Compiled by Arkansas Bureau of Legislative Research, Office of Tax Research, 1992.

because of rampant corruption and major scandals. In short, lotteries have already had a long history in the United States and have only recently been reintroduced by states, despite strong opposition from religious groups, those fearing their impact on gambling addicts, and those concerned with the regressivity of lottery revenues.

Notwithstanding strong opposition, lotteries have been popular among voters and have seldom been voted down (Miller, 1991). Strong support for the games has come from those anticipating financial gain, including retailers, advertising companies, and the organizations hoping to handle lottery operations and/or monies. In Georgia, for example, one of the largest contributors to the successful pro-lottery campaign was the 2,000-member Georgia Association of Convenience Stores. Lottery equipment vendors and those interests expecting to be major beneficiaries of the profits were also large contributors (Walston, 1992a).

The increasing use of state lotteries is testimony to their popularity at a time when pleas for new taxes find very little support. After a century of disuse, lotteries were established in New Hamsphire in 1964, New York in 1967, and New Jersey in 1970. Lotteries were started in four more states in 1972, and by 1991 were in operation in thirty-four states and the District of Columbia. Georgia and Texas have since joined that group. Georgia's lottery began operation in 1993, 117 years after the first Georgia state lottery was abolished (Walston, 1992a).

From 1980 to 1991, gross revenues from state lotteries increased from $2.1 billion a year to over $19.1 billion (ACIR, 1993: 106–107). As shown in Exhibit 5.13, net proceeds expanded from just over $1 billion in 1980 to $7.6 billion in 1991. Despite the growth in revenues generated by lotteries nationally, state revenue growth—as illustrated in Exhibit 5.14—has tended to be very uneven.

Certainly one of the major criticisms of lotteries, and a factor that has limited state reliance on them for revenues, is their vulnerability to economic downturns. That may be one reason why net lottery revenues accounted for only 0.6 percent of state own-source general revenue in 1980 and 1.8 percent in 1991. In 1991 lottery proceeds accounted for only 4.7 percent of Florida's general revenues, the highest percentage nationally and in a state without an income tax.

A major reason that lotteries do not generate more revenues is that they have exceedingly high administrative costs, averaging approximately 33 percent of the net take. Lotteries require a substantial outlay for tickets, computer resources, advertising, prize money, and other needs. Despite these costs, however, states have found that lotteries do generate revenues—no state has ever lost money, and some have netted millions of tax dollars.

More specifically, about half of lottery revenues are returned to players as prizes. In Georgia, for instance, the expectation has been that roughly 50 percent of gross revenues would be paid out as prizes, 15 percent would be overhead for the lottery agency, 5 percent would be paid to retailers as commissions, and 30 percent would be paid to the education fund for which profits are earmarked (Walston, 1992a).

States typically place lottery revenues in the general fund, though some states earmark at least a portion of the revenues. Of the states with lotteries, twenty-one dedicate at least part of the revenues, usually to fund education or economic development. Exhibit 5.15 shows the distributional patterns. Most recently, Indiana, Minnesota, and West Virginia have dedicated lottery proceeds to pensions, environmental programs, and education, respectively. Capital projects receive money in Colorado, Indiana, and Iowa (Fabricius and Snell, 1990: 9). Georgia is also typical in terms of earmarking lottery funds for education. Twelve of the thirty-four states that had lotteries in 1991 earmarked some or all of the revenues for education. Other states earmarked funds for transportation, capital projects, economic development, local government, environmental projects, senior citizens' programs, and property tax relief.

Lottery games take a number of forms, including:

- *Instant games* in which players scratch off coverings to reveal prizes or match winning numbers or symbols (such as poker hands).

- *Numbers games* in which players choose numbers (usually three or four) in hopes of matching winning numbers that are chosen daily or weekly.

- *Lotto games* in which players choose numbers (usually four to six numbers from a possible thirty to forty-nine numbers) in hopes of matching winning numbers chosen weekly. Typically, the lotto prize grows each week that there is no grand prize winner.

- *Draw lotteries* in which players buy numbered tickets and the winner or winners are chosen in a weekly or monthly drawing.
- *Subscription games* in which players purchase "subscriptions" to play and tickets are issued for each drawing.
- *Video lottery terminal games* in which players play card games or other skills games to win prizes. (Scott and Ryan, 1988: 316; Walston, 1993b)

Initially, states used draw lotteries, much like those used in the eighteenth and nineteenth centuries. Player boredom and the availability of new technologies, however, have led states to develop more games, and to increase their sophistication. Instant winner and numbers games were introduced in the early 1970s and lotto games were introduced in the early 1980s (Clotfelter and Cook, 1989: 100). Since that time, lotto games have become more and more sophisticated. In many states, players may choose their own numbers or have them chosen randomly by the lotto machine. The latter is often viewed as less interesting than playing one's own favorite numbers (such as birthdays, Social Security numbers, and ages), but it can speed up the process of choosing numbers and (according to lottery officials) increase the likelihood of winning because favorite numbers tend not to be drawn from the full range of possible numbers. Moreover, use of dates and ages increases the likelihood of multiple winners and shared prizes. The mind-boggling, multimillion dollar prizes from lotto games, particularly the Powerball game, which includes many state lotteries, are becoming familiar across the United States and draw consortiums of players from around the world. The controversy caused by an Australian consortium's winning the Virginia lottery by buying tickets with all the possible number combinations is indicative both of the size of the games and the intense competition for winning strategies. Recent rulings, too, have questioned the purchase of state lottery tickets from brokers (third parties), rather than directly from state licensed vendors.

Video lottery terminals (VLTs) are growing in popularity and were in use in Louisiana, Montana, Oregon, Rhode Island, South Dakota, and West Virginia in 1993 with some expectation of approvals in New York, Indiana, and Missouri. The VLTs look like slot machines and variations include draw poker, blackjack, and keno. Critics fear that such skill games can be more compelling for those addicted to gambling and video games. In other words, VLTs may encourage more playing by those addicted to gambling and those less likely to begin playing otherwise. In 1989 South Dakota was using 6,600 video lottery terminals, one for every 109 state residents, and collecting 90 percent of its lottery profits from the machines (Walston, 1993b).

Lotteries raise a number of religious, social, economic, and political issues. For many, gambling is a moral issue, and lotteries represent government sanctioned and promoted gambling. Others believe that lotteries encourage gambling

Exhibit 5.13

State Lotteries, Net Proceeds, Fiscal Years 1980–1991

(Millions)

State	Where the Revenues Go	1980	1981	1982	1983	1984	1985	1986	1987	1988	1989	1990	1991
United States**		$1,057.4	$1,159.9	$1,526.1	$2,026.1	$2,684.5	$3,511.2	$4,690.6	$4,801.1	$5,610.2	$7,003.6	$7,430.3	$7,613.8
Alabama	No Lottery												
Alaska	No Lottery												
Arizona	Transportation			45.2	23.1	20.0	22.8	42.2	51.5	66.2	97.1	111.8	86.0
Arkansas	No Lottery												
California	Education							685.6	565.4	799.1	1009.7	924.1	774.6
Colorado	Parks and Recreation and Capital Construction				47.0	37.7	28.9	26.1	34.1	35.5	17.1	39.2	562.9
Connecticut	General Fund	60.8	55.5	62.5	73.8	97.0	128.0	165.6	187.2	195.7	193.7	207.6	197.8
Delaware	General Fund	6.3	7.7	8.5	10.0	13.0	13.9	15.5	15.8	19.4	23.8	25.1	25.3
Florida	Education									200.7	716.6	809.3	854.2
Georgia	Education												
Hawaii	No Lottery												
Idaho	Permanent Building Fund, School District Building Fund											24.2	16.2
Illinois	Education	35.8	87.0	141.5	214.9	378.0	514.4	545.1	540.6	485.6	587.3	581.0	583.9
Indiana	"Build Indiana" Fund											132.4	151.2
Iowa	Economic Development							26.3	27.5	35.5	44.5	42.2	38.3
Kansas	Economic Development									19.6	14.9	21.0	22.1
Kentucky	Education										45.7	61.0	54.4
Louisiana	General Fund												n.a.
Maine	General Fund	0.7	01.1	02.4	03.8	04.6	04.4	13.7	20.5	30.0	30.0	36.3	34.4
Maryland	General Fund	185.4	171.4	208.3	198.2	216.9	263.7	323.4	337.2	346.2	334.9	337.4	335.2
Massachusetts	Local Government	92.5	64.8	69.4	84.3	106.5	238.3	318.4	364.0	394.9	420.8	459.7	470.4
Michigan	Education	236	196.8	198.3	214.7	229.7	359.1	403.2	391.3	471.0	456.8	461.3	429.2
Minnesota	Environmental Trust Fund, Greater Minnesota Corp.											08.0	66.0
Mississippi	To Be Determined											n.a.	n.a.
Missouri	General Fund							80.0	61.4	53.5	65.4	69.5	65.4
Montana	Local Schools									07.6	03.0	05.6	04.5
Nebraska	Education, Environment											n.a.	n.a.
Nevada	No Lottery												
New Hampshire	Education	3.7	3.9	3.9	5.7	5.5	4.2	10.2	20.7	25.7	29.2	30.7	33.9
New Jersey	Education, Institutions	142.4	181.4	214.9	295.4	356.1	388.2	416.1	470.3	499.4	528.6	520.4	526.3
New Mexico	No Lottery												

State	Where the Revenues Go	1980	1981	1982	1983	1984	1985	1986	1987	1988	1989	1990	1991
New York	Education	83.3	97.0	179.0	268.8	380.8	572.0	567.2	614.1	640.7	752.2	841.1	944.6
North Carolina	No Lottery												
North Dakota	No Lottery												
Ohio	Education	35.7	112.2	150.5	146.5	244.6	336.4	380.9	371.2	532.9	651.1	606.4	635.6
Oklahoma	No Lottery												
Oregon	Economic Development												
Pennsylvania	Senior Citizen Programs	158.0	168.8	226.7	354.8	514.8	571.2	539.2	567.8	568.4	625.3	597.9	601.7
Rhode Island	General Fund	16.6	11.8	12.8	14.4	17.4	17.8	20.7	20.9	20.5	22.0	25.9	24.9
South Carolina	No Lottery												
South Dakota	General Fund									8.7	7.0	14.7	29.4
Tennessee	No Lottery												
Texas	General Fund												n.a.
Utah													
Vermont	General Fund	0.2	0.5	1.0	1.1	1.2	0.9	2.7	6.6	9.0	10.4	10.9	12.6
Virginia	General Fund, Capital Improvements										141.0	158.4	258.9
Washington	General Fund				69.7	60.7	47.1	65.0	79.2	82.3	105.7	94.6	98.7
West Virginia	General Fund							22.1	27.0	15.1	19.0	22.2	24.8
Wisconsin	Property Tax Relief										97.5	108.8	121.0
Wyoming	No Lottery												
District of Columbia	General Fund				12.6	26.8	36.1	41.4	41.4	44.2	55.7	55.0	55.0

n.a.—not available

**U.S. total does not include the District of Columbia

Source: U.S. Department of Commerce, Bureau of the Census, *State Government Finances:* (year), and unpublished data compiled by the National Conference of State Legislatures.

137

Exhibit 5.14
State Lottery Revenues, Annual Percentage Change, Fiscal Years 1980–1991

State	1980	1981	1982	1983	1984	1985	1986	1987	1988	1989	1990	1991
United States**		28.7%	30.2%	34.8%	31.0%	29.6%	36.8%	03.7%	21.4%	23.1%	09.0%	02.5%
Alabama	*											
Alaska	*											
Arizona	*			34.4	20.8	22.9	55.8	17.5	21.6	46	14.3	23.1
Arkansas	*											
California					14.1	10.5	3.5	20.7	50.6	24.6	5.8	16.2
Colorado					35.2	35.4	24.7	4.0	9.5	23.1	77.4	1334.6
Connecticut		9.2	12.6	11.5	9.8	17.2	6.2	14.1	5.0	3.6	5.9	4.7
Delaware		20.1	23.0	17.4				12.2	21.3	15.8	4.9	0.7
Florida										177.1	12.9	5.5
Georgia	*										n.a.	n.a.
Hawaii												
Idaho												33.1
Illinois		117.0	57.2	48.6	79.1	35.9	6.8	1.8	0.2	17.3	0.4	0.5
Indiana												14.2
Iowa								14.8	31.9	33.4	2.4	9.3
Kansas										3.8	5.2	5.3
Kentucky											58.6	10.8
Louisiana												n.a.
Maine		5.0	70.2	35.1	22.1	11.3	154.9	50.0	41.8	16.4	9.9	5.4
Maryland		1.6	18.5	2.3	16.1	26.8	5.5	4.7	6.7	7.8	8.5	0.6
Massachusetts		4.0	13.6	24.7	26.4	95.9	40.5	17.5	11.0	9.1	12.2	2.3
Michigan		5.0	4.2	6.1	6.1	51.7	12.8	0.6	19.3	3.6	1.6	7.0
Minnesota											n.a	723.5
Mississippi												n.a
Missouri								16.3	15.4	35.2	12.1	5.8
Montana										46.7	95.8	20.2
Nebraska											n.a.	n.a.
Nevada	*											
New Hampshire		24.4	0.0	29.5	17.9	11.7	123.8	73.4	26.8	15.2	8.1	10.5
New Jersey		19.4	21.4	36.1	22.4	9.2	7.2	12.8	5.1	6.1	1.9	1.2

State	1980	1981	1982	1983	1984	1985	1986	1987	1988	1989	1990	1991
New Mexico	*											
New York		20.0	76.3	49.5	37.9	46.5	3.1	10.4	7.6	18.2	11.4	12.3
North Carolina	*											
North Dakota	**											
Ohio		389.9	23.2	9.4	51.4	41.2	10.0	13.6	28.4	2.3	14.9	4.8
Oklahoma	*											
Oregon								14.9	59.5	3.0	3.9	12.6
Pennsylvania		102.2	33.1	57.5	39.7	4.8	22.2	1.2	7.6	8.9	1.4	0.6
Rhode Island		6.6	8.3	13.9	21.0	1.3	8.7	2.8	6.8	0.7	7.7	3.9
South Carolina	*											
South Dakota										20.3	45.4	99.5
Tennessee	*											
Texas	*											n.a.
Utah	*											
Vermont		20.7	52.2	8.6	18.4	8.9	140.8	103.4	38.7	12.3	8.9	16.1
Virginia											16.9	63.4
Washington					2.9	7.6	14.4	6.8	10.9	18.8	3.6	4.3
West Virginia								25.7	19.8	5.0	13.9	11.5
Wisconsin											27.6	11.2
Wyoming	*											
District of Columbia					58.8	31.1	6.4	0.0	3.7	16.3	4.5	0.0

n.a.—not available

*no lottery

**U.S. total does not include the District of Columbia

Sources: ACIR computations based on U.S. Department of Commerce, Bureau of the Census, *State Government Finances:* (year).

Exhibit 5.15
Earmarking of Net Lottery Proceeds, 1988

State	Net Proceeds (in millions)	Apportionment (in millions)	Purpose
New England			
New Hampshire	$25.0	$7.1	K-12 education
Rhode Island	23.6	7.1	Public Facilities Asset Protection Fund
		9.4	Budget reserve and cash stabilization
Mid Atlantic			
Maryland	N/A	17	Stadium Authority and General Fund
New Jersey	N/A	N/A	K-12 education and state institutions
Pennsylvania	802.1	802.1	Senior citizens programs
Great Lakes			
Illinois	524.4	524.4	K-12 education
Indiana			
Michigan	488.4	488.4	School Aid Fund
Ohio	522.2	522.2	K-12 education
Wisconsin	69.4	69.4	Property tax relief
Plains			
Iowa	34.9	29.6	Economic development
		5.3	Capital projects
Minnesota		N/A	
Southeast			
Florida	236.9	236.9	K-12 education
Virginia		140.0	Capital improvements and general revenue
West Virginia		18.0	Education, parks and senior citizens
Southeast			
Arizona	65.2	23.0	Local Transportation Assistance Fund
		7.7	County Transportation Assistance Fund
		34.5	General Reserve Fund
Rocky Mountain			
Colorado	33.0	16.5	State capital construction
		13.2	Local parks
		3.3	State parks
Idaho	10.4	5.2	State Building Account
		5.2	Public school buildings
Montana	7.2	7.2	K-12 education
Far West			
California	804.0	651.0	K-12 education
		97.0	Community colleges
		56.0	Other higher education
Oregon	51.8	51.8	Economic development programs

Source: Fabricius and Snell, 1990: 52.

by compulsive gamblers. There are also social differences discernible among the players. The middle-aged play more than the young. Urban residents play more than rural residents (likely due to the larger number of outlets in urban areas). There are positive correlations between playing lotteries and the proportions of college graduates and Catholics in the population as well (Scott and Ryan, 1988: 319–320). More important, lotteries may be very regressive in nature if the poor play lottery games more frequently than more affluent members of society. The evidence is contradictory, however; studies of Washington, Wisconsin, and Florida indicate that the poor do not play lotteries more frequently (Yenson, 1992); studies of New Jersey and Maryland indicate that they do (Branch, 1992; '' 'No' on the Lottery,'' 1992). Nonetheless, critics still warn about the negative impact on lower income residents, and the common wisdom (rightly or wrongly) is that the poor spend a larger proportion of their incomes on lottery games. One estimate is that lotteries are twice as regressive as state sales taxes (Scott and Ryan, 1988: 324).

The political issues include the control of lottery operations and the role of the state in encouraging the playing of lottery games. State lotteries are usually administered by a commission or board appointed by the governor. The fear of corruption strongly encourages the establishment of independent commissions, but privatization is still an option that states generally consider (Scott and Ryan, 1988: 319–320). Concern about corruption may be due in part to the growing industry that has come to dominate state lottery operations. It is common for administrators to move from one lottery to another, from state lottery agencies to lottery industry firms, and so on. The number of firms producing lottery equipment and developing new technologies is relatively small (Walston, 1993c). In a government operation for which credibility is all-important, even the suggestion of cronyism or favoritism can be politically explosive. The fear of corruption should lessen as state lotteries expand and mature, however. Pressures for more formal standards of conduct or ethics will likely increase. Then, too, as the industry itself grows, the closeness of lottery and industry officials will decrease.

To the extent that some segments of society tend to play lottery games more than others, there generally are concerns about just how much government promotion is appropriate. Many states spend about 3 percent of lottery revenues on advertising, but the percentage varies considerably from state to state. In 1992, $286 million was spent nationally by state lotteries. The more important issue is just how enticing the advertising should be (Walston, 1993d). Often it tries to appeal to player greed and fails to stress the long odds. Images of new millionaires are far more appealing than statistics concerning the one chance in several million of winning. To address the values issue, Clotfelter and Cook have proposed two alternatives to the revenue lottery that is highly promoted, revenue maximizing, and low payout (1990: 103–104). The first is a sumptuary lottery that has minimal promotion, less pervasive access points, and low payout. The second alternative is a consumer lottery, which is essentially a form of entertainment providing higher payout rates, and thus, placing less emphasis on revenue maximization. Clotfelter and Cook argue that both alternatives will get states out of the business of promoting gambling, while still providing entertaining games that raise some revenue. Service to the public, in other words, should be the goal.

Lotteries raise several economic issues. First, there is the question of regressivity. Whether the poor play lottery games more than the more affluent is questionable, although the common wisdom is that that is in fact the case. It may also be argued that because the poor play the games, they have less to spend for food, housing, and other necessities placing additional burdens on the state. Second, the earmarking of lottery monies for education or other public purposes may simply mean substituting lottery revenue for other state revenues, rather than making genuine increases in state funding for the earmarked purposes. Third, lotteries may also redirect spending, as people buy tickets rather than other goods, and thus reduce sales tax revenues (Scott and Ryan, 1988: 324–327).

In some measure, the impact of lotteries is uncertain. They certainly offer more entertainment value than property or income taxes, and for most people they are relatively painless. Politically, that is a winning combination for public officials unable to increase revenues from other sources. Politicians also fear that residents will drive to other states to buy lottery tickets or have friends and relatives do it for them. It has been estimated that Georgians purchased $50 million in Florida lottery tickets each year before the Georgia lottery began operations (Walston, 1993a: C5), and Georgia officials have high expectations of luring players from Tennessee, South Carolina, Alabama, and, when pots are large, north Florida. The potential for tax exporting is a compelling one for officials and taxpayers.

After increasing dramatically between 1970 and 1985, revenue growth—in terms of constant dollars—has leveled off. Clotfelter and Cook (1990) found that real per capita sales were $7 in 1970, $20 in 1975, and $38 in 1980. By 1985 sales had risen to $97 per person, but they were only $98 per person in 1988. In fact, between 1985 and 1988 lottery revenues grew more slowly than did tax revenues. In addition, lottery sales were down 21 percent in 1988, 23 percent in 1989, and 8 percent in 1990.

Studies have shown that lotteries compete with parimutuel wagering for expendable income dollars. This competition has a significant negative impact on other gambling revenues. In a study of the impact of the Ohio state lottery on race track betting in northern Kentucky, Thalheimer (1990: vi) found that on the average attendance was down by 15 percent, and the handle was reduced by 22 percent. Another study indicated that every dollar bet on the lottery reduces the average bet per person at a horse racing track 18 cents (Gulley and Scott, 1989: 92). Since states keep about 40 percent of lottery sales and less than 5 percent of parimutuel bets, they are financially better off with lotteries because they keep a much larger proportion of lottery net proceeds.

Lotteries, as yet, have not become major sources of state revenue when compared with other taxes, but the percentages of state revenue that they generate are increasing slowly. The more interesting issue is how the games escalate in terms of sophistication, size of prizes, and promotion. Players grow bored quickly and revenues drop off unless new games are introduced. That problem in itself may eventually kill the lotteries. But, for now, interest is high—particularly in the new lottery states.

Charges

Most state and local revenues come from taxes that are paid in part because governments have the legal and coercive capabilities to force payment. Not all revenues, however, are generated from taxes. In some cases, governments charge the public fees for goods and services produced and/or provided by them, generally based on average costs.

The Bureau of the Census defines charges as

amounts received from the public for the performance of specific services benefitting the person charged, and from sales of commodities and services except by government utilities and liquor stores. Includes fees, assessments, and other reimbursements for current services, rents, and sales derived from commodities or services furnished incident to the performance of particular functions. (U.S. Department of Commerce, 1990: A2)

As mentioned earlier, charges are a major revenue source for local governments. When charges are combined with special assessments and fees, the total user-based revenues represent about a third of the own-source revenues for local governments. Given the public's desire not to increase taxes, state and local governments are placing greater reliance on charges to cover expenditures.

Local governments rely on charges because they provide "more services amenable to charges and because the forces of tax revolts in the late 1970s and early 1980s placed local governments under greater fiscal stress" (Mikesell, 1991: 359). Larger local governments rely on charges more than do smaller ones. In general, charges provide over 15 percent of revenues raised by state governments and nearly 35 percent of those generated by local governments (U.S. Department of Commerce, 1991a: 2).

Because of the unpopularity of tax increases, state and local governments are turning to charges to generate additional revenues from traditional and nontraditional sources. Such charges are on the whole acceptable because they take the burden off the general taxpayers and place it on consumers—in accordance with the benefits received approach. Governments have been increasing their reliance on charges since the late 1950s, but their dependence grew most quickly during the 1970s. Exhibit 5.16 illustrates the rapid growth of local charges since the 1970s. Examples of charges at the state level include operations of state universities and colleges; toll roads; bridges and tunnels; and lotteries. Examples

Exhibit 5.16
Charges as a Percentage of Local Revenues

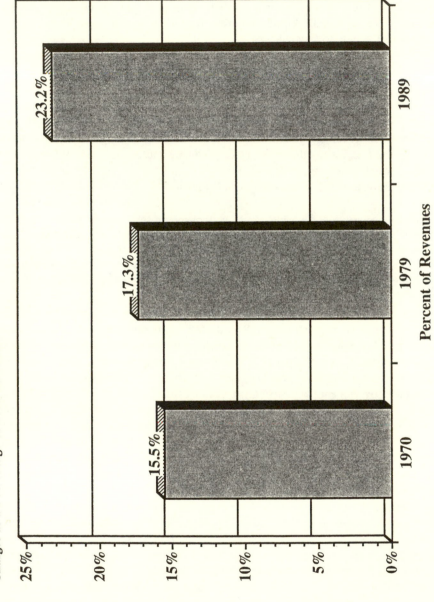

Source: Tax Foundation, 1992: 305.

at the local level include water; electricity; transit; natural gas; parking; garbage collection; cultural and recreational facilities; and libraries. An expanded list of charges is found in Exhibit 2.4, in Chapter 2.

Characteristics. Charges can be collected effectively or efficiently only for products or benefits with specific characteristics. In the first place, benefits received from products furnished by governments must accrue to identifiable individuals rather than to the public. Second, there must be a feasible and economical way to exclude nonpayers from receiving these benefits. Third, there must be an economical way to control usage. Many services, for example, are controlled by meters, fences, turnstiles, and decals. Finally, for the most part, charges can be imposed only on products that are consumed voluntarily, although some charges, such as special assessments and building permit fees, are compulsory. (By contrast, taxes are compulsory payments for public products that do not vary with levels of consumption.)

Charges also can be exported beyond governmental jurisdictions. That is, persons can be assessed charges for products furnished by governments regardless of where they reside. For instance, those who use municipal water are charged for its use whether or not they live within the city.

Costing. The degree to which charges are intended to cover costs varies among governments and products. Paying charges, however, is similar to purchasing private products, with two major exceptions. First, charges frequently do not cover the full cost of furnishing the product; often the remainder is paid from general revenues. This situation is particularly prevalent when the product is perceived to be a useful social good, such as a recreational facility. Second, charges sometimes cannot be levied because state or local laws prohibit such levies. Public schools are examples of products for which, by law, consumers are not charged.

In any event, charges do help defray part, if not all, of the costs of furnishing products. And consumers of the products, not the public, pay for them. Moreover, charges allow governments to estimate how many consumers are willing to pay for governmental products, and how much they will pay.

With federal aid to state and local governments unlikely to increase in real dollars anytime in the near future, with increased demands for governmental products, and with voters reluctant to increase taxes, state and local governments continue to rely on charges to finance many of their private goods and services.

Despite this increased dependence, for a variety of reasons charges probably will never become a major source of revenue for either state or local governments. The primary reasons are that

- many charges for governmental products cannot recover the full cost of providing those products.
- legal limitations often prevent governments from levying charges.
- charges can block access of some who are unable to afford products perceived as useful social goods.

REFERENCES

Advisory Commission on Intergovernmental Relations (ACIR) (1993). *Significant Features of Fiscal Federalism.* Vol. 2. Washington, D.C.: Advisory Commission on Intergovernmental Relations.

—— (1987). *Local Revenue Diversification: User Charges.* Washington, D.C.: ACIR.

Alt, Ronald (1990). "Trends in State Taxation." In *Book of the States, 1990–91.* Lexington, Ky.: Council of State Governments.

Bland, Robert (1989). *A Revenue Guide for Local Government.* Washington, D.C.: International City Management Association.

Book of the States, 1992–93 (1992). Lexington, Ky.: Council of State Governments.

Bowman, John, and John Mikesell (1983). "Recent Changes in State Gasoline Taxation: An Analysis of Structure and Rates." *National Tax Journal,* 33, June.

Branch, Taylor (1992). "Do Lotteries Prey on the Poor? Yes—Don't Let All the Industry's Numbers Fool You." *Atlanta Journal/Atlanta Constitution,* September 13, pp. G1, G2.

Clotfelter, Charles, and Philip Cook (1989). *Selling Hope.* Cambridge, Mass.: Harvard University Press.

—— (1990). "Redefining 'Success' in the State Lottery Business." *Journal of Policy Analysis and Management,* 9, no. 1, pp. 99–104.

Commerce Clearing House (1991). *State Tax Guide: All States.* Chicago: Commerce Clearing House.

—— (1992). *State Tax Guide: All States.* Chicago: Commerce Clearing House.

—— (1993). *State Tax Guide: All States.* Chicago: Commerce Clearing House.

Eckl, Corina, et al. (1991). *State Budget and Tax Actions 1991.* Washington, D.C.: National Conference of State Legislatures.

Fabricius, Martha, and Ronald Snell (1990). *Earmarking State Taxes.* Washington, D.C.: National Conference of State Legislatures.

Fiscal and Tax Research (1991). *Comparative Revenues, 1985 Through 1989, and Revenue Forecasts.* Little Rock: Bureau of Legislative Research, State of Arkansas.

Gulley, O. David, and Frank Scott (1989). "Lottery Effects on Parimutuel Tax Revenues." *National Tax Journal,* 42, March.

Hyman, David (1987). *Public Finance: A Contemporary Application of Theory to Policy.* 2nd ed. Chicago: Dryden Press.

McIntyre, Robert, et al. (1991). *A Far Cry from Fair.* Washington, D.C.: Citizens for Tax Justice.

Mikesell, John (1991). *Fiscal Administration: Analysis and Applications for the Public Sector.* 3rd ed. Chicago: Dorsey Press.

Miller, Andy (1991). "Lottery Lovers May Be in Luck in '92." *Atlanta Journal/Atlanta Constitution,* December 1, p. A3.

" 'No' on the Lottery." (1992). *Atlanta Journal/Atlanta Constitution,* October 20, p. A18.

Scott, Loren C., and Earl Ryan (1988). "The Economics of a State Lottery." In James A. Richardson, ed., *Louisiana's Fiscal Alternative: Finding Permanent Solutions to Recurring Budget Crises.* Baton Rouge: Louisiana State University Press.

Snell, Ronald (1991). "Traditional Highway Funding May Run Out of Gas." *Fiscal Letter,* 13, November/December.

"State and Local Highway Finance: Where Does the Money Come from and Why Isn't There Enough?" (1991). Denver, Colo.: National Conference of State Legislatures, LFP #78.

Tax Features (1991). September.

Tax Foundation (1992). *Facts and Figures on Government Finance*. Baltimore: Johns Hopkins University Press.

Thalheimer, Richard (1990). "The Impact of a State Lottery on the Demand for Parimutuel Horse Race Wagering and Attendance in Northern Kentucky and Southern Ohio." Department of Economics, University of Kentucky, Lexington, Ky.

U.S. Department of Commerce, Bureau of the Census (1990). *Government Finances*. Washington, D.C.: Bureau of the Census.

———— (1991a). *Government Finances*. Washington, D.C.: Bureau of the Census.

———— (1991b). *Statistical Abstract of the United States, 1991*. Washington, D.C.: Bureau of the Census.

———— (1992). *State Government Finances*. Washington, D.C.: Bureau of the Census.

Walston, Charles (1992a). "Lottery Foes Have Tough Job." *Atlanta Journal/Atlanta Constitution*, September 27, pp. A1, A14.

———— (1992b). "Lottery Support Comes from Businesses Due to Make a Profit." *Atlanta Constitution*, October 22, pp. A1, A16.

———— (1993a). "Chances to Play Will Be Everywhere." *Atlanta Journal/Atlanta Constitution*, June 27, pp. C1, C5.

———— (1993b). "Industry Betting on Electronic Games." *Atlanta Constitution*, January 25, p. B1.

———— (1993c). "It's a Small World in Lottery Business, Industry People Use Revolving Door." *Atlanta Journal/Atlanta Constitution*, June 6, pp. D1, D10.

———— (1993d). "Will Georgia's Lottery Ads Plug Luck or Push Greed?" *Atlanta Journal/Atlanta Constitution*, May 23, pp. A1, A7.

Yenson, Evelyn P. (1992). "Do Lotteries Prey on the Poor? No—Indigent Are the Least Likely to Play the Games." *Atlanta Journal/Atlanta Constitution*, September 13, pp. G1, G2.

6

Property Taxes

Property taxes are the principal source of revenue for most local governments in the United States, providing approximately 75.3 percent of local revenues, or approximately $161.7 billion in 1991 (ACIR, 1993: 114, 130). By comparison, property taxes represent a small and relatively insignificant percentage of state revenues—only 1 percent of those generated in 1990 came from property taxes (ACIR, 1992: 96).

During the last two decades, the percentage of local revenues derived from property taxes has generally declined, although this percentage showed a slight increase during the 1980s as local governments struggled with declining state and federal aid and increasing program responsibilities. More precisely, property taxes declined as a revenue source for both counties and cities, representing 84.9 percent of local revenue in 1970, 75.9 percent in 1980, and 74.5 percent in 1990 (ACIR, 1993: 130). Property taxes provided 97.5 percent of independent school district revenue in 1991, compared to 52.1 percent of municipal revenue and 74 percent of county revenue. And despite the slight decline in reliance on property taxes from 1980 to 1990, revenues from local property taxes rose 128 percent, largely attributable to increases in assessed values rather than to rate increases (Dearborn, 1993: 10–11).

While local reliance on property taxes has declined and revenues have increased tremendously, property tax burdens on individuals also have increased. Property tax revenues as a percentage of personal income rose from 3.3 percent in 1982 to 3.6 percent in 1990. These figures indicate that property tax burdens are increasing inasmuch as a tax is more burdensome when it takes a larger percentage of a person's income. In addition, property tax revenues in 1991 rose faster than either sales taxes or state and local receipts (*State Policy Reports*, 1992: 10). As federal and state governments continue to shift more and more programs to local governments, the trend of increasing property tax burdens probably will continue for some time.

In spite of the overwhelming reliance on property taxes by local governments, these taxes are quite unpopular. Surveys of public opinion conducted by the Advisory Commission on Intergovernmental Relations (ACIR) during the 1970s revealed that the public generally viewed property taxes as the ''least fair,'' especially when compared to income and sales taxes (Bingham, Hawkins, and Hebert, 1978: 99). More recent studies continue to confirm taxpayers' gross dislike of property taxes. Tax revolts in California and other states in the late 1970s and early 1980s certainly attest to public sentiment against property taxes. Some recent surveys indicate that the public is generally willing to pay more taxes—although not necessarily property taxes—to improve basic services such as education and public safety. In short, property taxes have very little political support, particularly when those paying property taxes tend to be among the most politically influential publics.

Undoubtedly, the relationship between property taxes and the services that taxes support has tremendous fiscal and political implications, as the state of California, for example, is painfully finding out. The tax revolt in the late 1970s, coupled with the restrictions placed on state and local governments by Proposition 13, is having traumatic effects on the California economy and on the delivery of a vast array of government services. Proposition 13 severely restricted state and local taxing authority, including limiting property taxes to 1 percent of assessed value, limiting the assessments themselves, and requiring a two-thirds vote of the state legislature to approve new taxes or expand old taxes, and a two-thirds vote in local elections to approve local taxes. The immediate effect of Proposition 13 was to reduce property tax revenue by 57 percent and to leave local governments without the fiscal resources necessary to maintain services (Mields, 1993: 17). While many Californians did not initially expect this proposition to have a major impact on the delivery of services by state and local governments, conflicts over program funding have pitted northern Californians against southern Californians, public education against other social programs, and higher education against primary and secondary education programs. Proposition 13 has had a profound impact and has certainly complicated recovery processes following the major earthquakes and fires in northern and southern California in the late 1980s and early 1990s. Similar problems have been experienced in other states and communities when property tax revenues have been reduced. Closing schools before the end of academic years, deferring maintenance on roads and public buildings, and other cost-cutting measures have become familiar.

Restrictions placed on the abilities of state and local governments to raise revenues have been so effective in discouraging spending that the conflict over what to fund and, more important, what not to fund has debilitated government programs. In 1992, for instance, conflicts between the governor and the California state legislature held up passage of the state budget and necessitated the payment of state employee salaries in vouchers (i.e., promises to pay). The vouchers were at least initially accepted by banks instead of cash, but the impact of cuts and uncertain financing of entitlement and social programs created tremendous hardship for public employees and their most needy clients. The uncertainty of payment and the fears of perpetuating voucher use eventually led many leading banks in the state to declare that they would not continue accepting vouchers. Soon thereafter, the impasse was resolved.

The strong opposition to property tax increases has forced many states and local governments to look for alternative revenue sources. Unfortunately, officials have had limited success in diversifying revenue sources. As a consequence, property taxes will likely provide the principal support for local services for the foreseeable future.

TAX PHILOSOPHY

Historically, property taxes were designed to tax income. In the early 1800s property taxes were levied on the rents on agricultural land collected by landowners and based on the surplus capital created via agricultural production (Buchanan and Flowers, 1987: 352–357). As long as the land was largely used for agricultural purposes, property taxes effectively were based on income. Land was a fixed and finite asset that could be readily identified and measured. However, as the number of land uses increased and some land was judged unsuitable (or less suitable in terms of productivity) for agricultural uses, questions arose concerning the degree to which landholdings represented income. Further questions were raised as buildings and other improvements to the land were included in the assessed value of the land. As long as land was a major indicator of wealth, property taxes achieved their purpose—to tax wealth. However, as other forms of income, such as stocks and bonds, became important sources of wealth, the major function of property taxes changed.

To be sure, property taxes still do tax a form of wealth—capital assets of individuals and businesses. Unlike income taxes, however, property taxes generally fail to recognize that some portion of a taxed asset is offset by debt (Hyman, 1983: 580; Rosen, 1985: 479). For example, real estate property taxes are the same whether the taxpayer owns the property outright or owes all of the purchase price to a third party, such as a mortgage company. (The determination of tax liability without regard for any offsetting debt is an issue today in terms of the negative impact on first-time home buyers.)

Moreover, as Bell and Bowman (1991: 87) point out:

- Property taxes are in part taxes on unrealized capital gains.
- There is no market transaction that determines the size of the tax base, thus governments must estimate it.

• Because property tax rates are set at a level needed to balance local budgets, they tend to fluctuate more often than income and sales tax rates.

RECENT TRENDS IN PROPERTY TAXATION

While the percentage of state and local revenues generated by property taxes has been declining until very recently, the absolute amount of money collected has generally been increasing, as shown in Exhibit 6.1. The reasons for these revenue increases are:

• Increasing market values due to inflation and other factors, resulting in higher valuations and higher taxes levies
• Increasing development, resulting in fewer parcels of undeveloped land
• Increasing investments in buildings and other improvements
• Increasing ratios of assessed values to market values due to better appraisal techniques, better assessment processes, more frequent reassessment, and more state equalization (Raphaelson, 1987: 204–205)

Then, too, simple changes in the technology of planning and mapping also are contributing to the expansion of property tax rolls. Aerial photography, for example, is making cadastral (tax plot) maps much more accurate (Raphaelson, 1987: 214–215).

Reliance on property taxes over time is illustrated in Exhibit 6.2. In 1990 school districts and townships depended more on property taxes to fund their services than did other governments. Except for these two governmental units, dependence on property tax revenues to fund expenditures is decreasing. Finally, state governments do not, and never have, depended much on property taxes to fund their services. (The federal government, of course, does not, and never has, levied property taxes.)

According to Bland (1989: 27), several other significant trends are affecting property taxes. Among them are the following:

• Per capita property tax burdens are generally declining for cities but not for counties.
• Property tax bases are being limited to real property; and residential property represents an increasing share of the real property tax base.
• Declining manufacturing activities and growing service activities have not reduced the amount of potential property subject to taxation.

Property taxes are levied on several types of property, including real estate and personal property. Exhibit 6.3 illustrates some elements included in each of these types. (Taxes on agricultural land, timber, and minerals are discussed later in this chapter.)

Exhibit 6.1
Growth in Property Taxes for Counties (in Millions of Dollars)

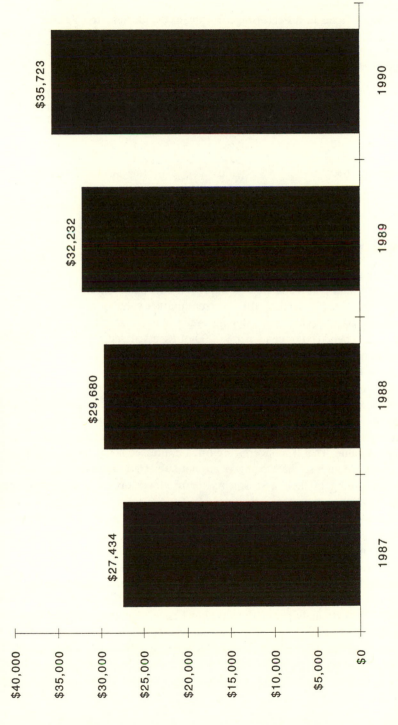

Source: U.S. Department of Commerce, 1992a: 3.

Exhibit 6.2
Property Taxes as a Percentage of Revenues, for Selected Years

(in Percent)

GOVERNMENT	1990	1985	1981	1977
STATE	1.9	1.9	2.0	2.2
LOCAL	74.5	74.2	76.0	80.5
CITY	50.9	79.2	53.6	60.0
COUNTY	73.3	75.5	76.4	81.2
TOWNSHIP	92.4	93.2	94.1	91.7
SCHOOL DISTRICT	97.5	97.3	96.1	97.5
SPECIAL DISTRICT	70.0	74.0	80.4	91.2

Source: ACIR, 1992: 126.

REAL ESTATE PROPERTY

Real estate property taxes are based on some measure of the current market value of land parcels as well as improvements made on the land. The assessed value may be 100 percent of the current market value or some percentage, such as 20 or 40 percent. The tax due generally is expressed in terms of mills (tenths of a cent) per $100 or cents per $1,000 of assessed value. Examples of effective and nominal residential property tax rates in large U.S. cities are found in Exhibit 6.4.

Determining the market value of a parcel of land is no small task unless that parcel or an identical one has been sold very recently. For that reason, political and economic debates concerning property taxes frequently focus on the effectiveness of the assessment process and the accuracy of the determinations of market value. That is, concerns are often expressed about the assessments being accurate enough so that taxpayers are not subjected to higher taxes just because of the timing of their assessments (or to lower taxes because their property values were assessed earlier).

Because properties that have not been sold in many years or that are undeveloped tend to be undervalued, periodic reassessment of property values is one of the most intensely political issues in state and local government today (Buchanan and Flowers, 1987: 364–365). Reassessment is a process by which states standardize both assessment processes and the criteria by which property values are ascertained in order to develop uniform and equal tax bases; as noted, it also is an extremely contentious political issue. The issues of reassessment and equalization are likely to arise more frequently because of the increasing influence of urban and suburban constituencies in state legislatures, coupled with more rapid turnover of properties and increased development of land in these areas, both of which result in higher property valuations and thus higher property taxes.

Exhibit 6.3
Types of Property

REAL ESTATE

LAND

Agricultural Land
Open Spaces
Timberland
Mineral Land

IMPROVEMENTS

Buildings
Infrastructure

PERSONAL PROPERTY

TANGIBLE

Inventory
Machinery
Vehicles
Jewelry
Furniture

INTANGIBLE

Stocks and Bonds
Insurance Policies
Bank Deposits
Accounts Receivable
Patents and Copyrights

Source: Bland, 1989: 30.

Valuation Approaches

Since there is no completely objective way to calculate the true market value of property short of selling it, the valuation process tends to rely on several different approaches. These approaches usually are written into law to elimi-nate—or at least reduce—subjective judgments and to lead to less variation in property values, thereby minimizing ill feeling among property owners. Ac-cording to Bell and Bowman (1991: 95), the American Institute of Real Estate Appraisers suggests that governments use a combination of three approaches: (1) market value, (2) income, and (3) cost. (Assessing agricultural property is discussed separately later in this chapter.)

Market Value Approach. Property appraisals are usually based on sales data from neighboring or similar properties, but it is often very difficult to find these benchmarks. A complicated but useful valuation technique uses multiple re-gression analysis to predict market value. The variables considered include lot size, location, square footage of living space, number of rooms, construction materials, and building type, such as two-story, ranch, or split-level houses. Depreciation generally is accounted for in the sales price. This method normally is used to value residential and commercial properties.

Income Approach. Income valuation measures property values according to

Exhibit 6.4
Residential Property Tax Rates in Selected Large Cities, 1990

City	Effective tax rate per $100 Rank	Rate	Nominal rate per $100
Detroit, MI	1	4.40	8.92
Milwaukee, WI	2	3.78	3.84
Portland, OR	3	3.32	3.32
Des Moines, IA	4	3.10	3.90
Newark, NJ	5	2.96	16.99
Philadelphia, PA	6	2.64	8.26
Omaha, NE	7	2.63	2.92
Providence, RI	8	2.55	2.55
Baltimore, MD	9	2.46	6.16
Manchester, NH	10	2.36	11.22
Sioux Falls, IA	11	2.27	2.52
Houston, TX	12	2.19	2.19
Jacksonville, FL	13	2.18	2.18
Bridgeport, CT	14	2.10	6.03
Atlanta, GA	15	2.08	5.20
Cleveland, OH	16	2.00	5.70
Boise, ID	17	1.92	1.96
Fargo, ND	18	1.78	39.59
Memphis, TN	19	1.77	7.09
Anchorage, AK	20	1.76	1.85
Portland, ME	21	1.74	3.75
Burlington, VT	22	1.65	2.29
Chicago, IL	23	1.63	10.20
Indianapolis, IN	24	1.62	10.79
Jackson, MS	25	1.47	14.73
New Orlenas, LA	26	1.46	14.65
Billings, MT	27	1.44	37.27
Wilmington, DE	28	1.31	1.69
Phoenix, AZ	29	1.31	13.08
Seattle, WA	30	1.30	1.36
Columbia, SC	31	1.26	31.42
Norfolk, VA	32	1.24	1.38
Louisville, KY	33	1.20	1.30
Wichita, KS	34	1.17	14.97
Charlotte, NC	35	1.15	1.34
St. Louis, MO	36	1.15	6.03
Denver, CO	37	1.12	6.76
Minneapolis, MN	38	1.11	10.16
Salt Lake City, UT	39	1.08	1.80
Oklahoma City, OK	40	1.04	9.45
Albuquerque, NM	41	1.04	3.11
Washington, DC	42	0.96	1.01
Little Rock, AR	43	0.95	5.08
Las Vegas, NV	44	0.88	2.50
Boston, MA	45	0.85	0.85
New York, NY	46	0.79	9.84
Casper, WY	47	0.71	7.50
Birmingham, AL	48	0.70	6.95
Los Angeles, CA	49	0.63	1.03
Charleston, WV	50	0.61	1.73
Honolulu, HI	51	0.48	0.48

Source: U.S. Department of Commerce, 1992b: 303.

their potential net earning power, as indicated by the capitalization of net income. This approach requires information on income and operating expenses for the valued property. After the net income is determined, it is capitalized at a rate of return prevalent in the market at the time of valuation.

Such rates are influenced by many considerations, including the degree of risk, market values with respect to future inflation, the prospective rates of return, historical rates of return earned by comparable properties, mortgage rates, and availability of tax shelters. Special consideration has to be given to these factors (American Institute of Real Estate Appraisers, 1983: 340). The income approach is used to value investment property such as commercial and industrial properties and apartment complexes.

Cost Approach. Cost valuation appraises property by determining the value of the land and buildings and then estimating replacement costs due to depreciation, deterioration, or obsolescence at the time of valuation. Thus, construction costs affect tax liabilities. This approach often is used for apartment complexes.

Despite the variety of valuation approaches available, the market value approach is still the most commonly used method. Governments also value property based on its use, hence open space and agricultural land are typically taxed at a lower rate than more developed parcels, while commercial property may be taxed at a higher rate than residential property. (See Exhibit 2.2 in Chapter 2.) A state-by-state breakdown of real and tangible personal property tax classifications and rates is provided in Exhibit 6.5. The differences in levels of taxation for residential, commercial and industrial, and telecommunications and utility properties are significant in some states, but not in most.

Exemptions

Governments also may levy lower tax rates on parcels of property located in certain specified areas, such as depressed or deteriorated urban zones, to encourage development (Raphaelson, 1987: 214). Besides differentiated rates, property tax exemptions frequently are given to hospitals, educational institutions, religious institutions, public housing authorities, government properties, and, increasingly, to areas being considered for industrial development. Approximately 75 percent of such property is tax-exempt in the United States.

Due to property tax exemptions, some governmental units may be negatively affected. To the extent that lower property tax revenues reduce money available for public services, governments with high proportions of exempted property may find it difficult to finance necessary services. Unfortunately, many of these exempted properties require high levels of service. For example, educational and governmental institutions and hospitals may significantly increase the governmental costs for fire service and solid waste disposal. Then, too, additional costs for building and maintaining major infrastructure to accommodate the exempted property owners may be required.

Exhibit 6.5

Basic Classifications of Real Property and Tangible Personal Property, 1991

State	Number of Classes Real	Number of Classes Personal	Residential Real	Residential Personal	Commercial/Industrial Real	Commercial/Industrial Personal	Telecommunication/Utility Real	Telecommunication/Utility Personal
Alabama	3	3	10 %	10 %	20 %	20 %	30 %	30 %
Alaska	1	1	100	X	100	100	100	100
Arizona	9	9	10	10	25	25	30	30
Arkansas	1	1	20	20	20	20	20	20
California	2	1	100	X	100	100	100	100
Colorado	6	1	14.34	X	29	29	29	29
Connecticut	1	1	70	70	70	70	X	X
Delaware	1	X	100	X	100	X	100	X
District of Columbia	5	1	100	X	100	100	100	X
Florida	1	1	100	X	100	100	Local	Local
Georgia	2	1	40	X	40	40	40	40
Hawaii	1	X	100	X	100	x	100	X
Idaho	1	1	50	X	100	100	100	100
Illinois	1	X	33.33	33.33	33.33	X	33.33	X
Indiana	1	1	33.33	33.33	33.33	33.33	33.33	33.33
Iowa	4	X	79	X	100	X	100	X
Kansas	4	5	12	X	30	20	30	30
Kentucky	1	1	100	X	100	100	100	100
Louisiana	5	5	10	X	15	15	10/25	25
Maine	1	1	100	X	100	100	100	X
Maryland	1	1	100	X	100	100	100	100
Massachusetts	4	1	100	X	100	100	100	100
Michigan	6	5	50	X	50	50	50	50
Minnesota	12	1	1.66	X	3.2/4.95	X	4.95	X
Mississippi	3	2	10	X	15	15	30	30
Missouri	3	9	19	X	32	33.33	32	33.33
Montana	11	13	3.86	X	3.86	3.86	12	12
Nebraska	1	1	100	X	100	100	100	100
Nevada	1	1	35	X	35	35	35	35
New Hampshire	1	X	100	X	100	X	X	X
New Jersey	1	1	100	X	100	50	100	50
New Mexico	1	1	33.33	X	33.33	33.33	33.33	33.33
New York	2	X	100	X	100	X	100	X
North Carolina	1	1	100	100	100	100	100	100
North Dakota	4	X	9	X	10	X	10	10
Ohio	2	3	35	X	35	27	35	100
Oklahoma	1	1	Max 35	Max 35	Max 35	Max 35	Max 35	Max 35
Oregon	1	1	100	X	100	100	100	100
Pennsylvania	1	X	Max 100	X	Max 100	X	Max 100	X
Rhode Island	1	1	100	100	100	100	100	100
South Carolina	6	4	4	X	6	10.5	10.5	10.5
South Dakota	2	X	100	X	100	X	100	100
Tennessee	4	3	25	5	40	30	55	55
Texas	1	1	100	X	100	100	100	100
Utah	5	1	66.9	X	95	100	100	100
Vermont	1	2	100	X	100	50	100	50
Virginia	1	1	100	100	100	100	100	100
Washington	1	1	100	X	100	100	100	100
West Virginia	3	3	60	60	60	60	60	60
Wisconsin	1	1	100	X	100	100	X	X
Wyoming	3	1	9.5	X	11.5	11.5	11.5	11.5

MV - market value
X - exempt

Source: ACIR, 1992: 140.

A federal program now reimburses local governments in federally impacted areas for at least some expense of public services, but states normally do not reimburse local governments for mandated services and exemptions. Exceptions, of course, do occur. Wisconsin reimburses Madison a percentage of the tax that would have been paid on state property in the city had it been taxable. Nevada gives Carson City an extra portion of state sales tax receipts to make up for tax-exempt properties.

Indeed, costs of tax exemptions for commercial and industrial properties, coupled with the need to furnish additional services and infrastructure expenses required for economic development, are increasingly being addressed in the economic development literature (Waugh and Waugh, 1988b: 112–113; Waugh, 1992). Much of this literature pleads with government officials to recognize the total costs that are being passed on to them by abatements and exemptions and suggests that some lost revenues be replaced. For instance, the federal government calculates such tax expenditures to gauge the impact of income tax deductions and exemptions. Similarly, state and local governments can use *shadow exemptions*—estimates of taxes that would have been levied if the exemptions were not given—to estimate the impact of their exemptions (Raphaelson, 1987: 224–225). These procedures can be used to determine how much revenue needs to be replaced.

Additionally, local governments are examining more closely the tax implications of certain kinds of development. Zoning board hearings on expansions of church property, for example, are more and more likely to find taxpayers voicing concerns about lost property tax revenues. Being church impacted is common in older communities that have many churches located in the downtown areas, and such impacts become more intensely political when large and growing percentages of the congregations are nonresidents. When property taxes represent a very large percentage of local revenues, abatements and exemptions that may reduce revenues are getting closer official scrutiny and engendering more public debate.

Homestead Exemptions

Notwithstanding the current concerns about property tax exemptions, property tax relief for elderly and lower income homeowners is becoming a major political issue, principally due to rising housing costs and inflation. In recent years, many homeowners have found that the value of their homes and, as a result, their property taxes have increased tremendously, while their household incomes have remained static or actually decreased in real terms due to inflation. In short, the value of their homes has increased on paper, but the only way to realize the actual value of their property would be to sell it. High property taxes have forced many homeowners on fixed incomes, particularly the elderly relying on Social Security and other fixed pension benefits, to sell their homes. Normally, state and local governments respond to this situation by offering homestead exemptions, usually by exempting a set percentage of the assessed value of the real estate or by reducing the assessed value by a specific dollar amount, such as $10,000, which in turn reduces tax liability.

One alternative to homestead exemptions that is receiving increasing attention, although it is not yet commonly used, is deferral of taxes until the sale of the property. Rather than exempting elderly and low income persons from all or some portion of their property taxes, a tax is levied based on the assessed value of the property, and then some portion of that tax (sometimes based on income) is deferred until the homeowners die or the property is sold. In essence, the deferred tax is levied on the homeowners' estate. The deferral keeps elderly and low income homeowners from losing their property or being forced to sell it and permits state and local governments to borrow monies against the antici- pated revenues (Hyman, 1987: 599).

In addition to exemptions and use value, other popular approaches to property tax relief involve:

- *Credits*—subtracting credit due from property tax liability
- *Refunds and rebates*—giving money back to property owners for specific, identified purposes such as spending to enhance property values
- *Freezes*—setting property tax rates and/or bases at a specified level and holding them for a period of time (Bell and Bowman, 1991: 106)

PERSONAL AND INTANGIBLE PROPERTY TAXES

Besides real property, governments also tax personal property, which is as- sumed to be an indicator of income. Basically, there are two forms of personal property. Tangible property includes automobiles, furniture, jewelry, and other items owned by individuals, and raw materials, inventories, and other items owned by corporations. Nationwide, approximately 60 percent of this type of property, however, is tax-exempt. Intangible property embodies items such as stocks and bonds, mortgages, and other financial assets. Intangible property, it should be noted, is less easily located by revenue authorities (and more easily hidden by owners); consequently, intangible property tax rates are generally low (Buchanan and Flowers, 1987: 361–362). Today, most intangible property is taxed as income rather than property. Thus, state and local governments rely less on revenues generated from tangible property than on funds raised from intangible property, though most state and local governments no longer tax personal property.

As illustrated in Exhibit 6.5, most states do not tax the personal property of individuals. Alabama, Arizona, Arkansas, Connecticut, Illinois, North Carolina, Oklahoma, Rhode Island, Tennessee, Virginia, and West Virginia are the only states that tax personal property. The taxation of intangible property varies widely among the states. Exhibit 6.6 indicates that twenty-one states levy intan-

Exhibit 6.6
Selected Features of Intangibles Taxation by State

State	Tax Levied	Part of General Property	Taxable Unless Exempt	Special Intangibles Tax	Tax Imposed on Individuals	Corporations
Alabama	Y	Y	Y		Y	Y
Alaska			Y			
Arizona			Y			
Arkansas			Y			
California			Y			
Colorado			Y			
Connecticut	Y			Y	Y	
Delaware						
Dist. of Columbia			Y			
Florida	Y		Y	Y	Y	Y
Georgia	Y		Y	Y	Y	Y
Hawaii						
Idaho						
Illinois			Y			
Indiana				Y		Y
Iowa	Y			Y	Y	
Kansas	Y			Y	Y	Y
Kentucky	Y	Y	Y		Y	Y
Louisiana	Y	Y	Y	Y	Y	Y
Maine						
Maryland						
Massachusetts			Y			
Michigan	Y		Y	Y	Y	
Minnesota			Y			
Mississippi	Y	Y	Y			Y
Missouri	Y		Y	Y	Y	
Montana			Y			
Nebraska			Y			
Nevada						
New Hampshire	Y			Y	Y	
New Jersey						
New Mexico						
New York						
North Carolina	Y		Y	Y	Y	Y
North Dakota	Y			Y	Y	Y
Ohio				Y		Y
Oklahoma			Y			
Oregon			Y			
Pennsylvania	Y	Y	Y	Y	Y	Y
Rhode Island	Y			Y		Y
South Carolina						
South Dakota						
Tennessee	Y	Y	Y	Y	Y	Y
Texas	Y			Y	Y	Y
Utah			Y			
Vermont						
Virginia						
Washington	Y	Y	Y		Y	Y
West Virginia	Y	Y	Y		Y	Y
Wisconsin			Y			
Wyoming	Y	Y	Y		Y	Y
Totals	21	9	29	17	19	18

Source: ACIR, 1992: 154.

Exhibit 6.7
Details of Intangibles Tax Base by State

State	Base Items (see Key at bottom of table)	Number
Alabama	A,B	2
Connecticut	O	1
Florida	A,B,E,F,H,O	5
Georgia	A,B,C,D,E,I,J,K,L,M,O	11
Iowa	O	1
Kansas	A,B,C,D,E,F,H,I,O	9
Kentucky	A,B,C,D,E,F,G,H,I,J,K,L,M,O	14
Louisiana	A,B,E,O	4
Michigan	A,B,C,D,E,F,H,I	8
Mississippi	O	1
Missouri	O	1
New Hampshire	A,B,C,E,G,I,O	7
North Carolina	A,B,E,F,H	5
North Dakota	O	1
Pennsylvania	A,B,E,I,O	5
Rhode Island	C	1
Tennessee	A,B,C,E,H,I,O	7
Texas	O	1
Washington	N	1
West Virginia	A,B,F,G,I,K,M,O	9
Wyoming	O	1

Key to Intangible Base Categories (number of states)

A-Equities (12)	I-Other financial instruments (8)
B-Bonds (12)	J-Patents (3)
C-Deposits (7)	K-Copyrights and trademarks (3)
D-Cash (4)	L-Licenses (2)
E-Mortgages (10)	M-Franchises (3)
F-Accounts receivable (6)	N-Computer software (1)
G-Cash value of insurance policies (3)	O-Other (17)
H-Interest in trusts (6)	

Source: ACIR, 1992: 155.

gibles taxes, some on very specific items rather than on all intangible assets, and some on individual or corporate property but not both. Exhibit 6.7 identifies the specific items subject to intangibles taxes in each of the twenty-one states. Equities and bonds appear to be more typically taxed than other intangible assets.

ASSESSMENT PROCESS

As Exhibit 6.8 shows, the assessment process consists of two interrelated stages: property assessment and assessment adjustments. Each of these stages in turn includes various steps.

DeKalb County, Georgia, can provide us with an illustration of how property taxes are determined. First, the county sends out property tax statements in March or April of each year, and taxpayers have thirty days in which to appeal any changes in their assessments. A Board of Tax Assessors and a Board of Equalization review all appeals. The annual county property tax statement describes the sources of county operating funds, including the percentage generated by property taxes, and the percentages of property taxes generated by the four classes of real property. In 1991 property taxes accounted for 57.5 percent of

Exhibit 6.8
Property Assessment Cycle

PROPERTY ASSESSMENTS	ASSESSMENT ADJUSTMENTS
Taxable and tax-exempt property are determined	Estimated value is multiplied by rate to determine tax due
Legal owners are identified	Assessments are equalized by state
Estimated property value is ascertained	Tax due is adjusted for homestead and other exemptions
Property owners are notified	Notices are prepared and published
Appeals from owners are heard	Public hearings are held
Adjustments are reviewed and approved or disapproved by Board	Tax rate is set by Board
Final certified assessment is prepared	Rate is certified

Source: Bland, 1989: 45.

county operating funds, with 46.9 percent of that amount coming from residential property, 36 percent for commercial and industrial property, 13.4 percent from business personal property, and 3.7 percent from public utility property.

A detailed explanation of the tax due indicates that there are separate taxes (and separate millage rates) that support county operations, hospitals, county bonds, and the city (if the residence is in an incorporated municipality). Taxpayers in the unincorporated areas of the county also have a levy to support county schools. In terms of exemptions, DeKalb County offers a basic homestead exemption (currently $10,000) to property owners who are resident in the county, essentially meaning an exemption for owner-occupied property. Other exemptions from county and/or school levies are given to taxpayers who are elderly, low income, disabled, and/or disabled veterans with incomes below a specified state net income (not counting Social Security, retirement, disability, or pensions) or federal adjusted gross income (not counting Social Security, railroad retirement, or disability income).

In reality, these represent, to be sure, a complex set of exemptions. The calculation of tax due begins with assessing the value of the property (40 percent of market value in DeKalb County), subtracting exemptions, and multiplying the taxable value by the appropriate millage rate for each levy (See Exhibit 2.2 in Chapter 2.) The levies for county operations, hospitals, and so forth are added up, and the resulting amount is the tax due (DeKalb County Government, 1992).

Mortgage companies generally pay the property taxes semiannually or quarterly from escrow accounts. Since most taxpayers make small payments into escrow accounts each month, along with larger payments on the principal and interest on their loans, they may be aware of the level of taxation only when receiving annual assessments from local governments and when receiving state and federal income tax reporting information from their mortgage holders. Homeowners who have paid off their mortgages face the "sticker shock" of large tax bills without the mediating effect of escrow accounts.

EFFECTS AND LIMITATIONS OF PROPERTY TAXES

There is some question and considerable debate concerning whether property taxes, if based on accurate valuations and applied equally among properties, are too regressive. While nominal rates are uniform within classes of property, effective rates of property taxation vary according to how close the assessed values are to the real or market values—the wider the variance, the less proportional the rates. As noted earlier, there are decided tendencies to value newer properties higher than older ones, developed properties higher than undeveloped ones, lower price properties proportionately more than higher price ones, and commercial and industrial properties more than residential ones.

A recent analysis conducted for the National Conference of State Legislatures concludes that low income households carry the greatest burden from property taxes (Greenstein and Hutchinson, 1988: 171–172). The Northeast region of the country has the highest property tax burden when compared to other regions. The Northeast is characterized by high property tax rates and above average housing-to-income ratios. The South Central and South Atlantic regions have relatively low property tax burdens. The two regions thus have low property taxes and below average housing-to-income ratios (District of Columbia, 1991: 32). Exhibit 6.9 shows the estimated property tax burdens for a family of four by region.

The provision of homestead exemptions for the elderly and those with low income does little to reduce regressivity and property tax burdens unless income is a criterion for exemptions. While property taxes generally are assumed to be among the most regressive, some economists still argue that they are in fact progressive. The difference of opinion rests primarily on the issue of tax incidence; that is, *who bears the tax burden*? Are residential property taxes, when paid by homeowners, more or less regressive than the tax paid by rental property owners, which is passed on to the renters? Personal property taxes normally have been found to be regressive in the lower income ranges and more progressive in the higher income ranges (Bingham, Hawkins, and Hebert, 1978: 176–177).

The extent to which property taxation affects real estate development and business locations and expansions also is uncertain. As will be seen in Chapter 8, which focuses on economic development, taxes—including property taxes— generally have very little direct impact on business decisions to locate in particular states or communities. Property taxes are just one of the variables

Exhibit 6.9
Estimated Property Tax Burden for a Family of Four, 1990

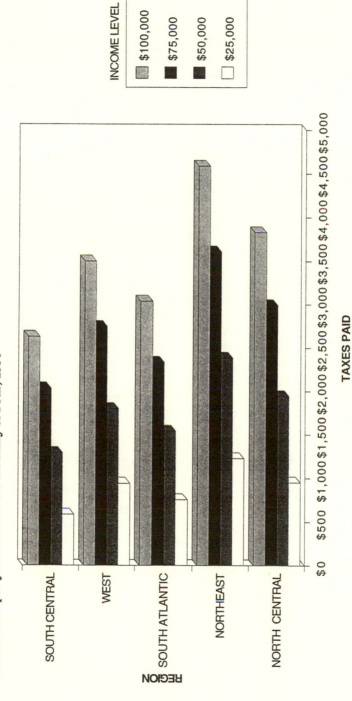

Source: District of Columbia, 1991: 35.

considered in making such decisions and are generally less important than the skills and availability of labor, access to raw materials, transportation for raw materials and finished goods, and distance to customers.

Intergovernmental competition, too, tends to encourage the development of comparable tax incentives, so states and communities seldom offer uncommonly attractive development incentives for very long before neighbors match the offer (Waugh and Waugh, 1988b: 216–218; Waugh and Waugh, 1988a). The low impact of property taxes on business relocation and expansion decisions, in this competitive context, does not mean that the taxes have no impact on business. Typically, property taxes are the single largest tax burden for manufacturing firms. Taxes on inventories of raw materials and finished goods can be prohibitively high. Thus, there is a national trend toward exempting inventories from property taxation (Vlaisavljevich, 1988: 185).

The assessment and taxation of inventories can present problems for tax authorities as well as for the businesses themselves, principally due to disparities caused by the timing of the assessments. New production processes minimize the reliance on large inventories of raw materials and components, therefore firms using such processes would have very little inventory subject to taxation. More traditional manufacturing firms and those with large inventories at the time of the assessment are at a decided disadvantage. Discount retail firms, for instance, appear to be choosing sites where inventory taxes are comparatively low, although it is uncertain whether their low prices make it difficult (or counterproductive) to pass property taxes on to consumers or whether such firms collectively find it convenient to locate near one another in communities that offer tax exemptions for inventories.

It must also be mentioned that there are arguments for having a two-rate system for property taxes to encourage real estate development. Proponents suggest that separate rates on land and improvements or buildings, with a higher rate on land, would discourage investors from holding undeveloped land and encourage commercial improvements. In essence, it would be more expensive to own land, whether developed or not, and less expensive to develop it. There have been municipal two-rate programs in Pennsylvania, most notably Pittsburgh, in Boston, and in Jamaica and some indications of success, although implementation (i.e., the separate valuations) may be problematic (Anderson, 1993). Notwithstanding the implementation problems, however, two-rate systems may offer some incentives for urban development.

AGRICULTURAL PROPERTY TAXES

Agricultural property taxation differs considerably from residential and other business property taxation. The taxation of agricultural property has historically been characterized by various types of preferential treatment. This preferential treatment normally takes the form of lower property tax assessments and/or rates on farmland, as well as sales tax exemptions on agricultural products and machinery. Moreover, farmers are frequently encouraged by state legislation to offset their income fluctuations with current production expenses and to convert income into capital gains in order to be taxed at lower rates.

These tax preferences commonly are distributed in direct proportion to volume of output, strongly suggesting that tax preferences favor larger farms with higher incomes. Since tax preferences often are capitalized into land values, they also reward landowners rather than nonlandowing farm workers. As a result of these preferences, then, agricultural taxpayers have lower tax burdens than do nonagricultural taxpayers.

Agricultural Tax Philosophy

Preferential treatment exists because of the wide acceptance of the doctrine of *agricultural fundamentalism*, which argues that food is a necessity and that its production involves degrees of risk and uncertainty due to a variety of natural and biological causes and to fluctuations in supply and demand. Consequently, farmers should be given tax preferences to compensate them for the risks and uncertainties involved in the production of agricultural products.

In addition, states rely on preferential treatment as incentives to attract outside capital. Such capital is needed to encourage mechanization, technological development, and resource mobilization, which in turn increases production. Nonagricultural capital, it is believed, will be attracted to agriculture because such tax preferences will reduce the effective tax rates of nonagricultural income or, in some instances, allow for the postponement of tax payments.

Trends in Agricultural Property Taxation

Property taxes are a major source of revenue for local governments in rural areas, even more so than in urban areas generally, and agricultural land accounts for a large proportion of their property tax base. Exhibit 6.10 shows the extent to which local governments are dependent on property tax revenues. Although property taxes as a percentage of total local revenues decreased in the mid-1980s, they have been increasing in recent years to the point that property tax revenues now represent almost 75 percent of local revenues.

As reflected in Exhibit 6.11, this pattern holds when property taxes are regionalized. While the New England states rely most heavily on property taxes, local governments in agricultural states in the Great Lakes, Plains, and Southwest regions also depend a great deal on property tax revenues.

Given this dependency on property tax revenues, local governments obviously are more affected by preferential treatment of agricultural land than are state governments. Exhibit 6.12 shows that states in the Midwest and the South have the most taxable acres of farmland and that they tax most of these acres—in contrast to the states in the western section of the United States. Furthermore, Exhibit 6.13 suggests that rural governments—especially those in counties with

Exhibit 6.10
Property Taxes as a Percentage of Total Local Revenues

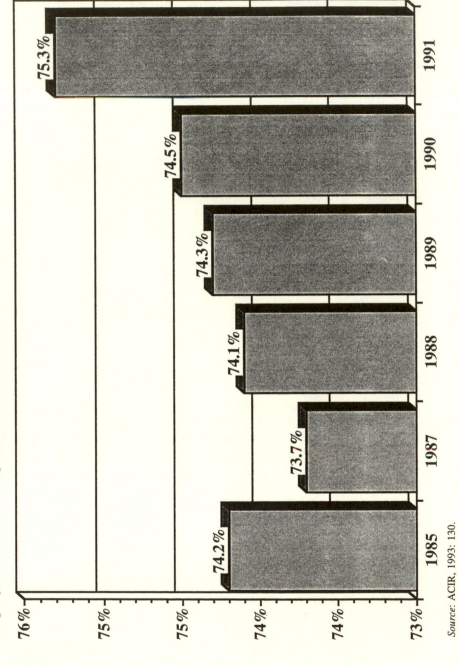

Source: ACIR, 1993: 130.

Exhibit 6.11
Property Taxes as a Percentage of Local Revenues by Region

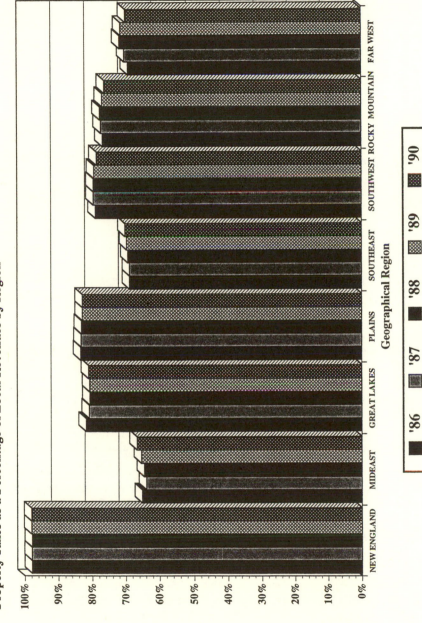

Sources: ACIR, 1992: 196.

169

Exhibit 6.12
Value of Acres in Farmland and Taxable Land and Buildings
by Region, 1987

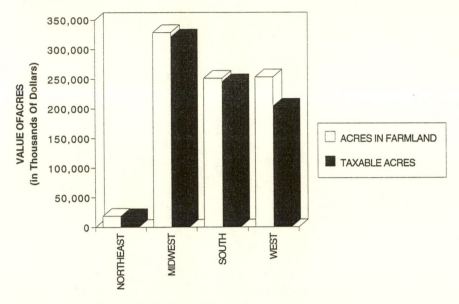

Source: U.S. Department of Commerce, 1990a: 5, 181.

less than 100,000 persons—rely heavily on property taxes, since their property tax bases are considerably smaller than the bases of the more populous counties, which have large residential, commercial, industrial, and utility properties. These exhibits suggest that any changes in preferential treatment of agricultural land would significantly impact local government revenues in agricultural areas.

Agricultural Property Tax Classification: Use Value Asessments

Of the tax preferences farmers receive, the most prominent and most controversial involves property tax assessments. Generally speaking, state and local governments group various types of properties and then assign different taxable values and different rates to those properties. Land used for agricultural purposes almost always has lower tax bases and rates.

As mentioned in Chapter 2, property normally is classified as either residential, commercial, industrial, public utility, or agricultural (see Exhibit 2.2). Property classifications and concomitant use value assessments have contributed to the acceptability of property taxes by rural residents and farmers. They have, of course, made property tax assessment more complex. In addition, a basic problem with classifications is that, once adopted, they continue to multiply, because classifications are not based on economic reasoning, but rather on political ex-

Exhibit 6.13
Percent Distribution of County Property Taxes by Population, 1989–1990

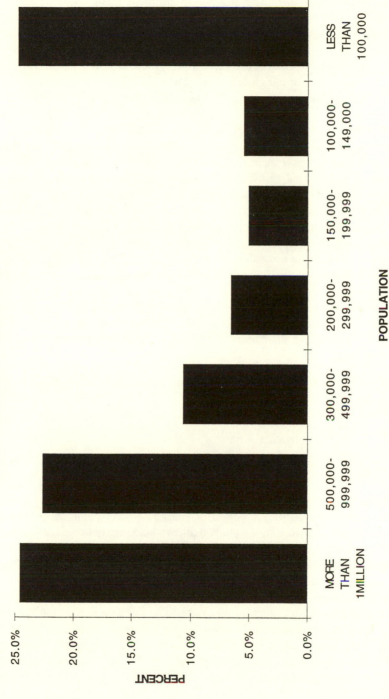

Source: U.S. Department of Commerce, 1992a: 5.

pediency. And since classifications generally lead to lower property taxes, it is much easier to add classifications than to eliminate them.

Use Value. Once classified, agricultural land, unlike residential property, is not assessed on the basis of its market value. Instead, farmland is assessed based on its value in farm use. Since the use value of agricultural land typically is lower than its market value, use value assessments generally lead to lower property tax liabilities for agricultural landowners.

Use value assessment is largely a tax abatement given to agricultural landowners based on the farming value of the land alone. Use value means that local governments are in effect lending money to farmland owners to produce products. In other words, use value assessments reduce the property tax base and presumably result in higher taxes being paid by nonfarmers. The consequence is an unequal distribution of tax burdens among local nonfarm landowners. (It might be appropriate for the state to compensate local governments for their tax losses, much as it does for school districts with state aid. The cost would then be shared by taxpayers statewide, instead of just locally.)

Use value assessments vary widely among states. By far the most prevalent way states determine use value of agricultural land is to capitalize income. The capitalization of income is based on the idea that the value of farmland equals the discounted present value of future income accruing to the land from farm production less property taxes on the land (Chicoine, 1986: 315).

Practically speaking, use value is determined by dividing the net income the land will generate in the coming year by the capitalization, inflation, and property tax rates:

$$NI/C+I+P$$

Where:
  NI = Net Income
   C = Capitalization Rate
   I = Inflation Rate
   P = Property Tax Rate

Net income is estimated from crop yields, commodity prices, input costs, and rental rates averaged over a period of years, the most common of which is a five-year span. This averaging method allows landowners to reduce the negative (and in some cases positive) impacts of economic and weather conditions. Exhibit 6.14 lists the steps used to calculate net income.

The capitalization rate is a multiyear—five, eight, or ten—average of mortgage rates based on new long-term loans processed by some accepted financial institution such as the Federal Land Bank. The inflation rate normally is a five-year average, also ascertained by an accepted financial institution. (Some states adjust both capitalization and inflation rates.) The property tax rate is derived from data supplied by local assessors. Exhibit 6.15 illustrates the process, including appeals, used to assess land values.

Exhibit 6.14
Steps Used to Calculate Net Income, Using a Five-Year Average

Step 1	Determine major soil regions of the state. Soil regions are as-certained by soil, climate, cropping patterns, and productivity.
Step 2	Determine the land capability classes for each soil in each county. The land capability classification system is a grouping of soils that shows the suitability of soils for most kinds of farming, crop rotation, and various farming practices.
Step 3	Develop a soil and land use pattern for each crop comprising 5% or more of the land in the region.
Step 4	Determine the income associated with each crop based on the five-year crop yield, the five-year average price paid for each crop, and government payments.
Step 5	Determine the costs associated with each major crop by (1) developing budgets for each region and land class based on production practices and five-year average input prices, (2) adjusting variable costs to land classes in the soil regions, and (3) determining fixed, management, and overhead costs.
Step 6	Subtract total cost from the total income to ascertain the per acre return.
Step 7	Determine the crop percentage for the major crops in the region by dividing the number of acres for each specific crop by the total number of acres for all major crops in the region.
Step 8	Determine the return percentage for each individual crop in the region by multiplying the cropping percentage by the per acre return for each crop.
Step 9	Determine the overall return by adding the return percentage for each major crop in the region.
Step 10	Calculate the average regional property tax per acre by dividing the total planted acreage by the total regional taxes.
Step 11	Subtract the average regional property tax per acre from the overall return *to get the net income* from the land.

Source: PEER Committee, 1990: 36.

It should be noted that agricultural landowners who change the use of their land during the fiscal year are liable for tax penalties, frequently the difference between the use value and the market value plus a nominal interest charge. When the land is converted to nonfarm use or sold for nonfarming purposes, the taxes on the difference between the use value and the value that the land otherwise would have been assessed at on an ad valorem basis become due, payable with usually no more than a two-year capture period.

Extreme fluctuations in use values adversely affect the stability of revenues. When use values of large portions of land fluctuate drastically from year to year,

Exhibit 6.15
Land Value Assessment Process

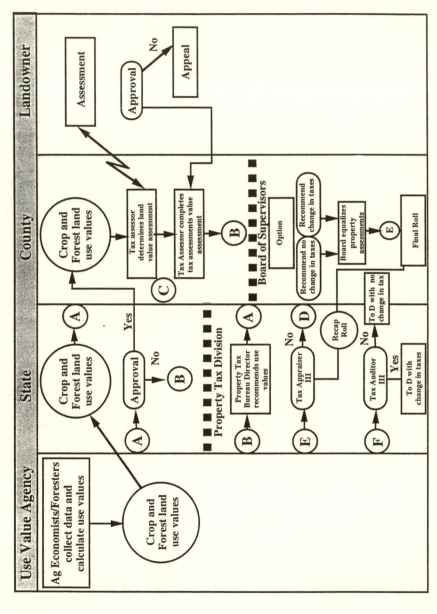

Source: PEER Committee, 1991: 21.

revenues cannot be projected accurately at given millage rates. In addition, farm-land owners find it difficult at best to estimate their property taxes, even if millage rates remain constant.

When use values vacillate excessively, a five-year averaging method designed to smooth some extremes may fail to account for the fluctuations because income or costs for the year that is dropped from the calculations often differ substantially from the income or costs for the year added to make up a new five-year period. In addition, if capitalization and inflation rates are averaged over a period of time longer than five years, the problems are magnified. The easiest solution to these problems is to use a longer time span, say ten years, to compute use values. Exhibit 6.16 is a schematic example of a ten-year averaging process.

In summary, agricultural taxation, as mentioned earlier, seldom pertains to a separate set of taxes; rather, it involves preferential tax treatment, especially for property and sales taxes. By the late 1980s the adoption of use value assessments and sales tax exemptions by state and local governments had become almost universal. They provided effective tax relief for agricultural landowners and producers.

These preferential treatments were adopted primarily because states regarded such taxes as indirect business taxes, which economic theory suggests, should be borne by consumers of the products. However, they are not. Instead, this preferential treatment entailed losses of tax dollars to both states and local governments and placed additional relative tax burdens on nonfarmers.

Embracing these preferential treatments means fewer tax dollars for state and local governments, particularly for primary and secondary education. The extent to which these treatments impact state and local governments depends on the importance of farming to the state and local economies and the importance of the nonfarming sectors to those economies. The challenge for state and local governments, then, is to find equitable ways to replace lost revenues.

CONCLUDING COMMENTS

While state governments and some local governments are not relying on property taxes as much as in previous decades, these taxes continue to be the principal source of revenue for most local governments and almost the sole source of revenue for many school and special districts. Despite problems of assessment and equity, property taxes have several advantages which, coupled with the lack of viable revenue enhancing alternatives, means that they will continue to be widely used. Besides being relatively inexpensive to collect, other principal advantages, according to Bland (1989: 43), are that they:

• Furnish a stable source of revenue
• Tax nonresident property owners, though these taxes may be shifted later to residents
• Are difficult to evade

* Finance property-related services
* Promote local autonomy

Continued reliance on property taxes has engendered considerable public opposition over the past two decades, but acceptance of alternative revenue sources has been elusive. Taxpayer groups mobilize at the mere hint of property tax rate increases and with every suggestion of periodic reassessment and equalization of property values. The most intensely political issues in local government may be property taxes and land use regulations (including zoning).

The major issues of property taxation continue to be the exemption of elderly, low income, and other specially identifiable property owners and the use of property tax deferrals and exemptions to achieve public policy objectives. As with many other government programs today, there is increasing pressure to target greater benefits for low income families and individuals. Measures of need, rather than age, are more likely to guide future exemptions. The deferral of property taxes, levying them on estates rather than on elderly property owners, may be the easiest and most popular approach that local governments can find. Concerns about progressivity and equity will likely encourage greater standardization of rates and assessment processes and more attention to need in the granting of exemptions and deferrals.

In terms of agricultural property taxation, the decline of the family farm and the growth of large-scale agribusinesses may encourage simplification of the assessment processes. In other words, the tax treatment of agricultural property may become more similar to the tax treatment of other business enterprises. The declining farm population, too, may lessen the pressure for special rates and exemptions.

Finally, *State Policy Reports* (1992: 7) lists four major ways to cushion property taxes:

* Clean up property tax administration by such measures as current value assessments.
* Adopt property tax deferrals—not exemptions—for the elderly and the poor.
* Preserve the property tax base against proposed new exemptions.
* Spread large utility, commercial, and industrial property tax bases among local jurisdictions to avoid inequities.

State and local governments need to address these factors.

Exhibit 6.16
Ten-Year Averaging Process

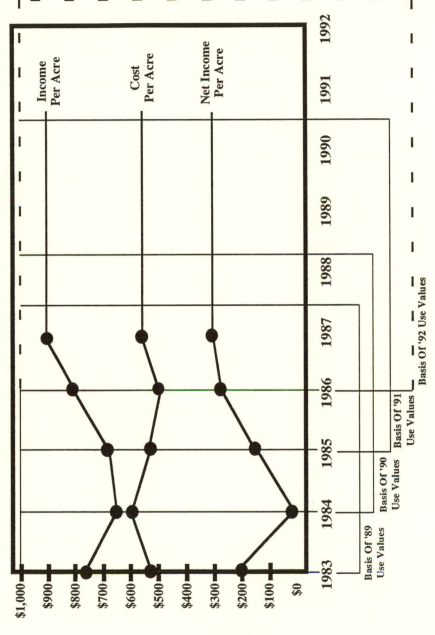

Source: PEER Committee, 1990: 12.

REFERENCES

Aaron, Henry (1975). *Who Pays the Property Tax?* Washington, D.C.: Brookings Institution.

Advisory Commission on Intergovernmental Relations (ACIR) (1992). *Significant Features of Fiscal Federalism.* Vol. 1. Washington, D.C.: ACIR.

—— (1993). *Significant Features of Fiscal Federalism.* Vol. 2. Washington, D.C.: ACIR.

American Institute of Real Estate Appraisers (1983). *The Appraisal of Real Estate.* 8th ed. Chicago: AIREA.

Anderson, John E. (1993). "Two-Rate Property Taxes and Urban Development." *Intergovernmental Perspective,* Summer.

Behrens, John O. (1993). "Assessments and Property Taxes: Today and Tomorrow." *Intergovernmental Perspective,* Summer.

Bell, Michael, and John Bowman (1991). "Property Taxes." In John Petersen and Dennis Strachota, eds., *Local Government Finances.* Chicago: Government Finance Officers Association.

Bingham, Richard D., Brett W. Hawkins, and F. Ted Hebert (1978). *The Politics of Raising State and Local Revenue.* New York: Praeger.

Bland, Robert (1989). *A Revenue Guide for Local Government.* Washington, D.C.: International City Management Association.

Buchanan, James M., and Marilyn R. Flowers (1987). *The Public Finances.* 6th ed. Homewood, Ill.: Richard D. Irwin.

Chicoine, David (1986). "Farm Taxes." In Steven D. Gold, ed., *Reforming State Tax Systems.* Denver: National Conference of State Legislatures.

Dearborn, Philip M. (1993). "Local Property Taxes: Emerging Trends." *Intergovernmental Perspective,* Summer.

DeKalb County Government (1992). *1992 DeKalb County Property Tax Statement.* Decatur, Ga.: Office of the DeKalb County Tax Commissioner.

District of Columbia (1991). *Tax Rates and Tax Burdens in the District of Columbia: A Nationwide Comparison.* Washington, D.C.: Department of Finance and Revenue.

Fisher, Ronald C. (1988). *State and Local Public Finance.* Glenview, Ill.: Scott, Foresman.

Greenstein, Robert, and Frederick Hutchinson (1988). "State Tax Relief for Low-Income People." In Steven D. Gold, ed., *The Unfinished Agenda for State Tax Reform.* Washington, D.C.: National Conference of State Legislatures.

Hyman, David (1983). *Public Finance: A Contemporary Application of Theory to Policy.* Chicago: Dryden Press.

—— (1987). *Public Finance: A Contemporary Application of Theory to Policy.* 2nd ed. Chicago: Dryden Press.

Jensen, David L. (1993). "Modern Technology for the Mass Appraiser." *Intergovernmental Perspective,* Summer.

Mields, Hugh, Jr. (1993). "The Property Tax: Local Revenue Mainstay." *Intergovernmental Perspective,* Summer.

PEER Committee (1990). *Report to the Mississippi Legislature: A Review of Use Value Procedures for Assessing Agricultural Land for Taxation Purposes.* Jackson, Miss.: Policy Evaluation and Expenditure Review Committee.

Raphaelson, Arnold H. (1987). "The Property Tax." In Richard Aronson and Eli Schwartz, eds., *Management Policies in Local Government Finance*. Washington, D.C.: International City Management Association.

Rosen, Harvey S. (1985). *Public Finance*. Homewood, Ill.: Richard D. Irwin.

Rourke, Richard W. (1993). "Assessment Innovation in Orange County, Florida." *Intergovernmental Perspective*, Summer.

State Policy Reports (1992). Vol. 10.

U.S. Department of Commerce, Bureau of the Census (1990a). *Rankings of States and Counties*. Vol. 2 Washington, D.C.: Bureau of the Census.

———— (1990b). *Agricultural Atlas of the United States*. Vol. 2. Washington, D.C.: Bureau of the Census.

———— (1992a). *County Government Finances, 1989–90*. Washington, D.C.: Bureau of the Census.

———— (1992b). *Statistical Abstract of the United States, 1992*. Washington, D.C.: Bureau of the Census.

Vlaisavljevich, Michael (1988). "State Business Taxes: The Policy and Research Agendas." In Steven D. Gold, ed., *The Unfinished Agenda for State Tax Reform*. Washington, D.C.: National Conference of State Legislatures.

Waugh, William L. (1992). "Transportation as a Variable in Regional Economic Development." In Robert P. McGowan, ed., *Economic Development Strategies for State and Local Governments*. Chicago: Nelson-Hall.

Waugh, William L., and Deborah M. Waugh (1988a). "Baiting the Hook: Targeting Economic Development Monies More Effectively." *Public Administration Quarterly*, 12, Summer.

———— (1988b). "Economic Development Programs of State and Local Governments and the Site Selection Decisions of Smaller Firms." In R. J. Judd, W. T. Greenwood, and F. W. Becker, eds., *Small Business in a Regulated Economy*. New York: Quorum Books.

7

Severance Taxes

When states decide to generate revenues from the production of marketable natural resources within their jurisdictions, they often levy severance taxes. Severance taxes are levies on the value or the quantity of marketable natural resources (oil, gas, coal, timber, fish, and other saleable minerals) extracted from land or water under state jurisdiction. Severance taxes invariably are compared to excise taxes because both are levied on particular products and normally earmarked for specific functions. The major difference between the two is that severance taxes are assessed at the time of production rather than at the time of sale.

Severance taxes may be known by a variety of other names, such as privilege, production, mining, minerals, license, or occupation taxes. Regardless of the name, they all have a tax base connected to marketable natural resources, a production value, and a rate associated with the production value. Multiplication of the base by the rate (less any specified credits or modifications) results in the severance tax liability.

Natural resources have distinctive characteristics that justify special consideration for taxation. Natural resources include a wide range of both depletable and reproducible resources. Reproducible resources can be replenished. Depletable but reproducible resources can be replaced, albeit not soon. But depletable and nonreproducible resources are irreparable losses.

Because they cannot be replenished, depletable resources generally are taxed somewhat differently than reproducible resources. While raising revenues is the foremost function of taxing both renewable and nonrenewable resources, depletable and slowly renewable resources also are taxed to conserve them. Severance taxes account for these myriad factors.

Severance taxes, therefore, are designed not only to generate revenues, but also to help slow the rate of natural resource depletion. For instance, if property with a valuable amount of timber is owned by a small producer, that producer may very well harvest it prematurely to reduce the assessed value of the land and thereby reduce the amount of property taxes paid. Such actions promote premature, and frequently unwise, harvesting of timber. If done on a massive scale, this would lead to a reduction in state revenues over a period of time.

Severance taxes are seen in some states as a ''new'' revenue source since historically they have not generated much money for most states. However, they have been around since the mid-1880s. Michigan enacted what was probably the first severance tax in this country in 1846, when it levied a special 4 percent tax on the value of smelter yields of copper and iron ore in lieu of local property taxes. In 1929, when oil and gas were found in significant quantities, the state imposed additional severance taxes on these products, also in lieu of local property taxes. Other early severance taxes were levied in Pennsylvania and Minnesota prior to 1900, and in Texas, West Virginia, Oklahoma, Louisiana, Kentucky, and Alabama before 1920.

TAX PHILOSOPHY

In most states, severance taxes are paid by producers for the privilege of extracting resources from the soil or water of the state. These taxes are based on the idea that marketable natural resources do not belong solely to producers, and that producers do not have the absolute right to exploit such resources because they belong to all citizens of the state, regardless of who owns the land on or in which resources are located. Thus, producers should legally be required to reimburse state residents for lost resources through severance taxes.

Severance taxes also came about as a reaction to difficulties experienced in assessing property taxes on lands possessing marketable natural resources. Obstacles encountered in assessing the realistic value of land with over- and underground natural resources, coupled with desires of state and local governments to derive revenues from such resources, led to the rapid adoption of severance taxes. (Since severance taxes are not normally considered property taxes, they are not subject to constitutional and statutory limitations applicable to property taxes—e.g., millage limits.)

States frequently—but not always—single out some natural resources for special taxation, partly because of special costs associated with their production (e.g., safety enforcement and environmental regulations) and partly because states believe that they have some degree of public ownership of these resources. Severance taxes are seldom levied to maximize efficient resource production, since such taxes are shaped in response to pressures of organized and unorganized interest groups which are benefited or hurt by the tax structures. Severance taxes, like other taxes, are created in the political arena by a variety of participants. States, accordingly, must ultimately balance the conflicting objectives of these groups.

To be sure, all taxes reduce returns of productive activities. However, lower taxes do not always result in increased productivity, especially when lower taxes lead to decreased spending for public infrastructure (e.g., transportation systems, education, and public services such as water and garbage collection) considered essential by businesses and industries that are deciding where to locate or expand. (See Chapter 8, which discusses taxes and economic development.) Failure to provide an adequate infrastructure can have a detrimental effect on the location or expansion of businesses and industries.

Some types of natural resource production rely on public spending more than others. The production of petroleum and natural gas, for example, demands comparatively few public expenditures, say, compared to coal, which relies heavily on public spending for roads, highways, and environmental program enforcement. Natural resource production is not the only business sector that utilizes publicly financed infrastructures. Retail stores rely on publicly financed streets, highways, and parking facilities. Manufacturing enterprises use streets, water and sewerage, and educational facilities.

Infrastructure costs frequently are used as a basis for taxing various natural resources. States, consequently, need to assess accurately costs associated with production as a basis for setting severance tax policies. When resource production imposes more costs than it pays, taxpayers in effect subsidize production. When infrastructure costs are computed in this manner, taxes also need to be sensitive to costs incurred after production has ceased. The severance of natural resources, for example, leads to reclamation costs. As production recedes, retraining and unemployment costs increase—at the same time revenues decrease.

Severance taxes must pay for the true costs of severing products from land or water. Of greatest significance are costs associated with providing government services to impacted areas; they are enormous, ranging from an array of reclamation projects to roads to water and sewerage. Social costs, too, are considerable and frequently immeasurable. Severance industries often employ transient workforces, and studies have shown that transient populations tend to have greater need for social and drug-related services which, to be sure, are expensive (Towe, 1981).

In recognition of these situations, some states dedicate at least a portion of severance revenues to trust funds established to compensate for the loss of nonrenewable (mineral) or slowly renewable (timber) resources. These funds provide money for infrastructure construction and economic diversification against the time when natural resources play out.

TRENDS IN SEVERANCE TAXATION

Revenues generated from severance taxes on timber and minerals amounted to $4.6 billion in 1990 (Tax Foundation, 1992:242). Exhibit 7.1 shows that, with the exception of the late 1970s and early 1980s, state reliance on these revenue sources has been decreasing since the 1960s.

Severance taxes by and large are not major revenue producers for state and local governments, accounting for slightly more than 1 percent of the operating budgets of most states. Fourteen states do not even levy any significant severance taxes. Exhibit 7.2 shows that of the thirty-six states levying severance taxes, Texas, Alaska, Louisiana, Oklahoma, New Mexico, and Wyoming receive the most revenues. Missouri, New Hampshire, Indiana, and Idaho raise negligible amounts of severance revenues. Obviously, Texas and Alaska are in unique positions with regard to taxation of oil and natural gas production. Their resource wealth, coupled with the amount of severance taxes raised, is sufficient to allow them to forgo reliance on other taxes (e.g., income taxes).

Severance taxes, as previously mentioned, are levied on marketable resources that are *severed* from the earth. The total amount of resources severed for production depends on the physical and geological characteristics of particular resources, thus making general trends difficult to estimate. As a result, taxes tend to be resource-specific, focusing mainly on the rate of extraction. Different taxes have different effects on extraction rates as well as affecting the point at which continued production is no longer economically viable. Exhibit 7.3 shows the theoretical impact of extractions on severance taxes.

The trend that stands out most sharply in the analysis of state and local taxation of natural resources is the great diversity in tax rates and bases among states that impose severance taxes. Exhibit 7.4 shows the different taxing units and unit values used, depending on types of producers taxed. Severance taxes, as illustrated in the exhibit, are concentrated in a few states, primarily in the southern and western sections of the country. They also are confined to a few products, basically timber, oil, coal, and metalliferous minerals.

Equitability of tax rates also varies considerably. The primary reason for this taxing diversity is that severance taxes generally are an accumulation of tax actions adopted over a period of time by a succession of government officials influenced by varying groups, and are not based on systematic analyses of tax policies.

TYPES OF SEVERANCE TAXES

Generally speaking, severance taxes are levied on resources as they are removed from land or water. These taxes normally are assessed on the value, volume, or quantity of resources severed. Translated into its simplest terms, this means that severance taxes are assessed either on a per unit or an ad valorem basis.

Exhibit 7.1
Severance Revenues as a Percentage of Total State Collections, 1950–1990

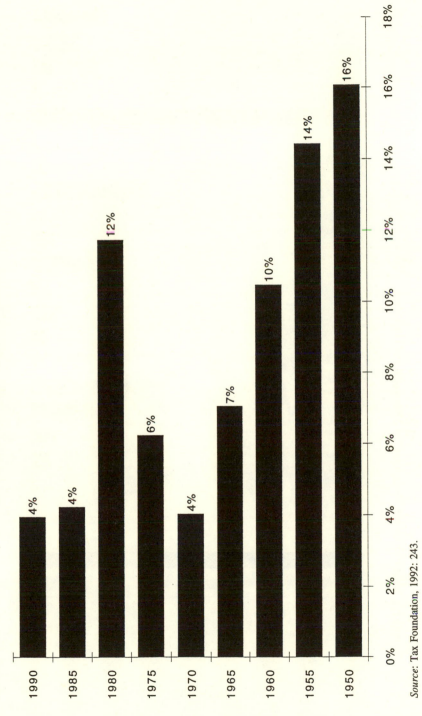

Source: Tax Foundation, 1992: 243.

Exhibit 7.2
States Generating Most Severance Revenues (in Thousands of Dollars)

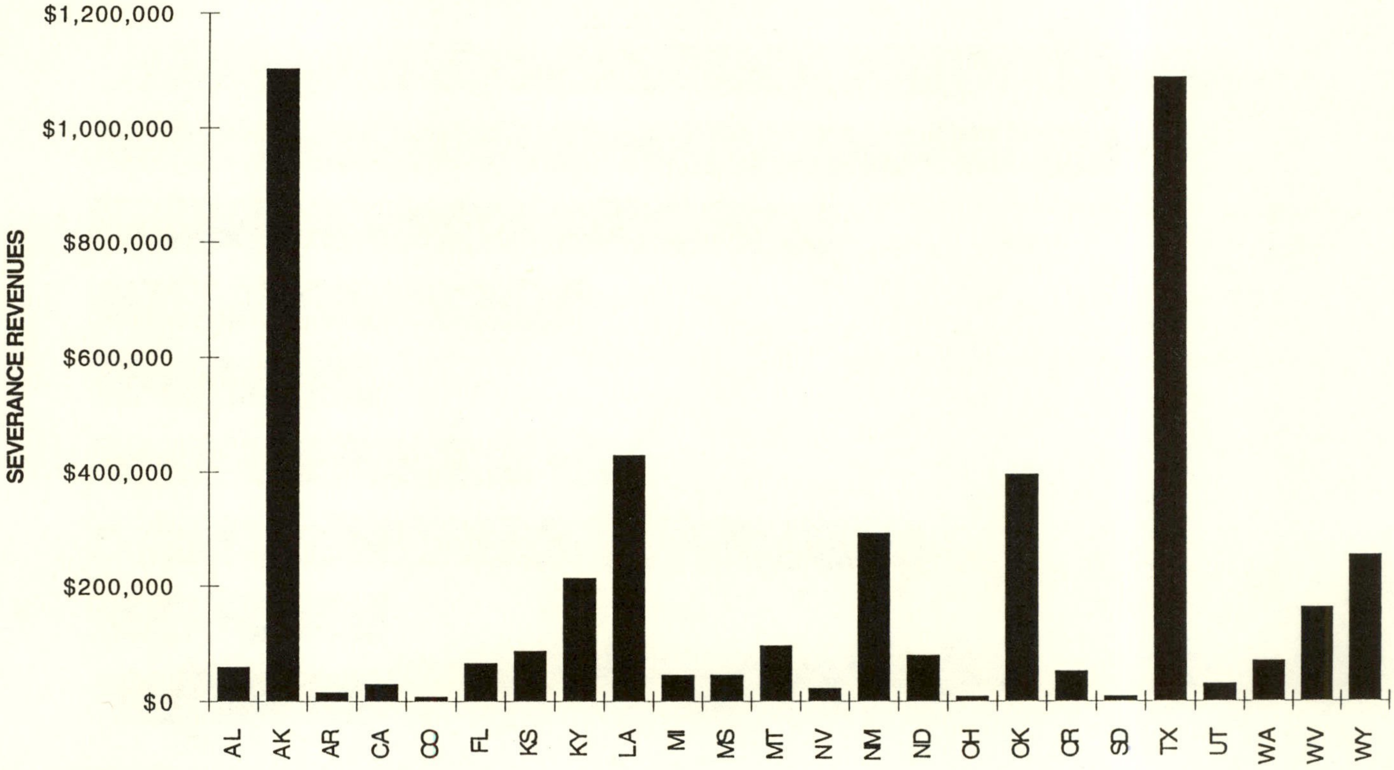

Source: U.S. Department of Commerce, 1992: 13.

Exhibit 7.3
Steps in the Processing of Minerals and Mineral Fuels Between Severance and Use of Consumer Goods

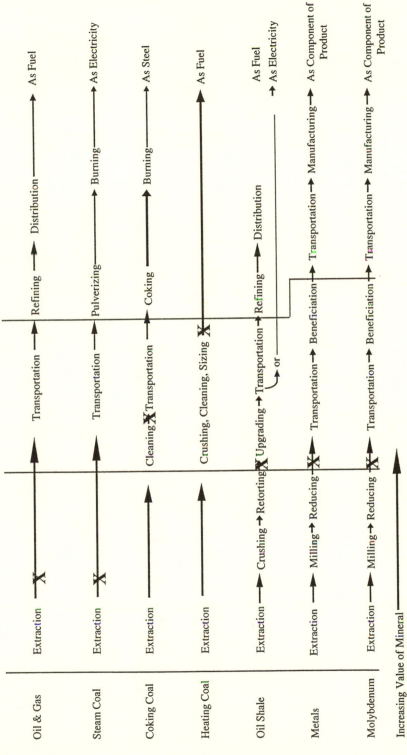

Increasing Value of Mineral ⟶
"X" Indicates Value of Mineral for Depletion Purposes

Source: Colorado Legislative Council, 1975: 22.

Exhibit 7.4
Basic State Severance Tax Rates and Bases, 1992

State	Product	Rate
Alabama	Iron ore	$.03 per ton
	Pine lumber	$.50 per 1,000 ft., $.75 per 1,000 ft. if sold as logs
	Hardwoods, cypress	$.30 per 1,000 ft., $.50 per 1,000 ft. if sold as logs
	Pulpwood, chemical wood, bolts	$.25 per cord (128 cubic feet)
	Pine ore mine props	$.75 per 1,000 ft.
	Hardwood ore mine props	$.50 per 1,000 ft.
	Piling and poles	$1.875 per 1,000 ft.
	Pulpwood chips	$.25 per cord (5,000 lbs.)
	Gum turpentine	$.15 per barrel (400 lbs.)
	Tarwood	$.125 per ton
	Cross ties	$.015 each
	Switch ties	$.025 each
	Other ties	$.125 each
	Oil and gas	10% of gross value of point of production
	Coal	$.335 per ton
	Lignite	$.20 per ton
Alaska	Salmon, canned at shore-based site	4.5% of value
	All other fish	3% of value
	Fish processed off shore	5% of value
	Oil	Greater of $.64 per barrel for old crude oil ($.80 for all other) or 15% of modified gross value
	Gas	Greater of $.64 per 1,000 cubic ft. (MCF) or 10% of modified gross value
Arizona	Minerals	2.5% of net severance base
	Timber	1.5% of value
Arkansas	Bauxite, barite, titanium ore, zinc, etc.	$.15 per ton
	Coal	$.10 per ton
	Iron ore, lignite	$.02 per ton
	Crushed stone, granite, sand, gravel, etc.	$.04 per ton
	Gypsum	$.015 per ton
	Timber products	$.178 per ton (pine); $.125 per ton (all other wood)
	Saltwater (used for production of bromine)	$2.45 per barrel
	Diamonds	5% of value
	Oil	5% of market value from wells producing 10 barrels per day or more; 4% if 10 barrels per day or less
	Gas	$.003 per MCF
California	Oil and gas	$0.025028 per barrel of oil and $0.025028 per MCF of gas

188

State	Mineral	Rate
Colorado	Metallic minerals	2.25% of gross income over $11 million
	Molybdenum ore	$.05 per ton
	Coal	$.36 per ton
	Oil shale	4% of market value
		2.13% of market value, gross income less than $25,000
		3.13% more than $25,000 but less than $100,000
		4.13% more than $100,000 but less than $300,000
Florida	Oil	8% of gross value; 5% of gross value for small well oil and tertiary oil; 12.5% additional for escaped oil
	Gas	$.126 per MCF
	Sulfur	$2.37 per ton
	Solid minerals	5% of market value, except phosphate rock ($1.57 per ton) and heavy minerals ($1.66 per ton)
Georgia	Phosphates	$1.00 per ton
Idaho	Ores	2% of net value
	Oil and gas	$.005 per barrel of oil or per 50,000 cubic feet of gas; additional 2% of market value
Illinois	Timber	4% of market value
Indiana	Oil and gas	1% of market value
Kansas	Oil and gas	8% of market value plus $.0135 per barrel of oil and $.0043 per MCF of gas
	Coal	$1.00 per ton
Kentucky	Oil and coal	4.5% of market value (minimum tax for coal is $.50 per ton severed)
	Other than coal or oil	4.5% of gross value less transportation expenses
Louisiana	Coal, other ores	$.10 per ton
	Lignite	$.12 per ton
	Gravel	$.06 per ton
	Marble	$.20 per ton
	Salt	$.06 per ton; $.005 per ton (for use in manufacturing)
	Sand, shells	$.06 per ton
	Stone	$.03 per ton
	Sulfur	$.92 per ton
	Timber grown on lands under reforestation contracts	6% of average stumpage market value
	Timber, other than virgin timber	5% of average stumpage market value (pulpwood); 2.25% (all other timber)
	Gas and natural gas liquids	$.10 per MCF
	Oil	12.5% of the higher of (1) gross receipts ICSS transportation expenses or (2) the posted field price
Maine	Minerals	Greater of the value of facilities and equipment multiplied by .005, the gross proceeds multiplied by .009
Maryland	Coal (open pit or strip mined)	$.09 per ton to state and $.06 per ton to county

189

Exhibit 7.4 (Continued)

State	Item	Rate
Michigan	Gas	6% of market value
	Oil	7.6% of market value; 5% of market value for stripper well crude oil and crude oil from marginal properties
Minnesota	Net proceeds from mining	2% of market value
	Taconite (iron sulphide and agglomerates)	$2.054 per ton ($.05 per ton for agglomerates)
	Semi-taconite and agglomerates	$.10 per ton ($.05 per ton for agglomerates)
Mississippi	Oil and gas	6% of market value plus $.035 per barrel of oil and $.004 per MCF of gas
	Saw logs; pine and soft wood	$1.00 per 1,000 ft.
	Saw logs; hardwood	$.75 per 1,000 ft.
	Lumber, including cross ties	$.75 per 1,000 ft.
	Poles, pilings, posts	$.036 per cubic ft.
	Pulpwood, except pine	$.225 per cord
	Pulpwood, pine	$.30 per cord
	Stumpwood or other distillates	$.25 per ton
	Crude gum turpentine	$.30 per barrel
	Salt	3% of market value
	All other timber products	$.75 per 1,000 feet or $.375 per cord
Missouri	Coal (surface mined)	$.45 per ton for the first 50,000 tons; $.30 per ton for next 50,000 tons
Montana	Coal—under 7,000 BTU/lb.	10% of market value (surface mined); 3% of market value (underground mined)
	Coal—over 7,000 BTU/lb.	15% of market value (surface mined); 4% of market value (underground mined)
	Metalliferous minerals	1.81% of market value over $250,000
	Gold, silver, and platinum	1.6% of market value over $250,000
	Oil	5.2% of market value
	Gas	2.85% of market value
	Micaceous minerals	$.05 per ton
	Cement	$.22 per ton; $.05 per ton for cement products, plaster, gypsum, or gypsum products
Nebraska	Oil and gas	3.35% of market value (2.35% from wells producing less than 10 barrels per day)
	Uranium	2% of market value over $5,000,000
Nevada	Minerals (excluding sand, gravel, and water)	2% if less than 10% of gross proceeds
		2.5% more than 10% but less than 18%
		3% more than 18% but less than 26%
		3.5% more than 26% but less than 34%
		4% more than 34% but less than 42%
		4.5% more than 42% but less than 50%o
		5% if greater than 50--o
	Royalties	5%
New Hampshire	Refine petroleum product	0.10%

190

State	Material	Rate
New Mexico	Potash	3% of market value
	Copper	1.25% of market value
	Molybdenum	0.25% of market value
	All other minerals	0.875% of market value
	Uranium ore	3.68% of market value
	Coal	$1.17 per ton (surface mined); $1.13 per ton (underground mined)
	Timber	5% of market value
	Oil and gas	7.08% of market value
	Gold and silver	0.2% of market value
North Carolina	Softwood saw timber, veneer logs, and bolts	$.50 per 1,000 ft.
	Hardwood saw timber, veneer logs, and bolts	$.40 per 1,000 ft.
	Softwood pulpwood, and other products	$.20 per cord
	Hardwood pulpwood, and other products	$.12 per cord
North Dakota	Oil	11.5% of market value
	Gas	$.0407 per MCF
	Coal	$.77 per ton
Ohio	Coal	$.08 per ton
	Salt	$.04 per ton
	Limestone, dolomite, sand, and gravel	$.02 per ton
	Clay, sandstone, shale, gypsum, and quartzite	$.01 per ton
	Oil	$.10 per barrel
	Gas	$.025 per MCF
Oklahoma	Asphalt, ores of lead, zinc, gold, silver, or copper	0.75% of market value
	Uranium	5% of market value
	Oil and gas	7.085% of market value
Oregon	Oil and gas	6% of market value
	Forest products	$1.64 per 1,000 ft. (more than 25,000 ft.)
South Dakota	Energy minerals	4.74% of market value
	Gold and silver	2% of gross receipts for the first $50 million and 1% over $50 million plus 8% of net profits from sale or royalties from sale of these metals
Tennessee	Oil and gas	3% of market value
	Coal	$.20 per ton
Texas	Cement	$.55 per ton
	Sulfur	$1.03 per ton
	Gas	7.5% of market value plus $.00077 per barrel
	Oil	The greater of 4.6% of market value or 4.6 per barrel plus $.005 per barrel

Exhibit 7.4 (Continued)

State	Resource	Rate
Utah	Gas	3.2% of value up to and including the first $1.50 per MCF and 5.2% over $1.50 per MCF
	Oil	3.2% of value up to and including the first $13 per barrel and 5.2% over $13 per barrel
	Metalliferous minerals	2.6% of market value above $50,000
Virginia	Coal	$.055 per ton (surface mined); $.045 per ton (deep mined)
	Pine lumber	$1.15 per 1,000 ft.
	Hardwood, cypress, and all other	$.225 per 1,000 ft.
	Pulpwood, chemical wood, etc.	$.475 per cord (pine); $.1125 per cord (all other)
	Chips manufactured from round wood	$.00986 per 100 lbs. (pine); $.00234 per 100 lb. (all other)
	Railroad ties	$.038 each (pine); $.01 each (all other)
	Lumber used in mines	$1.045 per 1,000 ft. (pine); $.2475 per 1,000 ft. (all other)
	Keg staves (pine)	$.038 per 400 inch bundle
	Keg staves (all other)	$.015 per 400 inch bundle
Washington	Uranium and thorium	$.05 per pound
	Chinook, coho, chum salmon and anadromous	5% of market value
	Pink and sockeye salmon	3% of market value
	Oysters	0.07% of market value
	Other food fish and shell fish	2% of market value
West Virginia	Coal	5% of market value
	Limestone or sandstone	4% of market value
	Timber	3.22% of market value
	Sand, gravel, other minerals	5% of market value
	Oil	5% of market value
	Natural gas	5% of market value
	All other	4% of market value
Wisconsin	Metalliferous minerals	3% of net proceeds greater than $250,000 but less than $5,000,000
		7% greater than $5,000,000 but less than $10,000,000
		10% greater than $10,000,000 but less than $15,000,000
		13% greater than $15,000,000 but less than $20,000,000
		14% greater than $20,000,000 but less than $25,000,000
		15% greater than $25,000,000
	Oil and gas	7% of market value
Wyoming	Oil and gas	0.4% of market value
	Uranium	5.5% of market value
	Underground coal	7.25% of market value
	Surface coal	9.5% of market value

Source: ACIR, 1993: 134–139.

Per unit production taxes, which are assessed on the amount of volume sold (e.g., barrel, ton, or cubic foot) rather than on the sale price, place a heavier tax burden on the producer of low quality marketable natural resource products than they do on the producer of high quality products. Taxes on units seldom make allowances for differences in the quality of the product. Low quality units may be worth less than high quality units, but producers still pay the same tax rates on the same bases. Low quality producers, as a result, absorb a larger percentage of the tax burden than do producers of high quality units. However, it should be noted that the tax burden on all qualities of severed products decreases as the price increases. In fact, the effective tax rate actually decreases as the price, and thus the producer's ability to pay, increases. In other words, per unit taxes do not respond automatically to price changes.

To overcome shortcomings of per unit taxes, states generally use ad valorem yield levies, usually gross or net production taxes. These taxes on the value of units correct for differences in the quality of products. Producers of natural resources that are worth less pay fewer taxes on identical production units. Further, these taxes embody the same percentage of the price of both low and high quality products. That is, the amount of taxes paid per unit increases as price (and ostensibly quality) increases. Conversely, tax revenues decrease as price and quality decrease.

As shown in Exhibit 7.4, *gross production taxes* are the most widely used type of severance tax. These taxes are based on the value of resource production and thus vary directly with the value of the commodity produced. Gross production taxes, therefore, are more responsive to prices, which often change rapidly (especially for minerals), and are more equitable for both the producer and the state. In addition, these taxes do not place a heavier burden on the producer of low quality products.

Net production taxes are similar to gross production taxes except that predetermined production expenses are deducted from gross revenues before taxes are computed. Deductible expenses normally include all production costs. They also may incorporate reclamation costs to encourage reclamation projects and interest expenses to promote borrowing for acquiring new capital assets.

Deductions discriminate against nondeductible expenses and guide spending patterns. Reclamation deductions, for instance, may cause producers to spend more money on such projects rather than on producing products that lead to higher outputs. Interest deductions may encourage the purchase of new capital assets, while decreasing labor costs and increasing unemployment. Moreover, when capital goods are purchased outside the state, deductions have the effect of transferring public funds to private, out-of-state companies. As a result, the state receives fewer tax dollars, while at the same time unemployment increases.

In some cases, a net production tax can be equivalent to a flat rate corporate income tax. As net income increases, the amount of tax paid also increases—a direct reflection of the producer's ability to pay. On the negative side, a net production tax seemingly rewards the inefficient producer at the expense of the efficient producer.

TAX EXPORTING

States attempt to export taxes whenever possible, that is, to shift the burden of taxation to those beyond their borders. Placing taxes on products that are destined largely for consumers in other states is seen as an economically and politically popular way of funding public goods and services for in-state residents without adding to their tax burdens. New York, for example, imposes a transfer tax on each transaction on the New York Stock Exchange. Florida derives nearly 40 percent of its revenues from sales taxes, paid in large part by visitors from outside the state. Approximately 80 percent of Kentucky's coal is sold to out-of-state electric utilities, so its severance taxes are borne predominantly by electricity consumers in other states. Putting a tax on severed, marketable natural resources that are sold principally to consumers outside the state does not necessarily mean that the full burden of a severance tax is shifted to consumers, however.

Several crucial factors contribute to a state's ability to export severance taxes. One is low in-state consumption of taxed resources. If most consumers reside outside the state, taxes can be readily and easily shifted to these out-of-state consumers. Conversely, if most consumers live inside the state, taxes hardly can be exported.

The ability to export severance taxes depends on a variety of factors, including market structure, taxing jurisdiction, elasticity of demand, supply of the taxed product, and location of the severing rights of the taxed product. In states unable or unwilling to export severance taxes, the tax burden is borne by their residents in the form of subsidies and/or by producers and their employees in the form of reduced profits and wages, respectively.

Two other interrelated factors affecting tax exporting are the price sensitivity of consumers and the availability of adequate substitutes. The extent to which out-of-state consumers continue to buy marketable natural resources depends on the price of the products, which are increased slightly by severance taxes passed on to consumers. Available evidence, however, suggests that only in exceptional circumstances do severance taxes affect the market price of severed resources.

Availability of substitutes seems to be a more inhibiting factor affecting tax exporting. If out-of-state consumers cannot obtain resources from producers in other states, or cannot substitute another resource, taxes can be easily exported.

These observations pertain to a competitive marketplace and thus must be modified in cases where few states control a dominant portion of a marketable resource. In such a situation these states can act together to tax producers, thereby making it unprofitable to purchase from one state instead of another. As the number of controlling states increases, such coalitions become more and more unstable because a variety of economic interests come into play.

Exhibit 7.5 displays severance revenues as a percentage of total state revenues. Severance taxes provide over 71 percent of Alaska's revenues, while that figure is almost 42 percent in Wyoming. Severance revenues represent at least 10 percent of total revenues in five other states. In these states severance revenues clearly exceed the amount necessary to compensate the states for any direct public costs. Severance taxes in these states, therefore, are undoubtedly exported to other states.

SEVERANCE TAX DISCRIMINATION

Tax exporting invariably creates severance tax discrimination among states. These disparities exist primarily because only a few states possess an abundance of marketable natural resources, and they tend to export some, if not all, of their severance taxes. For example, Montana's severance tax on all coal over 7,000 BTUs is 20 percent of the market value of surface mined coal and 4 percent of the market value of underground mined coal. Since over 90 percent of the coal mined in Montana is exported to midwestern states and Texas, these states are paying many of Montana's bills. (By contrast, 100 percent of North Dakota's coal is used inside the state.) Obviously, consumers outside Montana think the state's severance taxes are too high and should be reduced. This resentment can lead to serious economic conflict.

Tax dollars that flow into states rich in natural resources allow them either to reduce taxes on income, capital, sales, or property, or to increase the amount spent on public goods and services. Specifically, the revenues can be used to expand public services such as schools, health care, transportation, or social services, to name a few. Or they may be used to reduce taxes or offset tax increases. The problem, however, is that a few states benefit from these taxes, while consumers in other states ultimately pay them.

The primary question that often arises under such circumstances is, Should states with abundant marketable natural resources be allowed to generate revenues that exceed direct and indirect economic, social, and environmental costs? The answer is based on the answer to another question: Who shares ownership with producers? Is it the state or the country? If the state shares ownership, it should be free to set whatever tax rates and bases the marketplace will bear. On the other hand, if the country shares ownership, the state's tax rates and bases should be limited by Congress. Unfortunately, answers to these two questions have never been legally or philosophically resolved.

Inasmuch as severance taxes allocate differential burdens on various income groups and geographical regions, they have become a national issue, resulting in court cases concerning interstate tax discrimination. In addition, in the early 1980s various bills were introduced in Congress to limit the combined severance taxes to no more than 12.5 percent of a product's value. So far states are able to continue tax exporting practices.

This lack of resolve has led to consumer fears that states with abundant natural

Exhibit 7.5
Severance Revenues as a Percentage of Total Revenues

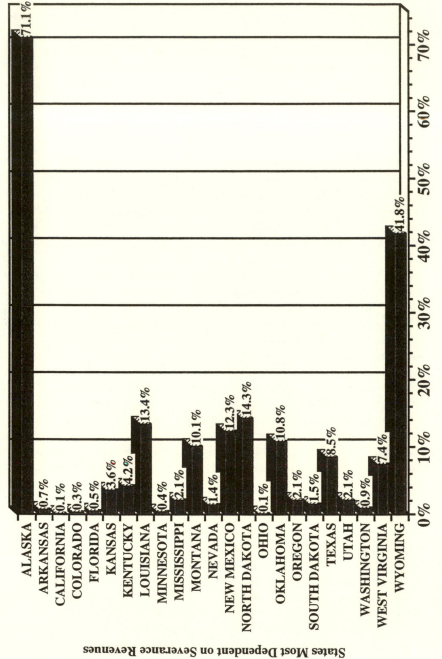

Source: U.S. Department of Commerce, 1992: 3.

resources will continually increase their severance taxes to an unreasonable level, further increasing fiscal discrepancies among states. These concerns are not based on economic reality, however. As mentioned earlier, states can successfully export severance taxes only when they are one of a few producers of marketable natural resources. Yet, these states cannot freely raise severance taxes to any level and still sell products. Consumers, after all, can purchase products from other states or even other countries—as some states are doing. Thus, the possibility of increasing severance tax discrimination is not as likely as some consumers' anxieties would warrant.

Earmarking

Most states earmark severance revenues to help defray costs associated with production. One of the major questions related to earmarking severance revenues, therefore, is how to distribute revenues. In Arkansas, for instance, 75 percent of the timber revenues are assigned to the state's local fund and 25 percent to counties. Of that 75 percent, 97 percent is distributed to the Forestry Commission. Montana's education trust fund allocates money to individual schools and other local infrastructure needs. Still other states distribute funds to research, regulation, reclamation, and community development projects. Mineral lands, in particular, earmark a substantial proportion of severance revenues for reclamation, since lands which are not adequately reclaimed degrade the quality of the environment, damage the beneficial use of land and water, and endanger the health and safety of the public. These negative impacts in turn lead to decreases in economic activity that often mean decreases in state revenues.

Distribution of severance revenues generated from timber is arguably somewhat different. The heavy loads of timber trucks cause considerable damage to local, especially county, roads. It therefore seems reasonable to increase the earmarking of these funds to local governments for road maintenance and repair.

Of the states that impose severance taxes, twenty-one designate at least a portion of them for specific purposes. Exhibit 7.6 shows that fourteen states earmark at least part of severance revenues for local government, seven for education, and five for conservation programs.

Since severance taxes account for only a small percentage of state revenues, increasing local government shares from, say, 25 percent to 50 percent could have a minimal effect on state budgets, but an enormous impact on local government revenues and expenditures. However, any amount of money taken from the general fund is likely to compound already existing fiscal problems.

Severance Tax Administration

Many agencies are directly and indirectly involved in state and local severance tax administration. Generally speaking, the agencies most immediately involved are state and local tax administrators expressly responsible for the taxation of

Exhibit 7.6
Earmarked Severance Taxes

SEVERANCE

Local Government	14	Alabama, Alaska, Arkansas, Colorado, Kansas, Louisiana, Minnesota, Mississippi, North Dakota, Oklahoma, South Dakota, Tennessee, Washington, West Virginia
Education	7	Kansas, Minnesota, Montana, Nebraska, Oklahoma, Oregon, Texas
Highways/mass transit	1	Montana
Health/welfare/human services	0	
Pensions	1	Oklahoma
Conservations	5	Alabama, Arkansas, Montana, Oregon, Wisconsin
Debt service/building funds	1	New Mexico
Regulation	2	New Mexico, Texas
Other	9	Alaska, Arkansas, Minnesota, Montana, Nebraska, North Dakota, Ohio, Oklahoma, Oregon

Source: Fabricius and Snell, 1990: 54.

severed resources. More specifically, local assessors are accountable for land valuation, and state revenue departments have primary responsibility for severance tax administration.

After severance taxes have been determined, the values are given to mill or mine operators, who collect taxes from producers at the time resources are delivered. This collection process is relatively efficient and cost-effective. It depends solely on mutual cooperation among state and local governments and producers of marketable resources.

TIMBER TAXES

Relatively little interest was shown in taxing timber before World War II. After the war, however, state and local demands for more revenues, coupled with rapid increases in timber values, led to expanded interest in the taxation of timber. This interest resulted in new alternatives to property taxes, one of which was severance taxes. (Since property taxes are covered in Chapter 6, they will not be discussed in detail here.)

Suffice it to say that while farmland crops bring in annual incomes to landowners, timberland owners have to pay taxes for many years (at least twenty) before they realize profits. Such landowners receive no regular income from the land until timber is cut. The speculative nature of timber growing (e.g., fires, insects, diseases, and value of timber at harvest time) also means that income generated is unpredictable. Additionally, property taxes sometimes encourage premature cutting, since these taxes *force* timberland owners to harvest early to minimize tax liabilities.

Timberland needs to be assessed on its use rather than its market value. This use value should be related to the productivity of the land. Productive capacity simply means that taxes are assessed on the land according to its ability to grow timber. In practice, however, it is extremely difficult to figure out how much timber land is capable of producing. These types of assessment practices, therefore, are still evolving in many states in order to implement more equitable tax bases.

Understanding severance taxes requires conceptually separating land and timber, even though land takes on a value because it has productive capacity. Timberland assessments require analyzing a sophisticated set of factors. Assessors ascertain the quality of the land, its accessibility, the type and value of timber the land is capable of growing, and the expenses involved in growing the timber. Other key factors affecting property taxes are the density of the timber stands and the cost incurred during the period of time between assessment and harvesting. These sophisticated assessments characteristically take place at intervals of no less than four years.

Timberland property taxes are based not only on these factors, but also on the age of the timber. Generally, timber is divided into three age classes. Reproductive timber is under twelve inches in diameter. These trees frequently are exempt from property tax bases, unless they are harvested—at which point the regular timber tax applies. The second category of timber consists of young growth trees—timber over twelve inches in diameter but not over a specified, say ninety years. Finally, old growth timber consists of trees over a specified age, again, say ninety years old.

Timberland, then, is subject to prevailing property taxes, while the timber is not taxed until harvested. In a sense, this separation represents a compromise between general property taxes and income taxes.

Timber Production

Exhibit 7.7 shows that the total value of timber harvested in the United States, and hence timber severance taxes, have been decreasing steadily since 1989. The most dramatic decrease, as displayed in Exhibit 7.8, has been in the production of softwoods, even though softwoods take less time to reproduce than

Exhibit 7.7
Total Value of Timber Cut

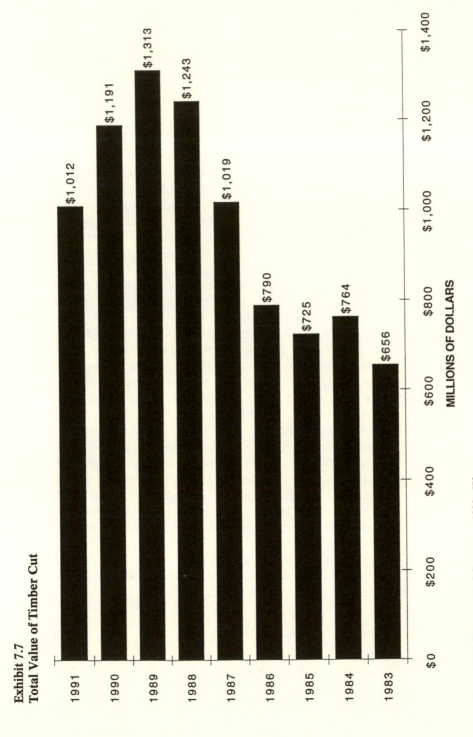

Source: U.S. Department of Commerce, 1993: 678.

Exhibit 7.8
Timber Production by Kind of Wood

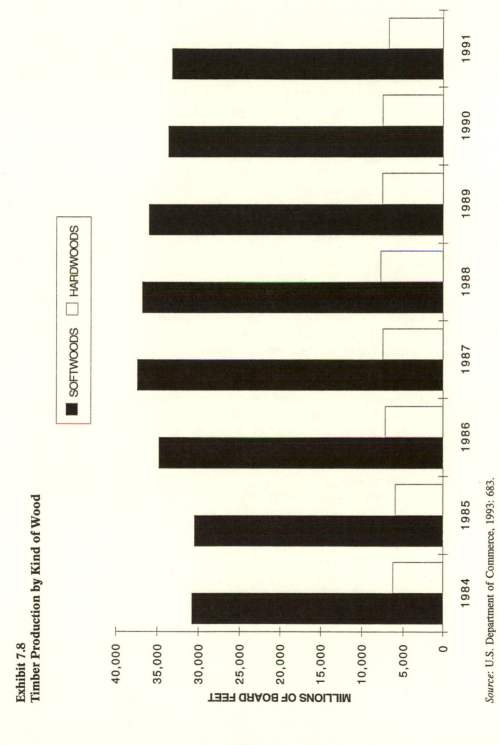

Source: U.S. Department of Commerce, 1993: 683.

201

hardwoods. Nevertheless, severance taxes on softwoods are generating much more money than are taxes on hardwoods.

As displayed in Exhibit 7.9, per capita consumption of timber products decreased from the early to late 1980s. Should 1988 be a bubble year and this decline continue, severance taxes on timber also may decrease and adversely affect those states which derive a sizable amount of money from timber taxes.

As mentioned earlier, not all states benefit equally from severance taxes on timber. Exhibit 7.10 shows that Washington, Oregon, and California generate more timber severance taxes than other timber producing states. Exhibit 7.11 illustrates that the Western states as a group produce more timber than do other sections of the country. However, since approximately 1987, Southern states have been expanding their timber production as Western states' timber production decreases. (Northern states do not generate much money from severance taxes on timber.)

Economic Strategy

Basic economic strategy of producers revolves around whether to cut timber selectively for continued income or to harvest all timber rapidly, liquidate speedily, and replant for future income. (The strategy selected will, of course, affect timber revenues.) The distinguishing economic feature of the latter choice is the great length of time required for timber to mature, although the time varies with the kinds of trees planted, the quality of the soil, the amount of rainfall, and the length of the growing season.

Given the length of time needed for maturation, many things can negatively affect timber harvesting and profits, which in turn influence timber revenues. Trees can be damaged or destroyed by insects, wind, and fire. Some trees will grow slower than anticipated. Finally, market conditions may change. The price of lumber may decline or not increase as forecasted, or interest rates may increase dramatically.

Moreover, timber taxes, like other severance taxes, are seldom paid until cash inflows from the sale of timber products are realized. Accordingly, taxing jurisdictions are not paid until some time after harvest periods, and they seldom know how much money they will realize in any given year because of the uncertainty of how much timber will be cut in that year. Timber revenues, therefore, may be quite unstable. State and local governments, as a result, cannot depend on timber taxes as a necessary revenue source.

Rates

Severance tax rates vary among states and types of timber products. As mentioned earlier, timber taxes, like most other severance taxes, are assessed on either a per unit or an ad valorem basis. Exhibit 7.4 shows that Alabama, for example, levies a per unit tax of 25 cents per cord on pulpwood chips and 50

Exhibit 7.9
Per Capita Consumption of Timber Products

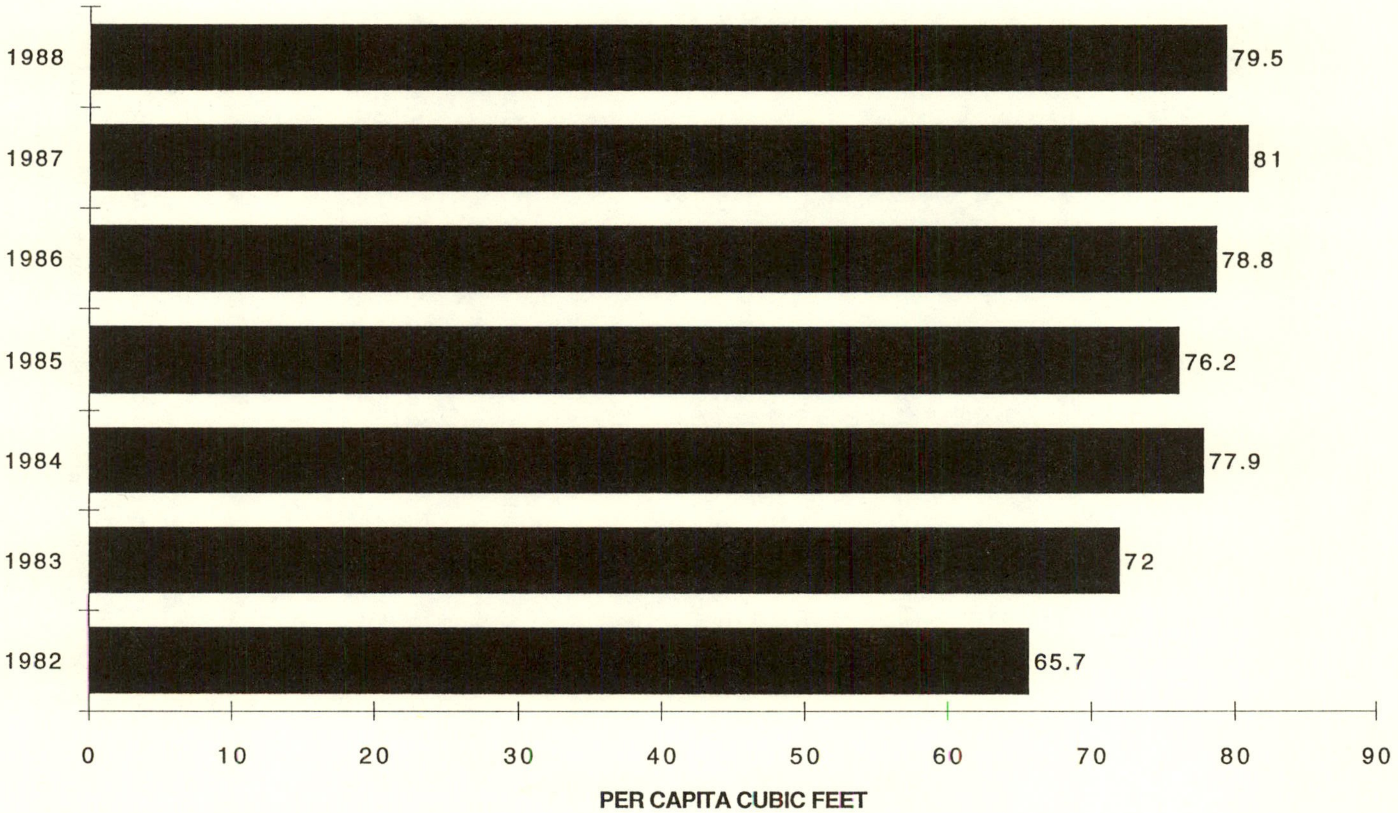

Year	Per Capita Cubic Feet
1988	79.5
1987	81
1986	78.8
1985	76.2
1984	77.9
1983	72
1982	65.7

PER CAPITA CUBIC FEET

Source: U.S. Department of Commerce, 1993: 681.

Exhibit 7.10
Timber Data, 1990, in Thousands of Dollars, States with over
15 Million Acres

	SEVERANCE	FEES	SEVERANCE TAXES AND FEES	ACREAGE
AL	$5,382	$2,978	$8,360	21,900,000
AK	$0	$7,755	$7,755	129,000,000
AZ	$0	$0	$0	19,900,000
AR	$3,547	$217	$3,764	17,247,000
CA	$22,588	$1,731	$24,310	32,500,000
CO	$0	$1,959	$1,959	21,417,000
FL	$9,467	$5,736	$15,203	14,980,000
GA	$0	$3,941	$3,941	24,100,000
ID	$206	$21,954	$22,160	20,200,000
LA	$4,712	$1,306	$6,018	13,883,000
ME	$0	$1,295	$1,295	17,600,000
MI	$0	$9,679	$9,679	18,220,000
MN	$0	$5,004	$5,004	16,700,000
MS	$3,660	$1,853	$5,513	16,980,000
MT	$0	$1,549	$1,549	22,500,000
NM	$0	$0	$0	19,019,000
NY	$0	$0	$0	18,500,000
NC	$1,540	$2,419	$3,959	18,710,000
OR	$51,156	$38,879	$90,035	27,362,000
PA	$0	$7,587	$7,587	16,800,000
VA	$1,458	$361	$1,819	15,438,000
WA	$69,257	$224,075	$293,332	16,842,000
WI	$0	$2,863	$2,863	15,351,000
TOTAL	$172,973	$343,141	$516,114	555,149,000

Source: Compiled by the Office of Tax Research, State of Arkansas, 1993.

cents per 1,000 feet on pine lumber. Louisiana, on the other hand, assesses producers an ad valorem tax of 6 percent on the average stumpage market value of pine timber.

If timber taxes are not assessed against a fixed quantity of the resource being extracted (per unit tax), the ad valorem tax rates apply to all timber products at 100 percent of their retail value at the time of harvesting, regardless of timber category.

MINERAL TAXES

Marketable mineral resources have been extracted since consumers were found for organic and inorganic matter. The amounts and types of minerals severed from the land depended then, as now, on demand, value, and cost of extraction. States, and to some extent local governments, always have regarded all marketable minerals as a special category of assets subject to taxes upon their extraction from land.

Exhibit 7.11
Timber Production by Region

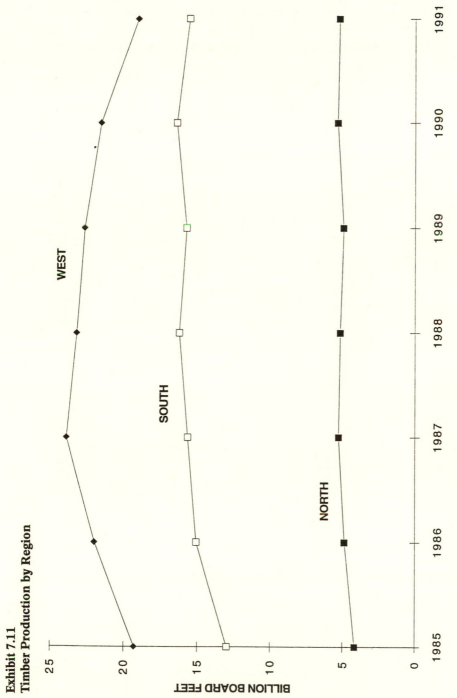

BILLION BOARD FEET

WEST

SOUTH

NORTH

25
20
15
10
5
0

1985   1986   1987   1988   1989   1990   1991

Source: U.S. Department of Commerce, 1993: 683.

Even though minerals are discussed collectively in this chapter, one should keep in mind that they essentially embody marketable fuels and metallic and nonmetallic ores. Mineral fuels are petroleum, natural gas, natural gas liquids, and coal. Metallic ores consist of elements such as aluminum, vanadium, and zinc, to name a few. Nonmetallic minerals are those used primarily in chemical and construction industries: they include clays, lime, phosphate, stone, sand and gravel, abrasive stone, cement, gypsum, and sulfur.

Severance revenues on minerals rose rather rapidly during the energy boom of the 1970s, as increased fuel prices boosted the values of energy-related minerals. This rapid increase influenced some states to expand tax bases and boost rates. (Nonfuel minerals did not experience a corresponding increase in values.) By the mid-1980s world fuel prices moderated, and the demand for and value of such minerals declined markedly.

As the value of mineral production began to fall because of the downward pressure on prices, state severance tax revenues also began to slump. A drop in the value of nonfuel minerals exacerbated this downswing. Recovery to 1970 levels is unlikely in the near future since mineral tax revenues are not expected to turn around soon, given the current state of severance tax structures.

Since property taxes are discussed more fully in Chapter 6, suffice it to say that the values of mineral lands are as difficult to assess as the values of timberlands. Land valuation depends on thickness of mineral seams, quality of minerals, cost of mining and transportation. With the aid of experts capable of measuring the quality and quantity of minerals by sample drilling, states can assess the value of mineral lands. Nonetheless, mineral values, and therefore the values of mineral lands, vary over time.

Furthermore, unlike timberlands, which can produce renewable resources, mineral lands cannot. Therefore, once minerals are taken from the land, the land is forever devalued. The assessed value of the land declines at a rate corresponding to the value of the minerals taken from the land, until eventually the minerals are economically irrecoverable.

The fundamental policy question is, Will tax policies hasten the removal of minerals from the land? Instead of discouraging the mining of minerals, general property taxes may have the opposite effect, encouraging mineral land owners to mine out from under the taxes. When property taxes stimulate production, they tend to depress rather than increase prices. This process in turn stimulates demand, which increases mining activities. To check production, states have come to rely on severance taxes instead of property taxes on mineral lands because severance taxes tend to be shifted to consumers, thereby cutting down on demand and thus conserving marketable mineral resources.

Mineral Production

Not all states benefit equally from severance taxes on minerals. Severance taxes are most prevalent in energy-producing states, where they account for an important share of the total tax revenues. Exhibit 7.12 shows which states generated the most severance revenues in 1990 from petroleum, natural gas, coal, and other metallic and nonmetallic minerals. Alaska, Texas, Louisiana, and Oklahoma produce the most revenues from oil and natural gas. Kentucky and West Virginia generate a substantial amount from coal. And Wyoming and Florida raise the most revenues from a variety of other minerals.

Exhibit 7.13 suggests that the value of oil and gas production in the United States—and hence mineral severance revenues—decreased between 1983 and 1986. Their production values have been slowly increasing since then. Coal and metal production have leveled off since 1983. The most noticeable increase has been in the value of nonmetal production (excluding oil, natural gas, and coal). Should this trend continue, it may affect those states which derive a considerable amount of money from severance taxes on minerals.

Mineral production has a history of boom and bust. As a result, severance revenues have reflected these patterns. Today, the bulk of severance revenues is generated by energy-related minerals. Until alternative fuels are marketed on a widespread basis, these severed minerals will continue to yield the most revenues. New technologies, though, offer potential for increasing severance revenues. Coal liquefaction processes, for example, are being developed; they combine coal under high pressure and temperatures with hydrogen-bearing substances to create synthetic fuels.

Economic Strategy

Producers' basic economic strategy gravitates around encouraging investment and development. High taxation of minerals, some contend, discourages investment and development. The extent to which severance taxes deter investment and development depends in large part on whether they are imposed on costs (gross) or surpluses (net). Theoretically, taxes imposed on producers will not hinder production as long as minerals are taxed less than 100 percent. In practice, however, producers have costs connected with severing marketable resources, and these costs obviously need to be deducted before taxes are assessed. Otherwise, producers will not have incentives to produce. Mining is a business that requires extensive outlays to *discover* the existence of minerals. Consequently, only the net value, some argue, should be taxed.

It is clear, therefore, that taxing net surpluses does not discourage production, while taxing gross surpluses may dissuade producers. Notwithstanding, difficulties are encountered in determining elements of necessary cost. Taxing minerals involves framing and administering laws that tax surpluses rather than costs.

Rates

Severance taxes on minerals usually are levied on either a per unit or an ad valorem basis and are assessed on producers. With the exception of coal taxes,

Exhibit 7.12
States Generating Most Mineral Severance Revenues, 1990

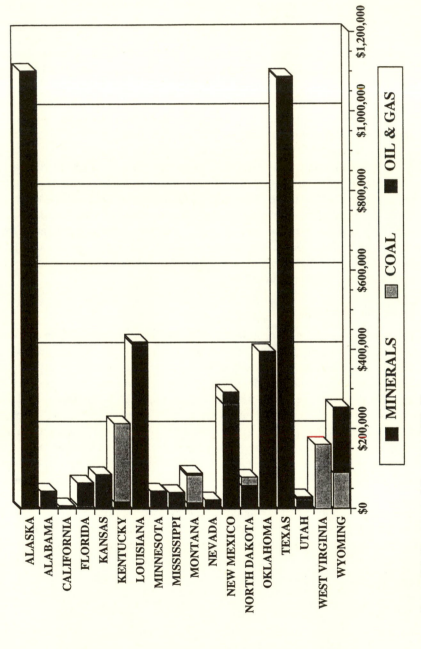

Source: U.S. Department of Commerce, 1992: 10.

Exhibit 7.13
Mining Production by Type of Minerals

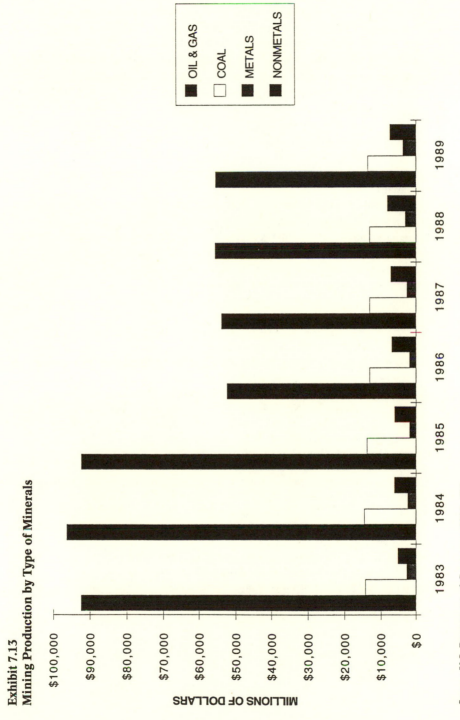

Source: U.S. Department of Commerce, 1993: 694.

209

which tend to be per unit taxes, most severance mineral taxes are levied on a fixed percentage of the market value of the extracted minerals. Some states tax the gross value of the mined minerals, while others tax net proceeds.

Exhibit 7.4 shows that Texas levies a 4.2 percent tax on the market value of oil and natural gas. North Dakota, on the other hand, assesses producers 77 cents per ton of coal. Remember that revenues based on units depend only on the quantity of mineral mined, whereas ad valorem taxes are based on a percentage of either gross or net value of mined minerals. Consequently, these ad valorem revenues vary with both the price and quantity of extracted minerals. Some states that levy per unit taxes—such as North Dakota and Minnesota— tie their unit-based severance taxes to price indexes in order to benefit from substantial price increases.

Though minor revenue sources, severance taxes offer the potential for generating additional governmental dollars. As state and local governments become increasingly interested in raising money from narrow-based taxes, severance taxes become appealing because at least a portion of the taxes are exported and paid by residents of other states or countries. Moreover, that taxation of severed resources not only raises revenues, but it also helps decrease the rate of exploitation.

REFERENCES

Advisory Commission on Intergovernmental Relations (ACIR) (1993). *Significant Features of Fiscal Federalism*. Vol. 2. Washington, D.C.: ACIR.

Colorado Legislative Council (1975). *Mineral Taxation*. Denver: Colorado Legislative Council, November, No. 214.

Commerce Clearing House (1992). *State Tax Guide: All States*. Chicago: Commerce Clearing House.

Fabricius, Martha, and Ronald Snell (1990). *Earmarking State Taxes*. Washington, D.C.: National Conference of State Legislatures.

Tax Foundation (1992). *Facts and Figures on Government Finance*. Washington, D.C.: Tax Foundation.

Towe, Thomas (1981). "Should the United States Limit State Severance Taxes?—No." *Fiscal Disparities*, Hearing before the Subcommittee on Intergovernmental Relations, July 15.

U.S. Department of Commerce, Bureau of the Census (1992). *State Government Tax Collections*. Washington, D.C.: Bureau of the Census.

——— (1993). *Statistical Abstract of the United States, 1993*. Washington, D.C.: Bureau of the Census.

8

Taxes and
Economic Development

One of the means of encouraging economic development most often mentioned in the popular press is state and local tax incentives. The press, and to a large extent the general public, presume that tax incentives have a significant and fundamental influence on business site selection decisions. This belief may explain the popularity over the last decade and a half of free enterprise zones and other tax incentive–based programs in political speeches and in economic development–related legislation, despite numerous studies showing that tax incentives are not very effective in stimulating economic development. Indeed, notwithstanding their evident popularity in the economic development literature, tax incentives are generally considered to have marginal influence at best on business site selection decisions as well as on other aspects of economic development (Duncan, 1988: 96; Waugh and Waugh, 1988a; Bland, 1989: 156).

To illustrate the relative importance of taxes in business decision making and to raise an important, but all too frequently forgotten, issue concerning taxes, it is helpful to examine the broad spectrum of factors that may influence site selection. Exhibit 8.1 shows the rankings of specific business site selection criteria by firm type; it is based on a 1984 survey of corporate chief executive officers (CEOs) in firms with relatively high research and development expenditures and likely to be in an *expansion mode* (Waugh and Waugh, 1988b). In these high tech firms, general tax climate was rated as the second most important site selection criterion by the chief executive officer of heavy manufacturing firms, fourth by the CEOs of light manufacturing firms, and seventh by the CEOs of both information processing and primary industry firms. The relatively high ranking of tax climate among CEOs of manufacturing firms is likely at-

Exhibit 8.1
Valuation of Site Selection Criteria by Firm Type (Rank order by means on 1–10 scale)

Criteria	Information Processing Firms (Rank)	Heavy Manufacturing Firms (Rank)	Light Manufacturing Firms (Rank)	Primary Industry Firms (Rank)
Labor: Skills & Availability	1.56 (1)	2.50 (5)	1.77 (1)	3.00 (9)
Potential for Expansion	2.50 (2)	3.00 (8)	2.62 (5)	2.62 (7)
Business Atmosphere of Community	3.00 (3)	2.60 (7)	2.69 (6)	3.92 (12)
State/Local Regulatory Practices	3.11 (4)	1.90 (2)	2.15 (3)	2.50 (4)
Cost of Land and Construction	3.22 (5)	3.75 (14)	2.85 (8)	3.17 (10)
Labor Costs	3.28 (6)	1.85 (1)	2.00 (2)	3.75 (11)
Tax Climate	3.31 (7)	1.90 (2)	2.38 (4)	2.67 (7)
Community Social Climate-Pleasantness	3.72 (8)	3.30 (10)	4.08 (12)	5.42 (13)
Proximity to Academic Institutions	3.89 (9)	4.90 (17)	4.85 (15)	7.67 (18)
Transportation Facilities	3.96 (10)	2.55 (6)	2.69 (6)	2.42 (3)
Cost of Living	4.06 (11)	3.15 (9)	3.62 (11)	5.67 (14)
Access to Markets	4.06 (11)	3.40 (11)	3.46 (10)	2.08 (1)
Proximity to Customers	4.11 (13)	3.70 (13)	4.62 (14)	2.17 (2)
Access to Raw Materials/Components	4.50 (14)	3.50 (12)	4.08 (12)	2.63 (6)
Recreation Facilities	4.50 (14)	4.74 (16)	5.67 (17)	6.67 (16)
Climate of Region	5.18 (16)	5.50 (18)	6.08 (18)	6.83 (17)
Energy Costs and Availability	5.56 (17)	2.10 (4)	3.00 (9)	2.50 (4)
Cultural Amenities	7.00 (18)	4.30 (15)	5.62 (16)	6.58 (15)

Source: Waugh and Waugh, 1988b: 226.

tributable to concerns about property, especially inventory, taxes (Bland, 1989: 156). However, representatives of the National Association of Manufacturers testified before Congress that tax incentives were actually of little value to manufacturing firms (U.S. General Accounting Office, 1982: 10). A better explanation of the rankings is the ambiguity of the term *tax climate*. A favorable tax climate does not necessarily mean low business taxes, inasmuch as low taxes usually mean low levels of public service (and a reduced quality of life). Low taxes thus do not provide the kinds of infrastructure and training that most businesses, including manufacturing firms, need to operate (Bland, 1989: 156). Consequently, it cannot be assumed that the high ranking of tax climate by manufacturing firms translates into the idea that low taxes will attract these firms.

To extend the analysis, Exhibit 8.2 shows the findings of a more recent U.S. General Accounting Office survey that included a broader sample of businesses. These data also indicate that financial or tax inducements are of little importance

Exhibit 8.2
Employer Ratings of Importance of Factors for Locational Decisions

Factor	Little or no importance	Some importance	Moderate importance	Great importance	Very great importance
Market access	68 14.5%	55 11.8%	78 16.7%	154 32.9%	113 24.1%
Community characteristics	89 18.9%	65 13.8%	135 28.6%	111 23.5%	72 15.3%
Site characteristics	96 20.3%	75 15.9%	110 23.3%	126 26.7%	65 13.8%
Government cooperation	129 27.3%	51 10.8%	99 21.0%	113 23.9%	80 16.9%
Transportation	123 26.0%	78 16.5%	95 20.1%	119 25.2%	58 12.3%
Real estate costs	143 30.6%	57 12.2%	122 26.1%	90 19.2%	56 12.0%
Financial health of region	139 29.7%	75 16.0%	105 22.4%	92 19.7%	57 12.2%
Quality of life	156 33.0%	71 15.0%	115 24.3%	89 18.8%	42 8.9%
Regulatory practices	162 34.8%	87 18.7%	114 24.5%	65 14.0%	37 8.0%
Miscellaneous taxes	179 38.2%	78 16.6%	103 22.0%	66 14.1%	43 9.2%
Labor force	217 45.9%	74 15.6%	84 17.8%	57 12.1%	41 8.7%
Financial inducements	277 59.7%	60 12.9%	64 13.8%	33 7.1%	30 6.5%
Technical assistance	311 66.5%	68 14.5%	64 13.7%	16 3.4%	5 1.4%

*Numbers with decimals are the valid percent of employers who responded.
Source: U.S. General Accounting Office, 1988: 76.

in making locational decisions. More specifically, almost 60 percent of the firms in this survey indicated that financial inducements were of little or no importance in their site selections. A study by Russell Smith (1986: 208) of firms in the Chicago area also concluded that many large firms have site selection criteria that are not very sensitive to government incentives at all. Smith argued that communities should only make those investments that will remain and be useful after the recruited firms have moved on, such as reasonable investments in infrastructure improvements and training programs. Notwithstanding the evidence of marginal impact, the use of tax incentives continues, and some research suggests that they are at least somewhat effective, although probably more effective in attracting smaller firms than larger ones (Rasmussen, Bendick, and Ledebur, 1983; Waugh and Waugh, 1988a: 120).

In general terms, the tax-related incentives provided by state and local governments are of three varieties. State economic development programs offer (1) broad-based tax incentives, (2) targeted tax incentives, and (3) selectively applied tax incentives, as well as a plethora of nontax incentives. Broad-based incentives are largely offered to all firms creating jobs or making qualified investments and are usually tied to the state's business tax structure. Credits, exemptions, and/or deductions are permitted for investment, research and development, job creation, depreciation of equipment and other assets, and other expenditures. Targeted incentives are used to reward specific businesses in specific locales, such as free enterprise zones, and are usually tied to a state's business tax structure. These incentives may only be available to new, small, expanding, or other types of firms and can be used to encourage the development or relocation of desired industries, such as high technology manufacturing firms, movie making, and research and development centers. Selectively applied incentives typically include different types of abatements such as those for property taxes as well as various other benefits from state government, local government, and/or special district revenue agencies (Pischak, 1989: 306–309).

Tax administrators prefer that tax incentives be as broad and as clearly articulated as possible to facilitate their administration. Indeed, they quite often suggest that state legislatures adopt simplified tax structures with lower rates, rather than narrower and more complex structures. Simpler and more certain tax structures, they imply, reduce compliance costs for firms and administrative costs for governments (Duncan, 1988: 84–94).

TAX INCENTIVE PHILOSOPHY

The expectation that tax and other financial incentives stimulate economic development by reducing the costs of doing business guides policy makers in many, if not most, communities and states. But the effectiveness of tax incentives is increasingly being questioned, and alternative incentives are being used more.

State governments design economic development policies to maximize economic growth, stabilize their economies, compete for a favorable distribution of the nation's economic activity, and redistribute income. That is, state policies seek to promote growth, encourage development among the state's regions and communities—particularly in the economically poorer areas—and compete with other states. Local governments, by contrast, seek to maximize their own growth and to discourage income redistribution, especially when they are more affluent than surrounding areas, or to encourage it if they are less affluent (Vaughan, 1979: 15–17). The importance of tax incentives to economic development, then, is related to their uses in the competition among states and communities. The pursuit of economic development incentives, with the objective of seducing corporate officials and luring their businesses to particular states or communities, has had and continues to have a profound impact on economic development policy making. The reality, however, is that policy makers copy the successes (and occasionally the failures) of other policy makers, and thus most advantages are short-lived. Tax rates and structures, after all, can be easily and readily copied. Unlike businesses, state and local governments have few secrets from their competitors. What cannot be copied are locale-specific factors, including everything from climate and cultural attractions to proximity to mountains, sea-coasts, and other desirable geographic features.

RECENT TRENDS IN TAXATION AND ECONOMIC DEVELOPMENT

During the 1970s and early 1980s, states and communities tended to pursue economic development with reckless abandon, particularly as they attempted to catch up with states that had implemented development programs a decade or more earlier. In the initial stages of the competition for new businesses, government development agencies most often used shotgun approaches, encouraging legislators and other government officials to load their programs with a wide variety of tax and nontax incentives with the hope of luring any and all businesses to the state or community. In essence, economic development programs offered cafeteria-style incentives. Tax incentives figured very prominently in those early development stages, despite the early warnings that taxes had little influence on business site selection decisions, and perhaps because indigenous firms also benefited from the incentives (Waugh and Waugh, 1991: 220). For example, as early as 1973 a study of utility company efforts to stimulate development found that the importance of tax considerations on the site selection decisions declined between 1967 and 1972, to the point where they represented tie-breakers rather than prominent assets for particular sites. Nonetheless, utility officials continued to mention tax-related factors to prospective clients (Lynch, 1973: 14).

The unfocused, or maybe very broadly focused, cafeteria approach is also evident in a 1981 survey that found forty-nine states offering industrial revenue bonds, forty-six subsidizing compliance with pollution control regulations, thirty-four providing property tax abatements, thirty-two providing loan guarantees, twenty-eight permitting accelerated depreciation of business assets, and twenty-five providing corporate income tax exemptions (Rasmussen, Bendick, and Ledebur, 1983: 21). The very diversity of tax-related incentives complicated the implementation and administration of the economic development programs for governments, and likely complicated the assessment of benefits by the firms themselves.

The next trend was a focus on so-called high technology industries. State and local governments attempted to create research centers similar to North Carolina's Research Triangle Park without regard for the long-term and costly investment required. Development programs included mechanisms to facilitate university-industry cooperation, including creative funding mechanisms to translate basic research into usable technologies and to cultivate entrepreneurial communities of public and private research and development organizations. Interest in high tech development waned somewhat once policy makers realized the cost of recreating North Carolina's success and the limited number and kinds of jobs created by such development (Waugh and Waugh, 1991: 231–232). For most states, competition with North Carolina's Research Triangle and California's Silicon Valley has been doomed to failure. High tech jobs are attractive but ill suited to the overriding needs of many, if not most, states. In other words, the high tech model does not necessarily provide an answer to such things as high unemployment.

By contrast, manufacturing firms create large numbers of skilled jobs, so the pursuit of high profile automobile assembly, electronics, and similar plants increased. Public investments in tax abatements, industrial revenue bonds, and other financial incentives fueled the competition. Illustrating the costs of site acquisition and preparation, training programs, and infrastructure improvements to attract businesses (not counting the tax incentives), a study by Milward and Newman (1987: 13–15) found the following:

- The state of Tennessee spent $33 million in 1980 to attract a Nissan plant, costing $11,000 for each of the estimated 3,000 employees in 1990.
- The state of Michigan spent $48.5 million in 1984 to attract a Mazda plant, costing $13,857 for each of the estimated 3,500 employees in 1988.
- The state of Tennessee spent $80 million in 1984 to attract a Saturn plant, costing $26,660 for each of the estimated 3,000 employees in 1990 (estimated to be reduced to $13,330 per employee when at full capacity of 6,000 employees).
- The state of Illinois spent $83.3 million in 1985 to attract a Diamond-Star plant, costing between $28,724 and $33,320 for each of the estimated 2,500 to 2,900 employees.
- The state of Kentucky spent $149.7 million in 1984 to attract a Toyota plant, costing $49,900 for each of the estimated 3,000 employees in 1988.
- The state of Indiana spent $86 million in 1986 to attract a Fuji-Isuzu plant, costing $50,588 for each of the estimated 1,700 employees, and an additional $25 million for 1,500 more jobs. The total was 3,200, $34,688 per employee.

The long-term costs of the tax and nontax incentives are still unclear. But if the competitions for the BMW assembly plant that ultimately chose a South Carolina site and the Mercedes-Benz plant that chose an Alabama site are any indication, states are still quite willing to make very large tax and nontax investments to gain new jobs. It should be noted, however, that South Carolina already had a high level of manufacturing employment (i.e., skilled workers) and a commitment to provide targeted training programs when the competition began (Waugh and Waugh, 1991: 231). Those attributes were likely of greater importance to BMW officials than the relatively low state taxes. The choice of the Alabama site by Daimler Benz in 1993 has generated considerable criticism within the state because of the high cost of infrastructure improvements and tax abatements, as well as the apparent agreement for the state to purchase thousands of the new Mercedes recreational vehicles assembled in Alabama. Whether the state investment outweighs the expected rewards remains to be seen.

Free Enterprise Zones

In the early to mid-1980s, there also was considerable enthusiasm, particularly among more economically conservative policy makers, for free enterprise zones, using tax abatements and regulatory relief as vehicles for stimulating economic development. The concept of enterprise zones was borrowed from the United Kingdom and was largely meant to encourage industrial and commercial development in distressed urban and rural areas and to create new jobs. In this country, the principal focus has been on urban areas. While enterprise zone legislation was not passed by Congress, despite strong support by the Reagan and Bush administrations, thirty-six states had developed enterprise zone incentives by 1992, and U.S. Department of Housing and Urban Development officials reported that those initiatives had generated over 260,000 jobs and attracted over $28 billion in investment capital between 1981 and 1991. Officials in Louisville, Kentucky, reported that that city's zone had generated approximately 14,000 new jobs and over $1.3 billion in new investments between 1983 and 1992. It is questionable, however, whether the tax incentives offered in the zones account for the new jobs and new investment capital (Deans, 1992).

A similar note is sounded by Elizabeth Gunn. Using data from a U.S. Department of Housing and Urban Development survey of local enterprise zone coordinators in 1989, Gunn concludes that the ''published research overwhelmingly suggests skepticism over the possibility that 'pure' enterprise zone incentives alone would generate enough investment and jobs to offset costs of administering the programs.'' She points to the increasing importance of quality of life factors and the more traditional factors of energy, access to markets, and labor as key to economic development (1993: 446).

During the 1980s, enthusiasm for enterprise zones was running high, despite the lack of hard evidence of success. By the end of the decade, the commitment by state governments to enterprise zone experiments ranged from 1 zone in the state of Michigan to 750 in Louisiana, and from zones of a few acres in some states to entire counties in Mississippi (U.S. General Accounting Office, 1988: 10–11). The criteria for establishing enterprise zones also varied tremendously among states and communities. It is not unusual, for instance, to find some of the most affluent sections of communities within designated enterprise zones, even though such zones generally are reserved for economically troubled areas.

In large measure, the enthusiasm for enterprise zones has now waned, although many still exist and more are being created. The principal finding of an early study of enterprise zones by the U.S. General Accounting Office was that tax incentives may influence businesses to move short distances, such as from the fringe of an enterprise zone into the zone itself (U.S. General Accounting Office, 1982: 10). The likelihood that tax incentives would lure businesses from distant communities or surrounding states was considered very remote.

Interestingly, the British experience is almost identical in terms of the limited effectiveness of enterprise zones in attracting new businesses and creating new jobs. A study of zones in Consett and Corby raises serious questions about those enterprises, as well as the Conservative government's development policy. The authors conclude that enterprise zones are the only option for local governments, given national policy, rather than a viable option for local redevelopment (Boulding, Hudson, and Sadler, 1988: 249–250). Much the same might be said of local governments in the United States.

A General Accounting Office study of Maryland's enterprise zones similarly found that, while financial incentives did affect business decisions, the incentives themselves did not necessarily lead to job creation or influence site selection (U.S. General Accounting Office, 1988: 4–5). The Maryland experience is illustrative of the enterprise zone experience nationally, particularly those implemented after some experimentation in other states. Maryland offered a tax credit of 80 percent of new property tax assessments for five years, new hire credits of $500 per employee, loan insurance of up to 100 percent, higher loan limits, a credit of $3,000 for hiring economically disadvantaged workers, and a credit of $1,750 for hiring laid-off workers (U.S. General Accounting Office, 1988: 48).

The ratings given each of these incentives, including the incentive package as a whole, by employers surveyed by the General Accounting Office appear in Exhibit 8.3. Clearly, the expectation was that the incentives would be of little to moderate importance, with somewhat less confidence in the credits for hiring disadvantaged and laid-off workers. Notwithstanding these expectations, the ratings were very mixed. By contrast, Exhibit 8.4 shows the ratings given by the participants in the Maryland program. They were considerably more enthusiastic about the property tax credits, new hire credits, and credits for hiring disadvantaged and laid-off workers. Still, the ratings varied considerably. The employers' ratings of the nonfinancial incentives appear in Exhibit 8.5. For the most part, employers were even less enthusiastic about the nonfinancial incentives. Interestingly, low ratings were also given to infrastructure improvement, simplification of government procedures (e.g., cutting red tape), and provision of employee job training.

While the current economic development literature still supports the inclusion of infrastructure improvements and regulatory relief in state and local programs, low ratings in the study of Maryland's enterprise zones are consistent with a shift to more demand-side incentives, such as human capital development, technical assistance, and marketing assistance. The economic development literature notes the problems attendant on excessive infrastructure improvement, tax abatement and deferral, and other investments, particularly for local governments. The di-

Exhibit 8.3
Employer Ratings of Importance of Maryland EZ Program Features

Feature	Little or no importance	Some importance	Moderate importance	Great importance	Very great importance	Not applicable
Property tax incentive	89 26.7%	34 10.2%	59 17.7%	72 21.6%	79 23.7%	130
Incentive package	102 28.1%	37 10.2%	97 26.7%	71 19.6%	56 15.4%	86
Loan insurance	120 34.6%	41 11.8%	56 16.1%	63 18.2%	67 19.3%	108
New hire credit	106 29.4%	55 15.3%	84 23.3%	61 16.9%	54 15.0%	99
Higher loan limits	128 38.0%	39 11.6%	61 18.1%	54 16.0%	55 16.3%	117
Disadvantaged hire credit	115 33.2%	61 17.6%	73 21.1%	52 15.0%	45 13.0%	112
Laid-off hire credit	120 35.6%	68 20.2%	68 20.2%	40 11.9%	41 12.2%	119

*Numbers with decimals are the valid percent of employers who responded.

Source: U.S. General Accounting Office, 1988: 77.

lemma is that local governments have limited means of providing demand-side incentives—tax abatements and infrastructure improvements are perhaps the most that they can offer to attract new firms and to keep established businesses (Reese, 1992: 2–5; Pischak, 1989: 313).

Property Tax Abatements

To this day, the most popular tax-related incentive for local governments undoubtedly is property tax abatement (Bland, 1989: 162). But it is uncertain how long it takes local governments to recover the lost revenues—or even if they can recoup such revenues—from such abatements. Exhibit 8.6 illustrates the levels of government-granting property tax abatements, the types of industries covered, the limitations of abatements to economically depressed areas, and the maximum period of the abatement. Data show that property tax abatements are granted in thirty states and are particularly popular in the South. The types of firms qualifying for abatements vary, but about half of the states using property tax abatements do so comprehensively rather than selectively. Similarly, slightly over half of those offering abatements do not limit them to blighted areas. More than half also provide abatements for periods exceeding ten years. Only the state of Florida requires voter approval for abatement awards. And Louisiana can grant abatements at the state level without local government approval (Bland, 1989: 164).

The Georgia experience may be illustrative of the practice of using property

Exhibit 8.4
Program Participant Ratings of Maryland EZ Program Features

Feature	Little or no importance	Some importance	Moderate importance	Great importance	Very great importance	Not applicable
Property tax credit	6 11.5%	1 1.9%	7 13.5%	19 36.5%	19 36.5%	12
New hire credit	9 15.5%	5 8.6%	14 24.1%	14 24.1%	16 27.6%	6
Disadvantaged hire credit	9 16.1%	6 10.7%	12 21.4%	16 28.6%	13 23.2%	8
Laid-off hire credit	12 21.8%	10 18.2%	13 23.6%	9 16.4%	11 20.0%	9
Loan insurance	14 28.0%	5 10.0%	10 20.0%	13 26.0%	8 16.0%	14
Higher loan limits	14 27.5%	5 9.8%	12 23.5%	13 25.5%	7 13.7%	13
Incentive package	6 10.7%	4 7.1%	14 25.0%	23 41.1%	9 16.1%	8

*Numbers with decimals are the valid percent of employers who responded.

Source: U.S. General Accounting Office, 1988: 77.

tax abatements for economic development purposes. State law permits the exemption of properties owned by industrial development authorities and other government organizations from property taxation. Almost all of Georgia's 159 counties have such authorities, and some have as many as three. By leasing property from an industrial development authority, a business can avoid property taxes altogether or have them phased in over time. When United Parcel Service (UPS) moved its headquarters to Fulton County in 1993, the building was financed by $100 million in industrial revenue bonds, and the development authority agreed that UPS would pay property taxes on only one-half of the value of the property for the first year. Thereafter, UPS' tax obligation would increase 5 percent each year until, after ten years, taxes would be owed on 100 percent of the property's value. That arrangement will save UPS $802,000 in the first year (1995) and approximately $4 million over the term of the agreement. Similarly, Dodge County provided a twenty-year property tax abatement to Gilman Paper Company, Emanuel County provided a seven-year tax abatement to Advanced Metal Components, Inc., and Effingham County provided a forty-year abatement to Fort Howard Paper Company. In the latter case, the paper company saves between $5.5 million and $9 million per year, based on the current tax rate, and it does not have to pay property taxes until 2027. Such abatements draw considerable criticism because of the costs to public schools and other services that are financed through property taxes and because similar tax breaks are not generally available to small businesses. In Effingham County, proponents of the abatement point to the 1,100 jobs provided by Fort Howard Paper Com-

Exhibit 8.5
Employer Ratings of Importance of Nonfinancial Incentives

Incentive	Little or no importance	Some importance	Moderate importance	Great importance	Very great importance
Infrastructure improvement	108 23.4%	81 17.6%	111 24.1%	91 19.7%	70 15.2%
Simplified government procedures	136 29.5%	87 18.9%	90 19.5%	86 18.7%	62 13.4%
Employee job training	167 36.2%	84 18.2%	92 20.0%	70 15.2%	48 10.4%
Community development corporations	163 35.6%	87 19.0%	100 21.8%	68 14.8%	40 8.7%
Low cost business consulting	202 43.9%	93 20.2%	84 18.3%	46 10.0%	35 7.6%
Foreign market, export assistance	345 76.2%	42 9.3%	35 7.7%	13 2.9%	18 4.0%

*Numbers with decimals are the valid percent of employers who responded.
Source: U.S. General Accounting Office, 1988: 78.

pany, while opponents point to the approximately $6 million in lost property tax revenue each year. It is also noteworthy that, as well as permitting property tax abatements sponsored by the industrial development authorities, the Georgia constitution also permits counties to exempt business inventories from taxation. By 1993 voters had approved *free port* exemptions in 125 counties (Whitt, 1993). Property tax abatements have certainly strained local public services heavily dependent on property tax revenues for support, but state and local development officials still argue that the abatements are necessary incentives for new businesses because other communities and states provide them.

Tax Increment Financing

Twenty-four states also provide for tax increment financing—using property tax revenues generated by redevelopment to finance improvements in an economically distressed area. Revenues representing predevelopment taxes are paid to the taxing authority (e.g., school district or local government), and the new or additional revenues are paid into a tax increment fund. Tax increment funds then are usually used to retire bonds issued to finance public improvements. The benefit to property owners in the tax increment district is that a portion of their taxes is used to make improvements in their own district and to attract new businesses. For businesses, federal tax credits for local property taxes reduce the burden from the increased property taxes (Bland, 1989: 165–166).

Exhibit 8.6
Statutory Provisions Governing Use of Tax Abatements

State	Local Governments Granting Abatements	Types Of Industries Qualifying	Limited To Blighted Areas	Maximum Abatement Period (Years)
Alabama	C,M	Most industries	No	
Arkansas	C,M	Leasehold interests	No	7
Colorado	N/A	Timber	No	30
Connecticut	M	Enterprise zones	Yes	7
Florida	C,M	Comprehensive	No	10
Hawaii	C,M	Required repairs	Yes	7
Illinois	C,M	Comprehensive	Yes	10
Indiana	M	Comprehensive	Yes	10
Iowa	C,M	Limited	Yes	5
Louisiana	P	Comprehensive	Yes	10
Maine	N/A	Certain mines	No	10
Maryland	C,M	Enterprise zones	Yes	10
Massachusetts	N/A	EDC property	No	7
Michigan	C,M	Limited	No	12
Mississippi	C,M	Comprehensive	No	10
Missouri	C,M	Comprehensive	Yes	25
Montana	C,M	Comprehensive	No	10
New Jersey	M	Comprehensive	Yes	5
New York	C,M	EDC property	No	10
North Dakota	C,M	Limited	No	5
Ohio	C,M	Comprehensive	Yes	15
Oklahoma	C,M	Manufacturing	No	5
Pennsylvania	C,M	Comprehensive	Yes	10
Rhode Island	M	Comprehensive	No	10
South Carolina	C,M	Comprehensive	No	5
South Dakota	C	Comprehensive	No	5
Tennessee	N/A	Electrical energy coops	No	4
Texas	C,M	Comprehensive	No	15
Vermont	M	Comprehensive	No	10
Virginia	C,M	Comprehensive	Yes	10

Note: C = counties, M = municipalities, P = parishes, N/A = information not available.

Source: National Association of State Development Agencies, *Directory of Incentives for Business Investment and Development in the United States, State by State Guide*, 2nd ed. 1986.

INTERSTATE TAX COMPETITION

A predominant fear of state and local officials is that their tax rate structures may be so out of line with those of other states and communities that businesses will flee to locations with the lowest tax rates or those offering the best tax incentives. For the most part, that fear is unfounded. In only a few cases has a tax structure created an inhospitable environment for business (Francis, 1988: 136). This fear was one of the principal arguments against the short-lived Florida sales tax on services. The critics argued that, until other states implemented similar taxes, service industries might find it advantageous to shift their operations to states without such taxes. The likelihood of many service industries fleeing Florida was rather remote, however.

Strategy and Policy

Interstate tax competition is exacerbating pressures to keep business taxes relatively low, or at least as low as surrounding states. That is, competition among and between states is making it difficult for states to shift tax burdens from individual taxpayers to business taxpayers. The need to keep a level playing field in the competition for new businesses has affected not only personal income tax rates, but personal property taxes through the definition of tax bases and assessment policies. As discussed in earlier chapters, states have reduced sales taxes on business equipment and property taxes on inventories (Vlaisavljevich, 1988: 178–185). They also have adjusted their corporate apportionment formulas to give more favorable tax rates to firms earning out-of-state and foreign-source income—to dissuade these firms from hiding income and simply to attract more large firms.

IMPORTANCE OF STATE AND LOCAL ECONOMIES

Economic development programs respond to specific economic problems, be they deteriorating infrastructure, high unemployment, and/or an unskilled labor force (Vaughan, 1979: 11–12). The economic development literature provides persuasive arguments for very narrowly targeted programs designed to address specific local needs (Waugh and Waugh, 1988b: 232–233).

A larger issue is the need for redistributing revenue sources, particularly from affluent suburbs to distressed inner cities. The need for tax base sharing (Vaughan, 1979: 12) is clear. However, political obstacles for the implementation of a tax base sharing program may be insurmountable.

The best known example of a tax base sharing effort is the Fiscal Disparities Program located in the Minneapolis–St. Paul metropolitan area. A strong regional planning organization was established in 1967 and, with passage of Minnesota's fiscal disparities law in 1971, the metropolitan area began an experiment to control development. The program was designed to lessen the unevenness of development in the area, to reduce economic competition among communities, and to discourage developmental sprawl. Each taxing unit contributes 40 percent of its post-1971 commercial-industrial tax base. The revenues thus contributed are allocated to communities based on their fiscal capacities. That is, communities with below average fiscal capacities (less post-1971 growth in commercial-industrial property values) receive more than they paid into the pool, while those with above average capacities receive less. In 1991, 157 taxing jurisdictions received more revenues than they contributed, and 31, most of them contiguous to Minneapolis, received less. The city of Minneapolis contributed $19 million in revenues to other communities, and St. Paul received $24.3 million more than it contributed. Over time, the percentage of the commercial-industrial tax base included in the program has grown considerably; it is estimated that it will be 34 percent by 1995. In short, the redistributive effect of the program is increasing, while there has been little change in the winners and losers in the program.

Although the program has evidently lessened the disparities among taxing jurisdictions somewhat, the impact on the competition for development is less certain. Politically, there are still more winners than losers, and opposition to the program still has to overcome the perceived benefits to the region as a whole (Goetz, 1992: 1, 7–10).

A tax base sharing system like that in the Minneapolis–St. Paul area may not be politically feasible in other metropolitan areas, but the need to address economic disparities among communities is critical. Economic interdependence and the importance of regional economies strongly suggest that disparities will have negative consequences for the most affluent communities as well as the least affluent (Ledebur and Barnes, 1992: 6). The spillover of economic problems, ranging from homelessness to crime to unemployment, from inner cities to suburbs is evidence of the existence of regional communities. Social and economic problems not addressed in poorer communities will eventually become problems in the more affluent ones. It is easier to deal with the problems while they are relatively small and localized.

RELATIONSHIP BETWEEN TAXES AND ECONOMIC DEVELOPMENT

Generally speaking, in the competition for new and expanding businesses, tax policies tend to be effective only as tie-breakers. Only when all other site selection concerns are considered equal by firms considering new locations and/ or expansion of facilities are tax policies seen as an important criterion (Bland, 1989: 156). While there is evidence that taxes may have some influence in general business decisions and, in some cases, in site selection decisions, there are more attractive incentives that can be offered by state and local governments. The key is to avoid having tax rates significantly higher than neighboring states and communities and tax systems that cause significantly higher compliance costs. The border state problem, discussed in Chapter 4, also holds true for tax systems generally. As the enterprise zone experience has shown, firms are willing to move short distances if there are significant differences in the tax rates.

The threshold at which taxes become important in a firm's site selection decisions is much less easily identified. For the most part, a firm's tax burden is reduced by the federal tax deduction for state and local property and income taxes (Bland, 1989: 156). The effect of tax incentives is that firms are often rewarded for behaving as they would have without tax incentives (Vaughan, 1979: 95).

The greatest value of tax incentives may be in their encouragement of capital investment and training of the labor force (Duncan, 1988: 95–96). The greatest drawback, apart from the apparent ineffectiveness of tax incentives, may be the loss of control over revenues that governments experience when granting abatements and other incentives (Pischak, 1989: 316–317). Also, if tax incentives are part of a state's or a community's economic development incentive package, firms may feel that they can negotiate favorable tax breaks simply by playing off one jurisdiction against another.

Loan Guarantee Programs

Many states encourage economic development through loan guarantee programs which, while not strictly tax incentives, permit specific, qualifying firms to borrow money at rates lower than they otherwise might find. Loan guarantee programs can provide new firms with start-up capital, which has been scarce since the 1970s. The principal concern, however, is the risk assumed by state and local agencies with such guarantees. If there is too little money available, loan guarantees might encourage more investment. If the risk is too high for banks and private lenders to invest, government loan guarantees may stimulate and temporarily support developments that will not be economically viable for long.

Community Improvement Districts

The number of private-public development authorities is also expanding. Community improvement districts (often called downtown management districts) typically involve property owners, commercial tenants, employers, and government agencies in the development of a city business district. While not strictly government tax programs, community improvement districts collect dues or taxes from participants for the improvement of their own areas. In some cases, because contributions are tied to local property taxes, tax administration is handled by local government revenue agencies. The participation of public officials in district governance, as well as the commitments made by local governments to these efforts, supports inclusion of these programs with other public economic development efforts. The apparent success of community improvement or downtown management districts is due to the financial support gained through the voluntary tax system to supplement and expand municipal services as well as to the level of commitment by the participants.

The concept of community improvement districts grew from special assessment districts used in many communities to pay for capital improvements, as well as from special public-private agreements to support newly developed areas and condominium agreements. Over 700 districts have been created in North America, and they have taken a variety of forms, ranging from Denver's Downtown Mall Management District, which was created for the construction and subsequent expansion of a mall, to Portland, Oregon's, 291-block Economic Improvement District. Due to changes in Oregon's property tax laws, the Portland district is now a voluntary association (Central Atlanta Progress, 1992: 4–5).

To participate in Philadelphia's Center City District program, businesses pay an annual fee. In 1993 the charge was 4.5 percent of the participant's property tax assessment. The district supplements government services. Uniformed personnel sweep sidewalks during the day and wash them at night. Uniformed community service representatives patrol the downtown business district to aid police and to assist residents and visitors. Representatives furnish retail security audits, conduct safety training, provide parade/events support, and dispense first aid (including cardiopulmonary resuscitation). Banners and other distinctive symbols are displayed throughout the district, and a newsletter is published quarterly to promote the district's image and to create a sense of community.

Similarly, the Central Dallas Association works with the city of Dallas and the Dallas Area Rapid Transit (DART) to improve the central business area through a downtown improvement district. The city has made a long-term commitment to provide resources and personnel necessary to maintain public services in the district and is providing assistance in dealing with specific problems, such as alcohol consumption and panhandling on the streets. City and DART efforts include street repairs, increased access to transit facilities, additional bicycle patrol officers, higher visibility for the police, more street cleaning, distinctive litter receptacles, and other services. Local businesses have agreed to a special assessment, not to exceed one-half mill. The program is administered by a nonprofit corporation and governed by a thirty-member board of directors representing the city, property owners, and tenants (Central Dallas Association, 1992).

A program proposed for the city of Atlanta may ultimately include four community improvement districts. Georgia law permits the establishment of assessment districts and authorizes their boards to levy taxes, fees, and assessments— not to exceed 2.5 percent of the aggregate assessed value of the property—and to sell bonds. The program proposal includes uniformed city guides, additional security for special events, equipment to assure more police patrols, litter pickup, sidewalk cleaning, marketing of the districts, brochures, special events, and some capital improvements (Central Atlanta Progress, 1993). Each community improvement district will have a nine-member governing board, with one appointed by the mayor, two by the city council president, and six by property owners in the district (Central Atlanta Progress, 1992: 6). While the initial proposal was for four districts, proponents expect a less ambitious program to be implemented first, focusing on the areas most in need of development.

Land Banks

Related to the tax-based economic development programs, land banks offer a mechanism to identify and acquire properties available for development. Land banks acquire title to abandoned properties, tax-delinquent properties that have not drawn buyers in local tax sales, purchased properties, donated properties, and transferred properties, and use them to encourage economic development. In the latter case, developers may arrange donations of property to the land bank, which waives the outstanding tax liability and sells the property back to the developers. Properties may be similarly donated to the land bank for use in an urban homesteading program (Harris, 1993).

It was through the Boston Redevelopment Authority, a land bank, that the Rouse Company acquired the abandoned cold-storage facilities near the Boston waterfront that became the Faneuil Hall retail and entertainment complex. The complex now pays $2.8 million a year in city taxes and $8 million in state taxes. Similarly, St. Louis' Land Reutilization Authority sold over 200 vacant lots to a developer who is building homes for low- to moderate-income residents (Dratch, 1993). In Georgia, the Atlanta Project is examining ways to speed up title searches so that the Fulton County/Atlanta Land Bank can make properties available for development quickly. The land bank has had considerable difficulty getting clear title to parcels and working fast enough to discourage tax sale investors from buying a few parcels critical to large developments and then holding them hostage. The potential benefits from the Fulton County/Atlanta Land Bank are manifest: in the fourteen communities targeted for development, 39 percent of the parcels are tax-delinquent, and the estimated loss in property taxes is over $12.6 million per year (Harris, 1993).

CONCLUDING COMMENTS

The popularity of tax abatement, enterprise zone, tax increment financing, and other tax-related incentives notwithstanding, taxes have only a marginal impact on economic development. Tax incentives have little influence on business site selection decisions. The exceptions to those generalizations occur when taxes are significantly higher in a neighboring jurisdiction. Individuals and firms will travel short distances to realize significant tax advantages.

While the usefulness of enterprise zones and similar tax incentive programs in stimulating development is questionable, there are indications that such programs can contribute to urban redevelopment when implemented in conjunction with other kinds of programs. Unfortunately, political support for enterprise zones tends to be strongest among those who oppose more demand-side investments in urban redevelopment. Designing and implementing more broadly focused developments requires more bipartisanship and less ideological conflict.

The most important tax issues are those related to problems caused by the disparities among tax bases, which leave some jurisdictions with too few resources to maintain services or to encourage development effectively, and with the need to target tax monies and tax expenditures to address specific local problems. Tax base sharing arrangements are difficult to implement. The use of community improvement or downtown management districts shows great promise, although their ultimate success may be due less to the additional tax support than to the level of commitment and the resulting sense of community. The use of land banks to identify and acquire tax-delinquent properties, assemble development-sized parcels, encourage development of low income housing and other desirable projects, and return properties to the tax rolls is also very promising for distressed communities. Land banks provide one-stop shopping for developers seeking inner city properties and can greatly reduce the developers' up-front costs.

In terms of other tax-related issues, certainly state and local governments are concerned about recent threats to the tax-exempt status of municipal bonds. If municipal bonds lose their appeal to investors, the resources available to local governments for capital improvements in all probability will be severely curtailed.

What is important to businesses and to the success of state and local economic development programs is the creation of hospitable and attractive tax climates. The objective should be sufficient business and individual taxes to support necessary public services, adequate infrastructure, effective human resource development, and a reasonable quality of life for the community. Tax rates can obviously inhibit economic development by being too high, but they can also inhibit development if they are too low.

REFERENCES

Bland, Robert L. (1989). *A Revenue Guide for Local Government.* Washington, D.C.: International City Management Association.
Boulding, Peter, Ray Hudson, and David Sadler (1988). "Consett and Corby: What Kind of New Era?" *Public Administration Quarterly*, 12, Summer.
"Center City District" (n.d.). Philadelphia (brochure).
Central Atlanta Progress (1992). *Proposal for a Community Improvement District for Downtown and Midtown Atlanta* (Draft). Atlanta: Central Atlanta Progress, Inc., June 16.
——— (1993). *Community Improvement District (CID) Proposal.* Atlanta: Central Atlanta Progress, January 26.
Central Dallas Association (1992). "A Downtown Improvement District for Dallas." Dallas: Central Dallas Association.
Deans, Bob (1992), "Zoned for Jobs and Growth," *Atlanta Journal/Atlanta Constitution*, June 8, p. A3.
Dratch, Dana (1993). "Concept Met with Success in Inner-City Boston, St. Louis." *Atlanta Journal/Atlanta Constitution*, August 3, p. E8.
Duncan, Harley T. (1988). "State Legislators and Tax Administrators." In Steven D. Gold, ed., *The Unfinished Agenda for State Tax Reform.* Washington, D.C.: National Conference of State Legislatures.
Francis, James (1988). "The Florida Sales Tax on Services: What Really Went Wrong?" In Steven D. Gold, ed., *The Unfinished Agenda for State Tax Reform.* Washington, D.C.: National Conference of State Legislatures.
Goetz, Edward G. (1992). "Tax Base Sharing in the Twin Cities." *Urban News*, 6, Spring.
Gunn, Elizabeth M. (1993). "The Growth of Enterprise Zones: A Policy Transformation." *Policy Studies Journal*, 21, Autumn, pp. 432–449.
Harris, Lyle V. (1993). "Land Bank Lags in Revitalization." *Atlanta Journal/Atlanta Constitution*, August 3, pp. E1, E8.
Ledebur, Larry C., and William R. Barnes (1992). "Metropolitan Disparities and Economic Growth." *Urban News*, 6, Spring. Abstracted from *Metropolitan Disparities and Economic Growth: City Distress and the Need for a Federal-Local Growth Package.* National League of Cities, March 1992.

Lynch, A. A. (1973). "Environment and Labor Quality Take Top Priority in Site Selection." *Industrial Development*, 142, March-April.

Milward, H. Brinton, and Heide Hosbach Newman (1987). "State Incentive Packages and the Industrial Location Decision." Paper presented at the Southern Political Science Association Annual Meeting, Charlotte, N.C., November 5–8.

Pischak, Kathryn A. (1989). "State Economic Development Incentives: What's Available? What Works?" *Municipal Finance Journal*, 10.

Rasmussen, David W., Marc Bendick, Jr., and Larry C. Ledebur (1983). "Evaluating State Economic Development Incentives from a Firm's Perspective." *Business Economics*, May.

Reese, Laura A. (1992). "The Role of Counties in Local Economic Development." Paper presented at the Annual Meeting of the Southern Political Science Association, Atlanta, Georgia, November 5–7.

Smith, Russell L. (1986). "Interdependencies in Urban Economic Development: The Role of Multi-Establishment Firms." In Dennis R. Judd, ed., *Public Policy Across States and Cities*. New York: JAI Press.

U.S. General Accounting Office, Comptroller General (1982). *Report to the Congress: Revitalizing Distressed Areas Through Enterprise Zones*. Washington, D.C.: US GAO, GAO/CED-82-78, July 15.

——— (1988). *Report to the Congress: Enterprise Zones: Lessons from the Maryland Experience*. Washington, D.C.: US GAO, GAO/PEMD-89-2, December.

Vaughan, Roger J. (1979). *State Taxation and Economic Development*. Washington, D.C.: Council of State Planning Agencies.

Vlaisavljevich, Michael. (1988). "State Business Taxes: The Policy and Research Agendas." In Steven D. Gold, ed., *The Unfinished Agenda for State Tax Reform*. Washington, D.C.: National Conference of State Legislatures.

Waugh, William L., and Deborah M. Waugh (1988a). "Economic Development Programs of State and Local Governments and the Site Selection Decisions of Smaller Firms." In Richard J. Judd, William T. Greenwood, and Fred W. Becker, eds., *Small Business in a Regulated Economy: Issues and Policy Implications*. Westport, Conn.: Quorum Books.

——— (1988b). "Baiting the Hook: Targeting Economic Development Monies More Effectively." *Public Administration Quarterly*, 12, Summer.

——— (1991). "The Political Economy of Seduction: Promoting Business Relocation and Economic Development in Nonindustrial States." In Melvin J. Dubnick and Alan Gitelson, eds., *Public Policy and Economic Institutions*. Greenwich, Conn.: JAI Press.

Whitt, Richard (1993). "In Lieu of Taxes' Looks Like Lulu of an Underpayment." *Atlanta Journal/Atlanta Constitution*, March 21, p. B2.

9

Tax Administration

Tax administration involves three generic functions. The first is preparing inventories of persons, corporations, and firms and collecting tax dollars from them as effectively and efficiently as possible. The second entails establishing and maintaining accounts of collected funds in formats that can be easily verified and eventually audited. The third is forecasting revenues so that budgets can be developed and balanced.

The administrative structure is crucial to the tax process because it is responsible for collecting, handling, and forecasting tax dollars necessary for governments to function properly. Special units and agencies are charged and entrusted by state and local governments to collect and maintain revenues. For instance, the administration of property taxes—a major revenue source for local governments—is governed by various state and local laws that designate collection and maintenance structures, processes, and procedures.

Specific structures and functions thus vary enormously according to state and local laws, the nature of the taxes levied, and among government jurisdictions. State governments normally have specific units, usually called revenue departments, designated to collect taxes. Counties and cities also have separate collecting and treasury units. School districts and special districts, on the other hand, often pay counties to collect their revenues. The structures and functions common to all tax administration are discussed in this chapter.

ADMINISTRATIVE STRUCTURES

Generally speaking, tax administration units—especially those entrusted to collect taxes—are organized either vertically or horizontally. Exhibit 9.1 schematically illustrates these two types of structures.

Categorical units consist of separate agencies set up to collect each type of major tax. Exhibit 9.1 shows separate agencies designed to collect income, sales, and motor fuels taxes. Each agency is responsible for all administrative aspects involved in collecting and maintaining its respective revenues (e.g., preparation, processing, data entry, depositing, verifying and auditing, and forecasting).

Functional units comprise separate agencies for each major tax function. Exhibit 9.1, for example, shows that one agency is charged with collecting all types of taxes, another is directed to process all types of tax returns, and still another is responsible for verifying and auditing all returns. Yet another agency forecasts revenues.

For the most part, governments do not use either one of these units solely. Most use a hybrid structure that attempts to incorporate and integrate the positive aspects of both categorical and functional units. It has certain marked benefits. The experience, knowledge, and information gained from administering one type of tax may be readily transferred to other types of taxes. Moreover, combining various specific functions into a larger, more diversified unit encourages sharing ideas and experiences.

Such integration allows units to collect and maintain revenues more efficiently and effectively. For example, the legal and statistical work entailed in tax administration can be shared among agencies. Assembly line techniques leading to greater productivity can be incorporated into tasks such as handling mail, keeping records, tracking correspondence, and conducting other routine matters. Auditing and verification also can be accomplished more economically.

Simply put, economies of scale are possible with hybrid units. Studies have shown that the amount of revenues collected increases, and the costs of those collections decline. Then, too, taxpayers seem more satisfied, primarily because an integrated system frequently fosters more consistent tax policies and procedures.

TAX COLLECTION

Regardless of the tax administration structure used, taxes are collected by a unit whose principal function is to collect revenues and turn them over to a treasury unit for maintenance and disbursement. The collecting unit generally is empowered by law to demand that all persons, corporations, and firms fully cooperate with it by supplying full and accurate tax information to allow for efficient and effective collection of revenues due the governing jurisdiction. Willful violations are punishable by fines and/or penalties, sometimes resulting in imprisonment.

Exhibit 9.1
Tax Administration Structures

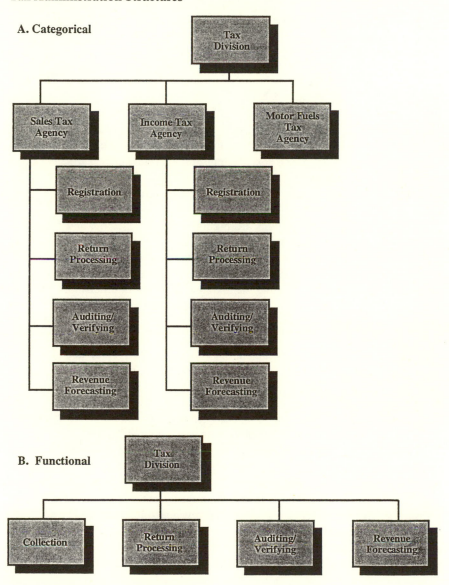

A. Categorical

Tax Division

Sales Tax Agency

Income Tax Agency

Motor Fuels Tax Agency

Registration

Return Processing

Auditing/ Verifying

Revenue Forecasting

Registration

Return Processing

Auditing/ Verifying

Revenue Forecasting

B. Functional

Tax Division

Collection

Return Processing

Auditing/ Verifying

Revenue Forecasting

Source: Adapted from Mikesell, 1991: 333.

The collection process entails a series of nonsequential steps, the first of which involves preparing inventory lists of persons, corporations, and firms that are required to pay or remit tax dollars to a governing jurisdiction. For property taxes, inventories consist of parcels of land with ownership designations. Sales and consumption tax inventories include establishments that must remit sales taxes they collect—minus collection fees—to state and local governments. Motor fuel taxes normally are remitted by distributors, though paid by consumers. Personal and corporate income tax inventories incorporate lists of individuals and corporations, respectively. Besides preparing these inventories, collecting units must update them monthly. Inventories, therefore, must be judiciously maintained.

The second step of the collection process involves determining the tax base and computing the tax liability. For both personal and corporate income taxes, incomes must be ascertained, followed by computation of the tax liability via assessment of statutory rates. Taxable transactions (purchases and sales) form the tax base for sales and consumption taxes; the tax liability is determined by applying the rates and exemptions to these transactions. Other taxes are computed in the same manner.

Incidentally, such computations are highly technical, specific, and often difficult. Their accuracy relies largely on forms developed and sent to taxpayers and remitters. These forms invariably are conflictive; that is, they contain contradictory elements of good tax administration. A good form must embody all of the principal elements affecting the tax base and rates in order to be accurate and precise. At the same time, the form should be simple and easy to read and complete. Accuracy and precision, unfortunately, can be attained only when simplicity is sacrificed.

After tax liabilities are ascertained, tax statements are readied showing each taxpayer's or remitter's name, address, tax due, parcel number (if real estate), and other pertinent information. A copy is sent to the taxpayer or remitter and a duplicate kept for the collecting unit's records. Most tax statements are mailed in installments that vary according to the type of tax and the taxing jurisdiction. Revenue returns may be due annually, quarterly, or monthly.

Money is collected, invariably via mail and electronic transfers. A recent development in the collection and maintenance of tax revenues is the increased use of electronic deposits and fund transfers. Such processes integrate collections and disbursements into electronic data processing environments. Besides permitting taxpayers and remitters to deposit revenues electronically in predetermined accounts in designated banks, credits and debts are automated electronically to increase productivity. Electronic processing also increases interest earnings by reducing the float time—the gap between the time tax statements are sent and revenues are received.

Upon receiving tax payments, collecting units issue receipts to taxpayers. When the total amount of taxes due is not paid, partial payments are noted on the statements and separate receipts are issued for the amounts paid. Control

Exhibit 9.2
Typical Record Files for Property Taxes

✔ <u>Master Card File</u> - A card file is prepared for all real estate taxpayers which include the parcel numbers of each piece of property they own or pay taxes on. These cards are filed with the real estate statements and are updated every year by noting the changes in the assessor's book.

✔ <u>Mortgage and Loan Company List</u> - A List of each mortgage or loan company paying real estate taxes in the county needs to be maintained. The list should include the name and address of the loan company and the parcel number of each piece of property that the company pays taxes on. A note should also be made if certain parcels are VA exempt.

✔ <u>Veterans Administration Exemption List</u> - A file of all property owners who are allowed either total or partial exemption from personal and real estate taxes should be maintained. This involves keeping a list of letters for the Veterans Administration stating the percentage of determined disability. A letter hab to be on file before any exemption can be granted.

✔ <u>Homestead Exemption List</u> - As an additional service to the taxpayer the collector could maintain a list of those persons 65 years or older and eligible for the Homestead Exemption. The tax is paid to the county, but the taxpayer is reimbursed by the State Revenue Office.

✔ <u>Delinquent Personal Tax Book</u> - This book lists all persons who are delinquent in paying their personal taxes. The book is prepared after the deadline of October 10. It is listed by city and school district and alphabetically by taxpayers last name.

✔ <u>Delinquent Improvement District Book</u> - This book lists all improvement districts in the county and which taxpayer's are delinquent in their taxes.

✔ <u>Ledger</u> - This is kept by the collector and lists all accounts that collect tax revenue in the county. This includes school districts, improvement districts, cities etc. Accounts are posted by month to show a monthly collection amount as well as a year to date total.

✔ <u>Journal</u> - The journal lists the date, control number range for check out, amount for each check out, and which account the money was deposited in. Every account is listed, totaled and balanced at the end of the mopnth.

✔ <u>Delinquent Improvement Redemption Certificates File</u> - When a taxpayer is delinquent in real estate taxes he has to redeem his property when the taxes are paid. A redemption certificate has to be completed and back taxes paid to complete the process of redeeming property. The certificates are a three part form with one copy to the property owner or tax payer - one copy to the improvement district collected for- one copy for the collectors file.

✔ <u>Deposit Slips</u> - Each deposit slip is a three part form with one copy staying with the check up- one copy in the master file (chronological order) - one is kept by the bank and returned with the bank statement.

✔ <u>Check Out Sheet</u> - This is a form which shows the taxes collected by various accounts for a certain period of time. A check out period could be one day or several days depending on the number of collections. This will vary with the collection schedule.

✔ <u>Post Card Reminders</u> - Several county collectors send out a post card after October 10 to all delinquent taxpayers in the county, both personal and real estate. This card reminds taxpayers to pay their taxes before the delinquent tax list is prepared and published in the newspaper.

Source: Association of Arkansas Counties, 1992: 4–2.

numbers, amounts of the checks, and respective dates are posted in appropriate tax books. Control numbers are sequential figures assigned to each transaction and generated by a validating process, thus making it easier to locate mistakes.

Various other records designed to oversee tax liabilities and payments are kept. Exhibit 9.2 lists some typical records county tax collectors use to keep track of property taxes.

State and local laws, more often than not, require collecting units to issue at least monthly settlements to treasury units. Collecting units are required to turn over promptly—usually within a few days—to treasury units all funds collected, whether taxes, charges, or fines. After depositing funds in various designated accounts and recording the settlements, treasury units approve the settlements.

The final step entails verifying delinquent taxes to see if taxpayers or remitters are complying with the laws. All taxes not paid must be certified for collection, and then according to law delinquents are notified. Certification involves listing the names of delinquents, the amount of tax dollars due, the penalties assessed, and the amount of interest charged, if applicable.

TAX MAINTENANCE

Revenues are maintained by treasury units whose primary responsibility is to manage and distribute tax dollars according to the law. Treasury units, therefore, receive tax collections, funds turned back to local governments by states, intergovernmental transfers, and grants-in-aid, as well as revenues from various other sources. They then distribute money as authorized.

More specifically, after receiving revenues, the units keep and issue accurate and detailed accounts of receipts and disbursements. Normally, treasury units also are required to issue monthly financial reports on the fiscal conditions of their governments. These units, then, are responsible for making full and complete settlements of governmental bills and employee salaries and wages. Then, too, when states collect money for substate governments, or when substate governments collect money for other substate governments, treasury units charge ad valorem commissions—in the neighborhood of 1 to 2 percent—for such assistance.

Transaction Records

Once funds are collected, treasury units deposit them almost daily in one or more banks, recording entries for each separate account. Exhibit 9.3 shows the principal records these units are required to maintain.

The *accounts ledger* lists every account the government has as well as all activities pertaining to each account, including deposits, sources of the deposits, expenditures, sources of the expenditures, dates of the transactions, and the number of each check or warrant. *Bank books* also are maintained; they contain the balances at each bank and show each account's deposits and withdrawals. The books, moreover, house information about transaction dates, check and receipt numbers, and daily balances.

Treasury units also keep *bond books* that have information about all longterm debt obligations. They list purposes of the bond issues, types of bonds, paying agents, amount of each issue, interest rates, and schedules of payment. *Receipt books* record all moneys coming into the government. Receipts are prenumbered and copies are sent to remitters.

With tax money coming in from an array of sources, these books need to be reconciled at least monthly. The *reconciliation forms* list each account in the

Exhibit 9.3
Four Major Transactions Kept by Treasury Units

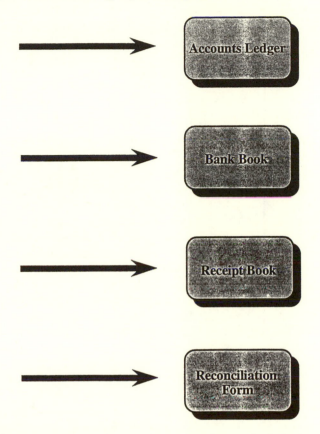

accounts ledger. For each account there are columns for balances, overdrafts, cash on hand, and the bank holding the funds. Monthly reconciliation is designed to make sure that bank statements, bank books, bank balances, and accounts ledgers balance.

Investments

Once tax dollars and other revenues are collected, the money is either spent or invested. While most tax dollars are used for governmental operations and capital expenditures, treasury units, from time to time, have idle cash to invest. Investing money yields interest. As more interest is earned, less revenue is needed from taxes. Consequently, wise investment policies help keep taxes from increasing as rapidly as otherwise would be the case. Exhibit 9.4 shows different types of investments use by state and local governments.

Because of the need for liquidity, these funds regularly are invested in cer-

Exhibit 9.4
Characteristics of Investment Instruments

Instrument	General Legality	Safety Factors	Liquidity	Relative Yield
U.S. Treasury bills	Most states permit.	Default risk free; custody sometimes difficult to arrange independently.	Immediately marketable (can be sold to obtain cash).	Typically the lowest yield.
U.S. Treasury notes	A few states restrict to short maturities.	Default risk free; same custody problems as T-bills. Price risks increase with maturity.	Generally marketable; price spreads widen on longer maturities.	Usually higher than T-bills.
U.S. Treasury bonds	A few states treat as outright maturities.	Default risk free; many public sector losses experienced in long maturity bonds	Marketable, but wider spreads exist in longer maturities.	Incrementally higher than notes, but often not in direct proportion.
Zero-coupon securities: a) STRIPS	Most states treat as outright ownership.	Considerable price risk for maturities over 5 years.	Less market than treasuries. Wirable through the Fed.	Often higher than coupon securities.
b) TIGERS, CATS, LIONS other depository receipts	Many states do not treat them as legal equivalent of the underlying treasuries.	The theoretical risk of depository failure; long maturity and price risk are major problems.	Sometimes poor; wide price spreads.	Usually higher than STRIPS because of limited market.

Instrument	General Legality	Safety Factors	Liquidity	Relative Yield
Federal agency discount notes	Some states require full faith and credit of U.S. government; these generally lack such guarantees.	No express federal guarantee; generally viewed as safer than longer-term agency notes and bonds. Federal "moral obligation."	Generally good; verify secondary market when you purchase.	Usually better than T-bills.
Banker's acceptances	A few states permit.	Good credit quality on top-name domestic BAs.	In large blocks, a secondary market may exist.	Generally higher than government securities.
State investment pools	25 states now operate.	Good diversification; some states do not mark-to-market however, and maintain long maturities.	Generally good; problems can arise if interest rates rise and the pool disintermediates.	Generally higher than short-term treasury securities.
Money market mutual funds	Some states permit.	Varies with the fund. Some are AAA-rated and hold only government securities. Constant $1.00 share price.	Institutional funds permit same day withdrawals and wire transfers; retail funds often do not.	Generally better than short-term government securities.
Municipal securities	Generally only in-state obligations permitted. Some states are amending laws to broaden authority.	Credit risk varies with issuer.	Poor. Only purpose is to invest bond proceeds.	Low. However, some high-quality bond issuers can buy tax-exempt, earn arbitrage profit, and keep it.

Exhibit 9.4 (Continued)

Instrument	General Legality	Safety Factors	Liquidity	Relative Yield
Government bond mutual funds and tax-exempt mutual funds	Very few states now permit.	Quality varies. Market price risk is primary risk. Should be no-load.	Can be liquidated, but losses will occur if interest rates rise.	Government bond funds often yield more than money market funds. Tax-exempt funds reflect lower rates in that sector.
Guaranteed investment contracts	Very few states now permit; generally for bond proceeds only.	Depends on insurance company. No federal insurance applies.	May be poor. Difficult to withdraw without losing earnings.	Sometimes higher than money market securities.
Federal agency bonds and notes	Some are full faith and credit, others are not. Certain states permit all; many permit only a few.	Default risk is greater than treasuries. Market price risk increases with maturities.	Often less liquid than other government securities.	Should be higher than treasury bonds of same maturity.
Certificates of deposit of banks and S&Ls	Many states permit in-state bank CDs. A few permit out-of-state CDs if insured or collateralized.	43 states require collateralization $100,000 federal deposit insurance per institution. 200 banks and S&Ls failed in 1987.	Most institutions penalize early withdrawal.	Erratic. Generally should exceed T-bills but some markets are uncompetitive.

240

Instrument	General Legality	Safety Factors	Liquidity	Relative Yield
Repurchase agreements (repos)	Some states permit explicitly; others by implication. Some impose rigid delivery requirements.	Safety improves with written agreements, delivery vs. payment, daily mark-to-market of collateral, and "haircuts."	Overnight/open repos are liquid; term repos are not.	Usually close to Fed Funds rate. Typically yields rise when securities dealer's inventories are large.
Commercial paper	Some states permit, usually with credit rating restrictions.	Unsecured corporate obligation under 270 days. Typically the greatest credit risk of money market securities.	Unless dealer agrees to redeem, liquidity can be poor. Usually held to maturity.	Higher than most other comparable maturity instruments.

Source: Miller, 1989: 124.

241

tificates of deposit, U.S. treasury bills, and/or money market certificates, all of which are insured by the Federal Deposit Insurance Corporation (FDIC). Investments are made for various periods of time, though the most frequent are thirty days, sixty days, six months, and one year. The period selected depends on the need for money, the degree of liquidity required, and opportunity costs. (Most governments maintain a thirty-day supply of operating money on hand.) These investments customarily are supervised by a depository board.

A sound investment strategy has two important facets. One is short-term investment of large amounts of money through purchase of certificates of deposit bought from financial institutions paying the highest rate of interest, usually via competitive bidding. The other facet entails depositing funds in investment accounts located in various institutions within the taxing jurisdictions.

REVENUE FORECASTING

Another integral function of tax administration is forecasting revenues. After all, government budgets and thus expenditures depend not on the amount of "hard" money currently available, but rather on the amount of money forecasted for the end of the fiscal year. Simply put, the function of a revenue forecast is to figure out the amount of revenues available so that a balanced budget can be developed and implemented. It basically tells governments how much they can afford.

Various forecasting techniques exist. All require an understanding of revenues and the economic factors and events affecting those revenues. For any technique or combination of techniques to be useful, however, it must meet two criteria (Liner, 1978: 32). First, it must be straightforward enough so that government officials untrained in statistics and/or economics can use it during the process of developing the budget. Second, it must require only data that are easily obtainable on a timely basis.

Most of the techniques are strongly influenced by time. That is, first and foremost, a time series trend must be computed. Then factors that contribute to any fluctuations in the trend need to be analyzed carefully before forecasts can be made.

Trends

The heart of most revenue forecasting techniques is trend analysis, and the nucleus of such an analysis is computing different patterns that comprise those trends. Essentially, a trend is a function of the multiplicative properties of three major patterns: long-term, seasonal, and cyclical. Such a trend is graphically depicted in Exhibit 9.5.

Long-Term Pattern. This pattern reflects gradual increases and decreases in the trend over a relatively long period of time, such as years. It normally is smooth and continuous, though it does not have to be linear. This pattern gen-

Exhibit 9.5
Long-Term, Seasonal, and Cyclical Patterns

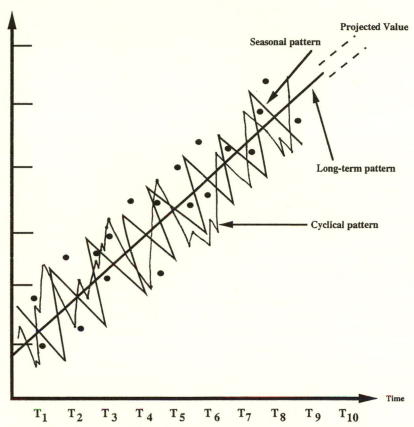

Projected Value

Seasonal pattern

Long-term pattern

Cyclical pattern

Time

T_1 T_2 T_3 T_4 T_5 T_6 T_7 T_8 T_9 T_{10}

Source: Adapted from Ronald John Hy, *Financial Management for Health Care Administrators*. Westport, CT: Quorum Books. Reprinted with permission of Greenwood Publishing Group, Inc., Westport, CT. © 1989 by Ronald John Hy.

erally dominates the other patterns, and therefore is by far the most important of the three. Because this pattern is so crucial, reliable and valid data are needed to project it.

Seasonal Pattern. This pattern consists of increases and decreases in the trend over a short period of time, such as several months. The seasonal pattern is a regularly vacillating trend that spans the time of the long-term pattern. Since the seasonal pattern occurs quite regularly, it is systematic and predictable.

Cyclical Pattern. The cyclical pattern is comprised of short-term periodic increases and decreases in the trend. It is a crucial component of trend analysis because it is used to project unsteady increases and decreases in the trend. Over time the trend tends to rise and fall at alternating periods of time, and the cyclical pattern accounts for the direction and intensity of that change. The central difference between the seasonal and cyclical patterns is that the former is more predictable because it occurs at regular time intervals.

Forecasting Techniques

Results of a 1991 survey conducted by the Federation of Tax Administrators illustrate the importance of revenue forecasting to state budgetary processes ("State Revenue Estimating Procedures," 1992: 38). Exhibit 9.6 summarizes the revenue forecasting practices among states. Twenty-eight states restrict the total amount of their appropriations to the forecasted revenues. Thus, increases in spending beyond forecasted revenues require concomitant cuts or increases in taxes to assure balanced budgets.

Twenty-four states designate a single officer, usually within the executive branch, to issue the official revenue forecast. Legislatures in these states perform only advisory functions. As of 1991, eighteen states assigned the responsibility of an official forecast to both the executive and the legislative branches. A few states require two groups to develop independent revenue forecasts and then reconcile their differences to arrive at the official forecast.

Besides relying on the aforementioned forecasting techniques, states, and often local governments, use formal and informal advisory groups to help interpret forecasts to reach consensus on forecasted revenues. Only six states formally review their official forecasts. The extent of the reviews obviously differs among states. However, many states formally or informally ask outside advisory groups from both academia and the private sector to review their forecasts before they become official.

All states periodically review their revenue forecasts when circumstances dictate. But only two states update forecasts as frequently as once a month. Exhibit 9.6 shows that fourteen states update forecasts quarterly, whereas sixteen states revise them semiannually.

Basically, three techniques are used to forecast state and local revenues: trend analysis, deterministic techniques, and econometric techniques. *Trend analysis* uses time series regression to forecast revenues. For certain revenues, time itself is a crucial, if not causal, factor. That is, fairly accurate forecasts can be made simply by assuming that revenues will increase or decrease over time at about the rate they grew or declined in the immediate past. Trend analysis, however, cannot estimate a *turning point* that might affect revenue generation; it will continue to project increases or decreases for a specified time period, irrespective of what might occur within the economy.

Trend analysis is especially useful for local governments with neither the time nor the money to develop econometric forecasts. It is particularly effective in forecasting revenues from fees, fines, and other minor sources of revenues.

Deterministic techniques are used to forecast revenues when tax dollars are generated via predetermined formulas. These techniques use factors other than

Exhibit 9.6
Summary of Forecasting Practices

State	Council of Economic Advisers	Forecasts Bind Budget	Forecasts Updated	Formal Review Process
Alabama	N	N	annual	N
Alaska	N	N	semiannual	N
Arizona	N	Y	quarterly	N
Arkansas	Y	Y	quarterly	N
California	N	N	3 times/year	N
Colorado	Y	N	quarterly	N
Connecticut	N	N	monthly	N
Delaware	Y	Y	6 times/year	N
Florida	Y	Y	semiannual	N
Georgia	N	Y	annual	N
Hawaii	N	Y	quarterly	N
Idaho	N	N	semiannual	N
Illinois	N	Y	quarterly	N
Indiana	Y	N	semiannual	N
Iowa	Y	Y	quarterly	N
Kansas	N	N	semiannual	N
Kentucky	Y	Y	as necessary	Y
Louisiana	Y	Y	quarterly	N
Maine	N	Y	semiannual	N
Maryland	N	N	as necessary	N
Massachusetts	N	Y	semiannual	N
Michigan	N	N	semiannual	Y
Minnesota	Y	Y	semiannual	N
Mississippi	N	Y	as necessary	Y
Missouri	Informal	N	as necessary	N
Montana	N	Y	as necessary	N
Nebraska	Y	N	semiannual	N
Nevada	N	N	as necessary	N
New Hampshire	N	Y	monthly	N
New Jersey	Y	Y	semiannual	N
New Mexico	N	N	annual	N
New York	Y	Y	quarterly	N
North Carolina	N	Y	semiannual	N
North Dakota	N	Y	semiannual	N
Ohio	Y	Y	semiannual	N
Oklahoma	N	Y	as necessary	N
Oregon	Y	Y	quarterly	N
Pennsylvania	N	Y	annual	N
Rhode Island	Informal	N	quarterly	N

Exhibit 9.6 (Continued)

South Carolina	N	N	4 times/year	Y
South Dakota	N	N	as necessary	N
Tennessee	N	N	semiannual	N
Texas	Y	Y	as necessary	N
Utah	N	N	quarterly	N
Vermont	Y	Y	semiannual	N
Virginia	Y	Y	quarterly	Y
Washington	Y	Y	quarterly	N
West Virginia	N	N	annual	N
Wisconsin	N	N	biennially	N
Wyoming	N	N	annual	N
Dist. of Columbia	N	N	annual	Y

*Biennial Budgets. The forecast horizon varies based on whether it is the first
or second year of the biennium.

Source: "State Revenue Estimating Procedures," 1992: 39.

time to forecast revenues. Deterministic techniques, however, are limited because they assume fixed relationships between inputs and outputs, which is not always the case.

Forecasting property tax revenues is a good example of where a deterministic technique can be applied appropriately. The total assessed value of a jurisdiction is the only variable factor in the formula, and it seldom changes drastically from year to year. Consequently, once the assessed value is ascertained, one only has to subtract the amount of the exemptions and multiply that product—the taxable value—by the millage rate to forecast property tax revenues.

State aid to public schools provides another illustration of an appropriate place to use a deterministic technique. State aid to public school districts usually is based on factors such as size of the school-age population, average daily attendance, size of the school district, cost for handicapped students, and cost of vocational education. While variations are found among states in both the number and types of factors and the degree of sophistication, the amount of state aid forecasted is ascertained by entering the appropriate figures into the formula.

Econometric techniques use principles drawn from economics and statistics—primarily multistep regression—and thus are highly complex conceptually. These forecasting techniques can yield a tremendous amount of information since they consider the simultaneous effects of several factors that ultimately determine forecasted revenues.

Designating econometric equations requires persons trained in economics, statistics, and taxation. Although expensive in terms of data collection and analysis, econometric techniques furnish results that are evaluated easily and systematically.

State econometric forecasting techniques require various steps. First, national economic and demographic forecasts are obtained from reputable national forecasting firms. Second, state demographic and economic forecasts are made, using changes and situations noted in these national forecasts. These state forecasts yield state revenue forecasts which are compared to budget demands. After this comparison, final budget allocations are constructed for legislative review and action.

The following eighteen factors are used most frequently in econometric equations to forecast state revenues (Economic Analysis and Tax Research, 1992: 4):

- U.S. Nominal Gross Domestic Product (GDP)
- GDP Deflator
- Real GDP
- Net General Revenues (NGR)
- Real Gross State Product
- State Personal Income (SPI)
- NGR % of SPI
- Wage and Salary Disbursements
- Nonfarm Income
- Farm Income
- Existing Home Sales
- Employment
- Wage and Salary Employment
- Manufacturing Employment
- Disposable Income
- Population
- Per Capita Income
- Real Personal Income

Exhibit 9.7 schematically illustrates how these factors are used with simultaneous equations to forecast state revenues. As the values of these factors change, the equations and their relationships to each other also are altered, resulting in modifications to forecasted revenues.

Although more costly than the other two methods, econometric techniques have several advantages. The most important is that the forecast is based on estimates of changing economic and demographic relationships rather than on monotonic change. This allows for a more accurate forecast. Furthermore, deterministic techniques usually include only a few causal factors, while econo-

Exhibit 9.7
Econometric Forecasting Process

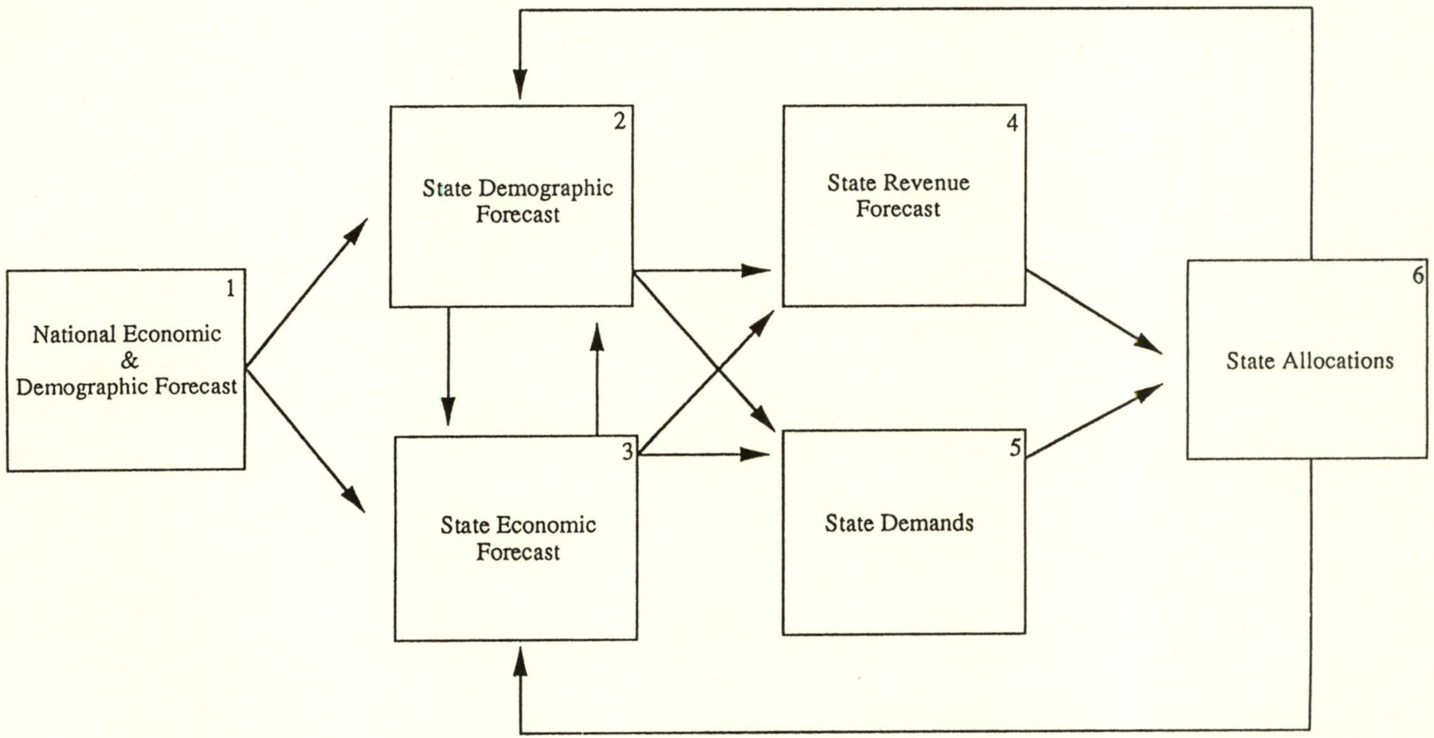

metric techniques use many more causal factors interacting simultaneously to affect revenues.

Summary. A combination of these three techniques furnishes the most accurate revenue forecasts. Econometric techniques are sensitive to changes in economic situations, whereas trend analysis and deterministic techniques are sensitive to underlying stable and economic relationships. Another reason for selecting a combination of forecasting techniques involves the desired trade-off between the cost of a forecast and the degree of accuracy needed.

The simpler techniques require less data and less time to produce. The more complex methods incorporate the effects of a larger number of factors acting on revenues, and thus, while furnishing more information, are more expensive. Tax management must use the combination that best balances the amount of information needed with the cost of that information. Regardless of which combination of methods is used, however, all methods rely on complex analyses of financial, environmental, and demographic data (Hy, 1989: 38).

While state governments tend to use combinations of econometric techniques to forecast revenues, local governments are more likely to rely on trend analysis. For the most part, trend analysis is more dominant in larger local governments (McCollough, 1990: 38). Although local governments possess the necessary computer hardware, software, and data bases to use econometric forecasting techniques, most tend to utilize spreadsheets and judgments of their revenue analysts. The more sophisticated econometric techniques are considered by smaller local governments to be too expensive and time-consuming, and simply cost-ineffective.

INGREDIENTS FOR SUCCESS

In the final analysis, tax administration in the United States rests ultimately on the honesty and integrity of taxpayers and remitters who by and large comply because (1) they are convinced that others also comply, and (2) they know that governments investigate, search out, and punish those who attempt to evade payments illegally. Taxpayers, furthermore, have become overwhelmed by government officials and a vast array of complex tax rules and regulations imposed on them.

As a result, good tax administration is built on the public's *trust* in the ability of governments *to collect and manage tax revenues* effectively and efficiently. This trust can best be attained by professional, objective, and uniform tax administration at the state and local levels, administration that demonstrates how well the tax system is operating.

Another valuable component of good tax administration is *commitment from top government officials* who first and foremost encourage hiring dedicated and hard-working personnel. Politically, tax administration is not an issue that sways elections. Nonetheless, it is important for these officials to let the public know of their commitment to effective and efficient administration—if for no other reason than to build up trust in the administrative mechanisms.

REFERENCES

Association of Arkansas Counties (1992). *Arkansas County Collector's Procedures Annual*. Little Rock: Association of Arkansas Counties.

Economic Analysis and Tax Research (1992). *Arkansas Fiscal Notes*. Arkansas Department of Finance and Administration, July.

Hy, Ronald John (1989). *Financial Management for Health Care Administrators*. Westport, Conn.: Quorum Books.

Liner, Charles (1978). "Projecting Local Government Revenues." *Popular Government*, 32, Spring.

McCollough, Jane (1990). "Municipal Revenue and Expenditure Forecasting: Current Status and Future Prospects." *Government Finance Review*, October.

Mikesell, John (1991). *Fiscal Administration: Analysis and Applications for the Public Sector*. 3rd ed. Chicago: Dorsey Press.

Miller, Girard (1989). "Investment Tools and Techniques." In Ian Allan, ed., *Cash Management for Small Governments*. Chicago: Government Finance Officers Association.

"State Revenue Estimating Procedures" (1992). *Government Finance Review*, August.

Conclusion

Most state and local governments are once again at financial crossroads. As happens periodically throughout the history of this country, state and local governments in some sections of the country are expanding vigorously and broadly, generating new jobs and trying to lessen poverty rates. Other areas are stagnating economically and demographically. They are losing people, which in turn means decreasing tax bases accompanied by decreasing revenues, normally without concomitant decreases in expenditures.

Though economic and demographic growth and decline create fiscal problems for state and local governments, by and large, problems associated with decline are more difficult to resolve than problems connected with growth. Growth undoubtedly necessitates additional revenues beyond those supplied by inflation. Decline, on the other hand, seldom means that governments need fewer tax dollars. Governments experiencing decline still have to spend nearly as much money as they did during periods of stabilization; yet their tax bases, and thus revenues, are shrinking.

OWN-SOURCE REVENUES

In either case—growth or decline—the current fiscal situations experienced by state and local governments are likely to result eventually in substantial changes in tax structures because both growth and decline necessitate revenues which may be beyond their fiscal resources that state and local governments currently are generating. At the same time, federal aid in terms of real dollars is decreasing. These two situations mean, quite frankly, that in the foreseeable future state and local governments will have to alleviate these fiscal problems by increasing their own-source revenues.

Increasing own-source revenues, however, creates a problem because over the past two decades the fastest growing states and localities are those with relatively low state and local tax burdens. Those with high tax burdens are growing more slowly. Consequently, adding new taxes and/or increasing existing taxes may very well increase tax burdens and slow economic and demographic growth, since such actions probably will increase the cost of living as well as the cost of doing business. Expanding own-source revenues without negatively affecting growth is one of the major tax issues state and local governments are facing.

According to Lieberman (1991:37), states and localities must address questions such as these:

- How high should taxes be?
- Who should bear the tax burden?
- Should taxes be used to promote economic growth?
- Should taxes be used to help particular segments of the economy?
- To what extent should revenues be used to ameliorate social problems?

TAX INCIDENCE

Another key issue state and local governments face is tax incidence. Deciding who should pay taxes and how much of their incomes they should pay has been, and will continue to be, a major issue. Basically, taxing consumption—through sales and excise taxes—affects only income that is spent, while income taxes, whether personal or corporate, are levied on earned income, irrespective of whether it is spent or saved. Since those with lower income normally spend a higher percentage of their income on necessities, they are hit harder by most consumption taxes than those with higher incomes. Consequently, most consumption taxes are considered regressive—even when low income persons are granted various exemptions.

State and local revenues, it should be remembered, tend to come from regressive taxes. Approximately two-thirds come from consumption taxes and various combinations of other taxes, charges, and fees, most of which are somewhat regressive and tend to be shifted to consumers. State and local governments are increasingly relying on charges, fees, and consumption taxes to expand their own-source revenues. As a result, lower income persons, as a group, are contributing—and will continue to contribute—a higher percentage of their incomes to state and local revenues through these taxes than are higher income persons.

About one-third of state revenues are generated from personal income taxes, which are seen as progressive. Higher income persons pay more in income taxes, thereby offsetting the lower consumption tax burden. This situation, however, is tempered by the fact that state and local income, wage, and payroll taxes can be deducted from federal income taxes, thus reducing the federal burdens of higher income persons. The progressivity of graduated personal income taxes also is reduced by the many deductions and credits that are allowed by states. Even though many of these deductions and credits are not regressive per se, they tend to benefit only those who itemize their taxes. Insofar as lower income persons tend not to itemize, they do not take advantage of deductions and credits; consequently, their actual tax burden is greater than that of higher income persons.

TYPES OF TAXES

Tax fairness, as previously mentioned, depends on which tax concept, or combination of concepts, one accepts. A tax is fair, some contend, if it is based on ability to pay; that is, higher income persons pay more taxes proportionate to their incomes than do lower income persons. Others hold that a tax is fair if everyone pays the same rate, regardless of income. Still others maintain that a tax is fair if only those who receive its benefits pay the tax.

Income Taxes: Personal and Corporate

Personal income taxes are based on adjusted gross income, which is used as a base to determine taxable income and ultimately to calculate taxes due. Adjusted gross income typically includes personal income and miscellaneous earnings, such as interest income, and excludes some forms of income, such as Social Security payments. Taxable income is calculated from adjusted gross income with reductions based on the state or local revenue structure's specified deductions and exemptions from income.

The primary argument in favor of these taxes is that the rates, exemptions, deductions, and credits can be tailored to individual groups based on their ability to pay. In addition, these taxes cannot be shifted.

Generally, personal income tax revenues for states have been increasing. This increase reflects either changes in graduated income tax rates or—most likely—growth (in both nominal and real terms) in personal income coupled with unchanging brackets (bracket shifting). This bracket shift affects the *ability to pay* principle of taxation. Taxes increase as individuals move into higher brackets, even when their purchasing power has not increased.

As a result of bracket shift, personal income tax structures are not distinguishing between middle and low income persons, and between upper and middle income persons. The only solution for bracket shifting is to index either brackets or rates. Otherwise, progressive income taxes in reality devolve into a flatter tax structure than was originally planned.

Having said this, one should realize that extensive disagreement exists over the direction of income tax reform, translating into fierce political opposition from those likely to be hurt by changes in existing policies, be they ordinary people or interest groups. Changing provisions for deducting mortgage interest and property taxes, for instance, might mean that individuals would pay more taxes and that the value of their housing would fall.

Corporate income taxes are profits-based levies on corporations that conduct business within states. These taxes normally do not apply to sole proprietorships, partnerships, or Subchapter S corporations, whose profits are taxed as personal income.

Corporate income taxes are based on the ability to pay principle. The major problem is that net income is an elusive figure, affected by different accounting methods. In addition, the precise incidence of the taxes is unclear. There is little agreement as to who actually bears the major burden of corporate income taxes. Most corporate tax liability appears to be passed to the consumer via higher prices, but some may be shifted to shareholders in the form of lower dividends and/or to workers in the form of lower wages and benefits.

Concern over the impact of business taxes on location and expansion decisions has resulted in slowing the growth of these taxes, despite evidence that such taxes are not important factors. It also has reduced the share of state revenues contributed by businesses.

Nevertheless, for obvious political and economic reasons, states and localities have protective attitudes toward certain businesses. Farm states, for instance, favor agriculture and agribusiness. Despite such preferences, governments still are interested in raising reasonable amounts of revenues at rates that appear competitive with other states. Politics require a reasonable ratio of business to nonbusiness taxes, even though most economists believe that consumers eventually pay most of these taxes.

Corporate income taxes also are complicated by multiple taxation. One of the most troublesome problems concerns taxing cash and stock dividends, particularly undistributed profits. Normally these profits are taxed twice—once as corporate income and again as personal income for those who receive dividends.

Consumption Taxes: Sales, Use, and Excise

Some consumption taxes are paid by consumers at the point of purchase, while others are paid in the form of higher prices. In addition, sometimes these taxes, like corporate income taxes, are shifted to stockholders and workers.

Consumption taxes are convenient to pay and efficient to collect. They also are used as a mechanism to export taxes to transient populations. When levied on vice and luxuries, they serve a sumptuary purpose. Consumption taxes quite often are criticized on the grounds that their incidence is regressive and frequently capricious. Tobacco and liquor are the favorite bases for excise taxes. The former is especially vulnerable to tax increases since it is both socially unacceptable and inelastic in demand. Collection of consumption taxes is impressively easy and inexpensive, although tax evasion in the form of bootlegging can be a serious matter.

Consumption taxes generate a significant amount of revenue. But state and local governments must constantly be aware of the impact of tax exemptions, which in many states are estimated to be half as much as the taxes generate. Moreover, exemptions normally are unevenly distributed, affecting certain parts of the economy more directly than others. Businesses, especially services and agriculture, are the primary beneficiaries. These exemptions generally are justified as tax incentives which stimulate economic development. When exemptions create or return jobs for residents, states can increase their revenues via increases in personal and sales taxes, and states can reduce their expenditures by lower unemployment compensation and other such costs. But tax incentives must be viewed carefully or more will be given away in exemptions than can be retrieved. While certain exemptions may be necessary, they impose a serious burden on the remainder of the tax base. Tax exemptions impact negatively on schools, quality of the labor force, and other infrastructures, since exemptions deprive state and local governments of needed revenues. And because of the tremendous growth in the service sector, exemptions for these businesses have a considerable impact.

Severance Taxes

Scarce and valuable natural resources have distinctive characteristics that justify special taxing considerations. They are either nonreproducible or slowly reproducible and relatively fixed in supply. Thus, depletion is an ever-present problem which tax structures must take into account.

The key problem centers on the deterrent effect of taxes on timber and mining production and on who should pay these taxes. Certain resources can be successfully taxed ad valorem, whereas others require per unit taxation. Timber, for example, is taxed on acreage and yield. Mines are taxed on production figures such as tonnage. Most states levy a per unit tax on severed resources. Experience shows, however, that ad valorem (percent of value) taxes are much more elastic (respond to market price changes) and most fairly compensate states for the diminishing supply of scarce resources. Indexing severance taxes also helps states and localities, since the infrastructure costs to support extraction remain relatively constant.

Almost all states levy severance taxes on the production or value of scarce natural resources. Such taxes attempt to balance the permanent loss to the state of these taxed resources. Frequently, states share these revenues with local governments. The revenues normally are earmarked for industry-related activities. In recent years, more emphasis has been placed on increasing severance *fees* rather than severance *taxes*.

Severance taxes can, and generally are, exported. Exporting takes place when persons or corporations outside the taxing jurisdiction bear at least part of the tax liability. It is likely to occur when a state or local government levies taxes on businesses that market a significant share of their production to nonresidents.

The success of tax exporting depends on the uniqueness and permanence of the taxed commodity.

Tax exporting reduces the cost of services to residents because the costs are shared with nonresidents who purchase the taxed products and who do not use the services. Tax exporting is a significant phenomenon in this country. States whose scarce, nonsubstitutable, and needed natural resources are an important part of their economic activities are high tax exporting states.

Property Taxes

Several reasons exist for the long-time dominance of property taxes as a major revenue source for local governments. They are stable revenue sources, easily collected and administered. Property tax bases, especially real estate, are not elusive. Land and buildings are fixed and cannot be moved to escape tax assessors and collectors. The stability and dependability of these revenue sources make them important to local governments.

The major problem with property taxes involves assessment, equalization, and rate fixation. The assessed value of real property lags behind its market value, and tax limitation movements have prevented collection of the full amount possible. Moreover, many governments tax the same base simultaneously. Thus, governments that rely on property taxes as a key revenue source are hard pressed to increase revenues because of the growing inelasticity of property taxes. This problems is further aggravated by the increasing number of property tax exemptions given for economic development, which can be expected to continue. Consequently, these revenues have not kept pace with governmental expenditures, meaning that governments have to look at other revenue sources, such as charges and fees.

Property tax burdens usually are borne by landowners. However, in some cases—rental, farm properties, timber, and mining land—such taxes are passed to consumers. In addition, when taxes are inordinately high, property values are lowered, and the costs are borne by landowners. That is, when taxes rise, land values may fall, and landowners may lose money. High property taxes also may discourage construction, leading to property shortages and decay.

In an attempt to address this problem, property taxes have undergone considerable modification in recent years, primarily involving limitations on rate increases, increases in exemptions, and implementation of classification schemes. Even though property taxes depend on inconsistent assessment procedures and are highly visible and regressive, they are here to stay. Not only are property taxes a stable and dependable revenue source, but they also are administered locally without help from states, giving local government some fiscal autonomy.

EXEMPTIONS, DEDUCTIONS, AND CREDITS

This discussion merely points out that, theoretically at least, most state and local taxes unquestionably are regressive. To reduce the degree of regressivity and to compensate for unequal tax burdens, most state and local governments exempt basic necessities such as food, utilities, and prescription drugs from sales taxes. They also may reduce fees on goods and services used most frequently by lower income persons, such as camping permits. Although these exemptions reduce taxes and fees for everyone, they have a far greater impact on lower income groups because a higher percentage of their income is spent on exempted items.

While some exemptions are given to lessen tax regressivity, state and local governments are quite prone to grant many exemptions which all too often serve particular interests. Personal income tax deductions and credits also account for additional lost revenue.

Exemptions tend to be so pervasive that some are added every legislative session, and hardly any are ever repealed. Exemptions become especially evident during legislative sessions that increase taxes. In other words, taxes and exemptions increase together.

Frequently, exemptions in general sales and use, excise, corporate income, and property taxes are implemented to encourage economic development. But, as pointed out in Chapter 8, tax exemptions play only a minor role in the locational decisions of businesses, and they play an even smaller role in business expansion decisions. Normally, state and local governments grant exemptions as incentives to businesses without conducting adequate research. They merely accept the claims of those seeking exemptions, even though such claims are not based on empirical evidence. Such actions cost state and local governments millions of dollars. Yet, most governments have no idea of exactly how much these measures cost them until after they are implemented. In addition to reducing revenues, exemptions, deductions, and credits hurt states and localities because the untaxed money or money returned via credits and allowable deductions is taxed by the federal government, meaning that revenues are shifted from states to the national government.

INTERSTATE DIFFERENCES

Earlier chapters have shown that state and local governments generate revenues from a wide variety of sources, from sales and income to consumption and severance taxes to an assortment of charges and fees. The proportion of revenue sources used varies from state to state. Some state and local governments rely heavily on manufacturing industries, others depend on finance and trade establishments, and still others generate substantial proportions of revenues from agriculture and mining interests. Some state and local governments are poor, while others are wealthy. As a result of such differences, no single tax structure can possibly be recommended for all states. The fundamental problem in analyzing state and local taxes, then, centers around adequately recognizing interstate and intrastate differences that require variations in major revenue sources.

For the most part, interstate differences revolve around reliance on general

sales and personal income taxes as well as charges and fees. Southern states
tend to have more state dominated fiscal structures. State governments finance
more local expenditures, which generally means that these expenditures are more
controllable and uniform and financed with more elastic revenues. In practice,
southern states depend more than other states on consumption taxes, charges,
and fees. Northern and midwestern states, in contrast, have more locally dominated fiscal structures, creating the potential for greater disparity among local
government expenditures and heavier dependence on property and personal income taxes.

Regardless of these differences, all states must deal with the impact of inflation (or deflation) on their economies. When governments do not index either
tax rates or tax bases, bracket shifting occurs. Simply put, when rates or bases
are not indexed to correct for price increases, taxpayers pay more taxes—the
effect being the same as if taxes were increased.

Increases in taxes, regardless of how they occur, reduce the amount of after-
tax spending power of individuals and businesses. When state taxes rise, for
instance, the amount of money flowing into state coffers increases, and the
amount available for private spending and saving decreases. Thus, different parts
of the state economy are affected accordingly since government purchases drive
some parts of the economy more than others. (The opposite, of course, occurs
when taxes are reduced or eliminated.)

In practice, this means that when additional tax revenues are paid with money
that would otherwise be used for private consumption, spending patterns are
shifted from households and businesses to governments. If extra taxes are paid
from savings, there will be less private capital available for investment and
production, leading to lower economic growth. Of course, if the state uses the
additional money to reduce or eliminate a debt, more funds will be available
for investment and production. In any event, tax increases, no matter how they
come, lead to different impacts on different parts of the economy. The precise
effect of tax increases (or decreases) on individuals is not so clear. This impact
tends to be viewed ideologically rather than economically.

Although it is always dangerous to generalize, economic liberals tend to believe that behavior is not very responsive to the tax system, while conservatives
take the opposite view. Liberals prefer taxes with low elasticities because they
can raise large amounts of money for public sector activity without having to
worry too much about charges that they are killing the goose that laid the golden
egg. Conversely, economic conservatives prefer taxes with high elasticities because this limits the volume of taxes that can be collected before serious efficiency costs are imposed on the economy (Rosen, 1985: 411). The debate
between these two groups is likely to continue for some time within the political
environment.

THE POLITICAL ENVIRONMENT

State and local tax structures are affected by the political climate as well as the economic environment. In other words, tax changes generally are ideologically and/or economically based and undoubtedly occur within a political context. Debates concerning taxation, from who pays to how they pay, often touch only peripherally on the economic impact of the taxes on the states or communities.

More precisely, state and local tax structures more often than not are products of the particular interests of the decision makers, the influence of special interests, and the attention of the electorate. While state and local governments are influenced by economics, there is no escaping the fact that tax levies and enhancements are largely formed by political processes that are often insensitive to broader economic issues. Self-interest may be the most compelling economic interest represented in tax debates, and the self-interest of the most influential segments of the electorate frequently win out over the interests of the whole. The political challenge is how to increase and diversify revenues without raising the wrath of the electorate, knowing full well that a significant segment will oppose any tax increase almost without regard to need.

Many of these particular interests are driven by demographic changes. In suburban communities, for example, demographic changes are creating new demands. Relatively low taxes attract affluent residents, and suburban flight brings more middle-class residents. Traffic congestion requires more expenditures to expand street and highway capacity, residents on fixed incomes demand more social and health programs, and upper and middle income residents demand enhanced educational programs for their children. Higher population densities require more land use regulation, building codes, and zoning restrictions. Crime follows population density and development. Soon, the problems suburbanites fled are being visited upon them and rural areas, too. Cities, towns, and counties are run over by development and struggling to keep up with demands for services. Such changes obviously are inevitable, notwithstanding the few places where residents have resisted development, discouraged in-migration, and used restrictive zoning and/or condominium agreements to control population density.

In spite of the tremendous impact of demographic changes, state revenues remain limited, and state fiscal woes are being visited upon local governments. A sense of deja vu exists. In the 1970s and 1980s governments wrestled with the mandate of *doing more with less* and in most cases resigned themselves to *doing less with less*. That is, in these two decades state and local governments lacked the resources and, in many cases, the inclination to address problems created by demographic changes, and they had to seek out federal monies and programs to solve local problems.

Today, local governments face added pressure caused by state and federal mandates to address problems ranging from overcrowded jails to water quality and from environmental protection to equal employment opportunity. While the mandates often are laudable in intent, they all too frequently are not accompanied by the funding needed to implement them. Local governments have to find fiscal resources within political environments to satisfy the mandates before they can address their own problems.

Trends in Revenue Enhancement

What we see is a changing, demanding, and challenging political environment that requires state and local governments to exhibit more and more fiscal creativity in expanding revenues. Annexing tax-generating property, attracting more residents and businesses, and encouraging development of higher income properties are some of the ways in which tax bases are expanded. Efficiency reduces costs; consequently, some governments and residents turn to city-county, city-city, or county-county consolidation as a way to avoid duplication of services and to achieve economies of scale. Exporting taxes also is seen as a way to increase revenues while reducing the likelihood of taxpayer revolts and election embarrassments. Governments seek to fashion charges and fees that favor residents over nonresidents, and sales taxes on items purchased by tourists and other travelers. Wage and payroll taxes are used to capture revenues from suburban and rural residents working in central cities. Wheel taxes are used to capture revenues from nonresident workers, shoppers, and students who drive and park in central cities.

While governments try to expand tax bases and increase efficiency to find more creative ways of collecting needed revenue, some taxpayers offer resistance. The tax revolts, including Proposition 13 in California, Proposition 2½ in Massachusetts, and Measure 5 in Oregon, are now familiar to most of us. The secession movements as taxpayers try to remove their communities from larger political units to reduce their tax burdens are becoming more familiar. Secessionist movements are attempting to separate the borough of Staten Island from New York City, the town of Long Island from Portland, Maine, and even northern California from southern California. And the list of secessionist movements is growing. In 1993 governments in several affluent Kansas counties threatened secession from the state over property tax increases (Mields, 1993: 17). By contrast, other municipalities have sought bankruptcy protection (e.g., Bridgeport, Connecticut, in June 1991) to reduce pressure for major tax increases (Boroughs, 1992). Other municipalities have seen the seizure of public property for failing to repay debts.

Additional pressures for state and local governments to borrow creatively, bypassing voters whenever possible, also exist. Some communities are mortgaging public assets to generate operating revenue. Other communities are selling public buildings and lands to get needed funds. Using municipal bonds to fund industrial development, capital improvements, and other large ticket items is a popular approach. Indeed, state and local governments continue to worry that federal lawmakers may change the tax-free status of municipal bonds, making them much less attractive to investors. *Certificates of participation* (COPs), which are publicly sold shares in long-term lease agreements, are increasingly being used. Then, too, governments avoid large outlays of money by leasing facilities initially to avoid submitting the expenditures for public approval (Whitt, 1992).

The list of new state and local taxes, charges, and fees is growing almost daily. Some taxes are short-lived because they are not successful in raising revenue, others precisely because they are too successful. The most familiar successful revenue enhancing method may be sales taxes on services, which are certainly growing in popularity despite the Florida experience noted in Chapter 4. Raising sumptuary taxes on tobacco products, alcoholic beverages, and other ''sinful'' products, and taxing legalized gambling, ranging from bingo games to state lotteries and from dog and horse racing (and parimutuel betting) to casino and riverboat gambling, are discussed with increasing frequency.

Less familiar, and perhaps rightly so, have been efforts such as Illinois' long-distance telephone taxes, the city of New Orleans' proposal to license Mardi Gras products, and California's ''Twinkie tax'' on snack foods. The Illinois tax has created a furor in the business community, particularly with the airlines that committed to Chicago's airports. The New Orleans proposal would, for example, let one of the major breweries buy the right to be the ''official beer of Mardi Gras.'' (Given that Mardi Gras is a private festival rather than a city-sponsored event, there are fundamental questions concerning who can license products.) New Orleans, like many other cities that have major events, incurs considerable expense for law enforcement and other city services; consequently, there are compelling reasons to seek new ways to pay for the extra services.

In the case of California's Twinkie tax, fundamental issues arose concerning how to distinguish between snack foods and regular foods. Problems of administration, coupled with substantial compliance costs that may outweigh the expected tax and health benefits, remain. Whether the extra sales tax on snack foods encourages better dietary habits is doubtful, but the desire to avoid adding a regressive sales tax to regular food items is commendable (Boroughs, 1992).

Indeed, using taxes to encourage desired behaviors offers some interesting opportunities for state and local governments to reduce environmental damage. Certainly ''green taxes'' levied on those who generate excessive solid waste, travel on highways during rush hours or in congested areas (as used in Dallas and several European cities), purchase gas guzzling cars, park downtown rather than using mass transit, use firewood that contributes to air pollution, use electricity during peak periods, and so forth may have more public appeal than more broad-based taxes. By discouraging such behaviors, green taxes are designed to reduce the need for additional spending on items such as highways, landfills, and parking lots.

Federal, state, and local authorities also are reviewing the granting of tax-exempt status in light of the tremendous growth of the nonprofit sector. It is estimated that nonprofit organizations generated around $500 billion in revenues and employed 7 million people in 1990. However, little is known about the economic impact and tax avoidance of the nonprofit sector. For state and local governments, tax-exempt status means that organizations avoid billions of dollars in local property taxes, state corporate taxes, and state and local sales taxes and gain access to tax-exempt bonds to raise their own revenue. The U.S. General Accounting Office estimates that state and local governments lose about $3.5 billion per year from nonprofit hospitals alone. The use of nonprofit organizations as a form of bank for corporate and private assets, the creation of for-profit subsidiaries by nonprofit organizations, and the clearly commercial activities of nonprofit organizations are attracting more Internal Revenue Service and state and local attention—possibly resulting in more revenues for state and local governments (Gaul and Borowski, 1993).

The simplest choice for state and local governments is to improve their current tax structures by making them simpler and more comprehensive. States can make income taxes more comprehensive by reducing the loopholes that give advantage to some taxpayers over others and simplify their tax codes to facilitate compliance. State and local sales taxes certainly can be more comprehensive if they are applied to services such as haircuts, dry cleaning, jewelry repair, parking, and lawyers' fees. There still can be additional taxes on sumptuary items such as tobacco and alcoholic beverages, coupled with exemptions for food and prescription drugs to lessen the regressivity of the tax. Similarly, a more comprehensive property tax would include virtually all property except that owned by tax-exempt organizations. Tax exemptions also might be reviewed. And governments can choose to defer taxes rather than offer broad property tax exemptions to the elderly. More comprehensive taxes, by their very nature, would be easier to understand and simpler to administer.

Political Leadership

Much of the choice afforded state and local governments will depend on federal policy and leadership. Federal actions, such as curtailing the use of tax-exempt municipal bonds, increasing (or decreasing) the practice of requiring compliance with unfunded mandates, introducing new revenue sources such as a value-added tax, and increasing (or decreasing) intergovernmental transfers, can cause ripple effects in state and local treasuries. Similarly, state actions and mandates have tremendous impact on local fiscal resources and tax enhancing options. Expanding local authority to tax can at least give local governments greater leeway to meet their needs.

Fiscal autonomy, according to Callahan and Johnson (1979: 134), can be improved when states:

- Use restraint in promulgating mandates on local governments without providing sufficient funding, when appropriate

• Make an effort to overhaul fiscal structures to make them more cost efficient
• Encourage selective and responsible tax increases
• Are sensitive to local fiscal problems

Political leadership must recognize that the tax burden on Americans is not particularly high when compared with other industrialized nations. Our taxes are substantially lower than those in Europe, Japan, and Canada. To the extent that our national, state, and local tax structures are part of the global economy, they offer considerable attraction to investors. The real question is whether state and local governments are collecting enough tax money to support the kinds and quality of public services that they want and need.

REFERENCES

Boroughs, Don L., with Sara Collins (1992). "The Ten Worst Economic Moves." *U.S. News and World Report*, January 27, pp. 54–59.

Callahan, John, and Joy Johnson (1979). "Fiscal Federalism and the South: A Legislative Agenda." In Richard Weinstein, *Tax Reform and Southern Economic Development*. Research Triangle Park, N.C.: Southern Growth Policies Board.

Gaul, Gilbert M., and Neill A. Borowski (1993). "Tax-Exempt Status Shortchanges U.S. of Billions." *Atlanta Journal/Atlanta Constitution*, May 9, pp. F1, F6.

Lieberman, Carl (1991). *Making Economic Policy*. Englewood Cliffs, N.J.: Prentice-Hall.

Mields, Hugh, Jr. (1993). "The Property Tax: Local Revenue Mainstay." *Intergovernmental Perspective*, Summer.

Rosen, Harvey S. (1985). *Public Finance*. Homewood, Ill.: Richard D. Irwin.

Whitt, Richard (1992). "Lifting the Lid on Public Debt." *Atlanta Journal/Atlanta Constitution*, September 20, pp. A1, A8–9.

Appendix A

Analyzing Taxes

This book compares state and local tax policies. But taxes often are analyzed as well as compared. Although how taxes are analyzed is beyond our scope here, this appendix focuses on the key components of tax analysis. Coupled with the basic analytical designs discussed in Appendix B, this section should give the reader some sense of the nature of tax analysis.

THE NATURE OF TAX ANALYSIS

A tax analysis is the systematic identification, examination, and evaluation of real and potential impacts of a tax on at least a segment of society. More precisely, a tax analysis is concerned not only with intentional but also unintentional and unanticipated consequences, whether beneficial or detrimental, which *may* result from the implementation or expansion of a tax. Concern with both intended and unintended consequences of a particular tax is central to an analysis because the intended effects are seldom, if ever, the only impacts of a tax. In fact, unanticipated aftermaths are often even more critical than intended outcomes.

Besides dealing with intended and unintended consequences, an analysis identifies target and spillover groups affected by a tax. Target groups are those segments of the population who are intended to be affected by the tax, whereas spillover groups are those other than target groups who are affected by that tax. (These two types of groups, it should be recalled, may be affected either beneficially or detrimentally.) An analysis then dissects intended and unintended consequences affecting target and spillover groups by looking at the extent to which a tax is achieving its objectives.

Need for a Tax Analysis Framework

A sound analysis must simplify reality without omitting integral factors. Such a simplification often relies on a conceptual mode of analysis called an analytical framework. When a framework is integrated into the analytical process, *more rational* analysis can be conducted. (Note that the emphasis is on *more rational*, not on *rational*.) The function of a framework, Gunnar Myrdal (1958: 35) once said, is to make an analysis more rational by ascertaining relevant facts and bringing them into their true perspective by clarifying the causal relationships between means and aims.

While it would be pretentious to suggest that a single hybrid framework could be applied with equal success to all types of tax analyses, there nevertheless are basic functions essential to all tax analyses. First, a framework should list a tax's objectives clearly and precisely. Failure to specify objectives categorically may lead to overlooking a tax's real achievements, a serious shortcoming when attempting to evaluate tax impacts. Without a systematic framework critically important factors can be easily underrated or even neglected. (Including all relevant factors is crucial to an assessment because omitted factors may frustrate an analysis.)

Second, a tax analysis framework should focus on relationships rather than causes, primarily because understanding the latter is a difficult, time-consuming task which is of limited utility to an analysis. When conducting a tax analysis, one need not determine causality. It is sufficient to comprehend that X is so related to Y that X will have an impact on Y. In other words, knowing what causes Y is not so important as understanding the degree to which X will affect Y. In many cases, discerning the cause of Y is not crucial to an analysis.

Next, a framework should deal with tax dynamics. Tax impacts are dynamic, not static. Therefore the element of time must be incorporated into a framework; otherwise, a tax will be viewed statically, not dynamically. As the second law of thermodynamics indicates, a static state can be achieved only by cessation of all activity. Since a tax does not exist in a state of suspended animation, a useful framework must examine a tax as if it were in a state of quasi-dynamic equilibrium, a condition in which the analyzed tax remains analytically static within a stipulated range of time but in which time is considered an important factor.

Finally, a tax analysis framework should rely on both qualitative and quantitative techniques. While scientifically rigorous quantitative analysis is important, there also is a pronounced need for a comparatively simple and completely practical model that strikes a balance between administrative exigencies and available information on the one hand, and strict methodological research requirements on the other. After all, an analysis frequently relies on information that is not quantitatively precise enough to meet the criteria that purely quantitative models require.

More important, however, is the fact that tax-related agencies, especially at the local level, frequently have inadequate and often unreliable data resources on which to make meaningful and significant determinations. Then, too, many factors exceedingly crucial to an analysis cannot be quantified. Some critical factors are not prone to quantification because they cannot be assigned cardinal or ordinal values. (Unintended outcomes, in particular, are difficult to quantify.) Hence, if only quantitative analysis is used, prominent factors will be omitted, either intentionally or inadvertently, often causing the assessment to be quite inaccurate.

Any tax analysis framework performing the basic functions just described also possesses inherent, and thus unavoidable, limitations. First and foremost, a model oversimplifies reality through a parsimonious process. It likewise narrows the range of reality to make the complex comprehensible. When reality is oversimplified by any conceptual scheme, the output frequently does not reflect the actual world, thereby making it difficult to determine which factors are integral to the analysis.

An even more important problem is the tendency to compartmentalize and thus fragment knowledge which is applicable to an analysis. The danger of fragmentation and compartmentalization is that once the pieces are separated, they are difficult to put back together. As Ian Mitroff (1972: 230) observed, "We are masters at teaching [ourselves] how to break a system into components (i.e., analysis), but we are poor in teaching [ourselves] how to put the components back together again (i.e., synthesis)." Needless fractionalization makes it next to impossible to put the parts back together because such a cognitive process focuses on components of a policy rather than on the wholeness of that policy.

Keeping these two admonitions in mind, tax analysts should realize that regardless of the utility and irrespective of the degree of sophistication of any framework, the exact impact of a tax will always be unknown, and there is little one can do about that fact. Thus, a certain amount of conjecture will always be involved in any analysis because paradigms are bound to omit prominent events and effects. The unexpected occurrence of uncontrollable factors, moreover, undoubtedly contributes to this lack of preciseness. (Tax analysis, after all, is based on an interplay between certainty and uncertainty.) At the same time, analysts must realize that oversimplification need not necessarily lead to an unreliable and inaccurate analysis. When an analysis includes the critical factors, the generalizations generated by the use of a framework will be highly informative. In any event, tax analysts must utilize a framework or be faced with the chaos of reality.

PROPOSED TAX ANALYSIS FRAMEWORK

The subsequent model is designed to help analysts simplify a highly complex, somewhat subjective, and quantitatively squishy process in order to analyze taxes systematically. The framework then is intended to help analysts look carefully at both a tax's accomplishments and failures. (By reviewing strengths and weaknesses of a tax, an analysis can furnish an inventory of data needed for progressive planning.)

Identifying Objectives

Since, as stated previously, tax analysis focuses on ascertaining whether a tax is achieving its objectives, such an appraisal must begin with a clear and precise statement of objectives. Defining objectives is by far the most important phase of an analysis because objectives provide parameters for the assessment. Put differently, specific and clear objectives furnish indispensable criteria for judging a tax's achievements and failures. It is only after objectives, no matter how controversial, have been established that analysts can determine how well a tax is performing. Ascertaining a tax's objectives is, not unexpectedly, a manifold task because objectives frequently exist in an inchoate form. The first charge, therefore, is to clarify the objectives, with measurement of those objectives to be determined later: before a tax's performance can be ascertained, analysts must have a clear sense of the nature of the activity being evaluated, an intricate endeavor since most taxes have multiple objectives—a situation that often creates dissonance among investigators.

Since a tax frequently has multiple objectives, objectives need to be classified according to some preconceived scheme in order to eliminate or at least reduce troublesome dissonance. Such a categorizing process, which is the initial phase of any systematic analysis, helps identify objectives more clearly and precisely. With the aid of a classification system, a substantial number of disparate objectives can be rationally reduced to manageable and comprehensible groups.

Various functional classification schemes can be employed. Generally speaking, tax objectives are handled most easily when they are categorized as either predominantly procedural or predominantly substantive. Procedural objectives are those associated with the administrative implementation of a tax, whereas substantive objectives are those related to the actual level of a tax's objective—realization. An objective is classified as procedural when it aims to improve internal administrative efficiency and effectiveness. Substantive objectives, on the other hand, are those intended to attain target objectives by concentrating on specific sociophysical targets within the scope of a tax. (Given this distinction, any examination of procedures without a concomitant assessment of substance is meaningless.) Although this dichotomy is not without limitations, it nevertheless is necessary, for analytical purposes, initially to place each objective—on the basis of prevailing tendency—in one of the two categories, even though an objective may actually fit into both classifications.

At this point, two caveats are worth mentioning. In the first place, the stated objectives may not be the only ones, since every policy has various informal, and in most cases unstated, objectives. Analysts, therefore, must be certain to list all crucial objectives so that they can determine which are first-order and which are second- and third-order objectives. Second, objectives seldom, if ever, can be perceived as either static or absolute inasmuch as environmental fluctuations force constant adjustments in and revisions of a tax. Difficulty generally is encountered when trying to determine tax objectives because of the dynamic nature of the environment in which a tax operates. (These limitations, it is felt, can be minimized if one uses the suggested classification scheme.)

Operationalizing Objectives

After categorizing objectives into a manageable number, analysts must operationalize them. *Operationalization* is a process whereby specific concrete performances are used to indicate the existence or nonexistence of an objective so that the degree to which a tax is meeting its objectives can be gauged. Operationalizing objectives is a formidable task because there usually is a variety of ways to measure each objective. Each operationalized objective must address two methodological points: (1) indicators used to verify an objective should fit its commonly accepted meaning, and (2) indicators should provide the most accurate verification possible.

The easiest way to assure that the criteria of reliability and validity are met is to choose indicators that have been used previously, rather than developing original indicators. (This statement is not meant to stifle creativity but to control it. There obviously are times when original indicators should be developed.)

Another technique used to operationalize an objective accurately is to form an index of several indicators. The principal reason for employing such an index is to exhaust, as nearly as possible, all the operational facets of an objective; no single indicator can do that. By using an index, procedural or substantive achievements and failures of each objective can be measured more accurately.

Whenever possible, indicators comprising an index should be quantified in order to be able to measure precisely how much of an objective is achieved (Hover, 1976: 85–93). But many objectives, though not unimportant, cannot always be operationalized with quantitative indicators. When such a situation occurs, indicators whose accuracy can at least be verified should be used; that is, their attainment or nonattainment can be confirmed by more than one person.

The important point here is that only when reliable and valid indicators are selected will the objective, whether procedural or substantive, be specific, explicit, and precise enough to gauge a tax's performance. In short, regardless of the type of indicators employed, it is essential to note that few productive analyses are conducted without using verifiable indicators.

Analyzing Tax Performance

Once objectives are selected and operationalized, the type of analysis to be conducted can be determined. Basically, two types of analysis—input/output and organization/process—can be used.

Input/output analysis relies primarily on aggregate resource distribution data to measure effectiveness and efficiency. Such data are integral to tax analysis because all data, even qualitative data, can be assigned at least nominal properties. This circumstance, coupled with the profusion of new high-powered statistical techniques, means that an array of powerful statistics can be used to analyze all types of data.

In spite of all its advantages, input/output analysis alone usually leads to somewhat incomplete tax analysis, primarily because it ignores the effect of structures and processes on tax performance. As a result, input/output analysis can be enhanced considerably (and omissions minimized) by combining it with *organization/process analysis*.

Such analysis uses verifiable, though qualitative, data to determine the direct and indirect linkages between target and spillover groups affected by a tax and agencies responsible for implementing that tax. Put differently, organization/process analysis reflects the extent to which administrative organizations and procedures influence tax performance.

Such an analysis is accomplished principally by reviewing the linkages among budgeting processes, target and spillover groups, clientele and interest groups, and any other group that might be interested in objective-realization. Once the tax objectives and method(s) of analysis are determined, the type and amount of information needed to verify the extent of objective-realization must be ascertained. The next step, then, is to find out where data are located as well as what techniques can be used to gather such information. Reasonably accurate and relatively complete and comparable data which measure effectiveness and efficiency can be gathered from various sources. Some essential *data sources* are as follows:

For Input/Output Analysis

Existing records and statistics—routinely collected agency information

Interviews and surveys—target and spillover group satisfaction

Field observations—professional ratings

Experiences of other governmental and quasi-governmental agencies—procedural and evaluative comparable data

For Organization/Process Analysis

Organizational structures—flow of authority and responsibility

Investment return—cost-benefit outcomes

Productivity—ratio of input to output

Resource capability

Technical—actual and potential state of technology

Financial—capital structure and availability of credit and equity

Physical—condition of equipment and utilization capacity
Human—skilled personnel and personnel policies

Information gathering should rely on routinely collected data since such a procedure can save time and money. However, diligence must be exerted because, until recently, recordkeeping and data collection traditionally have been given low priority in many governmental and quasi-governmental agencies; thus the data frequently are invalid, unreliable, and incomparable. Data, even when reliable and valid, are not always comparable because various agencies tend to collect them differently, a situation which reduces the usefulness of the information when conducting a tax analysis. Despite these shortcomings, existing records and documents usually provide the best available information required to conduct a tax analysis, especially over time.

In summary, the purpose of a tax analysis is to provide specific information about the consequences of a given tax, not to determine and isolate cause and effect relationships. When appropriately used, an analysis furnishes useful information concerning the extent to which structures and processes affect objective-realization. The assessment also furnishes some knowledge of the intended and unintended consequences affecting not only target but also spillover groups. Tax analysis, furthermore, allows for the comparison of intended outcomes with actual results by raising questions such as the following: Are the actual consequences more desirable than the expected results? Whose objectives are being met? What strategies should be pursued to reach objectives? Are major opportunities to achieve objectives being overlooked?

Translated into its simplest terms, tax analysis is a twofold process. First, tax performance is evaluated via input/output analysis, and then that assessment is modified with data obtained by means of organization/process analysis. Thus, tax analysis is an iterative procedure which involves examining the continuing interplay between formal and informal tax objectives and the structures and procedures designed to meet those objectives.

REFERENCES

Hover, Kenneth (1976). *The Elements of Social Scientific Thinking*. New York: St. Martin's Press. (For a simple yet sound discussion of the quantification and measurement of variables.)

Mitroff, Ian (1972). "Who Looks at the Whole System?" In Henry S. Brinkers, ed., *Decision-Making: Creativity, Judgements, and Systems*. Columbus: Ohio University Press.

Myrdal, Gunnar (1958). *Value in Social Theory*. London: Routledge and Kegan Paul.

Appendix B

Analytical Designs

Identifying objectives and developing tax performance data are only the first two phases of a tax analysis. Another equally important phase involves collecting data that can be analyzed logically and statistically to ascertain whether a tax is meeting its objectives and, if so, the extent to which those objectives are achieved. Using an analytical design is the best way to accomplish this task.

An analytical design is a plan indicating which tax performance data should be gathered, and when, so that comparative information is available to determine a tax's actual impact. An analytical design primarily suggests the type of baseline tax data that need to be collected. *Baseline tax data* are collected either prior to or independent of a tax's impact. Such data must be utilized because the only way to estimate the actual extent to which a tax is meeting its objectives is to compare tax performance data to baseline data. Post-tax performance data by themselves are relatively meaningless without baseline data.

An analytical design helps demonstrate that a tax is the primary, though maybe not the only, antecedent factor responsible for the difference between baseline tax data and post-tax performance data. (Such a finding usually is achieved by statistically controlling for other causal factors.) Finally, and perhaps most important, an analytical design helps to ascertain whether and to what extent a tax is meeting its objectives. (The difference between two sets of data is representative of the degree to which objectives are met.)

ANALYTICAL DESIGNS

An analytical design approximates classical experimental designs as nearly as possible but deviates from them when conditions do not allow for the random assignment of data to either experimental or control groups or for the manipulation of the physical features of the implemented tax. Such a design capitalizes on the fact that some form of baseline/post comparison always is possible and that myriad statistical techniques can be used when examining such a comparison.

Three types of evaluation designs are frequently used to conduct a tax analysis. The first design compares tax performance data gathered before a tax is initiated to identical data collected after tax initiation or expansion (*pre/post design*). Another design, which is particularly useful when pre-tax performance data are unobtainable, compares tax performance data gathered after tax initiation or expansion to identical data also gathered after a tax is initiated but which could not possibly be a consequence of that tax (*post design*).

The third type of design compares tax performance data collected after tax initiation or expansion to projected tax data (*trend projection design*). This later design compares tax data gathered after tax initiation or expansion to data that would have been expected if the tax had not been put into operation. (Such projections are made statistically.) Statistical techniques can be used with any or all of these analytical designs to gauge the extent to which the tax is realizing its objectives.

Pre/Post Design

The simplest and most inexpensive analytical design is a pre/post design. Perhaps because of its simplicity, it is the most commonly used of the three analytical designs presented here. A pre/post design utilizes tax performance data gathered *before* tax implementation or expansion as baseline data. These data then are compared to identical tax performance data collected *after* tax initiation or expansion. The difference between the two sets of data indicates whether or not a tax is meeting its objectives, and the degree of that difference represents the extent to which a tax is achieving its objectives. Moreover, when the intended outcome is stated in precise terms, the actual outcome can be compared to the intended outcome to gauge the success of a tax.

Exhibit B.1 depicts a pre/post design. To implement such a design, the succeeding steps should be followed:

- Select valid and reliable tax performance data that indicate the degree of realization of each tax objective.
- Obtain tax performance data for each objective as it existed *before* the tax was initiated or expanded (X_1).

Exhibit B.1
Pre/Post Design

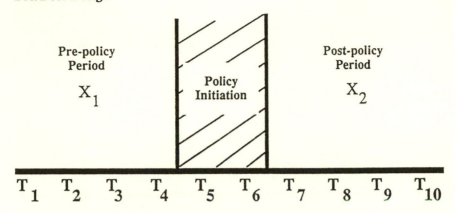

where: T = intervals of time (e.g., days, months, or years)

X_1 = performance measures gathered <u>before</u> policy initiation

X_2 = performance measures collected <u>after</u> policy initiation

$X_1 - X_2$ = estimated extent to which a policy is meeting its objectives

- Obtain identical data for each objective as it existed *after* a tax was initiated or expanded (X_2).
- Estimate the extent to which tax objectives are met by analyzing the degree of difference between pre and post performance data ($X_1 - X_2$).
- Control for the degree to which factors other than a tax affect the difference between the two sets of performance data.
- Compare the actual outcome with the intended outcome. (Execution of this step requires that the intended outcome be stated in specific enough terms to allow for statistical comparison.)

As mentioned earlier, a pre/post design is perhaps the most frequently used of all analytical designs, principally because it is quite practical and relatively inexpensive. The design requires little time, effort, and resources. About all that is needed is some planning prior to tax implementation or expansion so that baseline performance data can be collected prior to a tax initiation or expansion.

The major limitation of a pre/post design is that objective-realization due primarily to a tax can never be determined with a high degree of certainty. Using such a design can never absolutely assure anyone that the difference between pre and post performance data is attributable solely to the tax being evaluated, because this design does not allow the effects of environmental and maturational factors to be physically controlled.

Such a limitation, however, is not as serious as it seems; three precautionary actions can alleviate most potential problems. First, each tax objective can (and should) be operationalized with a number of performance data so that all facets of an objective are measured. The second action involves recognizing possible explanatory factors other than the tax and statistically controlling for them.

The third precautionary action involves utilizing a pre/post design only in appropriate situations. Put more precisely, such a design should be used only when the duration of a tax is short and the scope of its objectives is narrow. In addition, performance data used to operationalize tax objectives should be reasonably stable and certain to remain stable during the evaluation period. That is, performance data should not be distorted beyond normal by seasonal or cyclical changes. The key to employing a pre/post design is to use it only when the appropriate conditions are met and to make sure that all plausible explanatory factors are identified so that they can be controlled for statistically.

Post Design

Often a tax has to be evaluated when pre-tax performance data are unavailable. In such situations, a post design normally is employed. For baseline data, a post design uses performance data that are identical to post-tax performance data but that definitely are not a consequence of the tax being examined. A post design is similar to the pre/post design in that the difference between baseline and post data indicates whether a tax is achieving its objectives, and the degree of that difference represents the extent to which a tax is meeting its objectives. The actual outcome also can be compared to the intended outcome if the intended outcome is stated in specific terms. But a post design differs in that both sets of performance data are collected after initiation or expansion of a tax.

Although a post design does not use pre-tax data, it does use simulated control data which are similar, though not identical, to the control group of performance data used in experimental designs. *Simulated control data* are those which are as identical as possible to post-performance data but which obviously are not a consequence of the examined tax. As a result, baseline performance data must be carefully selected since it is virtually impossible to find identical data. Otherwise, any comparison will be simply meaningless and not especially credible. Exhibit B.2 exemplifies a post design.

Exhibit B.2
Post Design

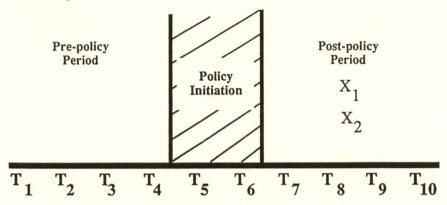

where: T = intervals of time (e.g., days, months, or years)

X_1 = performance measures which are gathered <u>after</u>
policy initiation and which are assumed to be outcomes
of the policy

X_2 = performance measures which are gathered <u>after</u>
policy initiation but which are not a consequence of the
policy (simulated control measures)

$X_1 - X_2$ = estimated extent to which a policy is meeting its
objectives

To implement a post-tax design such as the one depicted in Exhibit B.2, the succeeding steps should be followed:

• Select valid and reliable performance data that indicate the degree of realization of each tax objective.
• For each objective, obtain performance data that are assumed to be outcomes of the tax (X_2).
• For each objective, obtain simulated control data that are not outcomes of the tax and that are gathered at the same time as the post-tax performance data (X_1).
• Estimate the extent to which tax objectives are met by analyzing the degree of difference between simulated control data and post-tax performance data ($X_1 - X_2$).

- Control for the degree to which factors other than the tax affect the difference between the two sets of performance data.

- Compare the actual outcome with the intended outcome. (Execution of this step requires that the intended outcome be stated in specific enough terms to allow for statistical comparison.)

A post design should be employed only when no other analytical design is appropriate (e.g., when pre-tax performance data are unavailable), because the methodological flaws associated with a post design are substantial; the two most crucial pitfalls centering around selecting methodologically sound simulated control data and demonstrating tax causality.

Identification of methodologically sound simulated control data is by far the thornier of the two problems. The validity and reliability of the comparison of such baseline performance data with post-tax performance data depend almost solely on choosing virtually equivalent data. It is quite difficult, if not impossible, to locate performance data that are identical except for exposure to the examined tax.

The second methodological flaw inherent in a post design is that one can never be absolutely certain that the performance data attributed to the tax are in fact outcomes of that tax. It can only assume that the data are due primarily to the tax, an assumption there really is no way to substantiate. The possibility always exists that the data attributed to the tax are the result of other factors. However, if one can safely assume that a tax is the primary factor behind objective-realization and can locate methodologically sound simulated control data, a post design can be used to determine the extent to which a tax is meeting its objectives.

Despite these two intrinsic limitations, a post design often is used because no other alternative exists, especially when pre-performance data are not available. If caution is exercised in selecting simulated control data, this design can be useful.

Trend Projection Design

A trend projection design, the most powerful of the three analytical designs discussed here, is a refinement of a pre/post design (Hatry et al., 1973: 55). The principal difference between these two designs is that a trend projection design uses projected post-performance data rather than pre-performance data as baseline data. That is, post-performance data are compared to performance data that would have been expected had the tax not been implemented or expanded. Such a determination is made by gathering performance data at several different time intervals prior to tax implementation or expansion and projecting them by means of statistical techniques. The degree of difference between the projected tax performance data and the post-performance data represents the extent to which a tax is achieving its objectives. As with other analytical designs, the intended outcome can be compared to the actual outcome when the intended outcome is stated in specific terms that permit statistical comparison.

Unlike the first two analytical designs, in which performance data are compared at only one or two points in time, a trend projection design allows for the comparison of performance data at periodic intervals. It is preferable to gather and compare these two sets of performance data at several time intervals because performance data collected at a single time period seldom constitute an accurate sample of a tax's impact, especially when the tax being analyzed is ongoing.

To implement a trend projection design such as that illustrated in Exhibit B.3, the following steps should be used:

- Select valid and reliable performance data that indicate the degree of realization of each tax objective.
- Obtain performance data as they existed at several different time intervals prior to tax initiation or expansion (X_1 to X_5).
- Project pre-performance data (Y_1 to Y_3).
- Obtain identical performance data for each objective after tax initiation or expansion (X_6 to X_8).
- Estimate the actual extent to which tax objectives are met by analyzing the degree of difference between the projected pre-performance data and post-performance data ($Y_1-X_6, -Y_2-X_7, -Y_3-X_8$).
- Control for the degree to which factors other than the tax affect the difference between sets of performance data.
- Compare the actual outcome with the intended outcome. (As with a pre/post design, this step may be optional, since it requires the intended outcome to be stated in specific enough terms to allow for statistical comparison.)

At this juncture, a few observations are appropriate. Pre-performance data cannot be projected too far beyond the point of tax initiation or expansion; the further such data are projected beyond that point, the less reliable they become. Although convention fails to suggest the point at which projections become unreliable, the dominant position recommends that pre-performance data (baseline data) should not be projected beyond four or five time intervals (e.g., four or five days, four or five months, or four or five years, depending on the time interval used). Such a determination, however, should not be made capriciously; the decision should be based on an analyst's substantive knowledge of the examined tax.

In the past, trend projection design was used infrequently (particularly in state and local agencies) because of the high cost of data collection and data manipulation. However, with the increased emphasis on data collection, the recent establishment of state and local data banks, and the decreasing costs of computing systems, the expense of implementing a trend projection design is no longer prohibitive. Moreover, a trend projection design is exceedingly useful and quite powerful, especially when coupled with relatively sophisticated sta-

Exhibit B.3
Trend Projection Design

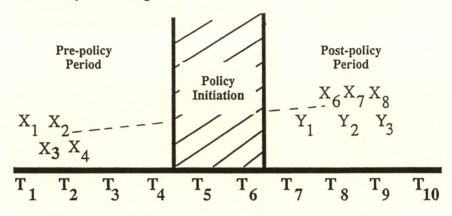

where: T = intervals of time (e.g., days, months, or years)

X_1 to X_4 = performance measures gathered at several different time intervals <u>before</u> policy initiation

Y_1 to Y_3 = projected performance measures (those that probably would have occurred had the policy not been implemented)

X_6 to X_8 = performance measures collected <u>after</u> policy initiation

$$
\left.
\begin{array}{l}
Y_1 \text{ to } X_6 \\
Y_2 \text{ to } X_7 \\
Y_3 \text{ to } X_8
\end{array}
\right|
= \text{estimated extent to which a program is meeting its objectives (at different time intervals)}
$$

tistical techniques such as linear and nonlinear regression analysis, time series analysis, and economic modeling.

A trend projection design oftentimes is the optimal tax evaluation design because (1) it places the analysis on safe methodological ground by forcing the comparison of a series of pre- and post-performance data gathered at different time intervals and perhaps collected under different conditions, and (2) it allows for the accounting of a wide range of factors such as maturation, trends, and events. These two requisites are especially important because more often than not an analysis is complex and ongoing and needs to be analyzed periodically rather than just once.

A trend projection design also helps guard against the predominant danger of accepting the findings of an immediate, one-shot tax analysis. More specifically, a tax analysis conducted almost immediately after implementation or expansion invariably finds that the tax is meeting its objectives. But if that same tax is evaluated two or three years after implementation or expansion, it is frequently discovered not to be achieving its objectives. A trend projection design guards against this phenomenon.

Despite its usefulness, a trend projection design needs to be refined by using it in combination with other types of analytical designs. For instance, the actual results of a trend projection design can be compared to those from another jurisdiction (simulated control data). By combining various analytical designs, certain methodological flaws in each of the combined designs can be corrected, resulting in a more reliable analysis. Since a trend projection design is a variation of a pre/post design, the same limitations and precautions for its use apply.

CONCLUDING COMMENTS

Determining which design is preferable depends on (1) the intended use of the results of an analysis; (2) the scope and direction of an analysis; (3) the resources required and available to conduct an analysis; (4) the level and amount of available performance data; (5) the level of accuracy desired; and (6) the feasibility of implementing the design. (No matter how methodologically sound, an analytical design certainly is inappropriate if it cannot be feasibly implemented.)

While not a hard and fast rule, the most appropriate analytical design is the one that minimizes the impact of factors other than the examined tax, permits a valid comparison between baseline and post-performance data, is inexpensive and feasible to implement, and provides useful information. Such a large order seldom can be filled by a single analytical design; therefore a combination of various designs should be used. Many variations and combinations of the designs presented here are possible. (Each possibility, of course, entails different costs and benefits.)

Regardless of which design or combination of designs is used to conduct a tax analysis, the succeeding steps should be followed when selecting a design:

- When a classical experimental design is inappropriate, use a combination of acceptable analytical designs.
- When only a single analytical design is used, rely on a trend projection design.
- When a trend projection design is not used, employ a pre/post design.
- Whenever possible, avoid using a post design by itself; and if such a design is used, combine it with other analytical designs.

REFERENCE

Hatry, Harry, et al. (1973). *Practical Program Evaluation for State and Local Government Officials*. Washington, D.C.: Urban Institute.

Appendix C

National and State Organizations and Information Sources

NATIONAL ORGANIZATIONS

Academy for State and Local Government
444 North Capitol Street, NW
Suite 349—Hall of the States
Washington, D.C. 20001
(202) 638-1445

Council of State Governments
Iron Works Pike
P.O. Box 11910
Lexington, Kentucky 40578
(606) 252-2291

Federation of Tax Administrators
444 North Capitol Street, NW
Suite 334—Hall of the States
Washington, D.C. 20001
(202) 624-5890

International Association of Assessing Officers
1313 East 60th Street
Chicago, Illinois 60637-9990
(312) 947-2069

Multistate Tax Commission
1790 30th Street

Suite 314
Boulder, Colorado 80301
(303) 447-9645

National Association of Counties
440 First Street, NW
Washington, D.C. 20001
(202) 393-6226

National Association of State Budget Officers
444 North Capitol Street, NW
Suite 328—Hall of the States
Washington, D.C. 20001
(202) 624-5382

National Association of Tax Administrators
444 North Capitol Street, NW
Washington, D.C. 20001
(202) 624-5890

National Conference of State Legislatures Headquarters
1125 17th Street, Suite 1500
Denver, Colorado 80202
(303) 292-6600

Office of State-Federal Relations
444 North Capitol Street, NW
Washington, D.C. 20001
(202) 737-7004

National League of Cities
1301 Pennsylvania Avenue, NW
Washington, D.C. 20004
(202) 626-3210

Tax Foundation, Inc.
One Thomas Circle, NW
Washington, D.C. 20005
(202) 328-4500

U.S. Advisory Commission on
   Intergovernmental Relations
1111 20th Street, NW
Washington, D.C. 20575
(202) 653-5540

STATE FINANCE DEPARTMENTS

ALABAMA
Director
Dept. of Finance
600 Dexter Ave.
Montgomery, AL 36130
(205) 242-7160

ALASKA
Director
Division of Finance
Dept. of Administration
P.O. Box 110204
Juneau, AK 99811
(907) 465-2240

ARIZONA
Director, Financial Services
Finance Division
Dept. of Administration
1700 W. Washington, Rm. 290
Phoenix, AZ 85007
(602) 542-1500

ARKANSAS
Administrator
Director

Dept. of Finance & Admin.
401 DFA Bldg.
Little Rock, AR 72201
(501) 682-2242

CALIFORNIA
Director
Dept. of Finance
State Capitol, Rm. 1145
Sacramento, CA 95814
(916) 445-4141

COLORADO
State Controller
Division of Accounts & Control
Dept. of Administration
1525 Sherman St., Ste. 250
Denver, CO 80203
(303) 866-3281

CONNECTICUT
Secretary
Off. of Policy & Management
80 Washington St.
Hartford, CT 06106
(203) 566-8070

DELAWARE
Secretary
Dept. of Finance
540 S. DuPont Hwy.
Dover, DE 19901
(302) 739-4201

FLORIDA
Director
Finance Division
Dept. of Banking & Finance
Capitol Bldg., Rm. LL22
Tallahassee, FL 32399
(904) 487-2583

GEORGIA
State Treasurer
Office of Treasury & Fiscal Services
1516 West Tower
200 Piedmont Ave., SE
Atlanta, GA 30334
(404) 656-2168

HAWAII
Director of Finance
Dept. of Budget & Finance
P.O. Box 150
Honolulu, HI 96810
(808) 586-1518

IDAHO
Administrator
Div. of Financial Management
Off. of the Governor
Statehouse, Rm. 122
Boise, ID 83720
(208) 334-3900

ILLINOIS
Action Director
Dept. of Revenue
101 W. Jefferson St.
Springfield, IL 62706
(217) 782-7570

Director
Bur. of the Budget
Office of the Governor
108 State House
Springfield, IL 62706
(217) 782-4520

INDIANA
Director
Budget Agency
State House, Rm. 212
Indianapolis, IN 46204
(317) 232-5612

IOWA
Director
Dept. of Management
State Capitol Bldg.
Des Moines, IA 50319
(515) 281-3322

KANSAS
Secretary
Dept. of Administration
State Capitol Bldg.
Rm. 263E
Topeka, KS 66612
(913) 296-3011

Director
Division of the Budget
Dept. of Administration
State Capitol Bldg., Rm. 152E
300 SW Tenth Ave.
Topeka, KS 66612
(913) 296-2436

KENTUCKY
State Budget Director
Governor's Off. for Policy & Management
Capitol Annex, Rm. 284
Frankfort, KY 40601
(502) 564-7300

LOUISIANA
Budget Director
Div. of Administration
Off. of the Governor
P.O. Box 94095
Baton Rouge, LA 70804
(504) 342-7000

MAINE
State Budget Officer
Bur. of the Budget
Dept. of Administration & Financial
    Services
State House Station #58
Augusta, ME 04333
(207) 624-7810

MARYLAND
Secretary
Dept. of Budget & Fiscal Planning
45 Calvert St.
Annapolis, MD 21401
(410) 974-2114

MASSACHUSETTS
Secretary
Executive Off. for Administration
    & Finance
State House, Rm. 373
Boston, MA 02133
(617) 727-8380

MICHIGAN
Director
Dept. of Management & Budget

P.O. Box 30026
Lansing, MI 48909
(517) 373-1004

MINNESOTA
Commissioner
Dept. of Finance
400 Centennial Bldg.
658 Cedar St.
St. Paul, MN 55101
(612) 296-9721

MISSISSIPPI
Executive Director
Dept. of Finance & Admin.
P.O. Box 267
Jackson, MS 39205
(601) 359-3402

MISSOURI
Commissioner
Office of Administration
State Capitol, Rm. 125
P.O. Box 809
Jefferson City, MO 65102
(314) 751-3311

MONTANA
Director
Budget & Program Planning
Capitol Station
Helena, MT 59620
(406) 444-3616

NEBRASKA
Administrator
Budget Division
Dept. of Administrative Services
P.O. Box 94664
Lincoln, NE 68509
(402) 471-2526

Auditor of Public Accounts
Budget Division
Dept. of Administrative Services
P.O. Box 94664
Lincoln, NE 68509
(402) 471-2111

State Tax Commissioner
Dept. of Revenue

P.O. Box 94818
Lincoln, NE 68509
(402) 471-5604

NEVADA
Controller
State Capitol
Carson City, NV 89710
(702) 687-4330

NEW HAMPSHIRE
Commissioner
Dept. of Administrative Services
25 Capitol St.
Concord, NH 03301
(603) 271-3201

NEW JERSEY
Director
Office of Management & Budget
Dept. of Treasury
33 W. State St., CN221
Trenton, NJ 08625
(609) 292-5258

NEW MEXICO
Secretary
Dept. of Finance & Administration
Bataan Memorial Bldg., Rm. 180
Santa Fe, NM 87503
(505) 827-3060

NEW YORK
Controller
Office of the State Controller
A.E. Smith Office Bldg., 6th Floor
Albany, NY 12236
(518) 474-4040

NORTH CAROLINA
State Budget Officer
Office of State Budget
116 W. Jones St.
Raleigh, NC 27603
(919) 733-7061

NORTH DAKOTA
Director
Office of Management & Budget
State Capitol, 4th Floor
600 E. Boulevard Ave.

Bismarck, ND 58505
(701) 224-4904

Director of Accounting
Office of Management & Budget
State Capitol, 4th Floor
600 E. Boulevard Ave.
Bismarck, ND 58505
(701) 224-2682

OHIO
Director
Office of Budget & Management
30 E. Broad St., 34th Floor
Columbus, OH 43266
(614) 466-4034

OKLAHOMA
Director
Office of State Finance
122 State Capitol
Oklahoma City, OK 73105
(405) 521-2141

OREGON
Administrator
Budget & Management Div.
Executive Dept.
155 Cottage St., NE
Salem, OR 97310
(503) 378-3103

PENNSYLVANIA
Secretary of the Budget
Office of the Governor
238 Main Capitol
Harrisburg, PA 17120
(717) 787-4472

RHODE ISLAND
Associate Director of Finance/Budget
   Officer
Office of the Budget
Dept. of Administration
One Capitol Hill, 4th Floor
Providence, RI 02908
(401) 277-6300

SOUTH CAROLINA
Executive Director
Budget & Control Board

P.O. Box 12444
Columbia, SC 29211
(803) 734-2320

SOUTH DAKOTA
Commissioner
Bur. of Finance & Management
State Capitol, 2nd Floor
Pierre, SD 57501
(605) 773-3411

TENNESSEE
Commissioner
Dept. of Finance & Administration
State Capitol, 1st Floor
Nashville, TN 37234
(615) 741-2401

TEXAS
Controller
Public Accounts
P.O. Box 13528, Capitol Station
Austin, TX 78711
(512) 463-4000

UTAH
Director
Budget Division
Dept. of Administration
2110 State Office Bldg.
Salt Lake City, UT 84114
(801) 538-1555

VERMONT
Commissioner
Dept. of Finance & Management
Agency of Administration
109 State St.
Montpelier, VT 05609
(802) 828-2376

VIRGINIA
Secretary of Finance
Governor's Cabinet
635 Ninth St. Office Bldg.
Richmond, VA 23219
(804) 786-1148

WASHINGTON
Director
Office of Financial Management

P.O. Box 43113
300 Insurance Bldg.
Olympia, WA 98504
(206) 753-5450

WEST VIRGINIA
Secretary
Dept. of Finance & Administration
State Capitol, Rm. E119
Charleston, WV 25305
(304) 558-2300

WISCONSIN
Administrator
State Executive Budget & Planning
Dept. of Administration
P.O. Box 7864
Madison, WI 53707
(608) 266-7996

WYOMING
State Auditor
State Capitol, Rm. 114
200 W. 24th St.
Cheyenne, WY 82002
(307) 777-7831

DISTRICT OF COLUMBIA
Deputy Mayor
Financial Management
441 4th St., NW, Ste. 1150
Washington, DC 20001
(202) 727-2476

STATE BUDGET
OFFICERS

ALABAMA
Budget Officer
State Budget Off.
Dept. of Finance
237 Alabama State House
Montgomery, AL 36130
(205) 242-7230

ALASKA
Director
Div. of Budget Review
Off. of Management & Budget

P.O. Box 110020
Juneau, AK 99811
(907) 456-3568

Director
Off. of Management & Budget
Off. of the Governor
P.O. Box 110020
Juneau, AK 99811
(907) 456-3568

ARIZONA
Director
Strategic Planning & Budget
1700 W. Washington
West Wing
Phoenix, AZ 85007
(602) 542-5381

ARKANSAS
Administrator
Office of Budget
Dept. of Finance & Admin.
P.O. Box 3278
Little Rock, AR 72203
(501) 682-1941

CALIFORNIA
Director
Dept. of Finance
State Capitol, Rm. 1145
Sacramento, CA 95814
(916) 445-3878

COLORADO
Director
Office of State Planning & Budgeting
114 State Capitol Bldg.
Denver, CO 80203
(303) 866-2980

CONNECTICUT
Executive Budget Officer
Budget & Finance Div.
Off. of Policy & Management
80 Washington St.
Hartford, CT 06106
(203) 566-5086

DELAWARE
Director

Off. of the Budget
P.O. Box 1401
Dover, DE 19901
(302) 739-4204

FLORIDA
Director
Off. of Planning & Budgeting
Off. of the Governor
1601 The Capitol
Tallahassee, FL 32399
(904) 488-7810

GEORGIA
Director
Off. of Planning & Budget
254 Washington St.
Southwest, Ste. 614
Atlanta, GA 30334
(404) 656-3820

HAWAII
Director of Finance
Dept. of Budget & Finance
P.O. Box 150
Honolulu, HI 96810
(808) 586-1518

IDAHO
Administrator
Div. of Financial Management
Off. of the Governor
Statehouse, Rm. 122
Boise, ID 83720
(208) 334-3900

ILLINOIS
Director
Bur. of the Budget
Off. of the Governor
108 State House
Springfield, IL 62706
(217) 782-4520

INDIANA
Director
Budget Agency
State House, Rm. 212
Indianapolis, IN 46204
(317) 232-5612

IOWA
Director
Dept. of Management
State Capitol Bldg.
Des Moines, IA 50319
(515) 281-3322

KANSAS
Director
Div. of the Budget
Dept. of Administration
State Capitol Bldg.
Rm. 152E
300 S.W. Tenth Ave.
Topeka, KS 66612
(913) 296-2436

KENTUCKY
State Budget Director
Governor's Off. for Policy & Management
Capitol Annex, Rm. 284
Frankfort, KY 40601
(502) 564-7300

LOUISIANA
Budget Director
Div. of Administration
Off. of the Governor
P.O. Box 94095
Baton Rouge, LA 70804
(504) 342-7000

MAINE
State Budget Officer
Bur. of the Budget
Dept. of Administration & Financial
   Services
State House Station #58
Augusta, ME 04333
(207) 624-7810

MARYLAND
Secretary
Dept. of Budget & Fiscal Planning
45 Calvert St.
Annapolis, MD 21401
(410) 974-2114

MASSACHUSETTS
Budget Director

Executive Off. for Administration
   & Finance
State House, Rm. 272
Boston, MA 02133
(617) 727-2081

MICHIGAN
Director
Dept. of Management & Budget
P.O. Box 30026
Lansing, MI 48909
(517) 373-1004

MINNESOTA
Commissioner
Dept. of Finance
400 Centennial Bldg.
658 Cedar St.
St. Paul, MN 55101
(612) 296-9721

MISSISSIPPI
Executive Director
Dept. of Finance & Admin.
P.O. Box 267
Jackson, MS 39205
(601) 359-3402

MISSOURI
Deputy Commissioner
Div. of Budget & Planning
Office of Administration
State Capitol, Rm. 124
P.O. Box 809
Jefferson City, MO 65102
(314) 751-3925

MONTANA
Director
Budget & Program Planning
Capitol Station
Helena, MT 59620
(406) 444-3616

NEBRASKA
Administrator
Budget Division
Dept. of Administrative Services
P.O. Box 94664

Lincoln, NE 68509
(402) 471-2526

NEVADA
Director
Budget Div.
Dept. of Administration
209 E. Musser St., Rm. 204
Carson City, NV 89710
(702) 687-4065

NEW HAMPSHIRE
Commissioner
Dept. of Administrative Services
25 Capitol St.
Concord, NH 03301
(603) 271-3201

Assistant Commissioner
Budget Office
Dept. of Administrative Services
25 Capitol St.
Concord, NH 03301
(603) 271-3201

NEW JERSEY
Director
Office of Management & Budget
Dept. of Treasury
33 W. State St., CN221
Trenton, NJ 08625
(609) 292-5258

NEW MEXICO
Director
Budget Division
Dept. of Finance & Administration
Bataan Memorial Bldg., Rm. 190
Santa Fe, NM 87503
(505) 827-3640

NEW YORK
Director
Division of Budget
Executive Department
State Capitol
Albany, NY 12224
(518) 474-2300

NORTH CAROLINA
State Budget Officer

Office of State Budget
116 W. Jones St.
Raleigh, NC 27603
(919) 733-7061

NORTH DAKOTA
Director
Office of Management & Budget
State Capitol, 4th Floor
600 E. Boulevard Ave.
Bismarck, ND 58505
(701) 224-4904

Deputy Director
Office of Management & Budget
State Capitol, 4th Floor
600 E. Boulevard Ave.
Bismarck, ND 58505
(701) 224-4904

OHIO
Director
Office of Budget & Management
30 E. Broad St., 34th Floor
Columbus, OH 43266
(614) 466-4034

OKLAHOMA
Director
Office of State Finance
122 State Capitol
Oklahoma City, OK 73105
(405) 521-2141

OREGON
Administrator
Budget & Management Div.
Executive Dept.
155 Cottage St., NE
Salem, OR 97310
(503) 378-3103

PENNSYLVANIA
Secretary of the Budget
Office of the Governor
238 Main Capitol
Harrisburg, PA 17120
(717) 787-4472

RHODE ISLAND
Associate Director of Finance/Budget
    Officer
Office of the Budget
Dept. of Administration
One Capitol Hill, 4th Floor
Providence, RI 02908
(401) 277-6300

SOUTH CAROLINA
Director
Budget Division
Budget & Control Board
2105 Pendleton St.
Columbia, SC 29201
(803) 734-1314

SOUTH DAKOTA
Commissioner
Bur. of Finance & Management
500 E. Capitol Ave.
Pierre, SD 57501
(605) 773-3411

TENNESSEE
Assistant Commissioner
Budget Div.
Dept. of Finance & Administration
309 State Office Bldg.
Nashville, TN 37234
(615) 741-2001

TEXAS
Director
Governor's Office of Budget & Planning
P.O. Box 12428, Capitol Station
Austin, TX 78711
(512) 463-1778

UTAH
Director
Office of Planning & Budget
116 State Capitol
Salt Lake City, UT 84114
(801) 538-1555

VERMONT
Commissioner
Dept. of Finance & Management
Agency of Administration

109 State St.
Montpelier, VT 05609
(802) 828-2376

VIRGINIA
Director
Dept. of Planning & Budget
P.O. Box 1422
Richmond, VA 23211
(804) 786-5375

WASHINGTON
Director
Office of Financial Management
P.O. Box 43113
300 Insurance Bldg.
Olympia, WA 98504
(206) 753-5450

WEST VIRGINIA
Director
Budget Division
Dept. of Finance & Administration
State Capitol

Charleston, WV 25305
(304) 558-2344

WISCONSIN
Administrator
State Executive Budget & Planning
Dept. of Administration
P.O. Box 7864
Madison, WI 53707
(608) 266-1035

WYOMING
Administrator
Budget Div.
2001 Capitol Ave.
Cheyenne, WY 82002
(307) 777-7203

DISTRICT OF COLUMBIA
Director
Office of the Budget
441 4th St., NW, Ste. 350-N
Washington, DC 20001
(202) 727-6343

Selected Bibliography

Aaron, Henry (1975). *Who Pays the Property Tax?* Washington, D.C.: Brookings Institution.

Advisory Commission on Intergovernmental Relations (ACIR) (1977a). *Improving Federal Grants Management. The Intergovernmental Grant System: An Assessment and Proposed Policies.* Washington, D.C.: ACIR.

———— (1977b). *State Limitations on Local Taxes and Expenditures.* Washington, D.C.: ACIR.

———— (1987). *Local Revenue Diversification: User Charges.* Washington, D.C.: ACIR.

———— (1989). *Local Revenue Diversification: Local Sales Taxes.* Washington, D.C.: ACIR.

———— (1990). *Local Revenue Diversification: Rural Economies.* Washington, D.C.: ACIR.

———— (1991). *State Taxation of Interstate Mail Order Sales: Estimates of Revenue Potential, 1990–1992.* Washington, D.C.: ACIR.

———— (1992–1993). *Significant Features of Fiscal Federalism.* 2 vols. Washington, D.C.: ACIR.

Allan, Ian, ed. (1989). *Cash Management for Small Governments.* Chicago: Government Finance Officers Association.

Alt, Ronald (1990). "Trends in State Taxation." In *Book of the States, 1990–91.* Lexington, Ky.: Council of State Governments.

American Institute of Real Estate Appraisers (1983). *The Appraisal of Real Estate.* 8th ed. Chicago: AIREA.

Anderson, John E. (1993). "Two-Rate Property Taxes and Urban Development." *Intergovernmental Perspective*, Summer, pp. 19–20, 28.

Aronson, Richard, and Eli Schwartz, eds. (1987). *Management Policies in Local Government Finance.* Washington, D.C.: International City Management Association.

Association of Arkansas Counties (1992). *Arkansas County Collector's Procedures Annual*. Little Rock: Arkansas Association of Counties.

Bahl, Roy W. (1980). *The Impact of Local Tax Policy on Urban Economic Development*. Washington, D.C.: U.S. Department of Commerce, Economic Development Administration, Economic Research Division, September.

Baroni, Gene (1993). "State and Local Taxes: The Burden Grows." *Journal of State Taxation*, 11, Spring, pp. 22–29.

Behrens, John O. (1993). "Assessments and Property Taxes: Today and Tomorrow." *Intergovernmental Perspective*, Summer, pp. 13–15, 23.

Berry, Frances Stokes, and William D. Berry (1992). "Tax Innovation in the States: Capitalizing on Political Opportunity." *American Journal of Political Science*, 36, August, pp. 715–742.

Bingham, Richard D., Brett W. Hawkins, and F. Ted Hebert (1978). *The Politics of Raising State and Local Revenue*. New York: Praeger.

Bland, Robert (1989). *A Revenue Guide for Local Government*. Washington, D.C.: International City Management Association.

Boulding, Peter, Ray Hudson, and David Sadler (1988). "Consett and Corby: What Kind of New Era?" *Public Administration Quarterly*, 12, Summer.

Bright, Janis (1990). "Local Government in Fight for Its Life." *Public Finance and Accountancy*, October 19, p. 3.

Buchanan, James M., and Marilyn R. Flowers (1987). *The Public Finances*. 6th ed. Homewood, Ill.: Richard D. Irwin.

Bucovetsky, Sam, and James Douglas Wilson (1991). "Tax Competition with Two Tax Instruments." *Regional Science and Urban Economics*, 21, pp. 333–351.

Cantor, Arnold (1978). "State-Local Taxes: Tilt in the Road to Equity." *American Federalist*, 85, December, pp. 1–8.

"Center City District" (n.d.). Philadelphia (brochure).

Central Dallas Association (1992). "A Downtown Improvement District for Dallas." Dallas: Central Dallas Association.

Chernick, Howard (1992). "A Model of the Distributional Incidence of State and Local Taxes." *Public Finance Quarterly*, 20, October, p. 572.

Chu, Roderick G. W. (1987). "The State of New York's Struggle with Tax Reform." *Tax Executive*, 39, Summer, pp. 349–353.

Citizens Research Council of Michigan (1987). *Outline of the Michigan Tax System*. Detroit: CRCM.

Clark, Timothy B. (1986). "Taking a Regional Stand: Much of the Tax Reform Debate Is Not Cast in Regional Terms, but Key Items Such as Deductibility of State and Local Taxes, Tax-Exempt Bonds, and Energy Taxes Are." *National Journal*, 18, March 22, pp. 696–702.

Clotfelter, Charles T., and Philip J. Cook (1989). *Selling Hope: State Lotteries in America*. Cambridge, Mass.: Harvard University Press.

——— (1990). "Redefining 'Success' in the State Lottery Business." *Journal of Policy Analysis and Management*, 9, pp. 99–104.

Cloud, David S. (1992). "High Court Points to Congress for Mail Order Tax Ruling." *Congressional Quarterly Weekly Report*, 50, May.

Colford, Steven W. (1991). "High Court May Open Ad Tax." *Advertising Age*, 62, October 14, p. 1.

——— (1992). "Landmark Case May Bring Mailers Tax Bill of $20B." *Advertising Age*, 63, January 6.

Colorado Legislative Council (1975). *Mineral Taxation*. Denver: CLC.

——— (1986, 1991). *Tax Handbook: State and Local Taxes in Colorado*. Report to the Colorado General Assembly. Denver: CLC.

Commerce Clearing House (1991). *State Tax Guide: All States*. Chicago: Commerce Clearing House.

Cowden, Dick, and Sarah Eilers (1991). "Will Enterprise Zones Make It to the End Zone? Will Kemp's Idea Finally Score?" *Business and Society Review*, Summer, pp. 58–61.

Cronin, John J., and Michael A. Pearl (1989). "Sales and Use Tax Nexus—1989." *Tax Executive*, July-August, pp. 349–352.

Davies, David G. (1986). *United States Taxes and Tax Policy*. Cambridge, Eng.: Cambridge University Press.

Davis, William E., and John E. Petersen, eds. (1985). *Tax Reform and Local Government: An Assessment of Reagan's Plan*. Washington, D.C.: National League of Cities.

Dearborn, Philip M. (1993). "Local Property Taxes: Emerging Trends." *Intergovernmental Perspective*, Summer, pp. 10–12.

DeTray, Dennis. (1981). *Fiscal Restraints and the Burden of Local and State Taxes*. Santa Monica, Calif.: RAND Corporation.

Dilber, Robert Jay (1985). "Eliminating the Deductibility of State and Local Taxes: Impacts on States and Cities." *Public Budgeting and Finance*, 5, Winter, pp. 75–90.

Distilled Spirits Council of the United States (1983). *Public Revenues from Alcohol Beverages, 1981/82*. Washington, D.C.: DSCUS.

District of Columbia (1991). *Tax Rates and Tax Burdens in the District of Columbia: A Nationwide Comparison*. Washington, D.C.: Department of Finance and Revenue.

Dolan, Thomas G. (1992). "Danger Zones: The Required Ingredient in an Enterprise Zone Is Enterprise." *Barron's*, June 22, p. 10.

Dubnick, Melvin J., and Alan R. Gitelson, eds. (1990). *Public Policy and Economic Institutions*. Greenwich, Conn.: JAI Press.

Due, John F., and John L. Mikesell (1983). *Sales Taxation: State and Local Structure and Administration*. Baltimore: Johns Hopkins University Press.

Dye, Thomas R. (1985). "Federal Tax Reform: The View from the States." *Policy Studies Journal*, 13, March, pp. 547–562.

Echer, Deborah, and Richard F. Syron (1979). "Personal Taxes and Interstate Competition for High Technology Industries." *New England Economic Review*, September/October, pp. 25–32.

Eckl, Corina, et al. (1991). *State Budget and Tax Actions 1991*. Washington, D.C.: National Conference of State Legislatures.

Economic Analysis and Tax Research (1992). *Arkansas Fiscal Notes*. Arkansas Department of Finance and Administration, July.

Fabricius, Martha, and Ronald Snell (1990). *Earmarking State Taxes*. Washington, D.C.: National Conference of State Legislatures.

Feenberg, Daniel R., and Harvey S. Rosen (1986). "The Deductibility of State and Local Taxes: Impact Effects by State and Income." *Growth and Change*, 17, April, pp. 11–31.

Feiock, Richard C., and James C. Clingermayer (1992). "Development Policy Choice:

Four Explanations for City Implementation of Economic Development Policies.''
American Review of Public Administration, 22, March, pp. 19–34.

Feldstein, Martin S., and Gilbert E. Metcalf (1987). ''The Effect of Federal Tax Deductibility on State and Local Taxes and Spending.'' *Journal of Political Economy*, 95, August, pp. 710–736.

Fiscal and Tax Research (1991). *Comparative Revenues, 1985 Through 1989, and Revenue Forecasts*. Little Rock: Bureau of Legislative Research, State of Arkansas.

Fisher, Ronald C. (1988). *State and Local Public Finance*. Glenview, Ill.: Scott, Foresman.

Fisher, Ronald C., John H. Goddeeris, and James C. Young (1989). ''Participation in Tax Amnesties: The Individual Income Tax.'' *National Tax Journal*, 42.

Fusi, Deborah S. (1989). ''Cities, Counties Improve Infrastructure, Increase Enterprise Zone/Tax Incentives.'' *Site Selection*, October, pp. 1244–1254.

Gade, Mary N., and Lee C. Adkins (1990). ''Tax Exporting and State Revenue Structures.'' *National Tax Journal*, March, pp. 39–52.

Genetelli, Richard W. (1991). ''Minimizing State and Local Taxes with Combined (Unitary) Reporting.'' *Journal of State Taxation*, 10, Fall, pp. 71–81.

Gillis, Malcolm, and Ignatius Peprah (1980). ''Severance Taxes on Coal and Uranium in the Sunbelt.'' *Texas Business Review*, 54, November/December, pp. 302–308.

Goetz, Edward G. (1992). ''Tax Base Sharing in the Twin Cities.'' *Urban News*, 6, Spring.

Gold, Daniel M. (1992). ''A Taxing Decision.'' *Adweek's Marketing Week*, February 24, p. 28.

Gold, Steven D., ed. (1986). *Reforming State Tax Systems*. Denver: National Conference of State Legislatures.

———, ed. (1988). *The Unfinished Agenda for State Tax Reform*. Washington, D.C.: National Conference of State Legislatures.

Gold, Steven D., and Sarah Richie (1992). ''State Policies Affecting Cities and Counties in 1991: Shifting Federalism.'' *Public Budgeting and Finance*, 12, Spring, pp. 23–46.

Goldberg, Gerald H. (1991). ''Federal Preemption of State Tax Policy.'' *National Tax Journal*, 22, September, pp. 293–296.

Gramlich, Edward M. (1985). ''The Deductibility of State and Local Taxes.'' *National Tax Journal*, 38, December, pp. 447–465.

Gruver, Gene W., and Lester A. Zeager (1990). ''Economic Incentives for an Urban Bias in Development Policies.'' *Bulletin of Economic Research*, 12, January, pp. 55–63.

Gulley, O. David, and Frank Scott (1989). ''Lottery Effects on Parimutuel Tax Revenues.'' *National Tax Journal*, 42, March.

Gunn, Elizabeth M. (1993). ''The Growth of Enterprise Zones: A Policy Transformation.'' *Policy Studies Journal*, 21, Autumn, pp. 432–449.

Guskind, Robert (1989). ''Round Two for Enterprise Zones.'' *Planning*, 55, September, pp. 1–5.

——— (1990). ''Enterprise Zones: Do They Work?'' *Journal of Housing*, 17, January-February, pp. 17–24.

Halstead, D. Kent (1978). *Tax Wealth in Fifty States*. Washington, D.C.: U.S. Department of Health, Education and Welfare, National Institute of Education.

Hansen, Susan B. (1983). ''Extraction: The Politics of State Taxation.'' In Virginia Gray,

Herbert Jacob, and Kenneth N. Vines, eds., *The American States: A Comparative Analysis.* Boston: Little, Brown.

Harris, Hamil R. (1992). "What Ever Happened to Enterprise Zones?" *Black Enterprise,* 22, April, p. 20.

Hellerstein, Walter (1992). "Supreme Court Says No State Use Tax." *The National Journal of Taxation,* 77, August.

Hough, Wesley, and John Petersen (1983). *State Constraints on Local Capital Financing.* Washington, D.C.: Municipal Finance Officers Association.

House, Verne W., and Douglas J. Young (1986). "How High Are Montana's Taxes?" *Montana Business Quarterly,* 24, Winter, pp. 2–10.

Howe, Edward T., and Donald J. Reeb (1990). "Major State and Local Taxes Imposed on U.S. Electric Utilities." *Journal of State Taxation,* 9, Summer, pp. 3–28.

Hudson, David M., and Daniel C. Turner (1984). "International and Interstate Approaches to Taxing Business Income." *Northwestern Journal of International Law and Business,* 6, Summer, pp. 562–614.

Hy, Ronald John (1989). *Financial Management for Health Care Administrators.* Westport, Conn.: Quorum Books.

Jensen, Donald L. (1993). "Modern Technology for the Mass Appraiser." *Intergovernmental Perspective,* Summer, pp. 21–23.

Kenyon, Daphne A. (1991). *Interjurisdictional Tax and Policy Competition: Good or Bad for the Federal System?* Washington, D.C.: Advisory Commission on Intergovernmental Relations, April.

Kleine, Robert, and John Shannon (1985). *Characteristics of a Balanced and Moderate State-Local Revenue System.* Denver: National Conference of State Legislatures.

Knapp, Elaine S. (1985). "States May Gain and Lose Under Federal Tax Reform." *State Government News,* 28, Fall, pp. 4–7.

Knapp, John L., and Tyler J. Fox (1992). "Local Taxation in Virginia." *University of Virginia News Letter,* 68, March, pp. 1–8.

Kolhauser, Richard (1988). "The Growth in State Taxes: A Review of the 1971–1987 Period." *Illinois Business Review,* 45, June, pp. 9–13.

Lappen, Michael D. (1989). "Financing the War Against Urban Decay." *ABA Banking Journal,* 81, January, pp. 18–19.

Laputz, Susan A. (1991). "California Offers Tax Incentives to Promote Economic Growth." *Tax Adviser,* 22, August, pp. 501–503.

Laschober, Mary A. (1989). "Is the Illinois State Lottery a Winning Ticket for the State?" *Illinois Business Review,* 46, February, pp. 3–8.

Ledebur, Larry C., and William R. Barnes (1992). "Metropolitan Disparities and Economic Growth." *Urban News,* 6, Spring.

Lee, Robert D., Jr. (1992). "Linkages Among Poverty, Development, and Budget Systems." *Public Budgeting and Finance,* 12, Spring, pp. 47–60.

Liebschutz, Sarah F., and Irene Lurie (1986). "The Deductibility of State and Local Taxes." *Publius,* 16, Summer, pp. 51–70.

Lile, Stephen E. (1979). "Tax Burdens in Louisiana: How Do They Compare?" *Louisiana Business Review,* 43, November/December, pp. 2–10.

Liner, Charles (1987). "Projecting Local Government Revenues." *Popular Government,* 32, Spring.

"Local Taxes, Federal Courts, and School Desegregation in the Proposition 13 Era." *Michigan Law Review,* 78, Fall, pp. 587–607.

McCollough, Jane (1990). "Municipal Revenue and Expenditure Forecasting: Current Status and Future Prospects." *Government Finance Review*, October.

McGowan, Robert P., and E. J. Ottensmeyer, eds. (1993). *Economic Development Strategies for State and Local Governments*. Chicago: Nelson-Hall.

McGuire, Therese J. (1993). "Jobs and Taxes: Do State Taxes Affect Economic Development?" *Comparative State Politics*, 14, June, pp. 24–31.

McIntyre, Robert, et al. (1991). *A Far Cry from Fair*. Washington, D.C.: Citizens for Tax Justice.

Marshall, Patrick G. (1989). "Do Enterprise Zones Work?" *Editorial Research Reports*, April 29, pp. 230–242.

Mields, Hugh, Jr. (1993). "The Property Tax: Local Revenue Mainstay." *Intergovernmental Perspective*, Summer, pp. 16–18.

Mikesell, John (1991). *Fiscal Administration: Analysis and Applications for the Public Sector*. 3rd ed. Chicago: Dorsey Press.

Miller, Gerald J. (1991). *Government Financial Management Theory*. New York: Marcel Dekker.

Miller, Mark (1989). "Inside an 'Enterprise Zone'; Miami's Example Shows Benefits Can Be Limited." *Newsweek*, March 6, p. 13.

Milward, H. Brinton, and Heide Hosbach Newman (1987). "State Incentive Packages and the Industrial Location Decision." Paper presented at the Southern Political Science Association Annual Meeting, Charlotte, N.C., November 5–8.

Morgan, William E., and John H. Mutti (1981). "Shifting, Incidence, and Inter-state Exportation of Production Taxes on Energy Resources." *Land Economics*, 57, August, pp. 422–435.

Morse, Ann, and Christopher Zimmerman (1990). *Efforts to Collect Sales Tax on Interstate Mail-Order Sales: Recent State Legislation*. Denver: National Conference of State Legislatures.

Mutti, John H., and William E. Morgan (1983). "The Exportation of State and Local Taxes in a Multilateral Framework: The Case of Household Type Taxes." *National Tax Journal*, 36, December, pp. 459–475.

National Conference of State Legislatures (1991). *State and Local Highway Finance: Where Does the Money Come from and Why Isn't There Enough?* Denver: NCSL, LFP #78.

National League of Cities (1985). *The Deductibility of State and Local Taxes: Implications of Proposed Policy Changes*. Washington, D.C.: NLC.

New York Department of Taxation and Finance, Office of Tax Policy Analysis (1991). *New York State Taxes and Fees: Fiscal Years 1990–91*. Albany: NYDTF.

"Not So EZ: Enterprise Zones, the Bush Administration's Cure for Urban Squalor, Will Be a Republican Version of Big-Government Waste." (1989). *The Economist*, January 28, p. 16.

Novak, Janet (1991). "Broke States Soak the Rich." *Forbes*, June 24, p. 35.

Ohio Department of Taxation (1986, 1987, 1991, 1992). *Ohio's Taxes: A Brief Summary of Major State and Local Taxes in Ohio*. Columbus: ODT.

Pagano, Michael A. (1986). *Tax Reform and City Capital Spending*. Washington, D.C.: National League of Cities.

Parhman, Linda (1989). "Enterprise Zones Renewed." *American City and County*, 101, June, p. 16.

Pechman, Joseph A., and Benjamin A. Okner (1974). *Who Bears the Tax Burden?* Washington, D.C.: Brookings Institution.

—— (1989). *Tax Reform: The Rich and the Poor.* 2nd ed. Washington, D.C.: Brookings Institution.

PEER Committee (1990). *Report to the Mississippi Legislature: A Review of Use Value Procedures for Assessing Agricultural Land for Taxation Purposes.* Jackson, Miss.: PEER Committee.

Pennsylvania Economic League (1989). *Revenue and Expenditure Comparisons: Philadelphia Versus Selected Major Cities.* Philadelphia: PEL.

Peters, B. Guy (1991). *The Politics of Taxation: A Comparative Perspective.* Oxford, Eng.: Blackwell.

Petersen, John, and Dennis Strachota, eds. (1991). *Local Government Finances.* Chicago: Government Finance Officers Association.

Phares, Donald (1980). *Who Pays State and Local Taxes?* Boston: Oelgeschlager, Gunn, and Hain.

Pischak, Kathryn A. (1989). "State Economic Development Incentives: What's Available? What Works?" *Municipal Finance Journal,* 10.

Pitts, Jennifer (1992). "Twilight Zone: Baltimore's Failed Enterprise." *New Republic,* 207, September 7, pp. 25–26.

Porter, Douglas R. (Director of Urban Land Institute, interview) (1990). "Infrastructure Financing Exceeds Impact Fees." *Custom Builder,* 5, March, pp. 51–52.

Price-Waterhouse, Inc. (1992). "Seeing Through the Fog of State Taxes." *Price-Waterhouse Review,* 36, no. 2, pp. 2–5.

Rafuse, Robert W. (1990). *Representative Expenditures: Addressing the Neglected Dimension of Fiscal Capacity. An Information Report.* Washington, D.C.: Advisory Commission on Intergovernmental Relations, December.

Rasmussen, David W., Marc Bendick, Jr., and Larry C. Ledebur (1982). "Evaluating State Economic Development Incentives from a Firm's Perspective." *Business Economics,* May.

Reeb, Donald J. (1982). "State and Local Taxes and Electric Utilities." *Public Utilities Fortnightly,* 110, August 19, pp. 29–39.

Reeder, Richard J. (1985). *Rural Governments: Raising Revenues and Feeling the Pressure.* Washington, D.C.: U.S. Department of Agriculture, Economic Research Service, July.

Reese, Laura A. (1992). "The Role of Counties in Local Economic Development." Paper presented at the Southern Political Science Association Annual Meeting, Atlanta, Georgia, November 5–7.

Ring, Raymond (1983). "Tax Exporting and Importing." *South Dakota Business Review,* 42, August, pp. 1–2ff.

Roginske, Charles J. (1992). "Effects of Chapter 11 on State and Local Taxes." *Journal of State Taxation,* 11, Summer, pp. 53–65.

Rosen, Harvey S. (1985). *Public Finance.* Homewood, Ill.: Richard D. Irwin.

—— (1988). "Thinking About the Deductibility of State and Local Taxes." *Federal Reserve Bank of Philadelphia Business Review,* July/August, pp. 15–23.

Rourke, Richard W. (1993). "Assessment Innovation in Orange County, Florida." *Intergovernmental Perspective,* Summer.

Rubin, Barry M., and Margaret C. Wilder (1989). "Urban Enterprise Zones: Employment

Impacts and Fiscal Incentives.'' *Journal of the American Planning Association,* 55, August.

Savage, David G. (1992). ''Legal Confusion over Mail-Order Taxes.'' *State Legislatures,* 18, August.

Smith, Lee (1989). ''Jack Kemp's Bad Idea.'' *Fortune,* November 20, p. 16.

Smith, Russell L. (1986). ''Interdependencies in Urban Economic Development: The Role of Multi-establishment Firms.'' In Dennis Judd, ed., *Public Policy Across States and Cities.* New York: JAI Press.

Snell, Ronald K. (1991). ''The Trouble with Earmarking.'' *State Legislatures,* 17, February.

''Soaking the Poor: Study Finds State and Local Taxes Very Regressive.'' *Dollars and Sense,* July/August, pp. 9–11.

Stanfield, Rochelle L. (1983). ''State Taxes Are Up, but Don't Worry—Federal Taxes Are Down by Much More.'' *National Journal,* 15, June 25, pp. 1320–1327.

Steiss, Alan Walter (1989). *Financial Management in Public Organizations.* Pacific Grove, Calif.: Brooks/Cole.

Stonecash, Jeffrey (1985). ''Are We Really Reducing State Taxes?'' *Empire State Report,* 11, June, pp. 9–10.

Stull, William J., and Judith C. Stull (1991). ''Capitalization of Local Income Taxes.'' *Journal of Urban Economics,* 29.

Tax Foundation (1989). *Tax Burden by Income Class, 1986–1987.* Baltimore: Johns Hopkins University Press.

———— (1990). *Facts and Figures on Government Finance.* Baltimore: Johns Hopkins University Press.

Thai, Khi V., and David Sullivan (1989). ''Impact of Termination of General Revenue Sharing on New England Local Government Finance.'' *Public Administration Review,* 49, January/February, pp. 61–67.

Thomas, Robert D. (1990). ''National-Local Relations and the City's Dilemma.'' *Annals of the American Academy of Political and Social Science,* 509, May, pp. 106–117.

Ulbrich, Holley H. (1986). *State and Local Taxation of Out-of-State Mail Order Sales.* Washington, D.C.: Advisory Commission on Intergovernmental Relations.

———— (1988). *Local Revenue Diversification: Local Income Taxes.* Washington, D.C.: ACIR, August.

U.S. Congress, Congressional Budget Office (1978). *Proposition 13: Its Impact on the Nation's Economy, Federal Revenues, and Federal Expenditures.* Washington, D.C.: U.S. Government Printing Office.

U.S. Congress, House of Representatives, Committee on Energy and Commerce (1982). *Coal Severance Tax Limitations: Hearings Before the Subcommittee on Fossil and Synthetic Fuels,* H.R. 1313, 97th Congress.

U.S. Congress, House of Representatives, Committee on Small Business (1983). *Employment and Investment Incentives for Small Business in Distressed Areas. Hearing Before the Subcommittee on Tax, Access to Equity, Capital and Business Opportunities.* 98th Congress, 1st Session, April 27.

U.S. Congress, Office of Technology Assessment (1984). *Technology, Innovation, and Regional Economic Development.* Washington, D.C.: U.S. Government Printing Office, February.

U.S. Congress, Senate, Committee on Finance (1984). *State Severance Taxes: Hearing*

Before the Subcommittee on Energy and Agricultural Taxation, 98th Congress, 2nd Session, July 24.

———— (1987). *Collection of State Sales and Use Taxes by Out-of-State Vendors: Hearings Before the Subcommittee on Taxation and Debt Management*, 100th Congress, 1st Session, November 6.

U.S. Department of Commerce, Bureau of the Census (1976). *State Tax Collections*. Washington, D.C.: U.S. Department of Commerce, Governments Division.

———— (1990a). *Agricultural Atlas of the United States*. 2 vols. Washington, D.C.: Bureau of the Census.

———— (1990b). *Rankings of States and Counties*. 2 vols. Washington, D.C.: Bureau of the Census.

———— (1992). *County Government Finances: 1989–90*. Washington, D.C.: Bureau of the Census.

U.S. Department of Housing and Urban Development (1975). *Property Tax Relief Programs for the Elderly*. Washington, D.C.: Office of Policy Development and Research, November.

———— (1979a). *Economic Development: New Roles for City Government—A Guidebook for Local Government*. Washington, D.C.: HUD.

———— (1979b). *Local Economic Development Tools and Techniques: A Guidebook for Local Government*. Washington, D.C.: HUD, September.

U.S. Department of the Treasury, Office of State and Local Finance (1986a). *Federal-State-Local Fiscal Relations: Report to the President and Congress*. Washington, D.C.: U.S. Government Printing Office.

———— (1986b). *Federal-State-Local Fiscal Relations: Technical Papers*. Washington, D.C.: U.S. Government Printing Office.

U.S. General Accounting Office, Report to the Congress (1979). *Proposition 13: How California Governments Coped with a $6 Billion Revenue Loss*. Washington, D.C.: US GAO, GGD-79-88.

———— (1988). *Enterprise Zones: Lessons from the Maryland Experience*. Washington, D.C.: US GAO, GAO/PEMD-89-2, December.

———— (1992). *Revitalizing Distressed Areas Through Enterprise Zones*. Washington, D.C.: US GAO, CAO/CED-82-78, July 15.

Vasquez, Thomas, and Charles W. deSeve (1977). "State/Local Taxes and Jurisdictional Shifts in Corporate Business Activities: The Complications of Measurement." *National Tax Journal*, 30, Summer, pp. 285–297.

Vaughan, Roger J. (1979). *State Taxation and Economic Development*. Washington, D.C.: Council of State Planning Agencies.

Vedder, Richard K. (1982). "Rich States, Poor States: How High Taxes Inhibit Growth." *Journal of Contemporary Studies*, 5, Fall, pp. 19–32.

———— (1991). "State and Local Taxes and Economic Performance." *Southern Business and Economic Journal*, 15, October, pp. 2–15.

Warner, David (1992). "Firms Could Face New State Taxes." *Nation's Business*, 80, January, pp. 23–24.

Washington Department of Revenue, Research and Information Division (1980, 1983, 1985, 1987). *Comparative State/Local Taxes, 1985, 1984, 1982, 1979*. Olympia, Wash.: WDR.

Waugh, William L., and Deborah M. Waugh (1988a). "Baiting the Hook: Targeting

Economic Development Monies More Effectively.'' *Public Administration Quarterly*, 12, Summer, pp. 216–235.

——— (1988b). ''Economic Development Programs of State and Local Governments and the Site Selection Decisions of Smaller Firms.'' In Richard Judd, William T. Greenwood, and Fred W. Becker, eds., *Small Business in a Regulated Economy*, pp. 111–126. Westport, Conn.: Quorum Books.

——— (1990). ''The Political Economy of Seduction: Promoting Business Relocation and Economic Development in Nonindustrial States.'' In Melvin J. Dubnick and Alan Gitelson, eds., *Public Policy and Economic Institutions*, pp. 221–234. Greenwich, Conn.: JAI Press.

Waugh, William L. (1993). ''Transportation as a Variable in the Site Selection Decisions of Firms.'' In Robert P. McGowan and E. J. Ottensmeyer, eds., *Economic Development Strategies for State and Local Governments*, pp. 134–145. Chicago: Nelson-Hall.

Wilkinson, Margaret (1992). *Taxation*. Hampshire, Eng.: Macmillan.

Worsnoop, Richard L. (1990). ''How Fair Is the Nation's Tax Burden? There Is a Lot of Evidence to Support the Popular Perception that Middle- and Lower-Income Families Are Now Paying More in Taxes While the Wealthy Are Paying Less.'' *Editorial Research Reports*, April 9, pp. 190–203.

Zuckman, Jill (1992a). ''Aid Bargaining Is Now Centered on Enterprise Zones for Cities.'' *Congressional Quarterly Weekly Report*, 50, June 6, pp. 1605–1606.

——— (1992b). ''Riots Resurrect Enterprise Zones.'' *Congressional Quarterly Weekly Report*, 50, May 9, p. 1253.

Index

Abatements, 214, 219
Ability to pay tax, 51, 253–254
Accounts ledger, 336
Ad valorem tax, 31, 83, 113
Adjustments, allowable, 36
Administrative structures, 232
Advisory Commission on Intergovern-
    mental Relations (ACIR), 56, 58, 62,
    63, 65, 71–72, 84, 87, 91, 94, 103,
    134, 149
Agricultural fundamentalism, 167
Agricultural tax: Property, 166–177;
    sales, 96–100; tax philosophy, 167;
    trends, 167–170; use value assessment,
    172–175
Alcoholic beverages tax, 124–126
Amusement tax, 127
Analytical designs, 273–281
Analyzing tax performance, 265–271
Amnesty, tax, 76–78
Assessment, Property, 30, 162
Association of Arkansas Counties,
    232
Atlanta Constitution, 91, 95
Attitudes about government, 18

Balanced tax policies, 48
Bank books, 236
Barnes, William, 224
Baseline tax data, 273
Benefits received tax, 27–28
Bond books, 236
Bonds, 42–43

Capital gains, 57–58
Center City District program (Philadel-
    phia), 225–226
Central Dallas Association, 226
Certificates of participation, 261
Classifications, Property, 29, 170–171
Community improvement districts, 225,
    227
Competitive bids, 43
Consumer Price Index (CPI), 76, 113
Consumption tax, 57, 111–112, 254–
    255
Corporate income tax, 38, 62, 254
Credits, 36, 256–257

Dallas Area Rapid Transit (DART), 226
Debt financing, 41

Deductions. *See* Exemptions and deductions

Deficit, 7

Deterministic forecasting techniques, 244–246

Disposable income, 13

Downtown Mall Management District (Denver), 225

Downtown management districts, 225, 227

Earmarking taxes, 197

Earnings, 36

Econometric Forecasting Techniques, 246–249

Economic development, 211, 214; taxes, 52

Employment, 9

Enterprise funds, 35

Enterprise zones, 211, 217–218, 227

Equal sacrifice, 26

Equity. *See* Fairness

Excise tax, 20, 111–112; Alcoholic beverages, 124–126; Amusements, 127; food and lodging, 126–127; lotteries, 129–143; motor fuels, 118–123; parimutuels, 127–128; rates, 113, 122, 124, 129; tax philosophy, 112; tobacco, 123–124; trends, 113–118

Exemptions and deductions, 23, 31–32, 91–100, 157–159, 214, 256–257

Expansion mode, 211

Fabricius, Martha, 118, 134

Fairness: ability to pay tax, 26; benefits received, 27; flat rate, 27

Federal Deposit Insurance Corporation (FDIC), 242

Fees and fines, 27, 32–33, 143–145

Fiscal disparities, 223

Fiscal outlook, 19

Flat rate tax, 27

Food and lodging tax, 126–127

Forecasting patterns: cyclical, 243–244; long-term, 242–243; seasonal, 243

Forecasting Techniques: deterministic, 244–246; econometric, 246–249; trend analysis, 244

Fort Howard Paper Company, 220

Framework for tax analyses, 267–271

Free port exemptions, 221

General obligation bonds, 42

Gilman Paper Company, 220

Goods and services, private and public, 17

Gross production tax, 193

Gross state product, 13

Homestead exemptions, 159–160

Identifying objectives, 268–269

Incentives tax, 214, 216, 224, 227

Income, 13

Income tax, 36, 51–80; adjusted gross income, 36, 53, 253; corporate, 38, 56–57, 62, 254; cost of capital, 56; deductions, 36, 54–55, 253; double taxation, 56; exemptions, 36, 54–55, 253; local, 63; personal, 36, 53, 253; piggybacking, 31, 65, 71; state, 62; taxable income, 36, 53, 253; tax philosophy, 53; wage and payroll, 36, 38, 65–71

Indexing, 51, 72

Industrial development bonds, 43

Infrastructure, 212

Input/output analysis, 270

Intangible property tax, 160

Intergovernmental aid, 1, 40

Interstate differences, 257–259

Interstate tax competition, 222

Investments, 237

Land banks, 226–227

Loan guarantee programs, 225

Local trends, 58

Long-term pattern, 242–243

Lotteries, 129–143; impact, 142; issues, 140–142

Mail order and direct marketing, 103–106

Market valuation, 29

Methods of sale, bonds, 43

Mineral production, 206–207

Mineral tax, 204–210; economic strategy, 207; rates, 207–208
Motor fuels tax, 28, 118–123
Multistage sales tax, 83

National Association of Manufacturers, 212
Negotiated sale, bonds, 43
Net earnings, 38
Net production tax, 193
North Carolina Research Triangle Park, 215

Operationalizing objectives, 269
Organization/process analysis, 270
Own-source revenues, 28, 251

Parimutuels, 127, 129
Payroll tax, 36, 38, 65
Per capita revenues, 1
Per unit production tax, 193
Per unit tax, 83, 113
Personal property tax, 160–162; intangible and tangible, 160
Piggybacking, 31, 65, 71
Political environment, 259–260
Political leadership, 262–263
Population growth, 9, 17
Post design, 276–278
Pre/post design, 274–276
Progressive tax, 51
Property classification, 29
Property tax, 28, 149–151, 256; agricultural, 166–177; deferrals, 160–161; effects, 164–166; exemptions, 157–160; limitations, 164–166; personal, 28, 160–162; real estate, 154–160; tax philosophy, 151; trends, 152–154; use value assessments, 172–175
Proportional tax. *See* Flat rate tax
Public utility tax, 100–102

Quill Corporation v. North Dakota, 103

Real property tax, 28, 154
Reassessment, 154–155; valuation approaches, 155–157

Receipt books, 236
Reconciliation forms, 236
Regressive tax, 51
Retail sales, 89–91
Revenue bonds, 42
Revenues: additional, need for, 20; forecasting, 242
Revenue enhancement, 23, 260–262

Sales tax, 31, 81–108; advantages and disadvantages, 32; agricultural tax, 96–100; collection and administration, 106–107; consumer services, 94; exemptions, 31–32, 91–100; food, 91, 94; gas and electric utilities, 91, 94; prescription medicine, 91, 94; retail sales, 89–91; tax philosophy, 82; trends, 84–89; wholesale sales, 89–91
Severance tax, 181–210; administration, 197–198; discrimination, 195; gross production tax, 193; mineral, 204–210; net production tax, 193; per unit production tax, 193; tax philosophy, 182–183; timber, 198–204; trends, 184
Simulated control data, 276
Single-stage sales tax, 83
Smith, Russell, 213
Special assessment districts, 225
Spending patterns, 17
Stamp tax, 124, 126
State tax trends, 58
Sumptuary Tax, 112

Tangible property, 28, 160
Tax administration and collection, 106–107, 231–232
Tax base, 27–29
Tax base sharing, 223–224, 227
Tax climate, 212
Tax expenditures, 54
Tax exporting, 194–195
Tax foundation, 120, 184
Tax incidence, 252
Tax increment financing, 221
Tax inducements, 212
Tax liabilities, 234

Tax maintenance, 236
Tax rate, 27
Taxable income, 36
Timber production, 199–202
Timber tax, 198–204; economic strategy, 202; rates, 202–204
Tobacco tax, 123–124
Trend analysis, 242–244
Trend projection design, 278–281
Twinkie tax, 261

United Parcel Service, 220
U.S. Bureau of the Census, 33, 58; charges defined, 143
U.S. Department of Housing and Urban Development, 217

U.S. General Accounting Office (GAO), 212, 213
Use tax, 102–107; mail order and direct marketing, 103–105; site determination, 105
Utility Tax, 35

Valuation approaches: cost, 157; income, 155; market value, 155
Value-added tax (VAT), 57, 83
Vertical equity. *See* Ability to pay tax
Video lottery terminals, 135

Wage tax, 36, 38, 65
Wholesale sales, 89–91

ABOUT THE AUTHORS

RONALD JOHN HY is a Professor of Public Administration at the Arkansas Institute of Government, University of Arkansas, Little Rock.

WILLIAM L. WAUGH, JR., is a Professor in the School of Public Administration and Urban Affairs, Georgia State University.

ISBN 0-313-28529-2

9 780313 285295

90000>

EAN

HARDCOVER BAR CODE